D0765327

MOUNTAINEERING IN THE ALPS
AN HISTORICAL SURVEY

MOUNTAINEERING IN THE ALPS

AN HISTORICAL SURVEY

CLAIRE ELIANE ENGEL

WITH A FOREWORD BY LORD HUNT

LONDON

GEORGE ALLEN & UNWIN LTD

RUSKIN HOUSE MUSEUM STREET

First published in 1950
as *A History of Mountaineering in the Alps*
New Edition, totally revised and enlarged 1971

© George Allen & Unwin Ltd, 1971

ISBN 0 04 796037 X

Printed in Great Britain
in 12 point Barbou type
by W & J Mackay & Co Ltd
Chatham

FOREWORD
BY LORD HUNT

As I write this Foreword to Claire Engel's story of alpine climbing since its earliest days, the annual summer campaign is about to start in our Western Alps. From now until mid-September the shock troops will be assaulting the great mountain walls, some of them attempting new routes of ever greater difficulty. Behind these tough Commandos, thousands of lesser men and women will be plodding up the well-trodden ridges, queueing from time to time beneath the more awkward passages, in a never-ending stream.

Long ago it was assumed that the last great Alpine problem had been solved; but year by year new achievements are recorded on vertical rock and steep ice. The history of Alpine mountaineering is still being written.

I doubt if the pioneers could have imagined the explosion of humanity onto the peaks, passes and glaciers on which they ventured, intrepid in their isolation, in those early days. The opening up of new approaches, the construction of mountain cabins and the mechanization which followed the growing popularity of the sport and thus contrived to make it even more so, provide a startling contrast with the lonely remoteness of the high valleys only a hundred years ago. But despite this contrast, however widely different their skills and ambitions and viewpoints, mountaineers through the ages have retained throughout Alpine history something basic in common to them all—an inner urge to get to the top.

Whatever may be felt by those who do not climb about this particular manifestation of the human spirit, I, for one, am thankful that the Alps, so accessible to so many, should still provide an outlet for personal discovery and endeavour, long after the pioneers first showed the way. The reason why we climb, even though it be on a peak which has been climbed countless times before, is precisely because it poses another question: 'Can I do it?' With the gathering years we add the adverb 'still'. The importance of that question is that it insistently demands an answer.

The history of the early ascents has always held a fascination for me since, as a boy of just sixteen, steeped in Whymper's *Scrambles Amongst the Alps*, I gazed at the Brêche de la Meije from our holiday inn at La Grave and imagined the first crossing of that famous pass in 1860. That year (1926) I followed in Whymper's footsteps across the Brêche, and two years later my mind was full of Boileau de Castelnau and the early attempts on the Meije itself as, with my Dauphiné guide Paul Jouffray from La Grave, I made the traverse of that splendid mountain from the Promontoire Hut. And so it has always been with me. Many years later, on Everest, I had this strong sense of history; our predecessors were very much in my mind as we climbed the mountain. Later still, in the Caucasus, at least part of the delight of our expedition with our Soviet friends was the feeling of treading in the traces of Freshfield, Mummery, Dent and other members of the Alpine Club who had pioneered some of the climbs towards the end of the last century.

Mountains may still form physical barriers which divide people, but they provide a spiritual link between climbers for which frontiers have no meaning. This link joins past with present, too. I am grateful to Mlle Engel for giving me the privilege of introducing her book to the thousands of readers who, whether they climb or not, will share my fascination for mountains and their meaning to men and women across the years.

JOHN HUNT

AUTHOR'S PREFACE

IN 1949 I wrote my *History of Mountaineering in the Alps* and it was published in the following year. This was relatively soon after the end of a war which had put most of the Alps out of bounds for about six years, though when things got back to normal, or something like it, in spite of many difficulties resulting from surviving war regulations and rationing, mountaineering revived and blossomed at once. It was quickly clear, however, that things would never be what they were in 1939, though it took a few years to realize that the moral and technical trends which had begun to take shape during the previous ten to fifteen years were sweeping through the mountain world.

The financial and social upheavals caused by the war had not left the sport untouched. The vast increase in travel, especially by air, and the general broadening of horizons, together with rising standards of living, opened up the Alps to men and women who probably would not have considered climbing them a generation earlier. They, too, brought new attitudes to the sport of climbing and easily absorbed the new techniques.

These trends were present but not developed when my *History* came out, though they became fact during the next few years. Everything was on the move and has kept moving ever since. Great changes took place in outlook, ambitions, methods. An outstanding pre-war mountaineer once prided himself on never having used a single piton: a remark which would sound now like extreme puritanism or, worse still, a lack of precaution when tackling tricky pitches.

For several years, the Alps—mostly the Dolomites and the Bavarian Alps—had been the happy, or occasionally tragic, hunting grounds of 'artificial' climbing specialists. Then began the quest for 'the last Alpine problem': five of them were solved before the outbreak of the war, but mountaineers immediately became aware of many more 'last problems'. They are still finding them.

New climbs themselves have created a new outlook. All over Europe, Alpine clubs have had to accustom themselves to new conditions and new climbers, and they have had to face their members' aims and needs in a more practical way. Guides have changed beyond recognition: a great many of these among the best do not originate from Alpine districts.

New techniques have, during the last twenty years, prompted the invention of a host of new devices. Since 1949, with the development of the nylon industry, even ropes have changed out of all recognition and have made a huge number of intricate ascents possible. *Jumars, griff-jiffe, descendeurs, gollots*—all these were unknown twenty-one years ago.

The outlook of the climbers themselves has also undergone a change, notably in the accentuation of rivalry. Rivalry was not unknown, of course, to the nineteenth-century mountaineers: we have only to recall Coolidge's disparaging comments on other climbers' achievements. But such feelings have become more and more pronounced as climbers aim at time records on newly discovered routes, and intricate variations on established ones.

For these reasons alone my *History* needed complete readjustment, not only to incorporate new developments and achievements, which were so multifarious in these twenty years, but also to reassess the past in the light of the present. This re-evaluation involved the rewriting of many chapters, before I could begin to unfold the history of recent times. I went over all my former documents to take a more modern view of them and give them a correct perspective. I also added a good many new documents discovered since the publication of my *History*. More than two-thirds of the present volume is practically new: the book is no mere enlargement. For the same reasons, most of the iconography has had to be changed: photos taken twenty years ago look prehistoric when compared with those of recent times.

This book could not have reached its completed form without the constant help of Malcolm Barnes. I owe a great debt to the late Mr R. L. G. Irving, to General Jacques Faure, Colonel Klein, Colonel de Monicault, Professor Massimo Mila, Miss N. de Lavis-Trafford, M. Van der Kemp, curator of the Palace of Versailles, Baron Boileau de Castelnau, Dr Wyss-Dunant, M. Jacques Boell, John Wilkinson, Estcourt, Georges Sonnier, Jean Franco, Gaston Rebuffat, Bernard Pierre, Pierre Dalloz, Pierre Mazeaud, Hugh Merrick, Mr Nicholas B. Clinch, President of the American Alpine Club, Professor Basil Guy, who provided me with information or unpublished material.

I have found documents in many libraries to which I had access and I want to thank M. Gustave Vaucher, Honorary Director of the Geneva State Archives, the Keeper of the Swiss Alpine Club Library, M. Roger Pierrot, Keeper of the printed books department of the Bibliotheque Nationale, M. Borgeaud, Keeper of the Bibliothèque Publique et Universitaire of Geneva, M. Bourleaux, Keeper of the French Alpine Club Library.

C.E.E.

Les Praz de Chamonix
August 1970

CONTENTS

ILLUSTRATIONS

CHAPTER ONE

INTRODUCTION

I T was a slow process, lasting nearly two hundred years, by which man came at last to appreciate the high mountain landscape, with flame-like crags and snowy domes rearing their heads above the horizon. Yet, in spite of the fact that mountains have been explored and described over so long a period, today, when it is said that 'every Alpine problem has been solved' and when almost every great north face has been scaled, there is a suspicion that mountains are still, in a sense, a *terra incognita*. For the Alpine landscape still holds its element of mystery. When Dr John Forbes saw the Matterhorn for the first time in 1848, he wrote: 'Among the ideas that crowded the mind, those of Art and the Artificial came with the rest, and I am not sure if even that of oddness was entirely excluded'. The man who comes into contact with mountains for the first time is very likely to feel complex, confused impressions surging into his mind.

At first sight, mountains are the embodiment of disorder. Shattered boulders, gnarled trees, grey moraines ploughing their way through pastures and forests, scarred glaciers soiled with the black mud they have torn from the hillside, combine to form a tragic prospect. Travellers were not always repelled by such a show of brutal, irresistible force, but they usually complained of the lack of poise and proportion in Alpine shapes. Some found in mountains a kind of novelty, a relief from close contact with too tame a world. The keener minds among them went deeper and felt the stronger appeal of the high Alpine landscapes. Shelley and Sénancour, to name but two of the greatest, had the intuition of a higher order, a supreme architecture underlying apparent disorder. Shelley refers in *Mont Blanc* to 'the secret strength of things'; and Sénancour in *Obermann* speaks of an '*ensemble éternel*', when he is thinking of the great company of the everlasting hills. Though they had little in common, both men felt the manifold harmony of the landscape. Neither went very high—Shelley visited the Mer de Glace and Sénancour the Glacier de Soix, at the foot of the Dent du Midi; yet both had the revelation of what high mountains are like.

For the climber who responds to the appeal of Nature, such an experience is overwhelming. Mountains have a poise of their own. The three great glaciers which unite in the Mer de Glace, when seen from the top of the Grands

Charmoz, have the majesty of huge rivers winding down in broad regular curves. An ice wall leaves on the mind an impression of calm strength and haughty grandeur: such is the smooth precipice of the Mischabel group, the brow of which is crowned by the twin steeples, the Lenzspitze and the Nadelhorn.

Nightmarish landscapes are not infrequent in the Alps. A storm can turn the easiest mountain into a death trap. I shall never forget the impression of unreality I once felt when coming down the Matterhorn in a raging thunderstorm. The ridge, perfectly easy under good conditions, had become a yelling inferno where everything was dissolving into mud and water: holds seemed to break off at a mere glance; steps were washed away by a watery mixture of snow, sleet, hail and mud; the rope was frozen solid, it was impossible to hook it round a belay, and it set the loose stones rolling in every direction; an ice-cold wind was howling round the mountain; purple and yellow streaks of lightning flashed at frequent intervals, while the thunder roared with a dry echoless staccato. A kind of senseless fury was engulfing the mountains, and yet such an experience cannot destroy an implicit faith in their higher poise: they have a logic of their own, which is not after man's standard.

In the mountains time and space are different too. The slowness, the elaborate effort required to climb a mountain, have always perturbed the beginner. When he is defeated, he simply confesses his weariness and complains of it. Yet, while fighting against the mountain and against himself, he can grasp to the full the extent of passing minutes: 'The country where man is not hurried,' wrote Sénancour. Among the prisoners of war who escaped out of Italy in 1943 was a writer with no previous mountaineering experience, Sir Julian Hall. In October, when glaciers were in very bad condition, he had to cross the Felikjoch, one of the highest and most difficult passes into the Valais. Here is the striking way in which he expressed the excruciating heaviness of passing time: 'Every minute in the mountains is long, longer than an hour in sheltered places. For one cannot hurry. One goes at the pace of mountains—not of man—mountains whose life is eternal.'

A sort of unconscious asceticism has brought many men to the Alps; to win a victory over oneself adds a moral charm to the manifold delight of a big climb.

'We're not exultant but delighted, joyful, soberly astonished . . . Have we vanquished an enemy? None but ourselves. Have we gained a success? That word means nothing here. We have achieved an ultimate satisfaction . . . fulfilled a destiny . . . To struggle and to understand—never this last without the other; such is the law. We have only been obeying an old law, then? Ah, but it's *the* law and we understand—a little more,' wrote George Mallory, who was to disappear on Everest a few years later, 'obeying the law'.

Other aspects of the high mountain, such as colour and light, are equally disconcerting. One expects to find glaring and discordant shades and the hard outlines of a clear-cut horizon. And yet, in an air free from dust and vapour, where distances are blurred to the point of often confusing an experienced mountaineer, one sees only delicate hues—beige, ash-blue, mauve and russet hovering in a golden atmosphere. The great rock precipices are seldom black or even brown; all through the day they change from one colour to another. When Leslie Stephen describes a sunset on Mont Blanc, his prose reminds the reader of a water-colour by Turner. Of course, mountains provide the spectator with unbelievable crimson sunsets and green sunrises—the latter being the most ominous as they always portend a violent storm. When the storm breaks, the mountain world is contracted to flat brown or dark blue, in which the white glare of the ice adds to the impression of sinister fury.

Mountains are thus seen to exist in the realm of contradiction, so much so that writers who have tried to grasp the spirit of an Alpine landscape have been impressed by a constant opposition between its beauty and the sudden horror of which it is capable, between the love which mountains conjure up in many hearts and the feeling of hatred and despair which sometimes sweeps over the same persons among the same mountains. They have tried to solve the riddle. But the understanding of mountains comes only as a revelation. One would like to say that they dispense their grace, using the word in its theological sense; 'for many be called but few chosen'.

Much has been written about the ancient aspect of mountain worship and mountain love. From the earliest ages mountains have obviously puzzled their beholders who could not decide whether their influence was favourable or baneful. Greek gods lived on Mount Olympus, but Orpheus was torn to pieces by infuriated Bacchantes on the slopes of Mount Rhodopos. Similar traditions exist in every mythology.

There are many such instances in the Bible. It is easy to point to the religious importance of Mount Sinai, Mount Gilboa, the Hill of the Trans-figuration or Lebanon. Mountains are places where divine inspiration comes more frequently than elsewhere, but there is no connection between this and mountaineering. It would be a bad joke to claim Alpine qualifications for Noah on the ground that he made the first descent or landing on Mount Ararat. Yet the ancient form of mountain worship has many modern survivals. One of the oldest mountain pilgrimages on record is that of the Rocca Mellone, above Suza, where Bonifacio Rotario, a fourteenth-century hermit, carried up a heavy brass triptych dedicated to the Virgin. The top of the mountain is still visited once a year by a procession. Another mountain shrine is Santa Cruz, a hill commanding the harbour of Oran in Algeria. Though not very high, the hill is steep and pilgrims who visit it on Ascension Day have a stiff pull, especially under North African conditions; to make things worse, some of them climb on their knees. But this tradition has now vanished, like most other Christian traditions in North Africa. In the Alps, crosses or statues of the Virgin have been erected on several high summits: on the Meije, the Dru, the Grépon, the Dent du Géant, the Dom, the Matterhorn. From a mountaineer's point of view, the practice is highly dangerous: it adds to the considerable dangers already run by climbers in storms, as all these statues are of metal. The one on the Dent du Géant has been completely destroyed and that on the Grépon beheaded by lightning. I had to creep beneath the cross on the Matterhorn in stormy weather and thought it definitely un-comfortable. Yet, in spite of the difficulties incurred, the building of such shrines goes on, a remnant of the kind of exorcism which was still practised in the Alps two hundred years ago. We read that the glaciers at Chamonix were duly exorcised by a bishop at the end of the seventeenth century.

From time immemorial, of course, there has been what may be termed 'compulsory mountaineering': under this heading come many journeys across high passes. One of the earliest heroes of such exploits was probably Hannibal: Livy's account of this crossing is hair-raising and in paraphrase it has re-sounded through history. The grandest of all perhaps is that by Nathaniel Lee, in 1675:

> Like gods we pass'd the rugged Alpine hills,
> Melted our way and drove our hissing wheels
> Through cloudy deluges and eternal rills;
> What other ages so shall fain believe,
> Through burning quarries did our passage cleave,
> Hurl'd dreadful fire and vinegar infus'd,
> Whose horrid force the nerves of flint unlooz'd,
> Made Nature start to see us root up rock
> And open all the adamantine locks,
> Shake off her many bars, o'er mountains go,
> Through globes of ice and flakes of solid snow.

We do not know exactly which pass Hannibal crossed—possibly the present Col Lavis-Trafford—but whichever it was, the operation must have been very picturesque on account of the part played by the elephants.

In 1178 an English monk, John de Bremble, crossed the Saint-Bernard on his way to Rome, and his reaction was one of great distress. Sir Arnold Lunn quotes his fervent prayer: 'Lord, restore me to my brethren that I may tell them that they come not to this place of torment'. Twelfth-century monks were badly shod and John de Bremble was travelling in winter. Still, the terror he felt on slippery ground holds good for travellers in any period or wearing any kind of shoes. Medieval chroniclers have handed down to us the dire account of the way in which Henry IV of Germany and his family crossed the Mont Cenis on their way to Canossa in the middle of winter and in severe blizzards. No doubt the prospect of an interview with Pope Gregory IX did not make the landscape appear more inviting. Nothing but terror and hatred for mountains could be expected from such unlucky travellers.

And yet, despite an almost complete ignorance of mountains, a few hardy pioneers felt an impulse to climb them and even to express their admiration. Petrarch ascended the Mont Ventoux, Peter of Aragon climbed the Canigou and Antoine de Ville de Beaupré climbed the Mont Aiguille. The impulse which sent the latter on this very daring expedition was not, however, a poetic longing, but a military order from King Charles VIII of France: this was 'compulsory mountaineering' with a vengeance.

It would be unprofitable to seek in the annals of early mountain literature the first account of a climb undertaken for simple enjoyment. Josias Simler, Vadianus and other Swiss naturalists, gave descriptions of the kind, but it is difficult to ascertain who started the fashion. Climbs are as old as the hills, but climbs wilfully or gratuitously undertaken belong only to recent times. With the sixteenth century a few people raised their eyes to the mountains with more admiration and less terror than before. This was the birth of mountain literature, but not of mountaineering. The impulse to a very different activity took much longer to mature into a conscious desire to climb a certain peak.

PART I

THE APPROACH

CHAPTER TWO

STARTING POINT

MOUNTAINEERING was never an unrelated kind of activity, having no connection with contemporary trends of thought. When Christopher Columbus left Spain with his three ships in 1492, he was not answering a supernatural call: he was following in the footsteps of predecessors and making use of a knowledge accumulated through years of experience. A similar situation was to lead early mountaineers towards the summits.

The seventeenth century is a convenient starting point, for it marks the beginning of the historical epoch—from the mountaineer's point of view—and a few faint yet distinct notions become manifest in the writings of the time. Early in the century, literature had evinced a strong feeling for Nature. All the poets of the period, Andrew Marvell, George Herbert and Robert Herrick in England, Racan, St Amand and Théophile de Viau in France, wrote lovely poems to describe woodlands, gardens, rivers and fields. Yet hardly a mountain loomed on the horizon. When mountains were somewhat perfunctorily suggested, they were scarcely more individualized than the 'horned summits' of the sixteenth century, and no one dreamt of climbing them.

Mountain districts were well known so far as the valleys were concerned; travellers were crossing Alpine passes under compulsion more and more often. The political importance of Italy, and later of Switzerland, were attracting an increasing flow of visitors to those countries. But one can hardly call John Evelyn a mountaineer, in spite of his having crossed the Simplon in 1646 under winter conditions. He hated every minute of his ordeal, as did his pack horse, which narrowly escaped falling down a precipice, and also 'Captain Wray's nasty cur', which was soundly beaten for killing two goats belonging to natives of the district. Savoy, Dauphiny and the territories of the Swiss cantons and their allies, were mere squares on the European chessboard. Diplomats moved their pawns across them without being at all interested in their scenic aspects.

Early in the eighteenth century, Abraham Stanyan, the British Ambassador to Switzerland, was not quite certain whether the big rivers flowing through the country came or did not come from great heaps of snow and ice eternally hidden in mountain caves. He also explained that the local mountain goat was a very nimble animal called *shammy*. Other and more disconcerting creatures made Alpine travellers uncomfortable: these were the dragons. They flourished mainly round the Lake of Lucerne, hibernating in caverns on the slopes of Mount Pilatus, and were so numerous that the mountain was put out of bounds by local authorities. Other dragon families lived in the Saas Valley, in the Val Ferret and in the Grisons. In fact, there were few Alpine districts which could not boast of their own breed. These dragons were not man-eaters; they even welcomed absent-minded travellers who tumbled into their lairs when overcome with giddiness or liquor and they entertained them through the winter. When spring came and they left their winter quarters, they were kind enough to take off with their guests safely tied to their tails and fly them to some convenient landing ground. There is a slightly different legend in the Val Ferret. The local monster has a tail set with diamonds. Once a year, at midnight on Christmas Eve, it unhooks its tail to drink at a spring high up on the mountain side. Then is the time to seize the tail, make away with it and remain rich for life; but no one has yet contrived to be punctual and the dragon is still flying about with its jewelled tail. As late as 1723, J. J. Scheuchzer, a Zürich scholar who was a Fellow of the Royal Society, devoted a chapter of an extremely learned book to the description of the various Alpine dragons. He even asked himself whether wingless dragons were the females of the species or had to be placed in a quite different category.

There were few narratives of mountain travel except imaginary ones. When the heroes of journeys into the various Utopias imagined by Tissot de Patot or Gabriel de Foigny had to cross mountain ranges, they did anything except walk across them; they flew over, having wings tied to their shoulders, or they crept through underground passages. In a fairy tale by Mme d'Aulnoy, *The Blue Bird*, the Princess Florine climbed a steep ivory mountain with the help of small gold crampons given to her by a kind fairy: she tied them to her hands and feet and went up like the workmen who repair the wires at the tops of telegraph poles. Less fantastic travellers did not leave their native countries to see the mountains—or any other natural scenery. What they travelled for was to see collections of Greek and Roman coins or Renaissance paintings. Later in the century laboratories, collections of stuffed birds or sea-shells or baroque gardens were to attract a constantly increasing number of visitors. As for mountains, they were ignored by the great majority.

The age was much interested in science, but until the end of the century mathematics, not physics, was the favourite subject. It meant that the observation of Nature was of secondary importance.

In 1673, Justel, who was Louis XIV's librarian before he took refuge in

England as a Huguenot, reported to the Royal Society that a certain Capuchin monk had found in the vicinity of Geneva a mountain '*toute de glace et de cristaux*' (wholly made of ice and crystals). The monk had accompanied crystal hunters. This records an early glimpse of Mont Blanc, for there is no other ice-covered mountain near Geneva. Yet no one was much interested in the monk's discovery, or thought of following in his footsteps, and almost seventy years were to elapse before anyone troubled to write again about a trip to Chamonix.

And yet, at a time when no one seemed to be concerned with climbing mountains, one finds the following passage:

'It was as if I saw a bad man, dragged up by his guide to the top of a steep mountain. The man can do nothing unless helped by his guide; he follows assiduously in his footsteps until they are past the rocks and the abysses. When he is at the top, not only does he not reward his guide, but pushes him down a precipice and laughs while watching his fall.'

The writer is a Frenchman, J. F. Bernard; the passage occurs in his *Reflexions Morales*, published in 1711, a very dull book which does not deal with mountaineering at all. This gruesome episode is introduced only as a casual illustration. The author does not even stress the fact that a few extravagant persons can devote their activities to climbing mountains; he merely suggests that one should not behave like the scoundrel in the story.

CHAPTER THREE

FROM LABORATORIES TO MOUNTAINS

WHO were the pioneers? Where did they come from? They were not the inhabitants of mountain villages climbing of their own free will, for peasants never climb if they can help it; all the real pioneers were from the towns. The peasants feared the mountains, and in Alpine folk-lore mountains are alive with dragons and monsters of every description. This is true even of modern times, as witness the celebrated Valais monster which provided so much excitement in Switzerland in 1946: it was said to have murdered or mangled a large number of goats and sheep, but it was never seen by human eye, except by a nervous couple motoring down the Rhone valley, who mistook its shining eyes for the headlights of a car—or more probably the headlights of a car for its shining eyes. But in folk-lore proper, the mountains are full of evil. Murderous witches and wizards would hurl their victims down the Alpine precipices and the Devil lurked in many mountain districts: there is a Devil's Bridge across the Reuss near Andermatt, and a legend makes clear its unholy origin. Once, the Devil came flying over the Pennine Alps, carrying St Theodule and his brand-new bell from Rome to Sion, and they crashed on landing; the bell was not injured; neither was the saint, nor apparently was the Devil. A bas-relief on the façade of Sion Cathedral alludes to the legend.

Glaciers, according to legend, grow and swallow villages and meadows when a curse is laid upon them; it is said that some supernatural being cursed a mountain village above Kandersteg, the inhabitants of which had proved niggardly in their church offerings, and the glaciers covered the whole of the Blümlisalp as a result. The Wandering Jew crossed the Theodul Pass three times: on his first journey, he saw a flourishing city, on the second a deserted pasture, and on the third a vast expanse of snow and rock, barren for the rest of time. At Lucerne there was a law that forbade people to throw stones into a small lake on Mount Pilatus; it was said that the accursed soul of Pontius Pilate haunted the tarn and that when roused from sleep, he would raise terrible storms over the mountain and the lake.

The heroes of a few legends were the luckless ones who tried to scale threatening peaks that towered above their native villages. In the Saas valley the story is told of a man who tried to ascend the Mischabels. On the first night his bivouac fire was seen very high up, but nothing more was ever heard of him. Usually, these rash explorers go treasure hunting and are destroyed by demons who watch over hidden heaps of gold and gems. Curiously, the one legend of a successful climb belongs also to Saas: it tells how a native set out for a peak near the Fletschhorn and succeeded in climbing it despite an appalling wind. No one in the village believed his story. So, taking with him a cock and a dog and a cat, and having a heavy iron band fastened round his head, he set off again and succeeded in making his second ascent and coming down alive, though the three animals had perished. It is not clear why he took them up, nor what was the use of the iron crown.

On the Col de Balme, at the head of the valley of Chamonix, the twittering of a bird of ill omen is sometimes heard: but only by those whose death will occur within the year. When Whymper wanted to climb the Matterhorn, he was told that the spirits of the damned haunted the mountain and, according to Guido Rey, Valtournanche people still believed this at the beginning of the present century. Other restless spirits haunt the Aletsch Glacier, and a headless priest says Mass in the Riederalp Chapel. Similar legends developed quite recently: the Kien Hut above Randa, which was a convenient sleeping-place from which to climb the Taeschhorn, is said to be haunted, and guides always tried to avoid it. As this hut was built fairly recently and the Taeschhorn was not even climbed before 1862, the tradition is quite modern. Frank Smythe had a weird experience in a Valais hut round which he saw a yeti's footprints. As a final example, there is a ghostly caravan eternally coming up to the Monte-Rosa hut above Zermatt; numberless guides and climbers have heard the axes of these ghostly climbers tapping on the moraine below the hut and have even descried their lanterns. Such stories account for the constant terror conjured up by mountains in the hearts of people living in their shadow.

The prehistoric period of Alpine-lore, speaking from a mountaineer's point of view, is filled with the rumble of avalanches, a constant source of danger in ages when nothing could be done against them and a far from negligible one even at the present day, for villages have actually been buried under heaps of ice and rocks falling at unexpected seasons. Whole mountainsides have been known to break loose and overwhelm the regions below: such was the fall of the Rossberg above Arth-Goldau, of the Fiz above Servoz in 1741 and again in 1970, of the Diablerets above Derborence and of a part of the Altels above Schwarenbach.

People who lived near the glaciers invented numerous stories concerning them. It is a fact that in the seventeenth and eighteenth centuries glaciers were much larger than now, far less crevassed and consequently easier to cross. Cows used to be taken across some of them—the Mer de Glace for instance—to their summer pastures. In many valleys there were traditions telling of a blessed time when there were no glaciers and when it was possible to go from Courmayeur to Chamonix or from the Valais to Grindelwald on solid earth. In the middle of the eighteenth century the halcyon, glacierless era was supposed to have ended some eighty years earlier, and the oldest men in the valleys could remember their fathers having hinted that they had crossed the cols when they were children; but the glaciers crept down and people were now compelled to walk on ice. This was terribly dangerous, according to tales related to the early travellers and faithfully repeated by William Windham, Pierre Martel, von Haller or Justel's anonymous monk. If you crossed a glacier, you might well be swallowed up by a chasm which would suddenly yawn under your feet with a roar like thunder; with luck, however, you might escape by creeping along the bed of the torrent under the ice, to find your way out at the foot of the glacier. Sleeping on ice was fatal. Ice-towers, which were not yet called séracs, were likely to topple down if you even whispered in their vicinity. Glacier-water was reputed to be a cure for many illnesses.

Among dwellers in the Alps, one class of men had a better knowledge of the mountains than this: these were the chamois-hunters and the collectors of rock-crystal (one man usually combined both occupations). Having regard to the importance of rock-crystal in seventeenth- and eighteenth-century jewellery—its use for shoe and garter buckles, in sword-hilts and in the setting of mirrors, snuff-boxes and chandeliers—one realizes why literally tons of it were exported from mountain districts, and why there were so many collectors. Such men were to be found all over the Alpine regions, and they told wild tales of their adventures which fascinated travellers. One such story may be recorded. When—so they averred—they had to scale very steep crags, they climbed barefoot and, in order to stick to the precarious holds, they slashed the soles of their feet with knives, so that the blood, when drying, stuck to the stones and helped them to secure a sounder footing. How any sane person could believe or even invent such a story is incredible; and yet it survived until the beginning of the nineteenth century.

In mountain villages hunters were usually looked upon as erratic and notorious characters, dare-devils who risked—and often lost—their lives in courting danger. The chamois-hunter was to live a long and picturesque life in mountain literature, and it may be amusing to follow the course of this fantastic figure. It began with a passage in H. B. de Saussure's *Voyages dans les Alpes*:

26

'Is it possible to realize that chamois hunting gives rise to an almost irresistible passion? I knew a young man in the parish of Sixt. He was well built, with a fine face and had just married a charming wife. He actually said to me: "My grandfather died while chamois-hunting; so did my father. I am also sure that I shall die in the same way, and this sack here, which I carry on my back in the mountains, I call my winding sheet, being certain I shall never have another. And yet, were you to offer me a fortune if I abandon chamois-hunting, I would not do so." I made a few excursions with this man: he was amazingly strong and nimble, but his rashness was even more marked, and I was told that, two years later, his footing failed him on the brink of a chasm and he fell a victim to the fate he had been expecting.'

De Saussure's volumes were assiduously studied by all mountain lovers. The chamois-hunter became an Alpine hero and, in 1803, E. F. de Lantier, a third-rate French novelist who had read much and remembered all he had read, wrote *Les Voyageurs en Suisse*. It is almost an anthology. In the chapter entitled 'Of Various Alpine Animals', we find a passage in which de Saussure's text, quoted above, had been copied almost word for word, except that the young man died in six months. Then, in 1822, Samuel Rogers published a collection of poems entitled *Italy*, of which one poem is *Jorasse*, the name of a Chamonix guide:

> '"My sire, my grandsire died among these wilds;
> As for myself," he cried and he held forth
> His wallet in his hand, "This do I call
> My winding-sheet for I shall have no other."
> And he spoke truth. Within a little month
> He lay among these awful solitudes
> Taking his final rest.'

Two years—six months—one month: life and death were becoming more and more hurried!

Throughout the eighteenth and early nineteenth centuries, hunters played a leading part in all mountain narratives. They began to act as guides—there was no alternative—and, owing to the belief in the goodness of Nature cherished by the eighteenth century, they rapidly became idyllic figures, always ready to utter sanctimonious maxims of doubtful originality. Yet, if chamois-hunters knew the glaciers and ridges where they could track their prey, they never tried to climb mountains for the sheer love of doing so. As late as 1865, the Abbé Goret of Valtournanche, who played an important part in the story of the Matterhorn, wrote: 'The Mont Cervin, before which foreigners stood awe-struck, did not impress us.' A similar attitude prevailed all over the Alps. The Titlis is said to have been ascended in 1739 by Ignaz Herz, J. E. Waser and two other Engelberg men, but little is known about them and their exploit seems to be the one exception to a fairly general rule.

The pioneers of mountaineering came from a totally different quarter: they were scientists.

The age which produced them was even more interested in scientific research than the seventeenth century had been, and, without neglecting mathematics, was passionately fond of the natural sciences. Botany, geology, physics were effecting a closer contact between the spirit of man and Nature, enabling man to appreciate Nature's intricacy and his own power. Thanks to his newly-discovered dominion over Nature, it was felt that man was about to reach his life's true objective, happiness. The eighteenth century, a restless, tormented age, greatly preoccupied with the quest for happiness, sought for it along every path of knowledge. Could all natural phenomena be known, Nature would look like a perfect pyramid of smooth stones, the apex of which would be God.

Throughout the century, and even during the intervals when war made international communication difficult, scientists succeeded in keeping contact one with another, in bridging the diplomatic chasms. The whole century was intent on escaping from limits which were too narrow. Numerous islands—including Australia—were discovered and people began to realize that there were totally unknown regions even in the heart of Europe. It was thus that the exploration of the Alps began.

One of the heroes of the period was the naturalist. Great naturalists were among the people whose letters of introduction were as good as diplomatic passports, enabling their holders to travel freely through Europe. Another hero was the philosopher; a third was the doctor. As luck would have it, there were living in Switzerland two great naturalists, Bonnet and Saussure, two philosophers, von Haller and Lavater, and a great doctor, Théodore Tronchin—not to mention Voltaire and, at intervals, Rousseau. Von Haller and Saussure were leading authorities on Alpine subjects, and their reputation drew innumerable visitors to mountain districts. For a whole century, Dauphiny and the Austrian Alps were almost completely neglected, probably because no important scientist lived in Grenoble or Innsbrück.

Among the first scientists to interest themselves in matters Alpine were the brothers Deluc, Jean-André and Guillaume-Antoine, who have sunk into an undeserved oblivion, perhaps because they both outlived their glory. They were born respectively in 1717 and 1727; their father was a solemn bore whose chief concern was Genevese politics, the intricacies of which defy the patience of the best-disposed historian. The three Delucs were ardent admirers of Rousseau. The brothers entered history in 1754, when they sailed round the Lake of Geneva with their father, Rousseau and his mistress.

Now apart from their interest in Genevese politics, which was a family hobby, the Delucs were amateur scientists of some repute, and they began to think that the purpose of science might be advanced by an attempt to climb a high mountain, carrying a barometer to the top to read the air pressure, and by taking the temperature of boiling water at the summit. Accordingly they chose the Buet, a snow-covered peak which looks most impressive when seen from the neighbourhood of Geneva. Nowadays the mountain is nothing but a long grind up meadows, steep scree slopes and a small, almost level glacier. The going is never difficult but extremely tedious and one has to start from a very low valley. When the brothers Deluc made their first attempt, the worst part of the climb was discovering the way. The expedition took place in 1765, and they had to rely on the very inaccurate knowledge of peasants who had never been really high. Starting from Sixt the two brothers failed to reach the top, got stuck on steep grass slopes and discovered after a four hours' scramble that sheer precipices and a deep valley intervened between them and their goal. The barometer had been broken.

Five years of hectic Genevese politics prevented their renewing the attempt before August 1770. Their guide this time was an 'apprentice to a hunter' and was also a cheesemaker. These professions did not combine well and the man was abnormally clumsy too. It goes without saying that he lost his way. J.-A. Deluc slipped several times, and one of his companions became dizzy and had to give up the climb. When it was impossible to proceed further, the scientists started boiling water. Whereupon the cheese-maker roared with merriment and abruptly sat down on J.-A. Deluc's foot, which he badly twisted. Then without expressing the least regret, he went down to milk his cows, leaving his victims to follow as best they could. Deluc, who was in great pain, could only walk very slowly and the whole party had to spend the night out well above the highest huts. They were so tired that they managed to sleep a little, but were cramped and stiff when they awoke and had to wait some time before they could make their way back to Sixt.

The third attempt took place in September of the same year. The brothers now had a guide who happened to know his way, a certain Bernard Pommet. They slept again in the cow-sheds, were delayed there by bad weather and left early on the third day. This time they were successful. They went up and up, 'enjoying a multitude of agreeable sensations', and reached the last steep slopes. There was much snow.

'We were not shod for such an enterprise. But our guide, with his thick, hob-nailed boots, kicked the snow sideways as he ascended. In this way, he made little steps in the crust of snow which supported him, and by means of these we climbed up after him, supporting ourselves with our poles . . . We discovered the immense chain of the Alps, stretching for a distance of more than fifty leagues.'

The chief impression felt by the Delucs was that so much snow was to be seen all over the mountains that it was safe to assume that the Rhone, the Rhine, the Danube and the Po were never likely to run dry through drought. To the modern mind, the one redeeming aspect of the Buet is the stupendous view it commands. Mont Blanc, which usually appears almost level with the Aiguilles, seems from here to have stretched up its mighty bulk to display its shapely dome and flowing glaciers, while the soaring red granite turrets of the Aiguilles stop far below its brow. Behind the Chamonix range, waves of mountain roll away towards an immensely distant horizon. On their crests, amid hosts of other peaks, one descries the massive white shape of the Grand Combin, the thick-set pyramid of the Dent Blanche, the slender pyramid of the Weisshorn and the sharp summit of the Matterhorn. To the north, the bluish line of the Oberland fades into the sky. To the west, there is a vivid blue gap between two foothills: the Lake of Geneva between Evian and Lausanne. The whole prospect is at once striking and harmonious, but J.-A. Deluc, who loved mountains, did not know how to describe them. He was one of the first men to enter this mysterious realm, and he felt shy.

He little realized the dangers lurking in such unknown places. He suddenly discovered that he was boiling water on a snow cornice. Now Deluc did not retreat, for he explained that the added weight of his body and the boiler on the enormous mass of ice and snow were negligible. He was mistaken. Almost a century was to elapse before people discovered that cornices have to be approached with the utmost care and respect—if approached at all.

This successful ascent was not the end of the brothers' Alpine career. They had fallen in love with the mountains and continued to court them. Two years later, they returned to the Buet to make new experiments. While they were coming down, their barometer fell and was broken, an accident which occurs with almost tedious frequency in most of the narratives of the time, and which always plunges the man to whom it happens into the deepest gloom. The number of barometers that perished on mountain-sides is impressive and yet for years climbers never ventured up a mountain of any size without this cumbersome kind of luggage.

In 1773, having exhausted the charms of Genevese politics and tasted their bitter fruit, J.-A. Deluc, the elder brother, gave up this unsatisfactory pursuit and went to England. Eventually, with the help of the Baron de Salgas, a Swiss nobleman of French origin who was tutor to the Duke of Kent, he was appointed reader to the Queen and took up his abode at Windsor. In 1774 he was sent back to Switzerland to escort an intolerable German lady-in-waiting to the Queen, Fräulein von Schwellenberg, the person who was to make Fanny Burney's life at court almost unbearable. Climbing was out of the question, as poor Deluc could hardly escape from the lady's sight. After his return to England, he continued to take a keen interest in everything connected with the Alps. His brother, Guillaume-Antoine, went on exploring and sent long accounts of his expeditions to Jean-André. Once he returned to the neighbourhood of Sixt and climbed the next mountain to the Buet, feeling very sad because his former companion was not with him. On another occasion, in 1786, he went to the Col de la Seigne; he was caught in a storm, but a violent gust of wind cleared the view for a moment: 'The high summits', he wrote, 'could be descried, all white with fresh snow, through the gaps between the clouds; they appeared as many giants of an enormous size, as old as the world, who were at their windows looking down upon us, poor little creeping creatures.' The second part of the sentence is in English in the original.

For a long time the brothers had been accepted as outstanding scholars, and Jean-André was a Fellow of the Royal Society. Their scientific achievements were probably less striking than they themselves thought, but one thing cannot be taken from them: their keen unfailing interest in a mountain, the summit of which they reached in spite of hardship and danger.

The next mountain to be climbed was the Velan, a high snow peak which commands the Glacier de Valsorey at the top of the Val de Bagnes. The climb is incomparably more difficult than the Buet. The glacier which leads to the foot of the mountain is riven with crevasses, and then come endless slopes of ice and snow barred by walls of séracs. Eighteenth-century equipment made the going hazardous: shoes were insufficiently nailed; the crampons, when used, were of a very primitive kind, moreover climbers had to rely on alpenstocks, while their guides hacked steps with short-handled axes. Ropes, rarely used, were inadequately managed.

The man who succeeded in climbing the Velan was a priest of the St Bernard hospice, the Abbé Murith. He had been born in the near-by village of Sembrancher in 1742 and had taken holy orders in 1776. Murith dabbled in natural sciences; he was a botanist of some repute and an important local figure. He was acquainted with all the Genevese scientists and welcomed them when they came to his parish of Liddes or to the St Bernard, of which he later became prior. In the course of a visit to Geneva, he told his friends that he meant to climb the Velan, which was by far the most impressive peak in his district. He found two hunters who had some idea how to lead the climb, and the three men started on August 31, 1779, carrying food for several days and also the inescapable barometer—which, by great luck, was not broken. The hunters did not find the way and spent most of their time complaining of the heat and of exhaustion; they said they were home-sick and wailed that they would not go up one step more. Murith, who had an iron will, spurred them on, hacked steps and eventually dragged them up a steep ice pitch to reach the summit. When he was back at Liddes, he wrote triumphantly to Horace-Bénédict de Saussure to describe his climb:

'[Had you been with me] you would have enjoyed the most splendid spectacle of mountains and glaciers you can imagine; you would have been able to gaze on a wide circle of peaks of different heights, from Turin to the Little St Bernard, from the St Bernard to the Lake of Geneva, from Vevey to the St Gothard, from the St Gothard to Turin . . . But I cannot promise I will help you to enjoy so ravishing a view. In spite of my own intrepidity, I had too much trouble in gaining the summit of this wintry giant.'

Murith felt justly proud of his achievement. A few months later he wrote to the Genevese traveller Marc-Théodore Bourrit:

'The prospect from the Buet is magnificent [Bourrit had been up the Buet and was extremely touchy] but the Velan, which is hardly less than 100 toises lower than the highest point of Mont Blanc, would have delighted you; you would have seen the universe under your feet, the points and needles of the highest hills looking like a tumultuous sea . . . I believe I ascended one of the first great peaks ever climbed in Europe.'

He was right, and the fact that he emphasized is significant: in spite of his barometer, thermometer and the list of plants found on the highest rocks, Murith really climbed the Velan because he was attracted by the mountain. Scientific interest is not sufficient to account for it; he was clearly fascinated by the beauty of the great peak. Yet one aspect of modern mountaineering seems wholly absent from his motives: the craving for danger. Later on, as we shall see, he travelled extensively through the Alps and explored many little-known valleys. But never again did he attempt to ascend any high peak. Most of the early climbers specialized in one summit, and having climbed it

1. Napoleon's army crosses the Alps on its way to Marengo; aquarelles by Bagetti, Napoleon's official army painter. *Top*: At the St Bernard Pass on May 20, 1800. *Bottom*: In the fortified gorge of La Cluse, on May 21st. (Palace of Versailles)

2. *Top*: The Glacier des Bossons, by Woolett, 1777; the first accurate watercolour of the Chamonix Valley. *Bottom*: The Aiguille du Dru, by Sir John Hershel, 1821.

they gave up mountaineering for good. Not until the middle of the nineteenth century would climbers feel a continued impulse after a first great ascent and dedicate the whole of their lives—or at least of their summer holidays—to the mountains.

Another specialized climber was the Abbé Jean-Maurice Clément, also a priest of the Valais. He has left a name in history for two different reasons: he collected a fine library in his derelict vicarage of Val d'Illiez, and he climbed the Dent du Midi. The library was sold after his death, but I was lucky enough to discover a copy of its catalogue in the church of Val d'Illiez, in a chest of drawers full of old newspapers which had been torn to pieces by mice; these particular sheets of paper had proved too tough for them and were intact.

The story of the Dent du Midi is more complicated. Clément had been sent to Val d'Illiez in 1780; he was forty-six and heartily disliked both his work and his parishioners. He was on the worst possible terms with them and there were violent quarrels. Clément was endowed with a fiery temper and he felt horribly confined in his parish. He was a naturalist, owning about a thousand volumes of works on medicine and botany. Now Val d'Illiez is a dull place; there is nothing to be seen but the Dent du Midi, and this was why Clément conceived the idea of making the ascent. The officially accepted version is that he climbed the Haute Cime in 1784, a statement which is inaccurate.

According to a letter he sent to the *Journal de Lausanne* in December 1789, he had climbed 'two central peaks' of the Dent on August 22, 1788: 'The range has five summits, the furthermost, both east and west, being slightly lower than the two central ones. Tired to death, I reached the tops of the central ones . . . The weather was fairly fine.' Of course, he was carrying a barometer which gave most inaccurate readings. It is extremely difficult to guess what he meant by 'the two central summits' of a range of five, whether he meant the second and third or the third and fourth. The east and west summits are really much higher than the central ones. Modern topographers have divided the ridge into seven summits instead of five, so that, while it is almost certain Clément climbed some point, it is impossible to know which, for his account is too vague: 'My knowledge of natural history', he wrote, 'is not precise enough, and the time I spent on the top was too short to enable me to give a useful and interesting account of the things which struck me. It would require a second climb, which I shall never make unless with a companion.' After this he gave up mountaineering. The Dent du Midi is a somewhat unsatisfactory mountain, a foothill of crumbling rocks in a rainy district. It is perhaps not surprising that the Val d'Illiez was left to itself for a long time.

Among these pioneers of the Alps was one who succeeded in winning international repute; this was Marc-Théodore Bourrit. For over forty years he was in a very real sense the publicity agent for Mont Blanc. Born in 1739 in Geneva, he was of French Huguenot descent. A German traveller who met him, C. A. Fischer, wrote a lively description of his appearance: 'Bourrit's figure is long and thin, his complexion dark as a negro's, his eyes burning and full of genius and life; his mouth marked by a touch of mobility and good nature which inspires confidence.' Intellectually, he was far less attractive. A member of the Genevese middle class, he became a social snob and a prey to an almost morbid inferiority complex. He had imbibed a showy superficial culture and was immoderately proud of his many accomplishments. He was a painter and an engraver endowed with great accuracy and no talent; he read much and used to quote poets to uphold some lame scientific theory of his own, or borrow scientific terms to make his descriptions appear more impressive. As he had a good voice, he had been appointed precentor of the Cathedral choir and modestly wrote as follows: 'I have been told in Paris that my voice can compete with the finest in Europe . . . I daresay that when my passion for music gets the better of me, I may feel tempted to make myself known to the world.' The Church authorities used to complain bitterly that he was always absent in the mountains when required for a service. With no sense of humour, he was tortured by ambition. He sought to emulate his countryman, Jean-Jacques Rousseau, and was madly jealous of those who surpassed him in any way. Like most of his contemporaries, he was always ready to shed tears.

Once, arriving at the Montenvers above Chamonix and finding a vast concourse of tourists, mostly English, about to start for the Jardin de Talèfre with their guides, he began to preach a sermon to the guides:

'Put yourselves in the place of the strangers who come from the most distant lands to admire the marvels of Nature in these wild and savage aspects, and justify the confidence which they place in you. . . . In pointing out the various phenomena to their astonished eyes, you will rejoice to see people raise their thoughts to the omnipotence of the great Being who created them.'

The tourists and guides may, of course, have been impressed by this majestic flow of eloquence. As for Bourrit himself, he burst into tears as he stood between the Princess d'Hénin and the Paris lieutenant of police. But when he had a grudge against a rival, nothing prevented him from using the worst of weapons: libel, anonymous letters, slander and other unsavoury devices. His countrymen made endless fun of him; foreigners were more likely to fall under the spell of a man who could talk, gesticulate, weep, shout, or produce torrents of eloquence in weather fair or foul, and whom nothing could extinguish, not even the rain of Savoy.

Bourrit had one noble passion: his love of the mountains, to which he dedicated his life. From 1766 to 1812 he visited the Alps several times each year. He knew what high mountains were like, though he could never learn how to tackle them in the right spirit. He was afraid of running into dangers he did not understand; he would often demur at the last moment when starting on a long expedition, and yet a fortnight later he could again be ready to start. He dreaded the cold and climbed in fur-lined shoes which afforded a very bad footing. He dreaded the rain and carried a large red umbrella when crossing high pastures where cows and bulls spent the summer. He dreaded giddiness and used to lean heavily on his guides when climbing steep places. His companions, Murith, de Saussure and Paccard, and even his guides, were soon worn out by a man who climbed badly and talked so much. To make things worse, Bourrit used to take his dogs on his expeditions: Raton, Coco and Loulou were duly dragged across glaciers and moraines, and when they died, Bourrit had them stuffed.

His gift for publicity would have put to shame many of our modern advertisers. He wrote much, his style was bad and, in spite of the praise showered upon him, he dimly realized he was not a great writer. Consequently he stopped at nothing in advertising his climbs and his books. He flattered the current taste by discovering Golden Age valleys in the most unlikely spots, by praising the beauty of Alpine maidens, by building up the most fantastic scientific theories. He painted numerous Alpine water-colours which he managed to sell to Louis XVI, to Mesdames his aunts, to Lord Clive, the Emperor of Russia, the King of Sardinia, Prince Henry of Prussia and the Empress Joséphine. He begged a pension from the King of France and eventually got it, thanks to Buffon's help. The man was an overwhelming bore.

Yet he played a leading part in mountaineering history. His constant expeditions across the Alps took him again and again to Chamonix, Grindelwald, Courmayeur, the St Bernard and other well-known places, but he did more than merely cover classical ground. Once he went up the Val d'Illiez, met Clément and waxed enthusiastic over the Dent du Midi. On another occasion, when exploring the neighbourhood of the Gemmi, he went to Kandersteg and found the lovely Lake of Oeschinen. He made his way up the Val d'Anniviers and the Val d'Hérens, though on both occasions he was more interested in local customs than in Alpine scenery and completely forgot to look at the Dent Blanche or the Weisshorn. Another year, he mounted the Glacier de Valsorey, which was known only to the local chamois-hunters. Bourrit had conceived the idea that there should be a glacier at the head of each of the glens which come down to the main Rhone valley. After a few preliminary failures, he managed to secure the company of Murith and they ascended the Val de Bagnes towards Chanrion. They spent the night in a chalet where shepherds were making cheese, left early in the morning and, after a long trudge up pastures, scree slopes and moraines, came at last to the glacier:

'A new universe came into view; what words can I use to describe a spectacle which struck us dumb? How can I worthily describe the impression it made on our souls? It was a single stretch of ice of more than eight leagues in length surrounded on every side by ice mountains. This view burst in a single moment on our surprised and astonished sight. These prodigious mounds of ice, these mountains which seemed to touch the sky were serrated in innumerable ways.'

Bourrit was confident he could reach a crest from which one would be able to look down on Piedmont on one side and on the Rhone valley on the other, and he was very much surprised when he discovered that his way was taking him along the bottom of the ice trough, 'a long narrow gorge between two mountain ranges, the one covered with eternal snow, the other capped with huge mounds of loose scree, ice domes and crags'. There were no living things in sight, not even a chamois. The rays of a glaring sun played upon walls of rust-red granite and deep blue crevasses.

'The richness and variety of colours added to the beauty of the shapes. Gold, silver, crimson, and azure were shining everywhere, and what impressed me with a sense of even greater strangeness were the arches supporting snow-bridges over the crevasses, the apparent strength of which encouraged us to walk across. We were even courageous enough to stop in the middle and gaze down into the abyss.'

Behind his clumsy words, one feels the awe and admiration which Bourrit experienced when entering this virgin world, full of unsuspected wonders.

Bourrit actually found a new route up the Buet, from the valley of Valorcine. It was shorter than the one followed by the Delucs, though hardly less tedious. Bourrit's enthusiasm broke all bounds when he reached the summit and he clamoured to heaven and earth to witness and bless his triumph. He has been commemorated on the spot: a large boulder on the highest slope has been named after him 'La Table au Chantre', Bourrit being precentor *(chantre)* of the Cathedral of Geneva.

Being a constant visitor to the valley of Chamonix, he was a great favourite with the local people and he wished to ingratiate himself even further. He once wrote to the Bishop of Annecy to beg exemption from fasting for both natives and visitors: foreigners, he urged, might be induced to stay longer if they were not vexed by such regulations, and they would spend more money to the benefit of trade in the valley. No doubt the Bishop yielded to so persuasive an argument.

Few people ventured to oppose his overwhelming activity; the man did everything, knew everything and everybody and went everywhere—at least, if we are to believe the copious self-eulogies which he published. He labelled himself the 'Historian of the Alps', or 'Indefatigable Bourrit'. People who knew him well, like de Saussure, the Delucs and other fellow-countrymen, thought him a nuisance. He was hardly a gentleman and yet much is to be forgiven him, because he loved the Alps so much.

With few exceptions the early pioneers were not men of letters. Literature was developing along lines of its own, which hardly intersected the lines followed by science. Early eighteenth-century writers dreaded the mountains and ignored them as much as possible. Horace Walpole's dog was devoured by a wolf on the way up the Mont Cenis; Lady Mary Wortley Montagu suffered acutely from the cold when crossing the same pass; as a consequence, their accounts of their journeys were far from enthusiastic. Richardson ascribed to Sir Charles Grandison the following description of Savoy: 'a country equally noted for its poverty and rocky mountains'. Similar instances might be quoted by the dozen. On the other hand Thomas Gray, who travelled with Walpole, pitied the dog but was deeply impressed by the stupendous landscape of the Grande Chartreuse.

In 1732, the Swiss scientist and philosopher A. von Haller published *Die Alpen*. Haller was a Bernese patrician who had lived for some time in Bex, where he was able to gaze at the Dent de Morcles and the Dent du Midi. He had compiled a big work on Swiss plants, had travelled in Alpine districts to collect documents, and superintended the researches of several botanists, the Thomas family, among others, who were working under him. His poem, short and dignified, was mainly concerned with the moral and sociological aspects of the mountains: the age was obsessed by the ethical aspect of Nature and its influence on the soul of man, and mountain-dwellers, being primitive people, living very close to Nature, were consequently endowed with the fairest virtues. Haller's poem was translated into French, then into English and soon became one of the best-sellers of the century. But Haller's mountain-dwellers were not mountaineers and scarcely indulged in chamois-hunting.

In 1761, Jean-Jacques Rousseau published his novel *La Nouvelle Héloïse*.

One long section was devoted to a description of the hero's feelings when travelling through the Valais. The author might have known the Alps well. A native of Geneva, he had seen Mont Blanc during his youth, had lived in Annecy and Chambéry, had crossed the Mont Cenis to Turin, and on another occasion had returned to Switzerland across the Simplon. He had seen Monte Rosa and the Bernese Alps, and Mont Blanc from the neighbourhood of Sallanches, yet he never gave a first-hand description of any of them. At heart, he did not feel attracted to the mountains: they were too rough, too aloof from human standards, too devoid of human interest to attract him. Rousseau was obsessed with his own personality and could never free himself from it to the extent of merging his being into that of Nature. But he knew that mountains were becoming a background for literature. Sentimental readers might like to hear more about them. When he sailed round the Lake of Geneva with the Delucs, Rousseau obtained a good deal of information from the two sons who had just returned from a trip to Savoy. The young men worshipped the great writer and were only too glad to supply him with descriptions. One wonders whether they ever recognized they were the real source of passages like the following: 'There is something magical and supernatural in hill landscape which entrances the mind and the senses; one forgets everything, one forgets one's own being; one ceases to know even where one stands.' It is most likely that Rousseau drew his literary inspiration for such pages from Haller's poem and from the narratives of the Delucs.

When the *Nouvelle Héloïse* had become a best-seller and readers were shedding tears over its burning pages, scores of travellers went to Switzerland to see the places Rousseau had made immortal, but the practice of mountaineering did not benefit thereby. For such travellers the holy shrine was the Lake of Geneva, in the neighbourhood of Clarens and Meillerie. At the same time, places like Chamonix and Grindelwald were attracting a rising tide of travellers. Those who could not visit Switzerland or Savoy applied phrases which might have come from Rousseau to less illustrious ranges like the Alps of Dauphiny, the Pyrenees, and even the Vosges. But even in the Alps, few people ventured above the snow-line. The Montenvers was often the highest goal. Innumerable descriptions appeared in print; their writers raved, wept and went away relieved, first because they had been able to pay homage at the shrine, and then because they found it a rather disturbing neighbourhood. They hardly gave a thought to scaling the peaks.

There was one exception, the Duke of Hamilton, who went to the Mer de Glace with his tutor, Dr John Moore, and several friends and suddenly conceived the idea of climbing the Dru. 'Bounding over the ice with the elasticity of a young chamois', he reached the Nant Blanc side of the glacier and tried to scale the north face of the tall granite pyramid. One of his friends felt a sudden pang of jealousy and ran after him. Meanwhile 'the Duke had gained a considerable height when he was suddenly stopped by a part of the rock which was perfectly impracticable'. The other young man overtook him and they promptly agreed to come down. They had probably scrambled up over some easy rocks near the big Nant Blanc waterfall: it would have taken them hours to reach even the lower glacier at the foot of the Aiguille. No one repeated their attempt. One can sum up this phase of Alpine travel by saying that Rousseau's works did not lead to any Alpine discovery.

But there was one notable exception to the general indifference to high hills. Ramond de Carbonnière was a young lawyer from Colmar in Alsace, who visited Switzerland at the age of twenty-two when trying to forget an unhappy love affair. In 1777 he was seeking literary fame by means of a few sentimental poems, a wildly romantic novel and an historical play on a medieval subject. All these were failures. Ramond then translated into French and annotated Archdeacon Coxe's *Letters on the Civil and Political state of Switzerland*. The original was dull; Ramond's translation was more lively and, on the whole, fairly accurate; his notes were masterly. The book was widely read and Ramond achieved the literary fame he had been seeking. Strangely enough, Coxe was not pleased and they quarrelled, but this was of no importance either to Ramond or his readers. The young man now became secretary to the Cardinal de Rohan who, four years later, was to figure prominently— and notoriously—in the affair of the Diamond Necklace, which occasioned one of the crises preceding the French Revolution. Ramond himself played a mysterious though secondary part in it. His discretion, his natural dignity and prudent foresight served him well—for although a great deal of mud was thrown, none of it stuck to him. Yet he was involved in Rohan's downfall. He accompanied the Cardinal to Barèges in the Pyrenees, where they whiled away the tedium of exile. Eventually the two quarrelled. But Ramond had discovered the Pyrenees; he travelled through the whole range and ascended the Mont Perdu, thus crowning, more or less, a mountaineering career which had begun in the Alps.

Ramond is the first poet of mountaineering. True, he made no very high ascent in the Alps, but he had a vision and a keen feeling for mountain beauty. Once, when crossing the Joch pass after a heavy snowfall, he felt the magic of the high solitary world so few people had understood or even reached at that time:

'In front of us a long deep valley sank away into the distance; it was completely enveloped in spotless white snow. Here and there a few blocks of granite peeped out, looking like so many islands scattered over the ocean; the grim summits soaring above the valley were covered with snow and glaciers, which reflected the sun rays on all the shades of colour between white and blue.'

Ramond rarely indulged in long descriptions but, when he did, few writers could rival him. But he analysed what he felt when climbing and recorded his perception of the vague, slow, inarticulate, meandering thoughts which waver through the mind of the climber. To force oneself to precise thinking is impossible. Solitude, fatigue, the blessed relief of being at last able to cease moving weigh upon the mind; it subsides into musing, apathetic contemplation and quiet enjoyment of the current of time:

'The silence of these regions where nothing lives, where nothing moves, which are out of reach of the inhabited world, . . . contributes to deepen one's meditations and impart to them those sombre hues, that sublime note which they acquire when the soul hovers over the abyss of time. . . . Do not imagine that life can be painful for a single instant amid those desert places.'

Time and again he becomes conscious of the uncanny attraction of those mountain solitudes:

'Where is the source of their secret charm? What is the strange deep irresistible feeling that draws me to those realms over which my fellowmen have never established their dominion?'

It was the indefinable attraction of the hills that he thus felt and ventured to express.

His work contains not only descriptions and articulate feelings. He discovered a message: how to solve or at least to apprehend the riddle of a world which was to survive the ruins of a doomed century: 'My soul, oppressed with the deep realization of the ruins brought about by the ages, found nothing but wreckage within and without . . . and then everything became clear and order appeared where there had been only confusion . . . Imagination is terrified at the onslaught of the ideas of immensity and eternity.' Either by experience or through his vivid, manifold imagination, Ramond grasped most of the elements which endow mountaineering with its powerful fascination: the opening up of totally unknown regions the appearance of which could not even be suspected by non-climbers, the call of adventure and danger, the realization of the meaning of complete solitude, the sensation of going back to a time when the world was purer and more merciful because less lived in. Though he wrote at great length about chamois-hunters in his first book, he rapidly dismissed this stereotyped aspect of mountain life. His Pyrenean guide, Rondo, was a good fellow who was terrified by the initiative of his daring patron and was responsible for one or two failures on the Mont Perdu.

Ramond's experiences during the Revolution were unpleasant. A member of a party whose deputies for the most part died on the scaffold, he had several narrow escapes and was imprisoned three times. He probably owed his life to the fact that he remained during the greater part of the time in the Pyrenees, far away from Paris. Mountains were for him at once a refuge and an inspiration during the worst of the years he had to live through. The woman with whom he was in love died after a long illness. All through his life, Ramond closely and successfully kept secret the part he had played in the affair of the Diamond Necklace: of this affair all that survived was a poison ring, one of the three made by Cagliostro for himself, for Ramond and for the Cardinal. Ramond eventually became a scientist, a geologist and a topographer of repute, a member of the French Academy of Sciences, a prefect under Napoleon, and a remarkable tutor. He achieved the glory he had aimed at in youth and found that its taste was bitter. One thing remained alive in him: his passion for the mountains.

His books conveyed a message to a variety of readers. They were beautifully written, leading the mind by slow stages to the realization of entirely new notions. There was something strange and very disturbing about them which accorded with the mood of a restless period. Ramond's translation of Coxe's letters was used as a guide-book by the two great poets of the period, André Chénier and William Wordsworth. Ramond was not only a pioneer of mountaineering; he also brought mountaineering within the range of literature.

CHAPTER FOUR

MONT BLANC

I F you are looking from Dijon, from the Puy de Dôme or from Lyons in clear weather, a faint white shadow, assuming the shape of a high cone, looms up on the horizon, hardly more distinct than a cloud. From Neuchâtel, whence the Alps are seen to stretch along in an endless line, parallel to the general direction of the lake, this same white cone shows up at the western end of the range, supported on both sides by satellite mountains of almost perfect symmetry. But at Geneva a whole ice world comes within sight. Snow slopes descend from the cone, while a lower dome leads the eye down to the forests below. Fantastic rock steeples, coloured purple or dark blue by distance, soar up on the left of the mountain. Though dwarfed by the huge snowy mass, they have an unexpectedly and unbelievably beautiful architecture. At sunset the whole range is steeped in a red-gold glow which deepens to scarlet with turquoise shadows. The intervening foothills, with their forests of beech and pine, give a dark frame to this majestic landscape.

From time immemorial the great mountain had impressed those who gazed on it. As early as 1444, the Basle painter, Conrad Witz, placed it in the background of his *Miraculous Draught of Fishes,* which is now in the Geneva museum. But it did not acquire a name for more than three centuries. The whole range was vaguely referred to as 'Hoary Alps' *(Alpes chenues),* 'Horned Alps' *(Alpes cornues)* or, worse still, 'The Accursed Mountain' *(Le Mont Maudit).* A party of English travellers went to Chamonix in 1741 and did not even notice the mountain, which is not surprising: the valley is narrow and foreshortening has the effect of dwarfing the high summits. A year later, in 1742, a Genevese traveller, Pierre Martel, made the same trip and wrote in his account: 'The two other western peaks are the Aiguille du Mont Mallet and . . . Mont Blanc, which is the westernmost summit. The latter is deemed to be the highest amongst the *Glacières* and possibly the whole of the Alps.' Thus was Mont Blanc born to the world. But the names Mont Maudit and Mont Mallet did not disappear; the former travelled slightly to the east and was ascribed to the summit next to Mont Blanc, the latter retreated to the head of the Mer de Glace.

In 1760, a young Genevese scholar visited Chamonix for the first time. His name was Horace-Bénédict de Saussure; he was twenty years of age. His

birth and family connections, his upbringing, learning and natural gifts com-
bined to make him one of the most remarkable and appealing personalities of
the period. He belonged to the Genevese aristrocracy, a small, exclusive and
cultured class, all the members of which were related to one another. De
Saussure had been a brilliant student and was hardly twenty-two when he was
appointed Professor of Natural Philosophy at the Geneva Academy. He was
handsome, witty and refined, had been brought up by supremely intelligent
parents and was married to a charming and very rich girl, with whom he was
deeply in love. They were to have three children and de Saussure's home life
was peaceful and happy to the end. The one disturbing element in his otherwise restful personality was his passionate love of mountains, which was to
raise to a position of celebrity one who, but for such an incentive, might not
have been more than a distinguished naturalist. It eventually cost him his life:
de Saussure died at fifty-nine, worn out by his Alpine journeys.

Before his first trip to Chamonix he wrote to Haller, the Bernese naturalist
and poet: 'I am desperately anxious to see at close quarters the great Alpine
summits which look so majestic from the top of our (Genevese) mountains.'
When he reached Chamonix for the first time, he immediately became aware
of several interesting facts and he fell in love with the valley which was to
become almost his second home. He explored the lower hills and glaciers and
made an official annoucement, offering a reward to the first man who should
reach the summit of Mont Blanc. It looked like a casual offer and probably
was. At that time, de Saussure did not suspect the difficulty of the climb nor its
scientific importance.

Although de Saussure now resumed his work at the University, he had
resolved to devote his life to the study of the mountains. Year after year he
returned to Chamonix, but also visited most other Alpine districts. In the
course of these journeys, he kept minute diaries which he wrote twice over:
first while in his coach or on horseback or, if on foot, when making a halt.
These rough notes were rewritten at night in the inn. A third stage was reached
when he used these notes in the first draft of a book he began very slowly to
compose a few years later, checking the references and going over his
expeditions again so as to ensure complete accuracy. In 1768–9 he visited
England, which he felt was a country after his own heart. Two years later he
went to Italy and spent several months in Naples and Sicily as the guest of
Sir William Hamilton; but as soon as he was back in Geneva, he resumed his
Alpine expeditions. The great work of his life was to be a long scholarly
description of the mountains, in the course of which he hoped to unravel the
mysteries connected with their formation. The eighteenth century was intent
on solving the various riddles of the universe. It was tireless in building up

scientific and political systems, the bases of which were often no more substantial than a flash of the imagination. De Saussure, although anxious, like his contemporaries, to find the key to many problems of natural science, was a slave to minute observation and just lacked the touch of imagination which would have turned his exceptional talent into genius.

The people of Chamonix did not take very seriously the offer he had made in 1760 and again in 1761. Pierre Simon, who had been one of his guides, made two half-hearted attempts, first up the Glacier des Bossons and then from the back of the Mer de Glace, but he was quickly discouraged and nothing more was done for thirteen years. Local terrors and superstitions were too strong. Another figure now appeared on the stage: Marc-Théodore Bourrit. He came to Chamonix in 1766 for the first time and immediately started collecting information. Hearing of the promised reward for the first ascent of Mont Blanc, he caught fire; he had not the slightest wish to compete for the prize himself, but he wanted Mont Blanc to be climbed and hoped to derive some literary repute from his narrative of the feat. He wrote several books about the valley, all of them including long discussions of the feasibility of the ascent. He spoke of it, lectured on it and exerted himself so much that, on July 13, 1775, four guides attempted the climb.

When one looks at Mont Blanc from the bottom of the valley one perceives an obvious way up to the higher glaciers: the long spur of forest and rock which projects far into the ice and is called the Montagne de la Côte. Higher up, a logical route would lead across a not very steep but much crevassed glacier, then past the foot of a few dark rocky islands and up two big snow plateaux. The last part of the climb was obviously much steeper and more confusing. Accordingly, the four guides went up the Montagne de la Côte. They started late, were slow and had much trouble in crossing the crevassed glacier—the part known as the Jonction—when the heat of the day was melting the bridges and turning the snow into a quagmire. The view was beautiful, but the top of the mountain looked as remote as ever. Plodding through soft snow, the men came to a hidden crevasse and one of them narrowly escaped a bad fall. They could stand no more and thoroughly discouraged, tired, sunburnt and almost snow-blind, they came down, after having probably reached the lower part of the Petit Plateau.

A few weeks later, the third of the principal figures in the drama of Mont Blanc made his appearance. Michel-Gabriel Paccard was the youngest son of the Chamonix notary and a cousin to two of the men who had just failed to climb the mountain. He was eighteen and was pursuing a course of medical studies in Turin. Ten years later, de Saussure was to describe him as 'a handsome youth, full of intelligence, fond of botany, creating a garden of Alpine plants, wanting to climb Mont Blanc or at least attempt it'. He had already attempted it. In September 1775, a young Scottish landscape gardener named Thomas Blaikie, who was in quest of Alpine flowers and seeds arrived at Chamonix with letters of introduction for Paccard's father. Paccard's three sons took charge of him and showed him all the lower glaciers, while Michel-Gabriel took him to the Montenvers. Then after a night spent in a cowherd's hut at Blaitière, they crossed the three glaciers at the foot of the Aiguilles, then the Glacier des Bossons and the Glacier de Taconnaz and mounted the lower slopes of the Aiguille du Goûter. This last part of the expedition was nothing less than an attempt at reconnoitring a route up Mont Blanc along the crest which is so obvious from Chamonix. Blaikie did not suspect this and was chiefly interested in the flowers he had found in the troughs of the moraines. Both young men were very tired when they came down by the Glacier des Bossons.

In 1779 an unknown Frenchman made a rather futile and unsuccessful attempt. Three guides tried again in 1783 and failed near the Petit Plateau; then Bourrit himself began to move. He was now torn between a violent desire to be the first man on the top and a secret terror of fatigue, cold and the mysterious dangers lurking on the mountains. De Saussure wrote: 'M. Bourrit is even keener than I to conquer Mont Blanc.' Consequently, Bourrit staged his own attempt. According to the fashion of the time, he was bound to carry scientific instruments. He begged de Saussure to lend him his barometer and met with a polite but firm refusal: barometers were expensive and de Saussure rightly doubted Bourrit's skill in handling them. He next invited another Genevese naturalist, Dr H. A. Gosse, to come with him, and met with a second refusal. Finally, he succeeded in finding a companion in Michel-Gabriel Paccard.

The young student had now become a doctor. He had passed his examinations in Turin, and then gone to study in Paris, where he had met Bourrit who was selling his pictures and trying to make the acquaintance of the leading French scientists. The two men had already met at Chamonix. Paccard was then hardly twenty-two and had trusted Bourrit to the extent of confessing his literary hopes and plans. Bourrit probably thought the young man would be a convenient companion on a climb and would be content with a secondary part. But Paccard had matured; he had developed a strong will, a dry sense of humour and a most assertive spirit. His portraits display stern regular features, a high forehead, a long, slightly crooked nose, an intelligent, hard, straightforward look. Paccard was full of energy and courage; he was touchy and did not suffer fools gladly; he was cultured, and a gentleman at heart. Bourrit had none of those qualities, except touchiness.

On September 15, 1783, Bourrit, Paccard and three guides ascended the Montagne de la Côte, but now a few clouds gathered and, according to Paccard, 'Bourrit did not dare to set foot on the ice.' The young man made up his mind never again to climb with 'Indefatigable Bourrit'. In 1784 he reconnoitred the other face of Mont Blanc, at the top of the Glacier du Géant, and confessed that the route looked extremely difficult. He was right, for some of the most perilous climbs on the Alps are made in this part of the range. Then, in September 1784, with two guides, Paccard made a new attempt on the Aiguille du Goûter—climbing by the north arête and not by the face he had followed with Blaikie. In spite of very bad rocks and a broken barometer, he reached a point high above the Tête Rousse. He gave up the attempt at the end of the afternoon, when the weather was changing; but he wrote to de Saussure to describe the expedition.

Meanwhile, the great naturalist had become thoroughly convinced that Mont Blanc could be climbed, would be climbed and that he himself must climb it. He could not gaze at the mountain from Geneva without feeling something akin to guilt or pain, and this because he was not actually fighting his way up the icy slopes, but was simply, though anxiously, watching the various climbers who were trying to find a route. On September 16, 1784, Bourrit made another attempt, this time by the route on which Paccard had just failed. He started complete with dog, drawing material and four guides. A little below Tête Rousse, he felt cold and mountain-sick, and therefore sat down to sketch; this was the end of the attempt, as far as he was concerned. Seeing that he would not go a step further, two of the guides started climbing the Aiguilles du Goûter and in six hours reached the Dôme du Goûter. It was too late to go on, and what they saw was not encouraging: it was the Arête des Bosses, which was much too difficult for eighteenth-century mountaineers. In fact, it requires good nails, possibly crampons and an ice-axe. The two guides built a cairn—one wonders what it was made of, as there are no stones there—and then came down to tell their story to Bourrit. On the way down to Chamonix, Bourrit wrote a highly-coloured description of the episode, which provoked Guillaume-Antoine Deluc, who hated him, to write as follows to his brother in England: 'Bourrit has just given a manuscript redaction of his new attempt on Mont Blanc . . . The title is very funny and so are several paragraphs of the text. It is easy to see it has not been corrected by his friend Bérenger.' There will be more to say of Bérenger later on. Deluc wrote his letter in English.

After the guides' climb things looked more promising. De Saussure thought there was now a reasonable hope of getting to the summit though it was impossible to avoid having Bourrit in the party. What complicated matters was that Bourrit was now taking a son with him, and the son was as much of a hindrance as the father; he was twenty-one, extremely cocksure and proud of his accomplishments as a mountaineer. The summer of 1785 was very wet and the party had to wait until mid-September, a rather late moment. De Saussure arranged for a rough hut to be built at Les Rognes, at the foot of the Aiguille du Goûter. The first evening had a dreamlike beauty and de Saussure felt happy and restless as his eyes dwelt on the wonderful landscape with its changing hues under the fading light. On the following morning, the cold compelled the party to wait until six o'clock. Bourrit, as usual, dreaded the cold and attempted to climb in furred boots. They climbed for five hours, very slowly, over loose snow-covered rocks. At about twelve, de Saussure's guide called for a halt, went ahead to see what it was like and reported heavy fresh snow everywhere. It was unanimously agreed to give up the attempt. Everybody was tired, the Bourrits to the point of exhaustion, and these two staggered down leaning heavily on their guides' arms. De Saussure spent a second night alone in the hut, making observations.

The aftermath of the climb is not negligible as it affords an example of an unhappy but frequent habit of unsuccessful climbers to place the blame of failure on the other man. Bourrit with considerable impertinence wrote to de Saussure:

'Sir, I happen to have eyes and also ears, and they have revealed to me that the way in which you came down was not the happiest. You might have fallen backwards and broken your skull . . . As to *my* mode of coming down, I followed the prudent advice of [my guide] . . . I allow my heart to speak freely as it is good and honest.'

De Saussure, with great restraint, replied that he did not mean to hurt Bourrit, but was he not going a little too far? On the following day Bourrit's son sent de Saussure a long paper on how to come down a mountain:

'Sir, do you not envy me my twenty-one years? Who will wonder if a youth of this age, who has nothing to lose, is bolder than a father of a family, a man of forty-six?'

De Saussure's reply was a model of cool courtesy.

'A moderate amount of boastfulness is no great crime at your age . . . You say you descended agilely. It is true, you descended agilely enough on the easy places, but in the difficult places you were, like your father, leaning on the shoulder of the guide in front and held up behind by another . . . In no language in the world can that style of progress be termed agile climbing.'

As autumn was now closing in, a further attempt was impracticable that year. On June 7, 1786, a team of three guides again tried to ascend the Dôme du Goûter from the Chamonix side. The leader was François Paccard, a cousin of the doctor; an elderly man who had taken part in the unsuccessful expedition of 1775, he had also been William Coxe's guide. The three men slept at the top of the Montagne de la Côte, where they were overtaken by Jacques Balmat des Baux. We now meet the fourth principal character in the drama. Balmat was not a guide, but a chamois- and crystal-hunter; he was twenty-four years of age, clever, even cunning, and in dire need of money. It seems that his colleagues did not like him and his appearance on the Montagne de la Côte was not welcomed Yet the four men continued the ascent together. They were hoping to meet two guides who were coming up from the St Gervais side, but the latter had encountered difficulties and did not arrive until the Chamonix party had already left. The Chamonix men climbed steadily up long slopes covered with fresh snow, frozen hard at this early hour. They eventually reached the small rocks where the Vallot hut now stands and were terrified when they saw so near at hand the sheer precipices on both sides of the Arête des Bosses; they built a cairn and most of them felt mountain-sick. Balmat felt even worse; but he recovered and climbed a little higher in search of crystals. The quest was fruitless. On his return to the halting place, he found that the others had left—a sign that they felt little sympathy for the interloper. The weather was now becoming cloudy and Balmat started to descend. Although he failed to overtake the party he was able to follow the track they had left in the snow, finally reaching a broad crevasse which they had jumped; he did not dare to make the attempt and, as darkness was falling, he lay down on his rucksack and his snow-rackets to spend a most uncomfortable night. The others had been benighted on the Montagne de la Côte. At dawn, Balmat resumed his descent and reached Chamonix at eight. He was badly sunburnt and consulted Dr Paccard about the sad state of his complexion.

This new failure settled several important things: among them, that it was possible to sleep in the snow at a fairly high altitude without dying, and that the route above the Dôme—which is now the normal route—was unclimbable. These two discoveries were of great subsequent importance.

Now for three years Paccard had been surveying Mont Blanc through his telescope; he had planned a way to the top and was anxious to try it. Balmat wished to obtain the reward which had been offered. Each man needed a companion to act as a witness. Paccard for himself did not care about the reward: his was the disinterested attitude of the man who has dedicated his life to scientific research. He wanted to reach the summit to take barometric readings and also to feel what it was like at the top of a great mountain, although, as we must remember, climbing for the pleasure of climbing was unheard of at that time. So he offered to take Balmat as a porter. Balmat accepted, believing that Paccard intended to follow the Dôme route, and also because he himself had no alternative way to suggest. They set off accordingly, in the early afternoon of June 7, 1786. This adventure has often been related, and yet I think it is not superfluous to tell it once again, as the story has been frequently misrepresented, for one reason or another.

Climbing Mont Blanc by the usual route is not considered particularly interesting today. Under good conditions, it is no more than a long steep walk over ice or snow. One hardly ever needs to use one's hands. The description given me by my Chamonix guide is accurate enough: 'You bow your head and you plod up like an ox for twelve hours.' But Mont Blanc is so huge that everything depends on the weather, which never remains good for long. A storm on Mont Blanc is always dangerous and sometimes fatal. The cold can be terrible; the wind turns the final slopes into a raging inferno; the lack of air in the big ice troughs of the plateaux causes many people, and even excellent climbers, to suffer from mountain-sickness. When Paccard and Balmat climbed the mountain, most of the dangers of the ice-world were unsuspected. The young men were carrying their alpenstocks, one blanket, a little food and Paccard's instruments. They had neither crampons nor axes nor rope. They did not suspect that there are hours during which glaciers and séracs are better left alone; they did not imagine how carefully they must probe snow-bridges to test their strength; they hardly thought of the risk of avalanches.

Paccard and Balmat went up the Montagne de la Côte, as usual, and spent the night under big granite boulders which are still known as the Gîte à Balmat. They left at four in the morning. The weather was splendid, yet difficulties were immediately encountered. Owing to the hot summer, most of the snow had already melted: crevasses were gaping, snow-bridges were insecure—they had to wind their way up through a maze of crevasses. It took eight hours to reach the last rocks above the Grands Mulets. By this time Balmat was very tired and Paccard kept urging him on; he even took on his own shoulders his disheartened porter's pack. Balmat was feeling the height and the heat: he now wanted to abandon the attempt and suggested he should return to help his wife nurse their sick baby—their little Judith was very ill and actually died that very day, but Balmat might have thought of this before he started. The crossing of the Grand Plateau was exhausting; the melting snow often gave way under the men's weight. They were blinded by the glare; they took turns at breaking the trail. By five o'clock they had passed the Rochers Rouges, where two choughs stared at them. The afternoon was wearing on; they looked for some rocks where they might bivouac, but there were none within sight, so they plodded on, having made up their minds to reach the summit at any cost and if necessary to come down by night. The wind began to blow; yet they staggered on and eventually reached the summit: 'Paccard called me and I followed,' wrote Balmat later. Paccard reached the top at 6.25 and Balmat ran up the few last steps to stand beside him.

Meanwhile the whole population of Chamonix was looking at them through telescopes. Paccard tried nervously to make a few observations; he knew they would not be of much value, for he was very tired, very cold and feeling giddy on account of the height and lack of food. His hands were frostbitten, his eyes red, swollen and painful. After half an hour, the two young men started running and sliding down: they had barely two and a half hours of daylight left. But after sundown the moon lit them on their way, though such pale blue deceptive light hardly enables one to discern the lie of the land accurately. It was almost midnight when they reached the top of the Montagne de la Côte. The cold had frozen the snow and they did not flounder it in as before. All the crevasses had been avoided but the barometer was broken. So they wrapped themselves in their one blanket and were so tired that they were able to gain a little sleep. They came down to Chamonix early in the morning; Paccard was almost completely snow-blind.

By mere chance, de Saussure had provided the party with several reliable witnesses. Two travellers, Baron von Gerdsorf and Baron Meyer de Knonau, a French Knight of Malta of Swiss origin, had called on him in Geneva a few days earlier, and he had sent them to Chamonix, provided with plenty of information about the valley and what was taking place. They had seen the two climbers on their way up and later on at the summit. The following day, they climbed a mountain opposite Mont Blanc to make a sketch of the climbers' tracks in the snow; then they returned to Geneva to break the news. Meanwhile, Balmat too had hurried to Geneva to tell his story to de Saussure and to obtain the reward; he had taken François Paccard with him as a witness. Another Chamonix guide, Pierre Tairraz, had also gone to see de Saussure.

The naturalist immediately went into action and arrived at Chamonix on August 18th. He wrote to a friend: 'My head is so full of my plans that I feel tired and almost sick if I forget them even for a moment.' He went straight to Paccard's home, where he heard that the young man was again on the mountain with one of his brothers as a guide, trying to find a route up the other side of the Glacier des Bossons. As soon as Paccard returned, he arranged with de Saussure to take barometer readings in the valley while the older man was on the mountain. Then de Saussure collected his guides and left for Mont Blanc. But the weather, which is usually unsettled after August 15th, broke completely and de Saussure was once more defeated. He returned for a long talk with Paccard, who related his climb down to the smallest details. De Saussure wrote two accounts of it, one in his diary and the other in a letter to a friend. The two travellers, who had returned to Chamonix, also wrote a report of what they had seen on the day of the climb.

De Saussure went back to Geneva. He was far too intelligent and broad-minded to feel the slightest pang of jealousy against Paccard. To him it was perfectly natural that a man much younger and better trained than himself should have been first on the top. The Genevese scientists Charles Bonnet, Pictet, and others spread the news. Several newspapers told the world how a man had succeeded in carrying a barometer to the top of Mont Blanc. Paccard, who was thinking of writing an account of his climb, now sent out a terse, well-written advance note. De Saussure had a parcel of the notices which he distributed among his friends, several of whom, like Lord Palmerston, Sir William Hamilton, and the Duc de la Rochefoucauld d'Anville, sent in their subscriptions.

Suddenly, the whole appearance of the situation underwent a change: Bourrit had shown his hand. He was insanely jealous of Paccard's victory Had de Saussure been first, he might have tolerated it, but he could not bear the thought of having been forestalled by an insignificant village doctor of twenty-nine, whose name would become world-famous as soon as his book was out. Consequently, on September 20, 1786, he published a *Letter on the first journey to the summit of Mont Blanc,* an extremely perfidious document containing slanders cleverly directed against Paccard. According to Bourrit, Balmat had been the leader and the hero throughout the climb; he had been the first on the top, he had had to drag Paccard up with him, he had been grossly underpaid, and so forth. It appears that, for this, Balmat had supplied a few suggestions and Bourrit had worked them up. Now, owing to Bourrit's celebrity, the *Letter* was widely circulated. De Saussure, who had been shown the text, not only protested but compelled Bourrit to scrap the first edition and bring out a second one which was slightly toned down. Bourrit tried to play for time. He put out various lame suggestions, such as that the party had not reached the real summit, that Paccard's book would be valueless, that it would be badly written, that it would contain contemptuous remarks about de Saussure, and so on.

There had meanwhile been trouble in Chamonix. The guide François Paccard had been imprisoned for one day for using strong language about Bourrit. But the *Letter* was eventually altered, though Bourrit had been most reluctant to give in. He wrote furiously to de Saussure, trying again to pre-judice him against the young doctor. He added: 'If I had felt that I was wrong in publishing my letter, I should have done it anonymously.'

Paccard sent two articles to the *Journal de Lausanne* to correct the false impression created by Bourrit's statements and, in May 1787, he published two certificates signed by Balmat, stating the real facts. Bourrit did not react, but the newspaper was not widely read, whereas his *Letter* was. Paccard's manuscript, which was now ready, was sent to the Société Typographique de Lausanne. But the director of the firm was J. P. Bérenger, a well-known Genevese who happened to be an intimate friend of Bourrit—he usually corrected the latter's deficiencies in style. Bérenger did all he could to prevent the books's appearance, asking Paccard to make endless alterations to his text and then going to sleep over the alterations. On May 31st, according to a letter from Paccard to von Gersdorf, no progress had been made, while the sly *Letter* had prevented the young man from finding a sufficient number of subscribers.

In Chamonix, Balmat had come to believe the lies he and Bourrit had con-cocted together. On July 8th Balmat began abusing Paccard in the village inn, accusing him of having forged the two certificates. Probably he was drunk. Paccard lost control of himself and knocked him down, whereupon Balmat complained to Bourrit, who had just arrived in Chamonix and was relating his own deeds of prowess to Meiners, an unbearable German professor who was subsequently to slander de Saussure. But Bourrit no longer had any interest in Balmat: the man had served his turn by helping him to damage his rival's reputation and to kill his book.

A few days later, de Saussure arrived in Chamonix, intent on climbing Mont Blanc and also—be it said—on calming the disturbance. On August 3rd he reached the summit of the mountain. There was now no room for Pac-card's book. With much dignity the young man stepped out of the limelight. He went on climbing; according to Deluc, he may have climbed Mont Blanc again. In 1788 he related his story to a Danish writer apparently without passion or bitterness: he had been lucky and the weather had been fine. He did not complain and did not even mention his unpublished written account.

The story of the first ascent of Mont Blanc is a strange and sad one. A whole century was to elapse before justice was done to Dr Paccard. Throughout the nineteenth and well into the twentieth centuries Balmat was supposed to be the hero and Paccard was made to cut an almost grotesque figure. By the end of the nineteenth century, however, English, American and Swiss scholars began to realize that the matter was not so simple, but it needed the com-bined efforts of C. E. Matthews, Dr Dübi, D. W. Freshfield, H. F. Montagnier, E. H. Stevens, Graham Brown, Sir Gavin de Beer and myself to put things in their true light. I had the good luck to discover several important letters in the Saussure archives, which enabled me to bring this rather intricate story to a conclusion. One thing remains unexplained: what happened to Paccard's manuscript? His diary, which is preserved in the Alpine Club, briefly mentions his first climb but does not relate it. The archives of the Société Typographique de Lausanne, which was to publish his book, have disappeared. The house of his descendants in Chamonix was flooded by the Arve in the sixties; furthermore, one of his grandsons is reported to have destroyed whole basketfuls of old papers and it is likely that the doctor's rejected manuscript was among them. Nothing whatever is known of it.

Early in the summer of 1787, Balmat made several attempts to find another route up Mont Blanc. He failed twice and at last succeeded on July 4th, with two other guides. But his new route was not better than the old one. It led from the Petit Plateau to the eastern arête, but like the one he had previously followed, it was under the constant threat of a huge crumbling wall of séracs. The one person who vaguely suspected the risks incurred in such places was Paccard himself, who warned de Saussure against the danger of avalanches on the plateaus.

On July 8th, de Saussure left Geneva for Chamonix, escorted by his wife, his two sons and his two sisters-in-law. The whole family was much worried by the prospective climb and wanted to be as near as possible while it took place. As soon as they arrived in Chamonix, the rain began. Saussure ordered his men to build two rough huts, one on the top of the Montagne de la Côte, the other on the highest rock above the Grands Mulets; he also made preparations for erecting a large tent higher up. He read the Iliad in Greek and waited. Bourrit and his sons arrived and the rain continued. Dr Paccard's father fell into a small torrent and was drowned; Bourrit made a speech at the burial; the rain went on. De Saussure read his barometer and felt extremely nervous. On July 31st, the wind suddenly blew the clouds away and the sun set in a welter of crimson and golden light. De Saussure spent part of the night getting ready in secret, as he did not want to make his wife more anxious than he could help. On August 1st he left with eighteen guides at seven in the morning.

Many accounts of his climb have been published; de Saussure wrote an excellent one and Bourrit wrote several based on de Saussure's notes. I propose to give a different account, the one by G. A. Deluc, written for the benefit of his brother in England. He had received all his notes from a

Genevese doctor who had had the story from de Saussure himself after his return from the mountain. This was Dr Odier, who had been summoned to Chamonix to attend a sick English traveller. On August 10th Deluc wrote:

'On the 3rd of this month, M. de Saussure reached the summit of Mont Blanc. Here follows what I heard from Dr Odier who was in Chamonix on that very day and talked with him when he came down. It transpires that he refused to have any one with him but the men he required, so that Bourrit had to remain below. [Saussure] left on the 1st with his valet and eighteen men. They spent two nights out, the first before reaching the snow-line, and the second on the snow, probably at the foot of some rocks at about 2,000 toises. Saussure had a hut big enough to hold them all. All the men he had to take with him had emphatically refused to spend a night out in the snow at such a height. They carried up plenty of straw for themselves and two mattresses for him. They dug the snow round the tent and tightly cemented it on the outside. There is some talk of the thermometer being at $3\frac{1}{2}°$ but M. Odier does not remember whether it was during the second night or on the top. I should say that it was during the night; they all lost their appetite and had to force themselves to eat.'

Let us imagine what the first part of the climb had meant for de Saussure. The eighteenth century, though toying with ideas of primitive life, had a strong taste for comfort and fastidiousness; de Saussure himself was the most civilized of men and had always had to make a great but silent effort to endure an unpleasant mountain bivouac. The unappetizing appearance and taste of the food taken out of haversacks made of hairy leather, the wine bottles circulating among the whole party, all these things made him thoroughly uncomfortable, the more so as he had to avoid hurting the feelings of his guides. Throughout the ascent, most of them exasperated him. They were really terrified, feeling the presence all round them of unknown dangers. It was always difficult to get them to move or to prevent them stopping for trifling reasons. They had left the Montagne de la Côte much too late, the snow soon began to melt and de Saussure was greatly relieved when they reached clean ice after ploughing for hours through soft snow.

Above the Grands Mulets there was a halt for lunch which seemed endless. The party was now on almost virgin ground. The Petit Plateau had been lately swept by an avalanche. Higher up, while preparations were made to erect the tent, de Saussure thought of the two men who had been there before him: 'When I picture to myself Dr Paccard and Jacques Balmat', he wrote, 'arriving towards nightfall in this wilderness without shelter, without hope of help, without even the assurance that man could live at the height they were hoping to attain, and yet persevering undaunted in their adventure, I admired their resolution and their courage.'

De Saussure himself was feeling mountain-sick; he was thirsty, hot, feverish and breathless. In the overcrowded, overheated tent the hours passed like a nightmare. Unable to sleep, he at last went out. Reading his notes today, one cannot help recollecting one's own experiences in a packed hut during the night before a big climb: an endless night through which it is impossible to sleep. One's limbs are cramped and stiff, and the heat and nervous excitement combine to bring on a splitting headache, until one feels that it will never be possible to recover control over one's exhausted body and shake it into action. Growing at last exasperated with lack of sleep, one rises as silently as possible and creeps out of the hut to breathe in the cold night air and look at the silver moonlight shining over the glaciers that lie between the hard black shadows of the rock-faces.

In the morning, the party was again late. Eighteenth-century guides could not be expected to get up at two or three in the morning. They were on the move by six and the long steep slopes proved an endless nightmare. De Saussure had to stop every few minutes to recover breath. Two guides gave up the climb and returned to the tent; the others plodded on for five hours and it was past eleven when they reached the top. De Saussure was exhausted.

'At the moment when I reached the highest point of the snow that crowned the summit, I trampled it with a feeling of anger rather than pleasure. Moreover my object was not merely to reach the highest point; I was bound to make observations . . . which alone could give value to my venture and I was very doubtful of being able to carry out more than a portion of what I had planned.'

An ideal passionately contemplated for years always tastes somewhat stale in achievement, for the reality is always less attractive than the dream. De Saussure had been vaguely hoping for some scientific revelation, a sudden discovery of the whole geological formation of the Alps. But no revelation came. A sea of mountains appeared to be dissolving into the shining midday haze. Clouds were boiling up. And the mountain ranges rose and broke in successive waves to the distant horizon. Thoroughly tired and giddy, the naturalist fought heroically for four hours, as he struggled to set down his notes and read his instruments.

We return to Deluc's narrative:

'They reached the top by 11.30 and remained there until 4. When they were perceived on the top, all the telescopes in Chamonix were turned that way and all the bells were rung. Then Bourrit left, to reach the place where the caravan was to sleep when coming down, hoping that some of the guides would go up again with him, but none wanted to. They all said they were badly in need of rest . . . M. de Saussure had a belt to which were tied several ropes held by several men to avoid accidents and help him up.'

Deluc is the only person to speak of de Saussure's rope. It is very likely he is right, as he had accurate information. De Saussure himself never mentions the rope, but for years people were slightly ashamed of being tied to one.

When he came down, de Saussure was greeted rapturously by his wife, who had sent him at his first bivouac a charming letter scribbled on rose-coloured paper. A young Polish nobleman, Laurent Dzieduszycki, who was in Chamonix for a few days, happened to meet the home-coming caravan and described it in his diary:

'The route up Mont Blanc had been known since the previous year when Dr Paccard, the Chamonix doctor and his two [sic] guides had reached it [the summit]. M. de Saussure had with him eighteen guides and his valet. They were all seen through telescopes on the 3rd, at 12. All the bells in Chamonix proclaimed the event . . . When he was going up, four guides went in front to kick a path in the snow. Several were seen lying down on the snow for four or five minutes to rest . . . There is nothing but ice and snow on the summit of Mont Blanc.'

De Saussure's victory was an epoch-making event. He was already one of the best-known men in Europe and Mont Blanc added new lustre to his fame. He was elated. Meeting a Bernese friend while on his way to Geneva, he ran up to him, shouting: 'Do congratulate me! I *have* climbed Mont Blanc!' Within a few weeks he published a *Brief Relation* of his climb; it is likely he hurried through the work, not wishing to take risks with the egregious Bourrit. Up to that date, few naturalists had gone so far—or so high—to look for proofs of their hypotheses. His climb put de Saussure on the same level as La Condamine or Sir Joseph Banks, who had both accomplished dangerous journeys to South America. After a former unsuccessful attempt, de Saussure had already been congratulated by the Prince de Ligne, Lord Palmerston, Murith, Bjelke (a well-known Swedish naturalist), and Marsilio Landriani (an Italian scientist). After the 1787 climb, letters of congratulation poured in from every side: from the Duchess of Bourbon (Philippe d'Orleans' sister), the Duc de La Rochefoucauld d'Anville, Landriani again, and others. He was elected a Fellow of the Royal Society and his *Relation* was translated into English and Italian. The vast non-climbing public now became aware of the importance of mountaineering: such efforts were clearly worth while, since a well-known scientist had taken so many risks and endured so many hardships to reach the top of a mountain. There was more to the high mountains than an idyllic setting for shepherdesses and kind-hearted chamois-hunters.

As for de Saussure, his subsequent climbs were almost as daring as the previous ones. He wanted to find some high place where he could stay for some time and make more observations than on Mont Blanc and under less trying circumstances. He thought of the Col du Géant. Now this col, leading from Chamonix to Courmayeur, is not exceptionally difficult to cross. It was much easier in the eighteenth century, when glaciers were broader, higher and consequently less crevassed than they are today. For one thing, the large ice-fall above the present Requin hut was probably much tamer. Yet it was hard enough for badly-equipped amateur mountaineers. In 1784 it had stopped Dr Paccard when he was reconnoitring. Three years later, just before de Saussure climbed Mont Blanc, Abraham Exchaquet, who was exploiting some lead mines lower down the valley, made an attempt to cross the col. He was not a scientist and had the daring to confess that he climbed simply because he liked it. He took with him Thomas Ford Hill, a young Englishman who also had a cult for the mountains to which he added an equally romantic love for the study of Celtic poetry. Hill had been the witness of one of the first mountain accidents, when his friend Lecointe, a young Genevese banker, had slipped and fallen on the moraine of the Charmoz, at the foot of the aiguille of that name, and been killed. In spite of this depressing experience, Hill returned to Chamonix. He was, according to de Saussure, who met him, 'the most clumsy of amateurs', and, ascending the Glacier du Géant with Exchaquet, he was such a drag that the climb had to be abandoned before the ice-fall was reached. The guides suggested to Exchaquet that they would find a route and let him know when the crossing could be safely made. But no word came from them and, on June 27, 1787, Exchaquet arrived at Chamonix. He was told that his guides had left, probably for the col, so he obtained two other men and hurried off on their tracks. He did not find them, which is hardly surprising when one considers the great breadth of the glaciers, but he made the col apparently without any difficulty and he descended to Courmayeur. There was much snow in 1787 and the séracs were probably in good condition.

As one might expect, Bourrit now intervened. Sorely tried by Paccard's success on Mont Blanc, he thought to achieve revenge by being the first across the Col du Géant. But he found that two parties—the guides' and Exchaquet's—had already forestalled him. He eventually crossed the col on August 28th with one of his sons and four guides and immediately started to crow about his achievement: 'The difficulties of Mont Blanc are nothing compared with the difficulties of this passage . . . The crossing is the most audacious expedition which has yet been made in the Alps . . .' And as a corollary he began making himself offensive to Exchaquet, by criticizing his Alpine qualifications or ignoring them. Exchaquet shrugged his shoulders and dropped the whole matter.

De Saussure started for the col on July 2, 1788, after most elaborate preparations. As he planned to spend a whole fortnight on the col, the tent used on Mont Blanc was inadequate, and he ordered a new one from a Widow Tilliard in Paris, who made tarpaulin tents 'highly recommended if one does not mind the smell'. De Saussure had with him his son Théodore, his valet (not the one who had been on Mont Blanc), and several guides. A young painter, Henry Lévesque, accompanied them up the lower levels of the glacier and painted two water-colours of the caravan, from which several engravings were subsequently made.

The attempt to camp for a long time at so high an altitude was even more daring than the ascent of Mont Blanc. Barely two years had elapsed since the days when people firmly believed that one night on the snow would be fatal. Before the construction of the large hotel and the telepheriques linking it to Chamonix and Courmayeur the Col du Géant was one of the most impressive sites in the whole range of Mont Blanc. The gap at the foot of the wild ridge crowned by the Dent du Géant opens over the broad steep Brenva Glacier. Beyond this rises a fantastically jagged granite wall. It soars up as a sheer precipice, describes two great peaks and then culminates in the summits of Mont Blanc de Courmayeur and Mont Blanc itself. The whole face is scarred with numberless rock buttresses, all of them covered with a glistening crust and overhung by masses of blue ice. Looking back towards the Mer de Glace, a snow plateau descends to the séracs through a steep snow-slope and a second plateau fissured with wide crevasses. The rocks are brown, red and golden when the weather is fine; dull blue, grey and purple when it is bad. Ice and snow assume the most extraordinary colours as the sun rises or sets: almond green, yellow, light pink, salmon, mauve or blue. They can look alternately lurid or as dull as plaster; their glare is never worse than when the sky is overcast. The whole landscape is more alive, more unsettled than the sea. Long clouds drive in the wind across the gaps between the peaks and hang upon the rock spires like muslin veils or mourning draperies. The mind of the beholder feels cut off from normality and has to find a new poise in harmony with the landscape. It is still an impressive scene, but no longer a peaceful one.

De Saussure felt elated. He loved the place and became quickly acclimatized. He could do a great deal of useful work without feeling depressed by the altitude. Whatever the state of the weather it inspired him to write ecstatic descriptions to his wife:

'These heights have done their best to make us regret them; we have had the most magnificent evening; all the peaks that surround us and the snows that separate them were coloured with the most beautiful shades of rose and crimson. The Italian horizon was girdled with a broad belt from which the full moon, of a rich vermilion tint, rose with the majesty of a queen . . . The snows and rocks, the brilliancy of which are unbearable by sunlight, present a wonderful and delightful spectacle by the soft radiance of the moon. How magnificent is the contrast between these granite crags, shadowed or thrown into such sharp and bold relief, and the brilliant snows! . . . The soul is uplifted, the powers of intelligence seem to widen and in the midst of this majestic silence, one seems to hear the voice of Nature and to become the confidant of its most secret workings.'

Things had not been entirely pleasant. There had been several violent storms; Exchaquet had turned up with a party of friends and it had required another storm to drive him away. Jacques Balmat, who was again de Saussure's leading guide, made constant blunders when carrying letters between Mme de Saussure and her husband, besides staying away for a whole week to have his portrait painted by Bacler d'Albe in Sallanches. One day, de Saussure discovered that all the food had gone; the guides had eaten it in order to compel their employer to leave. He had to make a hurried retreat to Courmayeur, thus curtailing his work. The guides had ransacked the food supplies so thoroughly that there was nothing to eat during the descent. Yet de Saussure loved every minute of the time he spent on the col.

On Mont Blanc his tracks were being followed. Hardly a week after his successful ascent a young English traveller, Mark Beaufoy, arrived in Chamonix. On hearing that the mountain had just been climbed, he at once decided that he too would ascend it. He collected ten guides—but not Jacques Balmat—and made the ascent in good time. 'He went up like a guide,' wrote Dr Paccard in his diary. Years later, Beaufoy explained that he had been impelled to go because man feels naturally urged to reach the highest places in the world: hardly more than four persons at that time had actually felt it. Beaufoy also said: 'I could not resist the inclination I felt to reach the summit.' This is a more likely explanation: he had already seen snow peaks in Switzerland. Becoming aware that it was possible to climb them, he thought it was worth while to try.

A few days later, Joseph Michaud, a young writer who was to lead an extremely eventful life, felt the same inclination. He took two guides who carried a ladder, ropes and food. He did not inquire about the condition of the mountain and he did not trouble to take a barometer. The party reached the Grands Mulets and slept in de Saussure's second hut—the one he had not used. Michaud, who had had no training at all, felt too tired to proceed when the guides urged him to get up on the second day, so he lounged away part of the morning on the rocks, warming himself in the sun and looking at the view; then he came down. This young man, who made no pretence to science, who planned his expedition in such a careless fashion, and, once having failed, admitted his failure with a shrug and did not boast or complain, is one of the first modern mountaineers.

One year later, Bourrit again tried to ascent Mont Blanc, but this great pleasure was to be denied him. He took with him two young men, William Woodley, who had come from the West Indies, and a Dutchman named Camper; they were touring Switzerland and Savoy together. Bourrit also took his younger son and the party had twenty-two guides. On the second day the weather deteriorated. Woodley and his party were quicker than the rest and they succeeded in reaching the summit in a raging blizzard. The two Bourrits and Camper had to give up when they were already fairly high. Bourrit was mad with rage and, when the others came down, he made a violent scene with Woodley although, as he wrote in his account of the climb, the young man had both feet badly frostbitten. This was Bourrit's last attempt on Mont Blanc; he did all he could to make his readers—and himself —believe he had reached the summit.

At this point of history Mont Blanc was more or less abandoned because of the troubled conditions prevailing in Europe. Yet in 1799 an extraordinary attempt was made on the mountain. Its hero was Elie-Ascension de Mont-golfier, a boy of sixteen, the nephew of the two Montgolfier brothers who had been the first men to go up in a balloon. The boy was born a year after the flight, in 1784; hence his cumbersome Christian names, which happened to fit him to perfection. He had been an *enfant terrible*; in 1798 he was placed in charge of a big silk-weaver in Lyons to be trained for a business career, as his uncles owned a large paper-mill in Vidalon and wished to take him into the concern. But the boy ran away from Lyons and eventually reached Chamonix, where he lived more or less on local charity. He grew fond of chamois-hunting; Jacques Balmat employed him as tracker in his expeditions and told him about his climb, showing him the route he had followed. The boy thought it would be interesting to try to climb the mountain. He collected a hatchet, crampons and food for five days, and without breathing a word to anyone he left one morning at two. The going was difficult and he was slow. He did not reach the hut until ten that night and spent a miserable time in the derelict shack; a storm broke and there was a heavy snowfall which continued well after daybreak. Then the wind turned to the north, the temperature fell and the sun shone through the clouds. Montgolfier resumed his climb but the going was worse than ever. He was sinking deep into water-logged snow, he was feeling the height, and it seemed likely that avalanches would begin to fall. He probably reached the Grand Plateau before giving up. He then spent a second night in the hut, weathered another storm and succeeded in descending alive. It is probable that this extraordinary lad was one of the first solitary climbers on record.

Jacques Balmat had played a strange part in the history of mountaineering. De Saussure never cared much for him and seems to have resented his attitude during the expedition to the Col du Géant. He was not taken on any of de Saussure's subsequent journeys. Balmat climbed Mont Blanc again with Woodley and then, probably disgusted by the weather and snow conditions he had encountered that day, did all he could to avoid further expeditions. His tales of past glories were meant to terrify Montgolfier. In 1802, he ascended the mountain again with a Russian gentleman, Baron Dorthesen, and his Swiss companion, Forneret. But in the same year he contrived to prevent a young English Officer, Colonel Pollen, from reaching the Grands Mulets, saying that the bergschrund was too wide—a rather lame excuse. The next year he prevented an anonymous Vaudois climber from starting at all. He made two more ascents, one in 1808 with several of his brothers, including a very young one, and Marie Paradis, a servant girl of the village; the other and last one in 1818 with Count Malczeski, a Polish traveller. Balmat then gave up serious climbing and devoted himself to searching for gold on lower mountains. He even went as far as the Val Anzasca. Eventually we find him leading mules across the Col de Balme or the Tête Noire.

It was in 1832 that Alexandre Dumas came to Chamonix, and accomplished some reporting. He sought out Balmat, primed him with drink and then made him talk about his first ascent of Mont Blanc. The outcome of all this was a brilliant piece of journalism. Dumas knew nothing of the story and could not check the accuracy of the old fellow's account now there was no one surviving who might have controlled his garrulity: de Saussure had died in 1799 and Paccard in 1827. He could describe things exactly as he wished they had happened. Dumas probably added frills of his own. He wrote a beautiful description of the conquest of Mont Blanc, unwittingly completing the nefarious work of Bourrit. This version was to be accepted as the complete truth until the time when a few scholars began to suspect its accuracy.

In 1834, Jacques Balmat was killed—possibly murdered—while trying to locate gold ore above the Glacier des Fonds, near the Pic de Tenneverges. It was the end of a chapter in Alpine history. Meanwhile, Mont Blanc had become well known and a score of climbers had reached its summit. For many years they had followed in de Saussure's footsteps, climbing by the *ancien passage*, blissfully ignorant of the dangers which constantly threatened the route. Then the mountain woke up and the first great Alpine tragedy took place in this very region. On August 18, 1820, a caravan of eleven persons, including a Russian doctor named Hamel, two Oxford students, J. Durnford and G. Henderson and their guides, was following the ill-fated passage. There was much fresh snow, the day was hot and the men were ploughing a deep furrow in the water-logged snow, when suddenly the whole layer tore itself free from the underlying ice, dragging the party down in indescribable confusion. The great white wave hurtled down the slope, grasping the men and their loads in its wild embrace, then stopped short and froze at once. Hamel, the two youths and three of the guides succeeded in extricating themselves from the deadly pressure. The five others had been hurled into a huge crevasse which was gaping at the foot of the slope. Two of them managed with help to break free. The three others had been smothered by the solidifying mass or killed in their fall.

This tragedy gave rise to violent controversies, but in truth no one, not even the best guide of the party, Joseph-Marie Couttet, knew enough about snow conditions. For seven more years parties still climbed by this death trap. Then, in 1827, the guides of Hawes and Fellows discovered a new and much safer route to surmount the last pitch of the mountain: the Corridor and the Mur de la Côte. Other guides had sense enough to understand the importance of the discovery. Henceforward, the two *anciens passages* were put out of bounds. Joseph-Marie Couttet, a survivor of the 1820 accident, eventually became Sir John Herschel's and John Ruskin's guide.

The list of early visitors to Mont Blanc is of peculiar interest. It shows that most of those who attempted to climb Mont Blanc were not only neither mountaineers nor scientists, but that they felt less and less concerned with their deficiency in the latter respect. Count Malczeski, who made the ascent at the age of twenty-five, had been an officer in the Polish regiments serving in the French army; he was a poet and a romantic figure. He described his climb twice, first in a letter to a Genevese magazine, then in a long footnote to his own poem *Maria*. John Auldjo, a young Scottish diplomat who was to die full of years as British consul in Geneva, went up Mont Blanc because he had liked the reflection of the mountain in the little lake of Chedde. Dr Martin Barry, a Quaker, loved very broad prospects and thought that the one from the summit would be very broad indeed. Dr van Rennselaer, an American, was 'doing Europe' and had already ascended Vesuvius and Etna. The Comte de Tilly, a French officer in exile, wished to be stirred by deep emotions. H. M. Atkins, a boy of nineteen, just wanted to do something interesting.

Women, too, ascended Mont Blanc. The first was the Chamonix maid-servant, Marie Paradis; though very tired, she managed to reach the top, and she later used her achievement to advertise her tea-room at Les Pèlerins. The second was Henriette d'Angeville, a canoness, who made the ascent in 1838. In spite of the fervent words she wrote about the mountain, there was nothing romantic about her: a spinster who loved Mont Blanc because she had nothing else to love. She had a clear, bold, haughty, precise mind; she succeeded in her climb by sheer will-power and became one of the lionesses of the season, a position she enjoyed, having a morbid passion for self-advertisement. In 1838, when the pranks played by the Baroness Dudevant (George Sand) were intriguing the public, Mme d'Angeville became madly jealous of that lady's glamorous reputation—and possibly also of the man's apparel which she paraded in Chamonix in 1836. So Henriette climbed Mont Blanc, simultaneously displaying a virile courage, hysterical tendencies and a climbing costume of checkered material, complete with wide trousers, long coat, huge feathered beret and a long black boa.

Climbers had ceased to carry barometers: they confessed they did not know how to read them. In 1827 Paccard offered his instrument to Hawes, who politely refused it. But several climbers made sketches: Auldjo, Atkins, Barry and Fellows painted charming water-colours. Auldjo's paintings enable the modern reader to realize the very unreliable ice-technique prevalent among the Chamonix guides of that time. The party breakfasted in the middle of a most dangerous snow-bridge; as a huge ice block bridged another crevasse, they crept along its flanks like flies on a window pane. Noticing a huge cornice, five or six of them went to its very brink to gape into the chasm below.

One of the striking aspects of those early climbs was the huge amount of food and drink that climbers took with them. Guides had made up their minds that the ascent of Mont Blanc should be celebrated with lavish and frequent meals all the way up and down. The first climbers had been much more modest: Paccard and Balmat took only a few slices of bread and pieces of cold meat which froze hard during the climb. The party of guides which climbed the mountain a week before Maria Paradis had some soup in a bottle and, as they wanted to drink it hot, they took a few pieces of charcoal with them to light a fire. Such Spartan fare soon fell out of fashion. Albert Smith gave the complete list of the provisions he bought for himself, his companions and his guides, and from this it is easy to understand why climbing Mont Blanc was so expensive. The quantity was staggering and included nearly 100 bottles of wine.

Mme d'Angeville had an equally large bill of fare. Very conscientious climbers took with them a live pigeon, not for roasting but to use as a homing bird and see whether it could find its way back across the glaciers. The experiment always failed. Dr Hamel had one pigeon on his ill-fated climb in 1820; it was carried in a pot, tied to the load of a guide, and the man happened to be one of the three who were lost in the big crevasse. Years later, a wing of the bird was recovered at the foot of the Glacier des Bossons. Mme d'Angeville's pigeon lost its way and never reached its native village of Les Praz.

Other useful implements were carried on climbs and mountain expeditions. Major Alexandre Roger always used an anti-flea-bag: it was a large silk bag into which he crept to avoid the various insects which inhabited the huts and inns. Auldjo and Atkins took their paint-boxes with them and Mme d'Angeville her writing pad. For years, climbers thought fit to carry 'a barometer, two thermometers, a telescope and a vessel to boil water'—this last to find the boiling point at the summit and not to make tea. Such was the list drawn up by Martin Barry. But his party forgot the methylated spirit for the boiler; a boy was sent back to fetch it from Chamonix and when he caught up it was discovered that he had been given nitric acid instead. When Dickens came to Chamonix, he tried to find a companion to climb Mont Blanc with, and failed.

As mountains became more widely known, a few people thought that something might be done to make climbing a less exhausting pursuit by having fixed bivouacs at certain places. We have to go many years back to trace the story of the first mountain hut. The man who first thought of one was a Mr Blair, who in 1779 gave four guineas for the erection of a small hut on the Montenvers. It survived until 1812; it is true it was built of excellent Chamonix granite, as no other stones were available on the spot. De Saussure slept in it when exploring the glaciers. But tourists were becoming more and more numerous and the hut was far too small. In 1792, a French diplomat, M. de Sémonville, saw the Mer de Glace and was entranced by its beauty; then he met Bourrit and fell under his spell. So he offered to pay for the erection of a new hut. But soon after he had made this promise, Sémonville was kid-

3. *Top*: An illustration from John Auldjo's *The Ascent of Mont Blanc*, 1827.
Bottom: De Saussure's Ascent of Mont Blanc, by Chrétien de Méchels.

4. *Left*: A drawing for Töpffer's *Voyages en Zig-Zag*, 1844: the Col d'Anterne ('*Orage dans la Montagne*').
Below: Monte Rosa from the Monte Moro, by G. Lory *fils* c. 1810.

napped by Austrian troops and could no longer devote his attention to the hut. As the old one was falling to pieces, Bourrit tried to unearth a new benefactor. He at last found a man of taste and talent, Desportes, the French resident in Geneva, who was a friend of de Saussure's and who now gave Bourrit 200 francs—a considerable sum of money—with the suggestion that the new hut should be a 'Temple dedicated to Nature': a half-classical, half-masonic title in keeping with the taste of the period. The town council of Chamonix and its mayor, Dr Paccard of Mont Blanc fame, granted Bourrit the necessary piece of ground. Now Desportes had made it clear that the new hut should be provided with hammocks, a fireplace, cooking utensils, first-aid dressings, a hatchet, alpenstocks and the indispensable barometer and thermometer. During the summer of 1795, Bourrit engaged a few workmen on the spot and the new hut was built. Bourrit's enthusiasm was such that he persuaded his daughter to work on it. True, the small building looked rather crooked, but it was quite picturesque. But erosion, which destroys mountains, does not spare temples, and by 1803 careless travellers had broken the mirror fixed above the fireplace, stolen all that could be moved, including the lock, and the Temple was a sad ruin. Both Desportes and Sémonville were far away, but Indefatigable Bourrit succeeded in finding a third benefactor in Doulcet de Pontécoulant, who had visited Chamonix and fallen in love with the mountains after escaping from Paris at the time when his party—the Girondins—had been outlawed. In 1797 he was again in exile for complicated political reasons; in Italy, he made the acquaintance of Bonaparte, who brought him back and, when he was first Consul, sent him to Brussels as prefect. From Belgium, Doulcet sent instructions and money to Bourrit; letters went backwards and forwards for three years; the Chamonix innkeeper Couteran was to supervise the work on the Montenvers, and he usually took plenty of time to do very little. Eventually, in 1806, the Temple was restored to its former glory, repainted, provided with two beds, chairs, tongs and bellows.

Meanwhile, Blair's hospice had crumbled to pieces. Slowly but surely in the years that followed, the Temple again began to lose its neat appearance and Bourrit once more grew anxious. Desportes reappeared, an exile now in Germany, following the fall of Napoleon. From Frankfurt, he wrote to Couteran, explaining how the Temple was to be repaired. The whole building was to be overhauled and the names of great naturalists were to be engraved along the cornice. Jaquet, an excellent Genevese wood carver, would attend to this last provision. He also wished to have his co-benefactors commemorated, and above all he wanted to know the price of the whole scheme. Couteran asked for 300 francs and again did nothing. Desportes sent several persons to stir him up, one of them being an English officer, Captain Walcott. At last, in 1819, the repairs were carried out and the town council duly thanked Desportes.

For years the small Temple was to be the one hut in the Alps built for the use of climbers. It was again repaired in 1840. Forbes and Tyndall were to use it as one of their headquarters when they were studying the Mer de Glace system of glaciers. It is the ancestor of all modern mountain huts.

CHAPTER FIVE
ELSEWHERE

ALL through the eighteenth century, and for years afterwards, there were three main mountain resorts, though it seems early to use so modern an expression: Chamonix, Grindelwald and Lauterbrunnen. In Grindelwald, tourists used to ride to the snouts of the two glaciers and there eat strawberries while they listened to the roar of an Alpine horn, blown by a bearded native. In Lauterbrunnen they looked at the Staubbach. When they felt very bold, they rode from one of those two villages to the other across the Kleine Scheidegg, gazing as they went at the wonderful north face of the Jungfrau. But the Bernese Oberland is a very rainy district, and any enthusiasm inspired by it had been somewhat diluted. From Chamonix they could climb anything from La Flégère to Mont Blanc.

Slowly new places were discovered. Of course, even the wildest valleys, forbidding places difficult of access, had always been known and visited by natives. High passes, like the Theodul or the Monte Moro were more frequented than the Simplon during the Middle Ages. In 1751, Needham crossed the Allée Blanche from Courmayeur to the Col de la Seigne. The valleys of Dauphiny, Valais and the Grisons all had their local history, archives and charters. Fir-cones of the Arolla pine are among the plants shown on the twelfth-century sculptures in the Abbey of Valère at Sion, from which town the Val d'Hérens leads to Arolla itself, the home of those splendid trees. But it took centuries for foreigners to venture into such recesses and become aware of their beauty.

One of the first valleys of the Valais to be opened to travellers was that of St Niklaus, with Zermatt at its head. Probably the earliest mention of the place occurs in a letter from Ricou to Haller in 1766. Ricou was a Vaudois naturalist who travelled up and down Switzerland collecting plants for Haller: 'As the mountains of Pratoborgno cover an almost immeasurable area,' he wrote, 'it is not possible to go everywhere . . . Those mountains are the highest I ever saw; their snow and ice are everlasting'. Pratoborgno is the old Latin name for the village of Zermatt. While Ricou mentioned expeditions to Stafelalp, Schönbühl and the Stockje, he did not even allude to the Matterhorn, which sounds incredible. Yet this lack of interest in the aspect of a mountain is not unique; for when William Windham went to

Chamonix in 1741 Mont Blanc escaped his attention. In Zermatt, as there was no inn, Ricou was housed by the vicar, a Frenchman from Alsace named Jean-Baptiste Rothärmel.

In 1777, some chamois-hunters from Gressoney, who had climbed to the Lysjoch, saw far down below them a glen surrounded by glaciers, a green island in the middle of wild snow expanses. The story was noised abroad and even reached the *Journal de Paris*, which gravely suggested that it was a valley of the Golden Age, a Happy Valley forgotten by civilization and lost to the world. But no one tried to find or visit it. It remained in that state, neither more lost nor more happy than any other valley, until 1789, when H. B. de Saussure at last opened it to the world.

De Saussure had heard the Lyssjoch story when he reached the place from the south, across the Theodul Pass. This expedition was as daring as the one to the Col du Géant. He had come from Courmayeur to Macugnaga, where he had spent ten days, mostly in bad weather, and ascended a few secondary summits from where he could see the route he meant to follow to the Theodul. Then, going up the Val de Lys, Val d'Ayas and Val Tournanche, the party reached Breuil, and after two days' rest made their way up the pass. The climb was long if not dangerous. From the col de Saussure saw the Matterhorn and wrote in his diary: 'Its shape is really that of a blunt pyramid —a pyramidal rock, the head of which is rounded.' From Zermatt, he wrote to Ramond to acknowledge the receipt of the latter's book on the Pyrenees: a polite, though slightly cold letter, and the only evidence we have that the two men were vaguely acquainted. De Saussure did not take Ramond very seriously as a scientist, while as a climber the younger man had not yet accomplished anything of great note.

In his *Voyages dans les Alpes*, de Saussure wrote what is probably the first extant description of the Matterhorn. He called it 'this wonderful rock' and went on:

'What a power has been displayed in breaking and sweeping away all that has been torn from that pyramid! For one sees no rubble heap at its foot; one sees only other summits, the sides of which, similarly scarred, suggest huge accumulations of shattered rocks; and yet there is nothing like that in the neighbourhood. Probably all that rubble, reduced to pebbles, stones and sand, fills our valleys and lakes where it has been washed down across the Val d'Aosta and Lombardy.'

Impressed by the strange beauty of the scenery and its immense scientific interest, de Saussure made up his mind to come back. He had to wait for three years before he could do so, but in 1792 he came once more and reached the Theodul on August 11th. A small hut had been built for him and his party. From the pass he started to climb the Breithorn, a fairly easy though long ascent. But he gave up the attempt and climbed the Little Matterhorn instead; Hérin, his guide, 'an intelligent and much experienced fellow,' was the only member of the party who was mountain-sick. Because the Zermatt people had been rude and inhospitable on the earlier journey, de Saussure did not descend that way, but went back through Breuil and the Val d'Aosta.

Such is the first real glimpse we have of the Matterhorn. As it is hidden at the top of a very long valley, the mountain was spared the inane comments lavished upon Mont Blanc, and also the childish though sometimes touching attempts to climb it. No shy amateur could even dream of ascending the terrible cliffs swept day and night by falling stones. De Saussure had not gone near enough to see that all the rubble had not been swept away to north and south, or that masses of debris lay there still, witness to the constant disintegration of the mountain. The Matterhorn was to remain almost untouched, even by writers, for more than fifty years; then the curtain would be withdrawn to reveal it as the most sensational mountain in the world.

A few years after de Saussure's visit, another well-known explorer arrived in Zermatt: this was Murith. He had done no real mountaineering since his ascent of the Velan, but he had specialized in exploring little-known districts. He had been associated with the Thomas family, a family of naturalists for whom botany was a passion bequeathed from generation to generation. The grandfather had worked for Haller; his son Abraham travelled with Murith, who later also took charge of the grandson. In 1795, Abraham Thomas wrote to Murith a flowery letter full of exclamation marks, to relate his journey to Zermatt: 'Would to God I could wield Gessner's brush or a poet's lyre! Then would I sing of my journey. Alas! I can but describe it as a mere botanist!' He went on in the same strain: 'You are faced with that splendid crag, the Matterhorn, which seems to pierce the sky with its haughty point.' But, completely bewitched by the wonderful flora of the valley, he forgot to look at other mountains. In 1803, Murith himself came to Zermatt with Louis Thomas, Abraham's son, a boy of nineteen. The priest went up to various places like Riffelalp and Winkelmatten, but he hardly noticed the Matterhorn: he also was much too absorbed by flowers.

One of the first English travellers to Zermatt was Cade, who visited the village and went up to the Theodul in 1800. Not being a botanist, he had time to notice the Matterhorn, 'a colossal obelisk, perfectly triangular . . .; the sight of such a mass of rocks, rising 4,000 feet above its base, baffles description.' In the year that followed, the curtain was occasionally lifted to offer glimpses of Zermatt and its mountains. In 1806, the Swiss naturalist,

Escher von der Linth, went up to the Theodul. On August 19, 1825, the painter William Brockedon crossed the pass from Breuil and was caught by the almost inevitable storm which breaks on or about August 15th and brings the summer to an end. His guide, Jean-Baptiste Pession, got him safely up the col and down to Zermatt in spite of a thick layer of fresh snow which had fallen on the glacier. Just for a few moments, a gust of wind cleared the view and Brockedon could cast a hurried glance at 'the vast mountain of the Monte Rosa and its enormous glaciers, the valleys beneath our feet sinking into indistinctness . . . and the beautiful pyramid of the Mont Cervin springing from its bed of glaciers.' Then the clouds came down and Brockedon had no time to make a sketch of the view: the Theodul does not figure in his *Illustrations of the Passes of the Alps*.

Before leaving the valley let us mention two more travellers, both Swiss. In 1830 and again in 1833, Alexandre Roger went to Zermatt, first from Breuil, the second time from Viège. He saw the landscape with a clear though angry eye, hampered as he was on both journeys by a dog, a barometer and an atrocious temper. In 1836, Dr Samuel Brunner, a Bernese who travelled as far as the Caucasus and Senegal, visited Zermatt and was entranced by the Matterhorn. He described the mountain from every possible angle, from Zmutt, from the Riffelalp, and from other places. When looking at it from the Schwartzsee, he suddenly conceived an idea which for thirty more years was considered fantastic: 'Coated in an armour of glaciers,' he wrote, 'the Matterhorn displays its snow-white flanks; were it ever possible to climb the peak, *here* would be the place to make the attempt.' Whymper himself did not realize this before the summer of 1865.

The next valley to that of Zermatt was however much more of a *terra incognita*. For unnumbered years people had avoided setting foot in that narrow glen which branches off at Stalden to disappear into the unknown towards a vaguely-defined snow mountain. The first traveller to give a few precise facts about the place was Abraham Thomas, who was sent there by Murith in 1795 and who was greatly impressed by the wild beauty of the valley, the lowering precipices, the huge waterfalls and the forests of larches and Arolla pines. He was shown from afar the small hamlet of Saas-Fee, an eagle's nest at the foot of the most stupendous cliffs in the Alps, and yet Thomas, who was enraptured by that secluded garden, hardly mentioned the peaks which watch above it. He had an eye neither for the dark granite walls of the Mischabels nor the soft white domes of the Allalin and the Alphubel. A few years later Murith himself crossed over from Zermatt with much difficulty. The third visitor was a Vaudois botanist and clergyman, Jean Gaudin, who descended the Monte Moro and described his climb and the flowers he found. Painters came later. In 1821 Gabriel Lory and Maximilien de Meuron made their way up the valley to collect material for the illustration of a book on the Rhone. They felt it was a terrible ordeal, as the valley was long and they had to sleep three times in flea-ridden chalets. The last part of the walk to the col was over steep hard névés and they did not like it at all. 'Here everything repels the visitor . . . the lodgings are atrocious, the going is tiring.' William Brockedon also came, on his way to the Monte Moro. This enterprising character, who loved the mountains, was impressed by the 'savage grandeur quite in accordance with the surrounding scenery'. But he was unlucky in many of his Alpine ventures: when he reached the Monte Moro, the pass was smothered under thick clouds and again Brockedon failed to see the view. Samuel Brunner visited the valley a little later and loved it; Alexandre Roger entered it by way of the Monte Moro, coming up from Macugnaga, and he quarrelled with everything, including the scenery.

The history of the other valleys of Valais is less eventful. Most of them were opened up by the men already mentioned, botanists who were explorers at heart but not mountaineers. It is surprising to find how long it took people to become aware of the presence of great mountains in the background of any landscape.

The Val Ferret, a large wooded valley leading up to an easy pass, stretches along the foot of the last beautiful peaks of the Mont Blanc range. The drawback of the place lies in its unsettled weather; it is probably the wettest valley in Valais. This may account for the fact that few visitors troubled to describe it. De Saussure followed it twice. Murith, though he never described it, certainly visited it, as the Col de Fenêtre at its head leads to the St Bernard hospice. Much later, in 1842, Töpffer took his pupils to the Col Ferret; they played pranks all through the night in the small Ferret inn, of which the regular customers were smugglers. Töpffer had a rather busy time, trying to keep the children from going beyond permissible limits, so that he completely forgot to look at the Tour Noir and the Mont Dolent, the two beautiful peaks which overlook the valley from the west.

Two valleys were to become illustrious in the annals of mountaineering: the Val d'Hérens and the Val d'Anniviers. In 1791, an anonymous traveller sent a paper to the *Journal de Lausanne* about a *Journey to Ivolena* (Evolène). This traveller was no writer, and there is much humour to be found where he certainly did not mean to be funny: 'Ivolena enjoys a delightful situation; one finds there a quarry of stones used for making ovens.' He had a most unpleasant time in the chief village, because the natives saw him writing notes on everything he heard or saw, and took him for a spy. He had great trouble in inducing the vicar to get him a bed and some food. He mentions 'the

71

mountains of the Arolla which are of a prodigious height', and adds: 'its glaciers are splendid'. There are three 'inaccessible points' which are now known as the Dents de Veisivi and de Perroc, and 'the Dent Blanche, which soars up as a triangular pyramid . . . The Dent Ronde at the top of the glacier is almost as high as the latter.' (This was probably the Dent d'Hérens.) He gave a precise list of the various passes which lead down to Piedmont or to the Val d'Anniviers, and of the various glaciers, the length of which is always very great. As usual the natives told him that years before it had been possible to cross into Italy over solid ground, but the tremendous increase of the glaciers had destroyed every path; one had now to walk over ice and it was often extremely dangerous. It seems that he had a good view over the huge expanse of ice and snow south of Ferpècle and Arolla, and that he was duly impressed by the wild prospect of peaks.

For a long time hardly anyone ventured near Evolène. Thomas and Murith went there in 1806; a Vaudois clergyman, the Doyen Bridel, may have explored the lower reaches of the valley in 1820; a Swiss geologist, Charles Godeffroy, went up to Arolla in 1838 and crossed several passes; the first English visitor was A. T. Malkin in 1839. Such was the slow beginning of the life of a place which was to become one of the great centres of mountaineering.

The Val d'Anniviers had been opened up by Bourrit, who had gone to Zinal probably in 1778. But he had been so much interested in an unusual aspect of local rural economy, and he had had so much to say about the beauty of the Anniviers women, that he completely forgot to look at the Zinal Rothhorn or the Dent Blanche. Murith, of course, ascended the valley, but as usual he was obsessed by flowers.

These two valleys—of Hérens and Anniviers—lead to very difficult passes, compelling travellers to cross miles of crevassed glaciers: no one but smugglers ventured into such remote places. Brockedon vaguely referred to them as being inhabited by unfriendly natives. But amateur mountaineers did not risk themselves in such places at a time when the Theodul or the Monte Moro were considered very dangerous. Yet, by the middle of the nineteenth century, all the southern valleys of Valais had been discovered, and it was realized with a shock that the great glaciers round Chamonix were but part of a huge system covering a whole district in the heart of the Continent. This region was full of mysteries. Maps were hopelessly inadequate; names were vague or non-existent. None knew exactly where the Weisshorn was, yet it was one of the most conspicuous peaks in the range and visible from the opposite side of the Rhone valley. Nevertheless, great efforts had been made to explore the lower reaches of the high mountains.

Mountaineering was already far advanced in the Western Alps when it was beginning in other districts. Here it progressed much more slowly. Neither in Eastern Switzerland nor in Austria did one meet with the galaxy of minor—though devoted—mountain worshippers who had played such important parts in Savoy or Valais. Secondary Swiss ranges were known to chamois-hunters, but no outsider had ventured there, nor was any to do so for a long time. The Grisons, for example, were hardly known to the outside world, though the Bernina pass had been much frequented up to the seventeenth century. De Saussure had ventured up to Chur in 1777, but did not go into the Grisons.

The leading personality in Eastern Switzerland was Placidus a Spescha, a monk from Disentis. He was born in Truns in 1752 and took orders in Disentis when he was twenty-two. He was sent to the Luckmanier hospice in 1781. He collected crystals and started reading the works of Swiss naturalists. De Saussure's books made such a strong impression upon him that he decided to explore the country round Disentis, an almost unknown district, its mountains still unclimbed and its geology a blank. He was to devote his whole life to this task. He was greatly hampered by the grave political difficulties of the period. The French Revolution had broken out, Switzerland had been invaded, the Grisons had become a battlefield. Eventually the Disentis convent was burned down, his collections were stolen by the French and he himself was taken prisoner by the Austrians and sent to Innsbrück.

He wrote that he found in the mountains all that a pious soul could wish for: 'While I climbed high mountains, I became aware of the almighty power of the Creator.' Whether he climbed to praise God and please his own soul, or merely to read his barometer, is not clear, but he made several important ascents, not to mention long journeys through unmapped districts. He climbed Piz Walhrein, Piz Urlaun, the Stockgron, the Oberalpstock and many other secondary summits. The climbs, though only moderately dangerous, were always difficult and Spescha had first to find his way to the foot of the mountain before the ascent could begin. Of course, the fact that there were no local guides could not be looked upon as a tragedy, when one remembers what had happened when there *had* been guides. Nothing deterred Spescha. Year after year he kept it up. At the age of seventy-two he attempted to climb the Tödi and failed. He died at seventy-eight, having opened up a totally new country. He had had many original ideas, one of which was a suggestion to found an Alpine club. He had noticed that large numbers of foreign travellers kept coming every year to Switzerland; they loved the country, and found it pleasant and healthy. Why not try and bring them all together? But first there was much to be done to make things more comfortable: for Alpine natives were usually repulsive boors, and hotels and hospices must be built in various places.

For many years after Spescha's death, nothing important was done in his district. But while he had been exploring the Grisons, another range had emerged from obscurity: the Bernese Oberland. Here history is very intricate indeed. The huge size of the main glaciers, the intricacies of the mountain buttresses, the fact that the approach took at least two days from the nearest hamlet, made climbing complicated and wearisome. It was difficult to recognize summits from far away and the weather in the Oberland is not good, to say the least. Clouds always hid parts of the view and, even with a cloudless sky, a novice experienced very great difficulties in recognizing a peak or in finding his bearings.

However, in 1811 Aarau naturalists attempted to climb the Jungfrau: they were the two brothers Meyer. Their father was a topographer. The brothers were learned men but, with what almost amounted to perversity at that time, they started to climb the big Oberland peaks without scientific instruments 'because these merely hampered a daring climber.' So cool a statement at that period required great strength of mind from the man who proffered it. The Meyers were abnormally tough people with considerable walking power. With two chamois-hunters, the brothers started from the Grimsel to climb the Jungfrau. The mere approach by an extremely roundabout route involved a tremendously long walk. The ascent of the glacier was a fairly intricate one; they made two bivouacs on the way, one of them in bad weather. On August 3rd they reached the summit of the Jungfrau. They felt perfectly well and happy on the top, where they planted a large black flag in a mound of snow; then they returned to the Grimsel.

There was some controversy about the climb, for no one had seen the flag. Consequently, the next summer—1812—one of the brothers, Gottlieb, returned and it is certain that the peak he then climbed was the Jungfrau itself. He had two guides with him and the route they found has since become the normal one for parties approaching from Concordia or the Jungfrau-Joch. They found a very bad bergschrund and had to creep across it by using the poles on which they meant to hoist their flag. The last slope afforded very bad going on steep ice. This time, the flag was duly seen from the Strahlegg and was not blown down for many years.

During the same summer another member of the family, Johann Rudolf Meyer, Gottlieb's nephew, a young man of twenty-one who was studying natural history in Germany, made a further important climb: he attempted the Finsteraarhorn. He was not the first to try to conquer the long snow slopes that lead to this splendid summit. In 1804, Servaas van de Graaf, a Dutch diplomat, poet and geographer, visited Switzerland and Savoy. He met Bourrit in Geneva, fell under his spell and, following his advice, went to Grindelwald and from there to the Grimsel. With two guides he climbed up to what he said was a very great height on the south face of the Finsteraarhorn and then had to give up; it was certainly a remarkable feat for a man of forty-seven who had never been up anything steeper than the slopes of the Montenvers at Chamonix.

Johann Meyer and his guides attempted the mountain on its eastern face, a very steep one. overhung in places by threatening séracs. They fought their way up for six hours until Meyer felt exhausted and abandoned the attempt. He sat down and sent his guides on. Owing to the relatively short time they were away, it is most likely they did not reach the real summit, but stopped at a secondary one—the Vorgipfel—and then came down to fetch Meyer.

De Saussure's example, which had inspired Placidus a Spescha and probably also the Meyers, was felt in places far remote from his usual playground. The mountains of Tyrol had been left undisturbed from time immemorial. They had not even been mapped and no one seemed to care much about them. Late in the eighteenth century two Austrian naturalists, Hacquet and Hohenwart, suddenly devoted books to the Gross Glockner district and eventually explored the lower slopes of the mountain, suggesting that the peak itself ought to be climbed. But Hohenwart mentioned the presence of ice precipices 'so terrible that the illustrious de Saussure himself would be frightened by them'. Then a most unconventional figure took command of the situation: Count Franz Altgraf von Salm-Reifferscheidt-Krautheim, Bishop of Gurk. He was a scholar but his interest in the mountains was not purely scientific. He wished to climb them for the pleasure of it, and he invited a large party to ascend the Gross Glockner with him. Most of his guests were learned men and priests, as was meet for a high church dignitary. There were eleven climbers with nineteen guides. The ascent was in itself not very difficult but on this occasion the weather was most unfavourable. The huge party was snowbound for several days in a hut and the actual climb proceeded along rocks covered with thick fresh snow, under a very cold wind. They failed once, then reached a lower summit. On July 28, 1800, Bishop Salm at last set foot on the main summit. He had fallen in love with the mountain and went back to it several times. The ascent of the Gross Glockner became before long a quite popular expedition.

The first ascent of the other great Austrian summit, the Ortler, was a piece of compulsory mountaineering. The Archduke John of Austria, seventh son of the Emperor Leopold, who made himself a name in history by the number of battles he lost, including that of Hohenlinden, where Moreau crushed his army, had on the strength of those high qualifications been appointed director-general of fortifications. Seeing on a map that the Ortler was set down as the highest mountain in Austria, he thought it would be useful to know more about it and specifically to have it climbed. He had neither the desire nor the capacity to undertake this himself, but he sent a Dr Gebhardt to discover geological data about the mountain and to make the ascent. Gebhardt took two chamois-hunters as guides and, in 1804, made numerous attempts to reach the summit. Luck was against him and he failed repeatedly. Then a third hunter, named Joseph Pichler, came forward. He asked first for a sum of money and for the help of certain colleagues, and having been granted both his requests, he set out with his companions on September 28th. They reached the summit in a howling blizzard. A year later, Pichler took Gebhardt to the top, this time in perfect weather. They built a great cairn so as to preclude dispute, as there had been rumour of Pichler having lied regarding the success of his first climb.

The next great peak to rear its head into mountain history was Monte Rosa. Its south face could be seen from Milan or Turin and it had been mentioned in many travel diaries. Some outlines of the mountain may possibly have been painted by Leonardo da Vinci into the background of the *Madonna of the Rocks* or other pictures, though there is but scanty evidence that Leonardo had climbed even a minor summit in the neighbourhood. De Saussure saw Monte Rosa from its very foot at Macugnaga and was not particularly impressed. But little by little climbers began to think that the mountain was beautiful and deserved a closer inspection. A long and protracted siege now began. Monte Rosa actually bristles with summits and they were to be conquered one by one. Count Morozzo of Turin was inspired by de Saussure's ascent of Mont Blanc and in the very year when the Genevese naturalist was in the neighbourhood of Monte Rosa, he tried to reach its summit. He did not go very high, and the mountain looked much too stern and steep to encourage him to proceed farther. The first serious attempt was made by the doctor of Alagna, Pietro Giordani in 1801. He reached the summit now called the Punta Giordani, climbing alone and writing on the spot an account of his feat; the text was eventually printed, then lost and rediscovered by mere chance much later. Giordani prided himself on having opened the way to knowledge and on having enabled future scientists 'to elicit the secrets of frozen nature'. When climbing the peak, he had arrived too late on the summit to have time to traverse to another, and night drove him away. Yet he had reached a very great height. Then came a long period during which European politics were far too stormy to encourage or even permit climbers to indulge in their pastime.

Monte Rosa was left alone for sixteen years. In 1817, Dr F. Parrot, a German scientist who had climbed in the Caucasus and had ascended Mount Ararat, reached the top of what is now known as the Parrotspitze. Two years later, J. N. Vincent of Gressoney climbed another summit, the Vincent Pyramid. The next peak—the Zumsteinspitze—owed its name to J. Zumstein, an Italian of Valaisian origin, who conquered it with two friends, including Vincent, in July 1819. Their climbing kit, including crampons, hooked alpenstocks, ladders, etc., was carried by two mules as far as the snow-line. The climb was more dangerous than difficult, as the party had to traverse under threatening walls of ice. They were not roped, thinking the procedure too risky, should a member of the party slip and drag the others down. They eventually reached their summit and basked in the sunshine, looking at the stupendous view and at a few silvery butterflies which had fluttered up to that great height. The silence of the great mountains, deeper than any other, made a deep impression on the men. They had great difficulties on the descent, because the afternoon sun had melted the snow on the slopes. Zumstein was anxious to return and climb other high points, but his desire did not materialize.

The next climber was an Austrian officer, Baron Ludwig von Welden. He was stationed in Northern Italy and had taken part in mountain warfare in 1815. Baron von Welden quickly came under the spell of Monte Rosa; he collected all available references to the mountain, went to look at it from every vantage point—from Gressoney, the Val Sesia, the Monte Moro—and then started to climb laden with the usual scientific instruments. On his fourth attempt he reached what is now known as the Ludwigshöhe on August 1, 1822. There were still other peaks to conquer, for Monte Rosa was a generous mountain which had means of rewarding many worshippers. It was also a kind mountain: there were no accidents during these early attempts and yet these pioneers were all nearly as inexperienced as those who had fought their way up the slopes of Mont Blanc.

Very slowly, tourists who had done some climbing in the Chamonix district began to feel attracted to other valleys. Why not go farther afield? Most of those early explorers were Englishmen and some of their attempts were daring and well planned. The timid, often childish impressions which had occurred in so many early accounts of the ascent of Mont Blanc now disappeared from their diaries. These pioneers knew something of the great ice-world they wished to visit: séracs and snow-bridges were still very surprising, but not completely unpredictable. Even the guides had acquired some knowledge and took precautions. They went so far as to rope up the members of the party, though not so far as to rope themselves *into* the party. Above all, climbers felt more deeply the grave joy imparted by the mountains. Bad conditions on a climb were often an added attraction and sometimes the humorous aspects of mountain expeditions was perceived and relished.

The Breithorn had been climbed for the first time in 1813 by a Frenchman, Maillart de St Sorlin, whose papers are still extant but unavailable. We have to limit outselves to the second ascent, which was made in 1821 by the astronomers John Herschel and Charles Babbage, with their Chamonix guide Joseph-Marie Couttet. Herschel's travel diaries belonged to his grandson, the Rev. Sir William Herschel, who allowed me to see them. John Herschel was twenty-nine when he made the ascent. Couttet had been his guide in Chamonix earlier in the year; he had a fine mountaineering record for the time, and had been in Napoleon's army as a *chasseur à cheval*. In 1820 he had barely escaped being killed on Mont Blanc when a fall of séracs drove most of Dr Hamel's party into a crevasse of the Ancien Passage, killing three guides.

John Herschel arranged to meet Couttet in Brig to climb what he took to be Monte Rosa, at the top of the Zermatt valley. Accordingly, they met on September 4, 1821. 'Savage scenery of the valley of St Nicolas', the astronomer wrote. On September 5th they left Zermatt over the Theodul Pass, went down to Breuil, then up 'Monte Rosa'. 'Magnificent view of Alps on Alps,' wrote John Herschel. 'Matterhorn to right, forming north extremity of a long ridge of snow peaks sharp as needles. . . . Superb sky, indigo blue'. They were on top by 4.30 p.m. and found 'dead and torpid bees on snow in descent', reaching the Theodul by sunset and Zermatt by eleven; 'moonlight over snow'. Babbage was deadly tired and was given some Madeira with eggs and milk. The Zermatt men they had taken as assistant guides were 'drunken and stupid' and had not provided mules, though they had been paid in advance. The party spent one more night in Zermatt, in the local priest's house. It was so flea-ridden that even Couttet got up in the middle of the night, and the following dialogue took place:

'Couttet, are you getting up?
'Yes, Sir. I am going to take water to the mule.
'Couttet, it seems that there are plenty of fleas here and very little sleep.
'Yes, Sir. I have counted several million of them.'

Accordingly, he went to sleep with the mule. As for Herschel, he did not sleep at all, as bells started ringing at midnight, 'like a thousand coppersmiths at work on a boiler'.

78

When back in England, on February 2, 1822, he wrote the Genevese astronomer Alfred Gautier that he had gone over all his figures once more and had discovered that one summit of the range surrounding the one he had reached actually towered above it. He added: 'And that I should suspect to be the loftiest peak in the southern chain of the Alps,' The truth dawned on him and he came to the conslusion that he had made a mistake and had climbed the Breithorn, not Monte Rosa.

In 1830, the Earl of Minto, who had climbed a little in the Chamonix range, came to Zermatt with his eldest son, a friend and seven Chamonix guides. He had the Breithorn in view, though he knew it had already been done. Yet his expedition was a landmark in mountain history, for his party was one of the first which had been formed according to modern conceptions: the tourists were not incompetent beginners, to be dragged along by exasperated guides utterly indifferent to the success of the climb and to their employers' feelings. These men knew and respected one another. Lord Minto's son was sixteen and all the guides loved him. The chief guide was again Joseph-Marie Couttet, who had been seven times up Mont Blanc and knew probably more about snow conditions than at the time of the Hamel accident in 1820, and among the others was Ambroise Paccard, the son of the great Dr Paccard. Good Savoy guides, who never speak anything but French, and usually their own dialect, manage to make themselves understood by anybody, either in German Switzerland or in the Himalayas. Accordingly, Joseph-Marie Couttet made friends with everybody in Zermatt and actually borrowed the vicar's hat to replace his own which had been snatched away by a gust of wind. A first attempt upon the mountain failed on account of bad weather, and the population was certain that the whole caravan had perished. Then the weather changed and the party left again for the hut on the Theodule pass. The next day, the climb was fairly easy, though Lord Minto was much impressed by the roping-up:

'The first process was to bind our gaiters firmly to our feet, so that no snow might enter between them and the shoe. We had already a pair of cloth trousers over our duck ones; the green veils were fixed upon our hats which we put over our nightcaps, and we had each a pair of blue spectacles to protect our eyes . . . Couttet now summoned us to come and have the cord attached to our bodies. There was something not altogether wanting in solemnity in this last ceremony, indicating a certain degree of peril in the adventure on which we were about to start and, though not quite so formidable as the last act of pinioning a malefactor before he is led out to the gibbet, an operation to which it bears some resemblance.'

The view was a failure. The summit was wrapped in mist and Lord Minto was probably relieved that he had not to go through the dreary process of making amateurish scientific observations. The party came down in high spirits, feeling that the whole of the climb had been a success. It had been excellent team-work.

Visiting new valleys became less and less of an exception. But why not cross fron one valley into the next by high glacier passes and open new ways of access right at the foot of the higher summits, instead of always descending into the depths of the valleys? Now the Valais offered many opportunities to climbers who liked to go as near as possible to the heart of the range. In 1828, a German scientist, E. H. Michaelis, crossed the Allalin Pass from Taesch to Mattmark and wrote an extremely vague account of his journey. The same expedition was attempted later by a young English botanist who lived in Switzerland, Robert Shuttleworth. He had explored the Alps extensively in quest of mountain flowers and on August 23, 1835, he left to cross this pass. His guides were two chamois-hunters who swore they knew the glaciers well and later confessed that they could not find their way. It was, so they tried to make out, entirely the glaciers' fault because the positions of their crevasses had been wickedly changed. The party reached the pass without difficulty: it is a broad snow-field from which the view is of striking beauty. But Shuttleworth had hardly time to enjoy it:

'We were soon enveloped in a thick and wet mist. All our endeavours to keep clear of the wide chasms were ineffectual and, having with great difficulty and much expenditure of time passed several covered only with a thin layer of snow which offered no resistance to the passage of our poles, we were obliged to give up the direction we had taken towards the right side of the glacier.'

Eventually the party was benighted. The prospect was far from pleasant since little food remained. They had no extra clothing and they were wet through after hours spent in the snow.

'We were therefore obliged to take up our quarters under a mass of broken rocks which afforded a sort of shelter to our heads and backs but not before we were so wet through that the tinder in our pockets had become perfectly useless and after several vain attempts we were obliged to give up all hope of lighting a cigar. Although much fatigued there was of course no prospect of sleep and the night was passed half sitting, half standing, in keeping each other awake, and in stamping with our feet to prevent their becoming quite benumbed. The fog turned into snow during the night and the cold was less intense than it would otherwise have been. The novelty of the position, the intense silence around us interrupted only by the rumbling of a dull low thunder and occasional reports of masses of snow or rock precipitated from the heights upon the ice beneath, together with occasional distant glimpses of the rocks and the bed of the glacier below us, lit up by flashes of lightning, afforded ample and not entirely disagreeable food for reflection. Our guides had recourse to sleep, to muttering of prayers, to occasional grumblings to pass the time, and one of them, who appeared never to have been in such a situation before, wished himself repeatedly back with his four-footed grunting companions in his snug chalet in the vale.'

At daybreak, they discovered that a thick layer of fresh snow had fallen during the night, apparently making impossible the descent of the steep glacier to Mattmark. It was already bad enough to retrace their steps to Taesch; they did not reach the valley before seven at night, horribly sun-burnt and almost snow-blind. And yet it seems that Shuttleworth had enjoyed his night out, on his precarious perch of wet rocks somewhere at the back of the Allalin; this new experience had made him aware of totally unexpected aspects of the mountains. His description of what was one of the first high-altitude bivouacs is most effective. He had become steeped in the uncanny, almost unreal atmosphere which mountains conjure up at night, in falling snow and drifting clouds. His portraits of his inefficient guides, who spent the night wailing and wishing themselves home, is extremely lifelike.

Another explorer, who was almost a mountaineer at that time, was Léonce Elie de Beaumont, one of the very few Frenchmen who cared for mountains. He was a leading geologist, a member of the Académie des Sciences, a Fellow of the Royal Society and a member of almost every scientific organization in the world. His strong will and fiery temper made him something of a terror to his learned colleagues. Yet he had a subtle sense of humour, and as early as 1834 he suggested that the next scientific congress should take place at La Bérarde: 'Members would camp under tents on the moraine of the Glacier de la Condamine; the thunder of ice pyramids crashing, one on top of the other, would greet their arrival and echo the toasts they would drink.' Elie de Beaumont was an excellent walker and visited most of the well-known Alpine valleys as well as those still almost unknown, Zermatt, the Maurienne, and Oisans, in his quest for scientific material. Hardly anybody had until then described La Bérarde. From one of his journeys he brought back a young Tyrolese guide, Stock, who remained with him in his Calvados castle for the rest of his life.

During the same period the majestic shape of the Meije appeared for the first time in a description by William Brockedon in his *Journals of Excursions through the Alps*. He had crossed many high passes and opened up new valleys; he was a passionate lover of mountains and in 1824 or a little later he went up to the Col du Lautaret:

'The snows and glaciers of Mont Lens burst upon us, lit up by the moon with a peculiar brightness, while the base of the mountain sunk into mist and indistinctness, produced a sublime and impressive effect upon the imagination rather than the eye, for it was aided by the deep and distant murmurs of the Romanche.'

The weather soon became bad and he was rain-bound in a dreadful hovel at La Grave. His amazement at the weird 'Mont Lens' under moonlight is one of the first tributes paid to the beauty of the Meije.

By the middle thirties a large part of the non-climbing public was aware of the fact that mountains could be, and sometimes were, climbed. Such feats led to glory—a rather incomprehensible kind of glory perhaps. Consequently, when Victor Hugo crossed the Mer de Glace, he took great care to relate the experience in his *Fragment de Voyage aux Alpes* and to make it sound as hair-raising as possible. He wrote in his guide's booklet: 'I hereby recommend Michel Devouassoud who saved my life.' Young Devouassoud had probably discovered that his patron wished at all cost to believe he had done something extremely dangerous when walking on this very tame glacier. He consequently took him along a short spectacular ice arête and everybody was much impressed by his skill and Hugo's courage. Devouassoud was more efficient than his patron thought: he went up Mont Blanc ten days later with Markham Sherwill, and again in 1834 with the Comte de Tilly.

At this time mountain glory was making a strong appeal to young men of romantic temperament. In 1833, a party of three Genevese students attempted to cross the Rossboden Pass from Saas-Grund to the Simplon. Their one Alpine implement was an umbrella—mercifully, a very strong one. They had a bad guide, bad shoes, no rope; they were terrified from the start. The tale told by Marc Viridet, the leader of the party, is a candid description of a mixture of complete incompetence and wild terror. Everything went wrong; they read bad omens in an inscription on a knife, they slipped and were stopped by the hardy umbrella at the very brink of a crevasse, they slipped again, they tore their shoes, lost their way and reached their goal very late, very wet, very tired, numbed with cold and fear, completely unnerved and having tasted to the bitter end all the unpleasantness provided by a badly-planned climb.

Viridet climbed no more, which is not surprising. Yet he did publish the story of his failure: it is a proof that most people saw something in mountain-eering. When Henriette d'Angeville had climbed Mont Blanc in 1838, she was adequately lionized in the Paris drawing-rooms and she drank the intoxicating wine of flattery to the full, feeling at last she was the equal of her unavowed rival, George Sand. Her contemporaries had realized—or thought they had—what her exploit meant. A new age was dawning.

CHAPTER SIX

GROWING INTIMACY

AN increasing interest in the mountains was becoming noticeable in several countries, though literature still fell very wide of the mark. A dying romanticism had discovered in mountains a complete set of sensational subjects: mediaeval legends, little Savoyard chimney-sweeps with their tame marmots, the glory of sunrise and sunset witnessed from the safe summit of the Rigi, St Bernard dogs, a revised version of the chamois-hunter and recollections of Byron and his name—which he had *not* carved—on one of the pillars of Chillon. Between 1827 and 1829, eight plays about William Tell were acted: one was Rossini's opera; another a tragedy by Sheridan Knowles, which was taken to Paris by Kemble and Harriet Smithson. In short, people had discovered everything but the mountains. All the great writers of the period visited the Alps or wrote about them.

This was the time when Dickens, Tennyson, Samuel Rogers, Matthew Arnold, Thackeray, Lamartine, Victor Hugo, Balzac, George Sand, Alexandre Dumas, Stendhal, and others visited the Alps. And yet no real inspiration had been found. Just as had happened seventy years earlier, a knowledge of the mountains would be recovered through scientific channels. The moment had come when, the lower reaches being already explored and more or less mapped, new lines had to be pursued.

The first scientists to accept the challenge and actually to start climbing were Swiss. As they lived near the Alps, they were more or less accustomed to these giant shapes as part of their everyday horizon. Mostly, they were unimaginative men, without fear of the vague dangers lurking in virgin wastes of snow. By 1830 there had been but one serious mountain accident, that which befell Dr Hamel's party on Mont Blanc in 1820. It is even possible that, to scientists who felt nothing but scorn for the legends and the superstitions kept alive in the high valleys, and who had had no intimation of the savage way in which mountains can react, climbing may have appeared as a hard, wearisome but fairly safe undertaking. At any rate, the early high-mountain expeditions were planned in a spirit of happy irresponsibility.

Of course, the scientific purpose of the climb was still the one valid justification. H. D. Inglis, when trying to make up his mind whether he would attempt the Gross Glockner, wrote in 1833: 'It is a positive act of egregious folly for one not moved by scientific motives to endure the pain and danger of an ascent greatly above the line of perpetual congelation.' After painful hesitations and a most uncomfortable night, he was prevented from performing the act of egregious folly by a welcome thunderstorm.

Several Swiss naturalists like Ignaz Venetz and Jean de Charpentier played a leading part in the discovery of the higher glaciers, but they were not mountaineers in the strict sense of the term; they went up many valleys but did not feel it necessary to ascend peaks in order to discover the means and modes of glacier progression. Another Swiss naturalist, Joseph Hugi, who began his mountain tours in 1828, was one of the first real mountain explorers and one of the first authors of mountain books after de Saussure to give long minute accounts of the kind of equipment required when climbing. He was mainly interested in geology and had travelled in the Jura and the Alps for seven years. He reconnoitred the approaches of the Jungfrau and found a route of ascent through the Rothtal, but was defeated by bad weather. So was an English party which attempted this route a fortnight later. The party consisted of Yeats-Brown and Francis Slade, with one guide, climbing without a barometer, simply for love of the mountains. Hugi wrote with contempt of this stupid waste of energy. It is very likely he never derived complete satisfaction from his own climbs; the district he specialized in is very wet, and though he keenly loved mountains, he either failed in his attempts or was drenched during his expeditions.

In 1828, Hugi tried to climb the Schreckhorn; his guide lost the way, they aimlessly wandered on the glacier and had to go down defeated. The next year, the same party tried the Finsteraarhorn, but once again the guides lost their way; one of them burst into tears and the other implored Hugi to tell them what to do. He decided that they would stay where they were until daybreak. But the weather grew worse, the sun rose behind a heavy curtain of cloud and snow, casting a faint wan light over an 'eternally wintry world', and the party had to give up. A new attempt with a new bivouac brought him to what is now known as the Hugi Sattel. The view was obscured by clouds and the way down the glacier was difficult on account of fresh snow. Eventually Hugi discovered winter mountaineering, or rather he discovered the mountains in winter, when he camped for several days in a hut above the Grindelwald glacier. He also attempted to climb the Eiger in January.

Hugi's achievements had shown what a daring and well-trained scientist could do. Now a party of Swiss geologists was to achieve far more than this a few years later: these were members of a team which, for several summers, camped in the 'Hôtel des Neuchâtelois'.

These men managed a successful and harmonious blend of true mount-aineering and scientific observation, although both were accomplished under very primitive conditions. The head of the party was Louis Agassiz, a young Neuchâtel naturalist, who was full of daring ideas but very hard up. His university career in Neuchâtel began, more or less, with a speech in which he put forward his own theories about glaciers, theories which were completely at variance with those held by the leading authorities of the time, among whom were Elie de Beaumont and the German, von Buch. Consequently, Agassiz had no choice but to take rapid measures to show that he was right and that the more illustrious men were wrong. The only possible way was to make a thorough study of glaciers, and the young man tried to find compan-ions and collect some sort of equipment. Because he was so short of funds, and the Academy of Neuchâtel could hardly give him more than moral support, he had to rely mainly on loans from friends or scientists (which were never repaid) and on the disinterested help of voluntary collaborators, the most important of whom was Edouard Desor, a German of French origin, who had been compelled to leave Germany on account of his too republican ideas and had been living for several years in dire poverty.

For two successive summers, Agassiz, Desor and two other young natura-lists explored various mountain districts, including that of Zermatt. Once they wanted to cross the Weissthor from Zermatt to Macugnaga, and were solemnly rebuked by their guide. The pass, the guide said, could only be crossed by pilgrims to the Sacred Mountain of Varallo, and since all the members of the Neuchâtel party were Protestants, the pass was barred to them. In 1840 they at last found the place which would yield a maximum of information: the Unteraar glacier, at the back of the Oberland. There were no huts of any description in the neighbourhood, and they built their camp in the middle of the moraine, under a big block which they rendered more secure by propping it up with a wall of stones.

Such was the 'Hôtel des Neuchâtelois'. The glacier, creeping along its course, was constantly dislocating the wall or crushing the stones. The whole place was draughty and wet. The floor consisted of mud, pebbles and ice, with a few straw-covered planks. A rug was precariously hung across the entrance of this cave to keep out the wind; but when a blizzard was raging, nothing could prevent the snow from pouring into the shelter, putting out the fire and sticking to clothes and blankets. Glacier streams always seemed to be ready to wash the whole camp away. Once this insecure shelter was almost swept off by the fury of the gale. During the first winter, their rock crashed on to the glacier. The following summer the party returned and, deprived of their rock, camped on the moraine, first in a tent and later in a wooden shanty. Food had to be brought from afar—from the Grimsel hospice or even from Fiesch in the Rhône valley.

In 1841, Agassiz and Desor visited the neighbourhood in March, in winter conditions. With the Grimsel hospice as headquarters, they roamed for three days on the glaciers and came down abominably sunburnt, almost snow-blind, dead tired and blissfully happy. They had obtained complete proofs of Agassiz's theories and they felt as light-hearted as schoolboys. An atmosphere of childlike gaiety surrounded the whole camp for several seasons, in spite of the trying circumstances under which they were living. Scientific work at such a height and at such a time was unbelievably difficult. Much had to be made out of very little. It was necessary to be accurate at all costs and yet one day, when Desor went out to retrieve a thermometer which had been let down into a crevasse, he pulled up a broom, because he had found the wrong string or the wrong crevasse.

The naturalists not only went on with their research but discovered first a taste, then a love and at last a passion for the mountains. Agassiz and Desor began by climbing the Jungfrau in 1841. The climb was a hard one, as there was an endless walk across glaciers to reach the place where real climbing began. Besides, they had much trouble in finding a ladder to bridge crevasses. They had no barometer, having already broken three and damaged a fourth during the season. Their guide, Jakob Leuthold, was competent and bad-tempered, and refused to accept advice from the men he was leading. A long succession of snow terrasses, a wide bergschrund and a very steep ice-slope led the party to the Rothtal pass; then they had to negotiate a thin steep ridge, during the ascent of which they were overtaken by fog. They were tired, depressed and giddy, but suddenly when they were wondering how much longer the ordeal would last, the fog lifted and a few minutes later they reached the top. This almost dramatic conclusion to a strenuous climb threw them into an ecstasy of joy.

'I remained but a few minutes on the summit,' wrote Desor, 'but it was long enough to make me certain that the view from the Jungfrau would never fade from my memory. After having carefully inspected the most striking aspects of this unique landscape, I hastened towards Agassiz, for I rather dreaded that such an overwhelming emotion would deprive me of my usual composure and I needed to feel the grasp of a friend's hand . . . I think we should both have wept, had we not felt shy.'

This emotional behaviour of men who were not addicted to displaying their feelings shows how deeply impressed they were by their experience. The endless prospect of glaciers, peaks and snow-fields, reaching to the southern horizon, the blue and green hills fading away into dim, boundless distances in the north, were completely new to them even after the weeks they had spent in the ice-world of the Oberland. There the lower hills had shut them in, while here, on this towering summit, they were feeling the freedom of air and sky. It was a new, unforgettable bliss.

In the following year—1842—at the end of another season on the same moraine, Desor attempted to climb the Schreckhorn. He was greatly surprised to see his guides keeping as much as possible to the rock ridges: early climbers had always preferred ice slopes. The worst part of the ascent was the crossing of an ice couloir, swept smooth by falling stones and waterfalls. Another steep ice-face brought the party to the knife-edged final ridge, up which they crept gingerly on all fours. Its summit was a small ice platform, standing aloof above tremendous precipices. But it was not the true summit of the Schreckhorn. Later, a careful reading of a more accurate map than the one used in 1842 revealed the fact that the party had only reached a secondary summit, the Gross Lauteraarhorn. The Schreckhorn was still a virgin peak and was to remain so until 1861, when it was ascended by Leslie Stephen. In his account of the climb, however, Desor had made a striking confession: 'The ambition', he wrote, 'of hoisting the first flag on the Schreckhorn, the one big Bernese summit which was still untrodden, was far too obvious for us to resist.' He tried to modify the statement by calling this longing a 'whim' and giving long explanations of the scientific importance of the climb; yet it was none the less a fact that he had climbed the lower Schreckhorn mainly because he thought it would be a fascinating experience.

In 1844 Desor ascended one of the three summits of the Wetterhorn. Two of his guides had already been up to reconnoitre the route. It was a long, fairly difficult climb. The party discovered a pleasant though hazardous way of sliding down ice slopes by using a ladder—their constant climbing companion—as a sledge enabling them to tear down slopes and fly over crevasses. The summer of 1845 was the last that the Neuchâtel party spent on the Aar glacier. Agassiz climbed another peak of the Wetterhorn, Desor did the Galenstock—and thus ended a picturesque association of many years. Agassiz left Switzerland to teach in the United States and Desor abandoned long mountain expeditions. Yet even apart from the considerable amount of scientific material they had collected during so many seasons, they had done useful work. Scientists had again shown the way up the high hills.

One of their climbing companions continued his visits to the Alps and thus bridged the gap between these early pioneers and the great climbers of the late fifties. This was Dollfus-Ausset, who had already ascended several peaks with Desor. He was a Frenchman from Mulhouse, where he owned a cotton-mill. He had his fair share of the stubbornness which belongs by tradition to Alsatians. An amateur geologist, he did all he could to help the Neuchâtel naturalists and then began to pursue research of his own. His thirteen heavy volumes on glacier history are an extraordinary mixture of accurate scientific notes, lists of illustrious visitors who called on him while he was camping on the Theodul Pass to make observations, bad poems—the worst being a dialogue between the Matterhorn and Monte Rosa—and accounts of his climbs. When he was sixty-five, he took his sons-in-law up the Finsteraarhorn and indulged in grandiose soliloquies on the summit: 'The soul communes in the infinite with those icy peaks which seem to have their roots in the bowels of eternity . . .' He had a fiery temper and did not suffer fools or guides gladly. His family and mountain companions were often terrified by this impressive and unpredictable personality.

Yet for various reasons the mountain adventures of Agassiz, Desor, Dollfus-Ausset or Hugi came but very faintly to the knowledge of the vast non-climbing public. They were hardly known outside Switzerland. Desor was a good writer, but his two volumes devoted far too much space to technicalities to be of much interest to the general public. Agassiz wrote only indifferently and Dollfus-Ausset's books were a maze in which readers very soon became lost.

But another scientist who had been associated with the Hôtel des Neuchâtelois, J. D. Forbes, proved to be the first great modern pioneer. C. E. Mathews, who knew him well, wrote this brief portrait:

'Forbes was certainly not an athlete and would probably have broken down under the stress of what would now be considered a really arduous expedition. He was pale, thin and had indifferent health, but his expression was singularly sweet and winning and he had the beautiful and refined manners of the old school.'

A scientist of high repute and a professor at Edinburgh University, he came to the Alps in 1839, when he was thirty. He had already travelled through the Tyrol and the Pyrenees, but he was now beginning to explore the High Alps from a scientific point of view. I do not intend to dwell on his discoveries, which were both important and numerous, nor on the theories he discussed with contemporary scientists, which were at variance with those of Agassiz, his former friend, and also with Tyndall's. These are not strictly relevant to mountaineering history. The important fact about Forbes is this: that he was the first man who opened up totally untrodden paths.

In 1839 and 1841 he went to Dauphiny, a province which hardly anyone had yet visited. He did not attempt to climb peaks, but several weeks of strenuous walking took him round the Pelvoux, the Meije and the Ecrins, and up and down numerous passes. 'The scenery is stupendous,' he observed. Villages were unpleasant and dirty, high chalets were still dirtier, the going was very rough and his party were often compelled to bivouac in the open or walk for sixteen hours. However, his guide, Joseph Rodier, was competent and intelligent. Forbes, who hardly ever indulged in descriptive writing, often remarked that the mountain prospects of Dauphiny were as wild and striking as the finest in Switzerland.

After his second visit to Dauphiny, he hurried across the Petit St Bernard, the Val Ferret and the Grimsel to the Aar glaciers: this was because in the previous year he had met Agassiz in Glasgow, and Agassiz had invited him to the Oberland camp. This new campaign was to provide Forbes with endless professional worries and many unforgettable mountain memories. The prospects of the climbing season were delightful. Forbes was a member of the party which went up the Jungfrau on August 28th. It was his first big climb and he felt perfectly happy on the high snows, though he thought the crossing of crevasses by means of a ladder was a slightly puzzling operation. He was not as emotional as Desor when treading the summit, and he did resent the visit paid by an eagle to the food basket they had left lower down on the glacier.

Forbes's sojourn on the Bernese glaciers convinced him that much was to be found in such surroundings before one could formulate a definite theory regarding glacier progression. He accordingly decided to make his headquarters at the Montenvers above Chamonix—and spend as much time on the Mer de Glace and the neighbouring glaciers as he needed to gather his material. In 1842 he passed two months in the old hut with his guide and friend, Auguste Balmat. He went to Courmayeur to see the southern glaciers of the range, crossing into the Val d'Aosta by the Col du Bonhomme and the Col de la Seigne and coming back to Chamonix by the Col du Géant.

Later in the same summer, he actually broke new ground by opening up the High Level Route, the glorious track which winds in and out over the great glaciers as far as Zermatt, Saas-Fee, the Simplon and indeed Austria. There are various ways of following it: by crossing the passes or traversing the summits. According to the weather and snow conditions, it can be quite easy or extremely dangerous. It is always a long expedition, and although the journey can be broken and resumed in any valley, it is strenuous. Forbes, having hurt his foot just before starting from Chamonix, rode down to Martigny. At the Grand St Bernard, he joined a friend, a Bernese professor of geology, and then, with Victor Tairraz of Chamonix and local guides whom they selected in each valley, they proceeded up the Val de Bagnes and crossed the Col de Fenêtre into the Valpelline. They returned north through the Col de Collon, which brought them to Arolla. This was almost new ground: it is practically certain that no foreigner had ever crossed this little-known pass, used only by chamois-hunters and smugglers. When the party was coming down near the foot of the mighty and majestic Mont Collon, yelling at the tops of their voices to start a reverberating echo, they noticed a corpse on the snow. It turned out to be that of a smuggler who had been caught in a blizzard the winter before and had died of cold and exposure. In spite of the bright, calm, summer day, Forbes was suddenly overwhelmed by a secret terror:

'We turned and surveyed with a stronger sense of sublimity than before the desolation by which we were surrounded and became still more sensible of our isolation from human dwellings, human help and human sympathy, our loneliness with nature and, as it were, the more immediate presence of God.'

Arolla consisted at that time of only a few chalets at the edge of a forest. While the members of the party were resting, a man called Pralong came and talked with Forbes. He suggested the very little-known Col d'Hérens as the best route to Zermatt; he, Pralong, happened to have crossed it several times. Forbes had vaguely heard of it and was attracted by the idea of going 'amongst some of the highest and most majestic peaks of the almost unknown district'. Accordingly, he accepted Pralong as his guide and went down to Evolène, as there was no possible accommodation in Arolla. It was almost worse in the lower villages, as the place was dirty and the natives unfriendly. Forbes's Bernese companion was so disgusted with the conditions that he went down by himself, leaving Forbes and his guides to attempt the crossing of the high pass.

They mounted by the Ferpècle valley, at the foot of 'jagged summits of which the most conspicuous is a sharp pinnacle called Aiguille de la Za'. The party slept in the last huts of Bricola and left very early in the morning , on a clear, cold night alive with stars. Pralong and Tairraz knew that glaciers must be crossed as early as possible, when the snow is still hard. The Mont Miné Glacier goes up by easy but endlessly long slopes and proved to be more difficult than they expected. Yet, as there was but little snow, it was possible to see the crevasses and zig-zag accordingly. While they were climbing, night turned to grey dawn, shades of yellow, green and pink slowly coloured the sky and the sun rose behind the Dent Blanche, sending long pale rays into the distance. Little by little, dark points began to peep above the eastern horizon: the perfect triangle of the tip of the Matterhorn, and then a slender point with small projections suggesting the ears of a cat, which proved to be the Dent d'Hérens. At nine they reached a summit overlooking the col, and the whole entrancing eastern prospect burst into view, a wild world of mountains, lit by the bright sun of a cloudless morning.

They were now to go down to the Zmutt glacier, but the ice-slope that leads to it was suddenly broken by a gaping bergschrund, the upper edge of which overhung the lower and was shedding icicles in showers. A decision had to be made at once, as the weight of the three men might easily have started an avalanche and carried them into the abyss. Accordingly Pralong, tied to the longest possible rope, was lowered down by his companions and managed to land rather precariously on the lower lip of the crevasse; then he helped Forbes down and lastly Tairraz. After this, reaching the glacier and then solid ground proved easy. Crossing a bergschrund is always puzzling, as one never knows how the snow edges will accept being trodden on: they can react in many disconcerting ways and Forbes's description of his experience is one of the most impressive as well as one of the first ever written on this subject.

After several days in Zermatt, Forbes started making the tour of Monte Rosa as he had made that of Mont Blanc. He went over the Theodul Pass and down to Breuil. In St Jean de Gressoney he met old Zumstein, who had climbed one of the summits of the mountain in 1819. Then, crossing from one valley into another, he reached Macugnaga, at the foot of the south face of the great mountain. The next day, he left to cross the Monte Moro. The pass is easy, but the Saas district was probably one of the worst mapped in the Alps—which meant a great deal. The Mischabel range, seen from this valley, made a powerful impression on Forbes. In spite of his various ascents, he was by no means a climber and he did not question the belief that all the peaks he had seen on the way were unclimbable. 'The redoubtable Saasgrat, a lofty chain of inaccessible snow peaks' was how he described them, and yet he was one of the men who knew most about the mountains.

He spent several more summers studying the Mer de Glace and the other Chamonix glaciers. In 1850 he climbed the Aiguille de la Glière above Chamonix and made the first crossing of the Fenêtre de Saleinaz, between the Trient and Saleinaz glaciers. In 1851 he visited Norway and its glaciers, but his health broke down and prevented him from making other important expeditions. Until the very end of his life he retained his passionate interest in the Alps. 'My heart', he wrote, 'remains where my body can never be. My yearnings towards the Colinton banks (where he spent his youth) and towards the Alps are much on a par—both *home-sickness.*'

He had been a pioneer of mountaineering and he was also a pioneer of mountain literature, as we may see from his *Travels through the Alps,* which was published in 1843. Although it was a large book, with many scientific chapters on the formation of ice, the progression of glaciers and so forth, it proved to be highly readable and was widely read. It was the first book dealing with extensive journeys through the High Alps. A second edition came out two years later. In 1855 Forbes removed the purely scientific chapters and published *A Tour of Mont Blanc and Monte Rosa* which again proved to be a bestseller. During the twelve intervening years, much had been learnt about the Alps, a new age was dawning; but the book is still one of the best ever written on the subject.

Mountaineering was no longer the expression of a vague aspiration without aim or technique. An ever-increasing number of people were attracted to the mountains, while stories of adventure and in particular a new book did much to enhance this growing interest.

In September 1854, Alfred Wills climbed the Wetterhorn from Grindelwald. He was twenty-eight at that time. He had discovered the Alps a few years earlier, when crossing the Col du Géant, and had conceived an immense enthusiasm for and longed to come into closer contact with the range. Being a lawyer and a naturalist, he felt no passionate interest in science; and although he had a certain knowledge of glacial phenomena he was not attracted by the idea of growing more intimate with glaciers—a fact which did not prevent his becoming Tyndall's companion. Wills did not limit himself to visiting the great climbing centres of the period. He built a chalet in the lovely and almost unknown valley of Sixt, north of Chamonix, called it 'The Eagle's Nest' and made it his headquarters. From 'The Eagle's Nest' he wandered in the mountains of Sixt and gave them their Alpine reputation. But it was his ascent of the Wetterhorn, a few years earlier, that had made him one of the best-known climbers of the period. It was not the first ascent of the peak, but the fifth or sixth; it was not even the first ascent made by an amateur, for Agassiz had been up the mountain ten years earlier. But it was the first ascent to inspire a well-written narrative, and it was Wills's clear, unaffected, colourful style that enabled him to describe it so vividly. His guide Lauener, as he approached the crest of the summit-ridge, had uttered a cry which was to prolong its echo through mountain literature: 'I see the blue sky!' The fact that Wills remembered this and noted it is a proof that he understood the secret and potent charm of mountaineering.

Wills explored many high glaciers in the course of his career. He visited the valley of Saas, from which he crossed to Zermatt by the Adler Pass; a few years later, he repeated Forbes's expedition along the High Level Route from Arolla to Zermatt; he also climbed Mont Blanc and Monte Rosa. There was nothing new in the ascent of Mont Blanc which he made with Tyndall in

1858, except that the party was caught in a dreadful blizzard which might easily have turned a difficult climb into a tragic one, had the leading guide, Auguste Balmat, and the other members of the party known less about the mountains and their dangerous caprices.

Meanwhile on Monte Rosa history had not been standing still. In 1842 an Italian priest climbed another secondary summit, which was called the Punta Gnifetti in his honour. But there were many fruitless attempts to reach the highest summit. Thus two French professors from Besançon, Ordinaire and Puiseux, in 1847, also the guides of the Swiss professor, Melchior Ulrich, in 1848, and the brothers Schlagintweit in 1851, all reached the Grenzgipfel and failed to go higher. The top, which is now called the Dufourspitze, was attained at last in 1855 by an English party of nine members, the two brothers Smyth, Stevenson, Hudson and J. Birkbeck whom he had trained, with four guides. It was the end of a long and protracted struggle. When Wills climbed the mountain in 1858 with Ulrich Lauener, who had been a member of the first party, the climb was still a very daring one.

On the Continent, too, a taste for mountain climbing was developing and timidly breaking its connections with science. Among the men who had ascended Monte Rosa, Dr Puiseux was one of the earliest French mountaineers; in 1848 he made the first ascent of the Pelvoux in Dauphiny, one peak of which was named after him. The Schlagintweits were well-known German geologists, who were to become leading Himalayan climbers. But the country where at an early date mountaineering became a recognized pastime was Switzerland.

In Switzerland, since the beginning of the century, there had been a widespread taste for long walking tours, ascending the mountain valleys and crossing the low cols, looking at the glaciers even if not actually crossing them. Schoolmasters would take their pupils on holiday trips, showing them the St Bernard, the Rhône Glacier, the Devil's Bridge, William Tell's shrines, the valleys of Grindelwald and Lauterbrunnen, and eventually of Chamonix and Zermatt. Töpffer shepherded troops of twenty or thirty boys through various parts of the Alps, and occasionally the boys stopped playing pranks, stealing cherries or slipping grasshoppers and caterpillars down each other's necks, to look at the scenery. The result of these expeditions was Töpffer's delightful *Voyages en Zigzag*, but there is no record that any one of his pupils ever became even a third-rate mountaineer.

Sometimes, it is true, very earnest schoolboys made similar excursions without the encouragement of a professor. Such were Hugi, Melchior Ulrich and Gottlieb Studer. In a few cases, a knowledge of the mountains was forced upon children at what we should consider a tender age. One of the more picturesque figures of the period was Joseph Imseng, the priest of Saas-Grund. He was born in the Saastal in 1806, and became familiar with the mountains when, as a boy, he was put in charge of the village goats. To deal with those wayward creatures, he developed a will of iron and a remarkable talent for organization. When he was appointed as priest of Saas-Fee in 1836, he set out to make his valley better known to the outside world and started by opening a hostelry in this wild and isolated spot. A few years later he was running three hotels, two in Saas-Grund and a third in Mattmark. They were dirty, but Imseng was a pleasant host, and this made up for a good deal. When Alfred Wills visited the valley he was struck by the great culture of the man who spoke good French and good Latin, knew the flowers, the rocks and the history of his valley and was an authority on topography. Imseng became the adviser of all climbing parties in Saas; he accompanied Engelhardt, Wills and Ulrich to Zermatt across the great passes of the Mischabel range, the Adler, Allalin and Ried Passes. He climbed the Nadelhorn alone but for his guide, the Allalin and the Flestchhorn with Ames, the Balfrin with the Spence-Watsons, and the Ulrichshorn with Ulrich; he attempted the Dom with E. S. Kennedy. At a time when women climbers took care to hide the fact that they were engaged in so rash an occupation, Imseng was the soul of courtesy to Mrs Freshfield, Mrs Cole, Lucy Walker, and the Misses Pigeon, and he did not think it at all strange that he should climb the Balfrin with Mrs Spence-Watson. All these climbers described his picturesque figure, with the greasy old cassock which he tied up when the going became tricky and which then displayed an equally old, and usually torn, pair of breeches. In 1869, Imseng's body was found in the Lake of Mattmark. The official version was that he had had a stroke, had fallen from the path, which was very narrow, and so had been drowned. The local tradition is different. According to this a guide, who was also a notorious poacher, was caught in the act by the priest; they quarrelled and the guide, who was an immensely tall fellow, knocked Imseng down—the priest then fell into the water.

Imseng had been the leading spirit in the opening up of the Saastal. It was the view of Wills that Imseng's memory should be honoured by giving the name of 'Imseng Pass' to the Adler Pass, the first crossing of which had been made by that priest.

All the early Swiss pioneers were cultured men. All of them were scientists of some description: Fellenberg and Oswald Heer were naturalists; Coaz was a forestry expert; Gottlieb Studer a topographer; Melchior Ulrich a naturalist and a topographer, besides being a theologian. Though most of them had taken to climbing while still young, there is no youthfulness about their books: one always feels that they climbed because they felt it was a national duty to discover and describe their own mountains. Few of them ventured outside Switzerland: in all their immensely long climbing careers, Studer and Escher von der Linth went but once to Dauphiny and to Savoy. As years went by and English parties became more numerous and enterprising, the Swiss pioneers vaguely resented their presence and, while doing less and less themselves, they sometimes made unpleasant observations in their writing. Yet they did not go so far as to show discourtesy.

They usually carried the time-honoured load of scientific impedimenta but the narratives they afterwards wrote were not over-weighted with geology or botany. On the other hand, they were very technical: those men were not professional writers and they were hampered by the necessity of coining a wholly new vocabulary and a repertoire of images and comparisons. They were steeped in the vague semi-religious and Germanic sentimentality of the first half of the nineteenth century, and often carried it into their writing to the point of indulging in tearful digressions on fresh air, mountain flowers, the pastoral life, and so on. They usually sang hymns on reaching the summit—it was a national habit. Gottlieb Studer went so far as to quote Ossian apropos of a bivouac on the Triftgletscher in the Oberland and Schiller on the Tschingelgletscher. All had a deep sense of the strangeness of the mountain world, but they felt slightly awkward when expressing it. The best writer of this group was probably E. von Fellenberg who was more alive than his contemporaries to the beauty and 'awfulness' of mountains. He also had a sense of humour. German-Swiss usually possess a strong though quite special feeling for the ludicrous, but these men rarely ventured to indulge in it when describing their climbs. Most of them died very old: Studer lived to be eighty-six, Ulrich ninety-one and Coaz ninety-six.

They made a considerable number of first ascents. As early as 1835, Oswald Heer had climbed the Piz Palü and the Piz Linard, two of the highest Engadine summits. In 1850, Johann Coaz ascended the highest in that district, the Bernina. Ulrich specialized in exploring the mountains of Valais and from 1847 onwards climbed principally above Saas-Fee. He was fascinated by the wonderful panorama which these heights command, came back year after year, crossed to Zermatt by several new passes and attempted Monte Rosa twice. He was fascinated, too, by the 'stark pyramid' of the Weisshorn. He also explored the Lötschental, into which he crossed from Kandersteg.

One of his climbing companions, Gottlieb Studer, began his Alpine career in 1875, by going up the Diablerets, a mountain which he likened to a 'snow-

5. *Above*: The Dent d'Herens, 1861, by W. E. Hall, in the possession of the Alpine Club.

Below: The same, 100 years later, showing change in glaciation. (Photo: Malcolm Barnes)

6. The Matterhorn, photographed from the air, showing east (left) and north (right) faces, with Hörnli ridge centre. Mont Blanc in the background (right). (Photo: Bradford Washburn)

covered comb'. He climbed mainly in the Oberland, specializing in the cross-
ing of high passes. He made the first ascents of the Tödi, the Wildhorn (with
Ulrich), and the Rinderhorn—an expedition which he afterwards described
in very bad verses. Later he went to the Valais and climbed the two Combins.
E. von Fellenberg also accomplished a number of hard climbs in the Bernese
Oberland: the Silberhorn, the Lauterbrunnen Breithorn, the Wellhorn, the
Weisse Frau and the Mönch, and he found a new route up the Schreckhorn.

The narratives of all these climbers read very differently from those of
their English confrères. One has the impression that mountain climbing was
not an adventure for them. They took the mountains very much for granted
and derived little excitement from the conquest of a new peak. They were
strangely insensitive to the menace of Alpine heights. However hard the
mountains they were attacking, these men seemed to be on a kind of friendly
footing with them—a feeling which they perhaps derived from a sense of
national possession.

New districts were now being discovered. Dauphiny timidly crept out of the
unknown. In 1839 the two brothers Magnin, who were chamois-hunters,
made the first ascent of the central Aiguille d'Arves. They were overwhelmed
by the stupendous view from the top, and were still more overwhelmed by
the difficulties they had to fight against when coming down.

New tendencies were appearing. A few climbers thought they could well
manage without guides, and this notion, when one considers the rather
questionable competence of many professionals, was not unsound. Among
those pioneers of guideless climbing were E. S. Kennedy, Charles Hudson,
who was to be killed on the Matterhorn, A. G. Girdlestone, and others.
Hudson, in particular, was one of the most daring climbers of the period. For
several years he concentrated on finding new routes up Mont Blanc. With
E. S. Kennedy, he attempted to force a way up the south face from the Vallée
Blanche. Here is an unpublished account of this attempt, taken from a letter
written by Kennedy to Coolidge in 1894:

'After leaving our sleeping quarters near the Rognon, I was the leading man,
the distinction having been conferred upon me for the simple reason that I
was the possessor of the map that had been roughly sketched by Professor
Forbes. We reached the ice shelf whence we would look down upon the
Grands Mulets and the plateau of glaciers between us and the Dôme du
Goûter. Thence Hudson was leader. We had no guide with us but were all
roped. A heavy storm was upon us, so loud was the roar of the wind that even

with mouth close to the ear of the next man, no word could be heard. Hudson with his customary determination, forced his way ahead, while *nous autres*, we five, allowed the rope to pass through our hands. He was soon out of sight and at the end of his tether, he then unroped and went a short distance further. Upon his return he reported that during a brief lifting of the mist, he had looked down the opposite side of the ridge of Mont Blanc du Tacul, and come to the conclusion that the passage ahead between the two peaks of the Mont Maudit was practicable. But the weather was so bad that we unanimously determined to return. I think this is a fair instance of the unwillingness to run great risks that characterized early Alpine explorers. We were all in capital condition and the difficulties before us were by no means insuperable.'

After this failure Hudson tried again by another route from St Gervais, in company with Grenville, Ainslie and the Smyth brothers of Monte Rosa fame. They safely reached the Arête des Bosses but, owing to a blizzard, they descended to the Grand Plateau and ascended thence by the normal route to the top. The narrow ice ridge was still considered too formidable an obstacle. Four years later Hudson and Kennedy, with a guide, started from Chamonix and climbed the ice-arête, but did not dare to come down by the same route; they thought the Mur de la Côte easier.

Another tendency which became noticeable towards the middle of the century was the compiling of accurate mountain guides. Ebel, Murray, and others had published books which, though still useful, were hopelessly out of date so far as mountains were concerned. Everything had to be done afresh and on new lines, minutely and at length. The man who carried it out was John Ball. After a parliamentary career, he devoted eighteen years of his life to the study of the mountains with a view to describing them, not in a literary way, but in a precise and topographical fashion for the use of future climbers. He himself was a good mountaineer and had made the first ascent of the Pelmo and the crossing of the Schwartztor from Zermatt to Macugnaga. Ball continued his work for years, with the assistance of many contributors who sent him notes on their own expeditions.

A time had now been reached when the best climbers were no longer interested in science. Hudson and Kennedy did not give a thought to the temperature of boiling water on the top of Mont Blanc. And though Wills devoted several pages of his books to botany, it was not because he was studying the flora of the valley of Sixt, but because he was fond of flowers. It was clear now that people were climbing mainly because they liked it, and were not concerned with hiding this essential fact.

How did public opinion react to this notable discovery? The number of travellers who knew Switzerland and Savoy, but had never set foot on a mountain or even thought of doing so, was still considerable. Some of them continued to believe they had been very bold in crossing the Mer de Glace. Yet a new notion had now dawned. One might derive glory from a new and perhaps dangerous expedition. In 1842 Longfellow published *Excelsior*, the tragic story of a high-minded though ignorant youth who was carried away by an avalanche when ascending the Grand St Bernard. Instead of the un-wieldy alpenstock, he had thought fit to carry 'a banner with a strange device', the use of which was stranger still, and his melancholy end was not without poetic justice. The moral of the story should have been a warning to high-minded people who lacked training, equipment and common sense, not to climb without a guide. But Longfellow's message was intended to be less cynical; it seemed to convey admiration for that passion for glory which had made his hero impervious to danger.

When Tennyson wrote 'Come down, O Maid, from yonder mountain-height' in Switzerland in the summer of 1846, 'great mountains had dis-appointed him', as he confessed to a friend. He could not imagine there would ever be girls to 'walk with Death and Morning on the silver horn', and a lady venturing among such surroundings was no more than a poetic dream, a Fairy who 'glides a sunbeam by the blasted pine' or 'sits a star upon the sparkling spire'. In spite of its negative attitude, his poem reveals a growing interest in the mountains. Yet Tennyson himself was never very keen on them. The Engadine bored him; when D. W. Freshfield suggested that he had better try the Val Anzasca, he went to Ponte Grande where he wrote *The Voice and the Peak* to the rhythm of the torrent which disturbed his sleep, but he never thought of ascending the Monte Moro in order to find a better view of Monte Rosa—which was the 'peak' of the poem.

Meanwhile new approaches were being discovered, all of them leading to the mountains. Some, it is true, were very circuitous. The great peaks were brought down to the level of humanity; thus a Genevese, Leonard Gaudin, had made a model of Swiss mountains which he modestly labelled 'a most extraordinary production of human genius and industry', and he put it on show in London in 1825. There was another show in Paris in 1832—a kind of diorama called 'The Valley of Chamonix'. Alexandre Dumas described it in the last volume of his *Impressions de Voyage en Suisse*. A similar panorama was displayed in London in 1835. Painted by R. Barford, who exhibited it in the Egyptian Hall and published an ornate pamphlet as a commentary, it was a large view of the range of Mont Blanc as seen from La Flegère. In 1852, Barford exhibited another panorama, this time of the Bernese Oberland as seen from the Faulhorn. And then Albert Smith took the stage.

This celebrated person brought something new into the history of mountaineering. True, it was a rather blatant kind of publicity, yet the man was so sincere, he loved the mountains so deeply, that a genuine nobility seemed to animate the spectacular kind of advertisement which he organized. He had been dreaming of the mountains from his childhood, when he had been given a copy of *The Peasants of Chamonix*, the one good story of a mountain accident which was accessible to children. While he was studying medicine in a desultory way in Paris, he escaped to Chamonix and fell in love with the valley and especially with Mont Blanc. From that day onwards, his aim in life was to climb the mountain. But the enterprise was expensive; Smith had no money and had to wait for better days. He took to journalism, became a member of the staff of *Punch* and started a kind of sideshow which he called the 'Ascent of Mont Blanc', based on the sketches made by Auldjo. Smith also wrote books in which there was always some reference to Mont Blanc and he eventually sent a heroine of *Christopher Tadpole* up the mountain, to face appalling dangers which he listed as:

'Fog freezing so hard, you can't get through it;
'Tumbling into great holes in the glacier, never getting out again for four and twenty hours and then coming up in the middle of the Lake of Geneva;
'Getting butted by wild chamois;
'And pecked at by eagles;
'Rolling down into Italy like a football, never once stopping except you pitch into a crevasse.'

Eventually, in 1851, his dream came true: he left for Chamonix. His companions were William Edward Sackville-West, E. Philips and G. C. Floyd, and they of course had guides and equipment, including numerous bottles of wine. The climb was a complete success and Smith deserved it.

On his return to London, Mont Blanc was made to pay. Smith hired the hideous Egyptian Hall, had a screen framed in the front of a cardboard chalet above a trough where zinc water-lilies floated in a manner which was considered realistic, and for nine years went on telling the story of his climb, making it more and more romantic as time went by, and showing on the screen slides which looked more and more like real photos. In 1855, Jean Tairraz, who had been one of his guides, brought him a pair of chamois caught near the Col du Bonhomme. The she-chamois was called Linda, after Donizetti's *Linda di Chamouni*. Another guide brought him several St Bernard dogs. The chamois and the dogs were exhibited at the Egyptian Hall and Smith presented Dickens with one of the dogs. Three girls in Bernese costumes, who were barmaids in Chamonix, came with the dogs; their appearance probably did much to convince the London public that Chamonix was in Switzerland. The girls and the dogs, though not the chamois, were presented to the Queen. Smith had already been summoned to Osborne by Royal command to show his slides to the Prince of Wales. In 1856, another Royal command brought him to Windsor. He was almost a national figure. D. W. Freshfield remembered being taken as a child to Smith's show. Smith had his sketches painted on fans, and musical compositions, such as *Les échos du Mont Blanc* and *The Mont Blanc Quadrille* were dedicated to him; he invented a game called *The New Game of the Ascent of Mont Blanc*. So many people saw his Egyptian Hall production that they realized that the summit of Mont Blanc was really accessible, and not after all as remote as another planet.

It would not be wrong, I think, to apply Geoffrey Winthrop Young's phrase, 'a mountain prophet', to Albert Smith. For, in spite of commanding personality and inspired language, prophets have not always been men of perfect taste. Smith was a minor prophet; but now, from a very different quarter, came the major prophet, and this was John Ruskin.

On the subject of mountains, Ruskin showed himself at his best and at his worst. 'The Alps were alike beautiful in their snow and their humanity and I wanted neither for them nor for myself sight of any throne in Heaven but their rocks and of any spirit in Heaven but their clouds.' Such was Ruskin's conception, a very noble one, beautifully expressed but leaving little to be discovered from a closer contact with the rocks of which they were made. 'The only days I can look back to as rightly and wisely in entireness spent, have been in sight of Mont Blanc, Monte Rosa or the Jungfrau.' But perhaps the strangest aspect of Ruskin's love for the mountains was his loathing of people who knew more about them than himself. When speaking of such persons the prophet flew into a passion and had recourse to an amazing vocabulary.

I do not propose here to describe the part he played in compelling his contemporaries to appreciate the beauty of mountain scenery. His gospel of the 'cathedrals of the earth' is well known: 'They seem', he said, 'to have been built for the human race as at once their schools and their cathedrals: full of treasure of illuminated manuscript for the scholar, kindly as simple lessons to the worker, quiet in pale cloisters for the thinker, glorious in holiness for the worshipper.' A more disconcerting aspect of his personality was his refusal to grasp the meaning of mountaineering proper.

It was one of the tragedies of his life that he allowed himself to be constantly watched and led about by his parents who carried almost to the point of insanity the domination which many Victorians exercised over their children. Much has been said about Mrs Ruskin's staying with her son while he was in Oxford and wrecking his marriage through her insane jealousy of his spirited young wife. She acted in the same way when Ruskin wanted to see the mountains from closer quarters than the terrace at Berne or even a valley floor. In Chamonix in 1844, Ruskin's father summoned the retired captain of the guides, Joseph-Marie Couttet, and explained that he wanted him to show his son the mountains; but dangerous or even strenuous expeditions were out of the question. Couttet was fifty-six and, though still a good guide, he thought the job was very attractive, easy and well-paid. The son was probably not very enterprising, but as he was twenty-five he was old enough to know what he liked. Consequently Couttet took Ruskin to the Buet; the weather changed while they trudged up from Pierre-à-Bérard and this dull summit was duller than ever, smothered under thick clouds. It is possible that such an experience quelled Ruskin's ardour from the outset.

However, he climbed no other high mountain. Couttet took him up most of the secondary heights in the range of Mont Blanc; they went to the Jardin de Talèfre, which Ruskin thought ugly and uninteresting; they ascended the Brévent, and the Aiguille-à-Bochard, and they walked along the foot of the four big aiguilles which tower above Chamonix, but Ruskin never dreamed of crossing the Col du Géant and the idea of climbing Mont Blanc never occurred to him. Yet Couttet might have spurred him on for, though officially retired, he led Dr Ordinaire to the top in 1846 and J. D. Gardner in 1850. Of course, Couttet knew his patron; though a good walker, young Ruskin was a failure when it came to climbing. Couttet was well-behaved and had the pleasant, courteous manners of many Chamonix men; yet he could not refrain from saying of Ruskin: '*Le pauvre enfant! Il ne sait pas vivre*' (Poor child! He doesn't know how to live!). Ruskin took it as a good joke; Couttet meant it literally and was right. Ruskin never dared to wander beyond the limit of altitude set him by his parents. Lack of initiative and—however strange this may seem as applied to so great a writer—lack of imagination always kept him below the snow-line.

He travelled widely through the Alps, but never went very high. He spent a whole month in Macugnaga; though he thought that the place was dull beyond words, yet he did not think of ascending the Monte Moro. He visited Zermatt at a fairly early date, was entranced by the sight of the Matterhorn, but did not feel impelled to climb higher so as to command a better view of the array of high peaks which surround it. He met Forbes at the Simplon hospice in 1844; the naturalist took him up a ridge in the neighbourhood of the hospice. Though Ruskin appreciated his companion's charm and his art of making every feature of the scenery seem alive and full of meaning, he was never tempted to make a similar expedition by himself. When one reads his mountain descriptions, one realizes that 'mountain' for him means any aspect of the landscape between 3,000 and 7,000 feet, the places he could and did reach. Higher levels were out of bounds and trespassers would have been prosecuted. Mountains for him were like stars: they are studied from afar, through glasses.

This is how he describes the Zmutt glacier, near Zermatt:

'. . . the whole scene so changeless and soundless; so removed, not merely from the presence of men, but even from their thoughts; so destitute of all life of tree or herb and so immeasurable in its lonely brightness of majestic death, that it looks like a world from which not only the human, but the spiritual, presence have perished, and the last of its archangels, building the great mountains for their monuments, had laid themselves down in the sunlight to an eternal rest, each in his white shroud.'

Stepping on such graves meant defiling them. And yet Ruskin did much to draw people to the high mountains. His precise and impassioned descriptions made many realize the beauty of the Chamonix Aiguilles or of the Matterhorn. He went one step further and actually showed what they looked like.

Ruskin was the first mountain photographer. 'The first sun-portrait ever taken of the Matterhorn,' he wrote, 'and as far as I know of any Swiss mountain whatever—was taken by me in the year 1849.' At that time it was a long and complicated process requiring skill, patience and the use of many chemicals which had to be carried by the photographer. One wonders what a dark room looked like in Zermatt at that time! It was, incidentally, through his photographic work that Ruskin met Dr Melchior Ulrich, the Zurich naturalist who had just crossed from Saas-Fee by the Alder Pass. Ruskin, having some quicksilver in his travelling laboratory, helped Ulrich to mend his barometer, which had been broken on the way. Ulrich relates the story in his still unpublished travel-diary. Ruskin also photographed several of the Aiguilles near Chamonix; such is the source of the magnificent sketches contained in *Modern Painters*. As early as 1852—just two years after the publication of the fourth volume—he was quoted side by side with Forbes and Tyndall in articles in illustrated papers.

A few years later French photographers, the brothers Bisson, climbed Mont Blanc with their cameras. Their expedition was long and difficult but their prints were splendid, and when they were exhibited in Paris Théophile Gautier wrote about them in wild enthusiasm: 'In spite of all the obstacles he raised on the way,' declared the poet, 'Mont Blanc has been unable to avoid being caught in the net of obdurate scientific research. Here he is, fierce and solitary, a prisoner in the narrow frame of a photographic plate.'

This growing knowledge of the mountains was no longer limited to the townsfolk who were attracted to the Alps. Natives, though more slowly, had become aware of the remarkable features of the mountains which overlooked their homes and they sought to discover more about them. These natives had now been promoted to the rank of guides, instead of being mere chamois-hunters. In Chamonix, as early as 1821, they had been grouped into a company under a chief guide. There are endless references to this rather notorious organization which was immediately immersed in forms, regulations, rules, notices and certificates which made every climb a terribly complicated affair. As soon as climbing parties became more numerous, the company did everything in its power to hinder them. Devising new climbs required imagination and foresight. Hardly any route was ever discovered by local peasants when not prompted or led by their patrons, and they usually did much to prevent the latter from having their own way. One of the exasperating rules of the *Compagnie des Guides de Chamonix*, was to compel any intending climber to accept the guide whose turn it was to go out, no matter what mountain and no matter which guide. Such a rule was the typical product of a demented bureaucracy; it was forced on the local people by Chambéry officials. But as accidents were not very numerous, it may be safely assumed that no one paid much attention to the *guide-chef's* decrees. Technically this rule is still enforced. Yet I have climbed for years in the Mont Blanc range, always with my own guide, whether it was his '*tour de rôle*' or not, having had only one violent quarrel with the *guide-chef*.

More often, the obstacle in the way of new ascents came from the guides themselves. In 1854, E. S. Kennedy and the Abbé Imseng wished to climb the Dom from Saas-Fee. Their idea was to go up one of the steep rock buttresses leading straight to the summit. Whether they would have succeeded is another question. The Dom is very high and the rocks are rotten. The climb would have required great endurance, much steadiness and perfect technique. The party had taken two Saas guides whose names are not given. They climbed to a height 'much above the lower Mischabels'—the still anonymous Lenzspitze and the Nadelhorn—according to Kennedy. Then the guides stopped and said that, owing to the steepness of the slope, they would not proceed any farther. Now, nothing untoward had happened; Kennedy and Imseng were good climbers, they were not slow and they did not mind the height. But the guides were bored, tired and afraid, and the climbers had to give in and come down. Two years later, certain Saas guides who may have been the same men—one of them was a Zurbriggen—similarly compelled A. T. Malkin to abandon his climb of the Stellihorn as they were unable to cope with the long though easy snow slope of this very tame mountain.

Guido Rey, who is so great an admirer of the guides of Valtournanche, confesses that in the sixties 'those patient, sturdy and courteous men were excellent mountaineers [i.e. inhabitants of mountain districts] but not guides'. There was much to be done.

When Forbes crossed the Theodul Pass his guide, Peter Dammater, took neither alpenstock nor hatchet, but an umbrella. This inadequate tool was supposed to shield its owner from a thunderstorm which seemed about to break, but Forbes knew more than his guide about the vagaries of lightning and curtly ordered him to close the umbrella. He was not a moment too soon, for the storm broke almost at once, right above the pass, and the iron spike of the umbrella might well have proved a perfect lightning conductor. Alexandre Roger, the Swiss topographer who also went to the Theodul in 1830, had a violent argument with his guide Pession, as the latter was unable to discover the gaps of the crevasses; moreover, Pession carried a small cask of wine for his private use and was thus unable to cope with his patron's luggage and barometer. Guides were peasants, who only knew how to carry loads and possibly to follow a leader.

Yet there were already remarkable exceptions. Desor and Le Pileur have drawn portraits of early guides who were worthy of their reputations. Le Pileur, a French scientist, climbed Mont Blanc in 1844 in very bad conditions. He and his companions were snowbound for several days in their tent on the Grand Plateau:

'Mugnier, while the blizzard was raging above the tent, was always ready to cope with any misfortune which might befall us, and he protested that nothing in the world would make him lose his appetite. But the one who was always remarkable for his quiet steady cheerfulness, for his talent for being prepared to face anything, for being happy about everything, was Auguste Simon. He is twenty-seven, six feet tall and as strong as Hercules.'

The best among the members of this first generation of guides was Auguste Balmat, Jacques Balmat's grand-nephew, a 'very intelligent and very worthy man' according to Forbes. He was strong, clever, an excellent mountaineer with perfect manners and a most winning way. According to Whymper, who knew him at the end of his life, he did not look like a guide, but rather like a lawyer or a doctor. Forbes became acquainted with him in 1842, at the Jardin de Talèfre; Balmat was then thirty-four. They travelled together for five years and once Balmat visited Forbes in England. He saved an American tourist who had climbed some way up on a steep rockface above the Montenvers and could not get down.

When Forbes had to give up climbing, he introduced Balmat to Wills and later to Tyndall. Balmat took the former up the Wetterhorn in 1854, and went with him to Saas-Fee, where they crossed the Adler Pass; he also climbed Mont Blanc with Wills and Tyndall in 1858. This was an appalling climb; the party was caught in a raging blizzard on the summit, and Balmat, digging in the snow with bare hands to bury a thermometer (they had forgotten their spade), was frostbitten. After a while, he calmly told Wills that his hands had lost all sensation. Wills, feeling very anxious, immediately warned Tyndall, who did not realize at once what had happened. Looking up from his notes Tyndall then saw that the guide's face was haggard with cold and pain. He made haste to pack and asked Balmat to hand him a magnet he needed for a last experiment. The guide dropped it; his hands could not grasp anything. The party left at once as the situation was growing very serious. Wills and Tyndall were terrified by the idea that their guide might lose both his hands if circulation could not be restored at once. Below the Mur de la Côte, they stopped to rub them with snow until, after a long time, the blood began to flow. Balmat suffered agony, though he said nothing and did not complain.

'I have witnessed some forms of acute suffering in my time, [wrote Wills] but such an exhibition of human agony I have never beheld, and I devoutly trust I never may again . . . Balmat was an old and honoured friend of mine long before this adventure; but could anything have increased my regard for him, it would have been the manly fortitude with which he bore suffering as severe as any human frame can undergo.'

Eventually Balmat's hands were saved; Tyndall wished to pay him more than the usual fee for the climb, but Balmat refused, and Tyndall therefore asked the Royal Society to find a means of showing how much the guide's courage and initiative had been appreciated. The committee agreed at once and presented Balmat with a camera: he was greatly touched by what he still considered a completely undeserved gift. When Balmat retired in 1861, Wills made him the keeper of 'The Eagle's Nest' above Sixt; he died there in 1862.

Ruskin's guide, Joseph-Marie Couttet, was perhaps less remarkable than Auguste Balmat; yet he was among the good Chamonix guides. He was an older man, having been born in 1792, and he had fought in Napoleon's armies before he took to guiding. He had been the head guide of several parties which had reached the summit of Mont Blanc—including that of Mme d'Angeville. He had climbed the Breithorn in 1821 with John Herschel, and again in 1830 with Lord Minto; he went again to Zermatt in 1851 with the son of Sir Robert Peel, recently Prime Minister, and he had been there twice with Ruskin. All those who had climbed with him mentioned his courage and endurance. He was very handsome and when old looked a most impressive man. He had some learning and published a short, well-written guide-book, *Chamonix, Le Mont Blanc, Courmayeur et le Grand St Bernard*. It is strange that Ruskin should have said that Couttet could hardly read or sign his name, as Couttet had signed the legal deed drawn up for Ruskin when the latter bought a piece of ground above Chamonix in 1862; besides, it seems hardly likely that Ruskin had not heard of his guide's literary achievement. Couttet remained his devoted man-of-all-jobs for over thirty years in spite of a few quarrels, and Ruskin was deeply moved by the news of his death in 1872.

Melchior Ulrich also had a trusted companion, Johann Madutz from Matt, near Glaris. Ulrich said he was 'faithful, careful and full of precautions', though he was on probably less intimate terms with his employer than the two Savoyards with theirs. Madutz had begun his climbing career with Oswald Heer in the Engadine, then he had travelled with another geologist, Escher von der Linth, in the Oberland, Savoy and Dauphiny. After this Ulrich took him to the Valais. Most of these expeditions were more concerned with trudging up valleys and crossing snow cols than actual climbing; still, Madutz had done Piz Palü, the Titlis, a secondary summit of Monte Rosa, the Nadelhorn, and other peaks.

One might mention many other names. This was the true dawn of mountaineering as we know it—a clear promising dawn. The opening of railway lines now enabled travellers to reach the Alps more quickly and less expensively. Trains took them to Basle, Geneva, Lucerne and even Montreux. Hotels were becoming bigger, more comfortable and more numerous. Several were built in what for long had been out-of-the-way places. In 1839, Lauber, the doctor of Zermatt, opened a little inn which was enlarged in 1852 and then purchased by Alexander Seiler, who made it the nucleus of his Monte-Rosa Hotel. I have already mentioned the opening of the various Saastal inns which were supervised by Imseng.

No mountain hut had been built since the erection of the refuge at Montenvers. On Mont Blanc mountaineers had been clamouring for years for some kind of permanent shelter on the platform of the Grands Mulets. At last a very small, very primitive shack was erected on the south side of this rocky island, and formally opened on September 21, 1853. Albert Smith had come specially from London for the occasion. There were fifty visitors, most of them smoking their pipes; the oven was drawing badly, and the climbers who spent the night there had some idea of what the Black Hole of Calcutta must later have been like. A few similar shelters were subsequently built in the Oberland.

It was no longer dawn but broad daylight. Great things were shortly to be expected.

PART II

'WHERE THERE'S A WILL . . .'

CHAPTER SEVEN

THE ALPINE CLUB

THE Alpine writings of Alfred Wills were a revelation. In his pages readers suddenly discovered a new realm opened to man's passion for adventure and discovery. New territories in the very heart of Europe were now explored and blank spaces on the maps filled in. From Wills's descriptions, in spite of his efforts to suppress the too glaring details, new landscapes were emerging: the steep ice-wall of the Wetterhorn and the threatening blue cornice; the couloirs grooved and polished by falling stones; the white fury of a storm howling over the crest of Mont Blanc; the shapes of contorted séracs below the Col du Géant; the 'sinister barrenness' of the Distel Alp above Mattmark, with a grey lake at the foot of two shining glaciers; the cold, clear nights, alive with stars, when the party leaves to start its climb; the huge expanse of ice and snow leading to the Adler Pass; the steep ice-glazed slabs of rock.

Few people, when hearing the word 'glacier' could imagine anything more threatening than the benign Mer de Glace in its lower reaches. Wills, and Forbes before him, had compelled their readers to realize how immensely varied in aspect, how beautiful, how constantly changing in moods and colours glaciers are. That ice is white, often blue or green, was known; but what of the 'black ice,' so very dangerous when found on a steep slope or on rock? People tended to think that mountain landscapes above the tree-line were black, white and grey; yet the new literature revealed that rocks could assume any and every colour: blue, red, green, purple, silver. Light and shadow, playing on those desolate slopes, endow them with ever-changing life and colour. But the message could not be heard by all; it was necessary to see as well as to read.

In 1856, Ames made the first ascent of the Allalin and the Laquinhorn in the Saas valley, and Hinchliff crossed the Weisstor. In 1857, J. F. Hardy, W. Mathews, Ellis and E. S. Kennedy climbed the Finsteraarhorn; John Ball climbed the Trugberg and, later in the season, the Pelmo. These are but a few of the first ascents, of which it would be easy but tedious to give a much longer list. They show how a taste for long and strenuous expeditions was becoming popular.

For several years, it had been fashionable to travel on foot or on mule-back through the Alps. Gilbert, Churchill and their wives had visited the Dolomites; the Freshfield family—including Mrs H. Freshfield—had made several expeditions through Savoy, Valais, and the Grisons, and Mrs Freshfield had written spirited accounts of their trips. Ladies were already taking to Alpine travel and more were to come. When Cicéri, the French painter, made his fine Alpine lithographs, basing them on Martens's photos, he always placed a number of human beings in his foregrounds: either tourists or peasants in inappropriate costumes—for instance, a girl in a Bernese costume at the window of an old chalet in Saas-Almagel. There were always one or two ladies in crinolines even on the Monte Moro or at the top of the Buet.

Two French climbers made a rather spectacular appearance in mountain history. One of them is J. Reynaud, the *agent voyer* of La Bessée, who met Whymper in Dauphiny, made a few big climbs with him and came flying over the bergschrund of the Col de la Pilatte, apparently kicked down by A. W. Moore to hurry him over the gap. Reynaud was infuriated by the hint and the accompanying sketch in Whymper's book; it is most likely that both were exaggerated, as the man was a good climber and Whymper's sense of humour was neither original nor subtle. Reynaud was an experienced mountaineer before he met Whymper and had widely explored the Dauphiny valleys. It is a pity that so little is known about him. The other enterprising Frenchman was a young—and regrettably anonymous—count whom Whymper saw making an attempt on the Aiguille Verte above the Mer de Glace. He was either mildly insane or extremely daring.

Mountaineering was becoming so notable a feature of life that the idea arose of founding some association which would bring together the now very numerous climbers, so that they could compare notes and exchange information about new ascents. It would be the best means of circulating references and details of routes, mountain conditions, etc. The idea was not completely new, for John Auldjo, the enterprising young diplomat who had climbed Mont Blanc in 1827, had already suggested how useful such an organization might be. He was still alive—he died in 1886—and yet it seems he did not react or, so far as is known, attempt to join the new association.

The idea did not take very long to materialize. It was born on a joint ascent of the Finsteraarhorn by William Mathews and Kennedy in August 1857, and took shape at the Mathews's home near Birmingham in November and the first meeting of the Alpine Club was held in December. Among the original members were Alfred Wills, E. S. Kennedy, T. W. Hinchliff, and John Ball. The latter was the first President, with E. S. Kennedy as Vice-President and T. W. Hinchliff as Secretary. As stated in the second paragraph of the rules, 'the object of the Club shall be the promotion of good fellowship among mountaineers, of mountain climbing and mountain exploration throughout the world, and of better knowledge of the mountains through literature, science and art.' As early as November 1857, W. Mathews and E. S. Kennedy had thought of asking Ruskin to become a member, but he had refused. Forbes was made an honorary member in 1859. At that time, there were already 134 ordinary members.

In order to give a wider scope to the club's proceedings and to make communications accessible to non-members, the club decided to publish a periodical. Accordingly, John Ball and then E. S. Kennedy brought out three volumes of *Peaks, Passes and Glaciers* in 1859 and 1862. In 1863, the *Alpine Journal* began to appear regularly; the first editor was H. B. George. It has never ceased publication over the last century in spite of two world wars, and it is by far the best mountaineering periodical in the world. It has played a leading part in the history of mountaineering, providing climbers with an exhaustive, up-to-date, well-written bibliography on every possible aspect of the question.

The sub-title of the *Alpine Journal* is 'a record of mountain adventure and scientific observation', which is the best possible summary of the lines along which mountaineering was to develop. The idea of putting 'mountain adventure' first shows how daring those pioneers were. It was still thought very strange, if not worse, to confess one wanted to climb any peak for sheer enjoyment or for love of adventure. And yet, to be perfectly honest, such is the chief incentive of any mountaineer. The Alps are an enchanted garden one is permitted to enter only for a few weeks every year, a dreamland which can be reached only at the end of a long, dreary, expensive pilgrimage. Even then the gate of the hill fortress can be suddenly banged into the pilgrim's face by a spell of bad weather.

Mountaineering in the eighteen-fifties had little in common with climbing today; there were no huts, of course, and every climb meant at least one high altitude bivouac with the added weight of enormous loads of brushwood for fire. Hard mattresses in huts even today are unpleasant and usually dirty, but in those days you had to make the most of stony hollows or, at lower altitudes, of heaps of hay in the highest chalets far below the snow-line, so that on the second day you were compelled to trudge for hours before actually reaching the first pitches of the climb. Crampons had been more or less forgotten. In fact, the very primitive iron spikes worn by Jacques Balmat and nineteenth-century chamois-hunters would have been worse than useless on the hard steep slopes of the Aiguille Verte or the Weisshorn. Ice-axes were just ordinary axes used on ice, and most of the early climbs were done with short-handled axes to hack out steps, and an alpenstock, which was supposed to help its owner to haul himself up, though there are few things more useless and dangerous than those long, heavy, smooth poles.

Rope-technique was in its infancy. Years of practice were needed before any rational equipment could be worked out. New inventions were amateurish, to say the least: Whymper's grapnel, for instance. Still, such hardships made early attempts even more fascinating, for there is no glamour in a victory too easily gained. Alpine summits were difficult to conquer—if it is at all possible to speak of 'conquering' a summit which is always apt to strike back with unexpected savagery, even though it has been climbed two hundred times. Most peaks were unknown topographically and could provide any surprise. Pioneer work in the mountains required passion, vision, optimism and strength, both moral and physical. As luck would have it, all the leading mountaineers were endowed with such gifts, to which they often added great literary talent at a time when no self-respecting person would have dreamed of indulging in slipshod style. Their articles and books gave both beauty and dignity to the new pursuit and the tradition held good. Another aspect of this pioneer work was its variety. Each climber had his own conception of mountaineering and wrote and climbed after his own style.

One of the leading personalities of the Alpine Club was Leslie Stephen, who joined it in 1858. He had come to the Alps, in 1857, when he was twenty-six. He had most of the physical gifts which enable a man to show himself at his best on a mountain. He could walk or climb for hours on end; he was long, thin, extremely steady on any ground and particularly on ice which, like most of his contemporaries, he preferred to rocks. He rather enjoyed going up or down the long steep snow slopes and did not feel unduly anxious or bored. Most of the early climbers seem to have felt that a climb which did not require the cutting of several hundred steps was not a *real* climb. In spite of his love for ice, Leslie Stephen was good on rocks and in fact did many great rock-climbs, some of them on hideously rotten scree, the Bietschhorn for instance. His knowledge of the Alps was extensive. He quickly developed a passionate love for them and worshipped mountains at any height, at any season, under any conditions. No mountain district was either too wild or too tame for him. He loved the dreary, dirty hamlets of the Upper Valais and could even find charm in Zinal under pouring rain. He went to far out-of-the-way places like the Dolomites and the Carpathians. He knew mountain history and was probably the first writer to allude to it in a scholarly book, *Hours in a Library*. But he loved high mountains above all, and enjoyed every minute spent among them. He was looking for adventure when climbing and had the courage to be a pioneer and to say so.

His first glimpse of the three big Oberland summits from the train when leaving Basle struck him like a challenge: he saw them as a forbidding wall and wanted at once to scale it—and he did. He once asked a friend to accompany him in an attempt on the Jungfrau Joch, 'which is a joch which cannot be climbed, so that we have to do it'. He had many narrow escapes and ran considerable risks on the Eiger Joch, the Schreckhorn or the Galenstock in winter. Of course, danger lurked everywhere on those great unknown peaks and Leslie Stephen knew it, but always refrained from expressing his feelings in too obtrusive a way. Describing a bad pitch on the Zinal Rothhorn he wrote: 'Our method of progression was not unlike that of the caterpillar who may be observed first doubled up into a loop and then stretched out at full length.' As the rocks were ice-glazed the caterpillars had certainly a most unpleasant time.

One can imagine the shower of gorgeous metaphors a follower of Ruskin would have lavished on a description of the snow couloirs of the Schreckhorn, the ice wall of the Jungfraujoch, the knife-edge arête of the Rasoir on the Zinal Rothhorn. But Leslie Stephen avoided above all any trick of style or thought which might have brought him in the wake of Ruskin, whom he knew and did not like. Ruskin had woven a golden net of shining similes round the Matterhorn, and it was more than enough. Leslie Stephen never allowed himself any violent or glaring image. A glance at his portrait, with a long flowing beard, a thin face with a high, deeply wrinkled forehead, and almost tragic eyes, and one realizes why he was a master of understatement; yet he was a humorist, too, and knew how to bring in a touch of humour at the right moment. It is true to life. Leslie Stephen could indulge in such effects:

'It was necessary to cut steps as big as soup tureens, for the result of a slip would in all probability have been that the rest of our lives would have been spent sliding down a snow slope and that the employment would not have lasted long enough to become at all monotonous.'

Yet he goes deeper still: 'Every step of an ascent has a beauty of its own.' Without becoming too solemn or too sentimental, he analyses the slow halting meditation in which the climber's mind often indulges during a long hard climb: disconnected thoughts which by degrees allow the mind to come nearer and nearer to a communion with nature:

'One felt as if some immortal being, with no particular duties upon his hands, might be calmly sitting upon those desolate rocks and watching the little shadowy wrinkles of the plain, that were real mountain ranges, rise and fall through slow geological epochs.'

Though an agnostic, his understanding of the spiritual aspect of nature is both delicate and powerful. He had felt in mountains a sort of revelation of a mystical realm you may conquer by using both your muscles and your vision. But he never wished to go further than mystical conquest and did not trouble himself about 'science' when climbing. Once, when going up the Blümlisalp, he had sacrificed to the gods of the period and taken a barometer; but the instrument shot out of the guide's rucksack and fell into the Lake of Oeschinen. So much the better, thought Stephen, who never again added this extra weight to his guides' loads. On the other hand, he once climbed Mont Blanc, following an unusual time-table so as to be on the summit at sunset and thus enable his companion Loppé to paint a landscape dyed gold and flame-colour by the sinking sun.

So we realize with a shock that the author of the *History of English Thought in the Eighteenth Century* and of the *History of Criticism*, the editor of that glorious mountain of historical documents, the *Dictionary of National Biography*, was also the man who climbed for the first time the Schreckhorn, the Zinal Rothhorn, the Mont Mallet, the Bietschhorn, the Disgrazia, the Blümlisalp, who crossed most of the high Oberland passes and found new routes up many peaks including the Allalin, the Lyskamm and the Weissmies. Sometimes both aspects of his genius overlapped. There is an amusing correspondence between himself and W. A. B. Coolidge, in which Stephen tried to discover the validity of the claim made for Sir Charles Fellows, that he had climbed for the first time some point of the Blümlisalp. Now Leslie Stephen always thought that he had himself made the first ascent of this rather tedious snow peak; accordingly, he suppressed the claim. He was in point of fact right and the Blümlisalp story was simply one of the numerous mountain legends which never die.

If Leslie Stephen was the hero of 'mountain adventure' in the heyday of mountaineering, John Tyndall was entirely devoted to 'scientific observation'. He had come rather late to the mountains, yet fell completely under their spell; but about him there is a grim kind of heroism which Leslie Stephen lacks in his conception of mountaineering. Had he lived under twentieth-century conditions, Tyndall would have gone in for north faces and Kangchenjunga. He had studied in Germany and imbibed something of the dark romanticism of a country which always wallows in a morbid love of tragedy. Once, coming to Saas-Fee and finding himself unable to climb the Dom, on account of fresh snow, he went with the Abbé Imseng and two younger priests to visit a cave above the Vispach, near an old mill. The roar of the torrent in the semi-darkness was sufficiently eerie and Tyndall suddenly started reciting long passages from Schiller's *Raüber*. One of the younger priests knew the play and joined in the recital while Imseng stared at them wide-eyed.

Tyndall as a rule kept his romanticism so well under control that it is not easy to detect it, but there is no other word to describe the state of mind of a man who specialized in most difficult climbs, who made various attempts on the Matterhorn and the first traverse of the peak, the first ascent of the summit subsequently known as the Pic Tyndall and also of the Weisshorn. He explored almost unknown Engadine glaciers, climbed Mont Blanc several times (and at least once under extremely severe conditions), and went up Monte Rosa alone, making the first solitary climb of the big peak and probably the first big solitary climb in the Alps. He had a house built at Bel Alp to enable him to live, looking at the magnificent prospect of the Monte Leone, the Mischabels and the Matterhorn. When he had to come to grips with a mountain in dangerous mood, he fought with perfect coolness, but one feels that he enjoyed pitting his strength against a strength seemingly irresistible. This is obvious in his description of the storm on Mont Blanc, of an avalanche on the Morteratsch glacier or on the Glacier du Géant. After the Matterhorn accident, he conceived a rather complicated device, involving an enormous length of rope, for trying to recover the body of Lord Francis Douglas, lost somewhere in the north face. It was never used. Mountains, for Tyndall, had almost human personalities: the Matterhorn impressed him with its 'moral savagery, wild untamable ferocity'. On Mont Blanc, the Grand Plateau had 'a strength and yet a tenderness which at once raised and purified the soul'. When victory was his, as on the Weisshorn, he was elated.

But being intensely Victorian, he never let himself go and he hardly ever allowed his love of mountains to come before his work as a scientist. A different attitude seemed to him a personal affront. His *Glaciers of the Alps* is divided into two parts, the first describing his climbs, the second his scientific observations. Forbes had not been so systematic. It is difficult to realize which part Tyndall wanted to lay stress on. Of course, there was some overlapping; he was trapped into using scientific terms when describing mountains: the colour of the Grands Charmoz reminds him of 'molten copper', the curvature of one of their fantastic turrets—probably the one later known as the Aiguille de la République—suggests 'ductility'. Science was for him a serious matter; he tolerated no joke about it and quarrelled violently with Forbes and eventually with Ruskin about their ideas of the progression of glaciers. These disputes went on for years.

Another quarrel has remained famous in the history of mountaineering. Leslie Stephen had never taken any interest in scientific research in the Alps; he often jeered at it and criticized the two scientific papers printed in *Peaks,*

Passes and Glaciers. Tyndall felt that the criticism in some remarks was intended for him, and reacted as to a personal insult. He refused to have his account of his climb of the Weisshorn published in *Peaks, Passes and Glaciers*, made it the main chapter of his own book, *Mountaineering in 1861*, and shortly after-wards resigned from the Alpine Club. In a way, it made things clearer. It showed one had a right to climb from simple love of mountains. It also showed one could do with one porter less—the one who had been hired to drag the barometer and the theodolite up and down the slopes. Geology, glacierology, botany were going to live lives of their own. They would still be associated with mountaineering, but mountaineering could also develop along its own lines.

These were essentially Edward Whymper's lines. One cannot imagine him tied to the tail of a barometer on the top of the Matterhorn—though some delay and careful reflections on this ominous arête might have changed the history of the mountain and also of his own life.

It has often been though that Whymper had a complicated personality, warped by the tragedy he experienced when little more than a boy (he was twenty-five in 1865). On the contrary, I think he gives evidence of a simple, straightforward personality, with none of the dualism one detects in the more cultured minds of Tyndall or Leslie Stephen. Frank Smythe, in his biography of Whymper, has published long extracts from his private diary. As far as they mirror his deeper self—and it must be remembered that one can unconsciously lie to one's diary—they give the key to his mind. As Geoffrey Winthrop Young wrote in *Mountain Prophets*, 'Like many Victorians, he matured early and modified little in later years.' His diaries show a clear-cut mind with very precise, though scanty, ideas, plenty of common sense, a dry sense of humour, little sympathy with his fellow-men, a great precision of vision and thought and an overpowering egotism. He was self-centred to the point of never even attempting to imagine what anyone might think of him. He was keen to pit his mind against something hard—physically or mentally—and see which was the harder. He eventually found that mountains did prove the harder in a terrible way and he gave up. But the contest had made him live the most exciting seasons of his life.

This accounts for the unusual vividness, the permanent power of sugges-tion of his great mountain book. He could have had no doubts about the lines on which he should express himself: he had but one line, the one he had followed when planning his expeditions and which he followed again when relating them. He never had to conceal parts of his feelings, to strive hard to withhold too poetic a spirit from his text or to give coherence to his conception of mountains. All he had thought about them came into his *Scrambles,* and it was not particularly subtle. Mountains usually struck him as a challenge. When he saw the Matterhorn for the first time at Zermatt in 1860, he felt more surprise than admiration and considered its shape was ugly. He asked Leslie Stephen what he thought of the Mischabels: 'He says he considers the view the finest thing he has seen.' Yet, Whymper never climbed in this magnificent range under the spell of which mountaineers are apt to fall.

Whymper may have been drawn towards the Matterhorn because several parties were already intent on its conquest. These were his simple reasons for climbing or, alternatively, because they were either virgin peaks or hardly known at all, as for instance the Ecrins, the Ruinette and the Verte. He never meditated about mountains; he did not try to peer into their timeless past or their future. Their geology interested him in only one respect: if the rocks were rotten, then stones were likely to fall. He put every fibre of his body, every fraction of his strength into his fight. He did everything within his power to conquer them and he loved every minute of the battle even when waging it under desperate conditions, as when he crossed the Moming pass below a wall of séracs. He saw himself as attacking a powerful being which was not completely cut off from human standards. He dimly imagined himself as a fighting Titan. There are almost mythological episodes in the *Scrambles*: Michel Croz hammering down the cornice on the Moming Pass, Christian Almer taking his incredible leap over the gap on the Barre des Ecrins, the endless fight up the ice couloir of the Verte—the Whymper Couloir—and the whole soaring epic of the Matterhorn. But Titans could be defeated, and Whymper was. He never attempted to write great descriptions: he relied on his sketches, which are both lively and precise.

His chief concern in mountains was man or, more exactly, himself. He always placed his own figure against a background of peaks: the grim square-jawed face with lowering brow, the visionary eyes of youth which became hard and unrelenting in later life. Yet I am not sure that the term 'visionary' is the right one: it is more likely that Whymper's dreamy expression in the photograph taken when he was twenty-two was simply due to the fixed stare necessary with the slow photographic exposures of those days. All through his life he maintained the attitude of a defeated Titan. His lectures on the Matterhorn left a vivid impression on the minds of boys who heard them. One day in the nineties, Guido Rey saw Whymper coming down the Theodul: the Italian writer was so overwhelmed with conflicting emotions that he does not seem really to have looked at the Englishman, but described in his book an immensely tall old man with snow-white hair. Now, Whymper was fifty-five at the time and always had slightly yellowish hair.

Much has been written about the Matterhorn accident; far too much in a way. And yet, as wild legends are constantly repeated, it seems necessary to tell the story once again.

From 1861 onwards, Whymper had been attempting to ascend the Matterhorn from the Italian side. He tried with guides, without guides and alone, and always failed for various reasons. The weather changed; the ill will of Carrel, with whom he had associated, brought all his endeavours to nothing; there was an accident. In July 1865, Carell again played him false. He was marooned in Breuil without guide or companion while Carrel was hurrying up towards the mountain at the head of a strong party; he was trying to conquer the Matterhorn for Felice Giordano, the Italian Minister of Finance, and he had succeeded in spiriting away all the men who might have helped the Englishman.

Whymper was brooding in his inn when a young man arrived over the Theodul with his guides. He was Lord Francis Douglas, one of the youngest members of the Alpine Club, who had climbed the Obergabelhorn a few days earlier with Peter Taugwalder *père*. Whymper approached Douglas, explained the situation and suggested they might go back to Zermatt and attempt the Matterhorn together from the Swiss side. Douglas agreed. Whymper was in such a state of mind that he would have offered to take anybody with him, provided he acquired the means to attack the mountain. Accordingly, the party recrossed the pass and reached Zermatt. As they entered the hotel, they ran into Michel Croz, Whymper's Chamonix guide, who had been compelled to leave Whymper because of an engagement with Birbeck, who fell ill and eventually passed him on to Charles Hudson. Hudson was at that moment in Zermatt and planning an attempt on the Matterhorn. A general meeting ensued: Hudson agreed to invite Whymper to join the party. There was one condition: that they should take with them Roger Hadow, the young companion with whom Hudson had ascended Mont Blanc. Whymper agreed: he would have agreed to anything just to be in Croz's party.

The whole group left Zermatt on July 13th. Taugwalder took his two sons as porters. One of them was not to go higher than the bivouac. They bivouacked higher than the site of the present Hörnli hut, left early on the 14th and the climb went well. The rocks, though rotten, are not difficult to negotiate, except above the shoulder, where there are now fixed ropes. On the whole, the climb was surprisingly easy. Right at the end, the party passed into the north face, where they had to scale a few unpleasantly smooth rocks.

By one-forty they were on the summit. During the whole climb Whymper had been racked with the terror of being forestalled by the Italians who were endeavouring to force their way up the south-west arête. Reaching the easy rocks on the roof, he untied his rope and he and Croz ran up to see whether the worst had happened: it had not. There were no footprints in the virgin snow, no cairn on the ridge. Whymper had won. He and Croz peered over the crest and saw the Italians far below: they shouted to them and threw stones into the abyss to attract their attention. They succeeded, but too well: Carrel thought the old legend was true, that the mountain was haunted and there were evil spirits on the top. The Italians retreated at once.

While resting on the summit, Whymper lived 'one crowded hour of glorious life' and made a sketch. They were not out of danger yet: the descent was still a great problem. The party roped again at random, just because they were anxious, and a fateful mistake was made. They had several ropes, among which was an old and very thin one which had been taken for use as a fixed rope on the rocks, if necessary. Acting at random, the guides picked it up and used it between Douglas and Taugwalder. As the professionals in charge of the climb, the three guides were much to blame. But Hudson, who knew well why he usually climbed without guides, ought not to have let them do anything without supervision. As to Whymper, he took no interest in the process and went on sketching, and this was another great mistake.

The party came down in the following order: first Croz, then Hadow, Hudson, Douglas, old Taugwalder, Whymper, young Taugwalder. Whymper was finishing his sketch while the others were coming down the first easy slope. He ran to overtake them, grabbed the rope handed to him by Taugwalder, tied it round his waist, handed the end to young Taugwalder, and down they went.

One thing must be borne in mind. When the tragedy occurred, Whymper did not see it: he was behind a rock. His surmises are probably correct, but they are only surmises. From the beginning of the descent, Hadow was showing signs of exhaustion. The boy was certainly at the end of his endurance. With Hudson a few days earlier he had done Mont Blanc in record time, and was probably still feeling the strain. Then, the Matterhorn had been another long ordeal. His shoes were worn out and made him slip constantly. At each step Croz had to make Hadow's feet secure, and to do so he had to lay down his axe so that he had no support himself. Suddenly, while Croz was turning round to continue the descent, after having made Hadow secure, Hadow slipped and both his feet struck Croz in the back. The guide lost his footing and fell headlong down the steep slope, dragging the boy after him. Hudson came next, then Douglas; none had time to react and the rope was not belayed, so that there were no means to check the fall. The whole thing was as sudden as a stroke of lightning.

Between Lord Francis Douglas and Taugwalder the rope snapped in mid-air: it was the old worn line. The four doomed men slipped out of sight down the north face, amidst avalanches of stones. Whymper had advanced to the front of his rock to see the last act of the tragedy. The bodies of Hudson, Hadow and Croz were recovered on the Matterhorn glacier; they were horribly mutilated. Lord Francis Douglas was never found: he had probably been torn to pieces while descending the huge precipice.

It is much too easy, after a century, to point out the numerous mistakes committed by all the members of the party. It was a serious error to tie seven men to the same rope on a rock-climb. It was equally serious that not one of the experienced climbers of the party—Hudson, Whymper or Croz— had supervised the roping up on the summit or, if they did, had allowed the old rope to be used. Above all, Hudson, who seems to have been the leader, was seriously at fault in insisting on Hadow's inclusion in the party and in not examining the state of the boy's shoes. If he had done so, he would have noticed that his nails were worn flat, which made them worse then useless, actually dangerous. The whole thing was done in a surprisingly careless, almost fatalistic way, a sort of 'come-what-may' spirit.

After the Matterhorn accident, Whymper walked under a cloud. He had been badly shaken by the death of his companions and the ordeal he had had to undergo during the subsequent days in Zermatt. More than anyone else, he realized that the four men had been killed *par bêtise*, as he wrote on a photo of Michel Croz which he autographed for the Swiss writer Charles Gos, who has shown it me. The two Taugwalders, father and son, did not interest him: he had hardly met them before July 14th, 1865. He knew Charles Hudson but little, though he was well aware that the clergyman was probably the best climber of his time. He was not really acquainted with the two younger members of the party and had seen Lord Francis Douglas for the first time in Breuil a few days earlier. As for Croz, they had climbed together for several summers, they respected each other, they had quarrelled over money matters and Whymper was not likely to feel friendly towards his guide or towards anyone else. After the accident, he stopped climbing new peaks—in Europe at least—but certainly not out of despair or remorse: he felt no despair and had no ground for remorse. But he had probably lost his nerve when hearing his four companions sliding rapidly to their death down the precipices of the north face. This is the frequent reaction of the surviving member of a party which has met with a fatal accident. But till the end of his life, Whymper remained a sort of Alpine figurehead and his book immortalized his fighting conception of mountaineering, his tireless strength, his egotism and complete sincerity. The new pursuit required some striking image to impress the world, and Whymper, standing like a bronze statue facing the Matterhorn, supplied it. It is possible to know and climb Mont Blanc without knowledge of de

Saussure: people assume that he is a gentleman who had had something to do with the mountain. But it is inconceivable that one should approach the Matterhorn without remembering Whymper. The French guide with whom I climbed it knew where the 1865 accident had occurred. In Zermatt I have often been asked whether Whymper was buried in the little English churchyard above the village, and people were almost shocked when I replied that his grave is in Chamonix.

During the infancy of strenuous mountaineering, a new tendency was already developing: climbing familiar mountains by new routes. Ascending any mountain was an adventure, a quest after the unexpected and the unknown, and though there were still numberless virgin peaks in the Alpine skies, a few of the most impressive giants were already becoming too familiar for enterprising climbers, Mont Blanc for one. Every one among the crowds flocking to Chamonix knew exactly where to direct a telescope to find the Grand Plateau or the Mur de la Côte. Something new had to be found. It was easy to come to the conclusion that a summit being almost a geometrical point, it was possible and even logical to find as many routes up to it as nature could provide. This led to the most fascinating discoveries.

One of the men who excelled in such quests was the Rev. Charles Hudson, one of the earliest and most efficient guideless climbers. He had a perfectly modern way of facing mountain problems. Instead of devoting only his summer holidays to the Alps, he seems to have been always on the lookout for something strenuous which might keep him in training. Once, when he was twenty-five, he climbed the Dôle above St Cergue in winter; he bivouacked on the Col d'Anterne in January; he lived for several months in the little village of Bionassay, at the foot of the glacier of that name, eventually attempted to climb Mont Blanc in winter, and was defeated only on the Aiguille du Goûter by fresh snow. During the Crimean War he went out to Sebastopol as a padre and, the war over, took a trip to the Caucasus and climbed Mount Ararat. Back in Europe, he endeavoured to find a new route, possibly several, up Mont Blanc. The account of the discoveries he made with E. S. Kennedy was published in *Where There's A Will, There's A Way*. They had opened the route leading up from St Gervais to the top of the mountain, though they had avoided the ascent of the steep, narrow Arête des Bosses du Dromadaire, which was to be followed a few years later by Leslie Stephen's party.

Hudson was endowed both with daring and prudence. He knew and respected the whims of high mountains. He had seen them take advantage of the slightest error. Once, on the Col du Miage, while he was climbing with Leslie Stephen, Tuckett, F. Mather, Birkbeck and guides, Birkbeck, the youngest member of the party, took off the rope during a halt and withdrew to a short distance. As he did not return, they followed his track in the snow and discovered that the boy had slipped and fallen almost 1,800 feet. He had not been killed, had not even been very severely injured, but his legs and back were completely flayed. He had remained conscious although suffering intense pain; Hudson did all he could to help him during the endless climb down to St Gervais and the drive back to Chamonix.

Hudson cared more for rock-climbing than most of his contemporaries, but he knew that it is almost impossible to judge a rock-face accurately from a long distance. He found a route up the Aiguille Verte over the rock-ridge a few days after Whymper's discovery of the ice couloir up the same peak; both routes afford magnificent climbing but are difficult and dangerous on account of their steepness and falling stones. On the Verte, Hudson was climbing with E. S. Kennedy and Michel Croz, and on the descent, Croz left Hudson as last man on the rope, knowing that he could trust his steadiness; this was perfectly normal with such a strong party. A week later, when coming down the Matterhorn, they roped up in the same way, but in the middle, instead of a hardy, competent climber like E. S. Kennedy, they had an exhausted boy who did not know how to negotiate the smooth slabs of the face with his worn-out shoes. Hudson was not the last man down; there was another very young man behind him, a good climber but without any notion of the management of a rope, as he had always climbed between two guides. Taugwalder was an unknown quantity, so that when Hadow slipped the well-known tragedy followed.

On the very day when Hudson met his death on the Matterhorn, four of his Alpine Club colleagues, with two of the best guides of the period, opened a new route up 'the wrong side' of Mont Blanc, by the huge, broken, Brenva glacier. The Aosta face of Mont Blanc had been described by numerous travellers who had all been overwhelmed by its beauty and by the uncompromising steepness of its glaciers and of the rock walls and spires which towered above them. Dark red granite pillars soar up like petrified flames on each side of the gaps through which fantastically crevassed glaciers pour down into the valley. The whole landscape has a haughty and sombre grandeur which cannot but impress a mountaineer; and the greatest skill and experience is necessary to pit one's strength against so redoubtable a fortress. The members of the 1865 party were of the highest order: A. W. Moore, Frank and Horace Walker, and G. Mathews.

A. W. Moore, the youngest member of the party, was already at twenty-four an experienced climber. Among other fine expeditions, he had made the traverse of the Barre des Ecrins with Whymper and Walker in 1864, and had been up Mont Blanc with a single guide—a feat still quite exceptional. In private life he was on the staff of the East India Company, became a civil servant when it was dissolved, and later Lord Randolph Churchill's private secretary. He was an ideal climbing companion: the man who never grumbles, who does not become nervous or restless when conditions are bad, and who, when a storm breaks, keeps a cool head and a sense of humour. He pretended to be a cynic: a safe though rather transparent kind of mask, but useful when climbing. He was the historiographer of the epoch-making climb on the Brenva and his narrative is among the finest Alpine tales in existence.

One of the worst pitches of the climb was an extremely steep ice-arête which had to be scaled after hours of strenuous fighting up long ice-slopes or zig-zagging between mazes of crevasses and séracs. The glaciers seem to have been in very bad condition in 1865. The Brenva ice-ridge was the steepest and narrowest the members of the party had ever seen, a kind of knife-edge on which it was impossible to stand: you had to straddle it like a horse and crawl up. Down each side was a sheer wall of hard blue ice into which no alpenstock could penetrate. While creeping along this fantastic arête, Moore wondered: 'What would be the result if any of the party chanced to slip?' And the answer was only too obvious. They wormed their way up slowly, carefully, and at last reached the place where the ridge merged into a slope of névé. There is nothing more nerve-racking than a very bad ice-pitch; going slowly seems to increase the danger by giving one more time to realize it, and a long wait before making a new move can make a climber both cramped and insecure. Going quickly is also dangerous, since it gives one too little time to sound the ice or look for a convenient spot to place one's foot. The Brenva party had no crampons, no ice-axes and hardly any means of properly belaying their rope. They had to trust to luck and to their good balance. Above the névé they were confronted by a 'great wall of ice running right across and completely barring the way upwards'. They had to force it, for there was no question of descending by the arête they had just climbed. So they fought their way on, constantly looking up to see if one of the huge ice blocks was about to topple down and crush them. It was late in the morning; the sun was high and the danger was increasing with every second that passed. Suddenly, the leading guide said something which Moore did not understand. He said it again and it turned out to be: 'It is all right.' Moore's comment was: 'That moment was worth living for.' This is one of the finest understatements in Alpine literature. In fact, the wall of séracs is the key to the climb, the arête being just one of its bad pitches, varying in difficulty according to the state of the ice.

Moore's companions, the Walkers, were also leading pioneers. The father,

Frank, who was fifty-seven in 1865, had a fine climbing record, and he was to go on until his very last days. In 1871, aged sixty-three, he climbed the Diablerets, Castor, the Felikjoch and the Balfrin, with the Matterhorn to crown his season. He died in 1872. His son Horace was slightly older than Moore, being twenty-seven in 1865. They had already made many big expeditions together: the Aiguilles d'Arves, the Brêche de la Meije, the Ecrins, the Roseg. Their association was to last for years and was to lead them to discover the pleasures of winter climbing. Finally, Lucy Walker, Horace's sister, was also a climber.

Shortly before 1860 people had become aware of the extraordinary fact that there were lady mountaineers. The notion probably came as a shock to mid-Victorian minds: it was so much out of keeping with their idea of the well-bred young lady. Lucy Walker took after her father and brother, sharing their passionate love of the mountains. She began climbing in 1858 and went on for twenty-one years, going up ninety-eight peaks, among which were the Balmhorn (first ascent), the Matterhorn and the Wetterhorn (first ascents by a lady). In 1858 the whole Walker family was in Zermatt and one can imagine the consultation which took place as they planned an expedition. Why should she not go with her father and brother? Could she do it? What about her dress and provisions? But the three Walkers came back from a successful climb, and a new vision of life opened out for the girl who was then twenty-eight.

According to notes which have been given me by one of her friends, she was in every other way the perfect Victorian young lady. She was not an athlete and her greatest asset, when climbing, was her unflinching will-power. She did not ride or fish or take walking tours. She indulged in no outdoor recreations but croquet. She was an expert needlewoman and read a good deal in several languages. She took an active part in the social life of Liverpool, where she lived with her parents. She was a charming hostess and a devoted friend.

When climbing, she never dreamed of dressing as a man; she used to wear a white printed dress to which some decent shape had to be restored after a strenuous expedition, a thankless task, no doubt, after a rock-climb or a long tramp down the last moraine. She always climbed with her father or her brother, or both, and one or two guides. Though Continental writers knew hardly anything about mountaineering, one of them met the Walker party and described it. He was E. de Laveleye, a Belgian economist and historian who visited Zermatt, tried to understand why men care for mountains and to a certain extent succeeded. One day he happened to be on the Theodul:

'We were extremely surprised when, creeping into this dark den [the hut] we saw a young woman endeavouring to dry her garments, soaked with water and crisp with frost, in front of a wretched fire. The guides told us she was a young English lady who travelled by herself. She was coming from the top of Mont Blanc and was going to the top of Monte Rosa; indeed, she climbed it a few days later. Her name was Miss Walker. A moment later, we saw her going away. She had two guides. One was going in front of her, the other behind, and a thick rope tied round her slender waist bound her to both hardy mountain natives. She was walking quickly, though floundering in the snow, and she was very soon out of sight behind a thick mist and sheets of drizzle driven by the blizzard.'

Now Miss Walker did in fact climb Mont Blanc and Monte Rosa in 1862, but I wonder whether the two 'hardy mountain natives' were not Frank and Horace Walker, or one of them and Melchior Anderegg, as Lucy never climbed alone with guides. The brief note quoted above, published in 1865, is one of the first descriptions of a climbing party by a French writer.

Most of these pioneers wrote books, or articles at least, if only to conform with the rules of the Alpine Club and put their notes at the disposal of future climbers. When reading such texts, one immediately feels that the writers' minds were obsessed by a major terror: that they might give way to a Ruskin-like verbosity. They had no desire to write treatises on mountain ethics and always dreaded anything which might resemble the passage about the tomb-stones of the angels who had gone to eternal rest on the Zmutt glacier, an uncomfortable place at the best of times. They knew far more about mountains than Ruskin, they had heard and understood the message of the Alps in its majesty and freedom, but they would not dream of preaching about it: it was among the sacred things not to be talked about. Consequently, their books wore an almost casual air, holiday notes jotted down in an apparently careless way: *Hours of Exercise, The Playground of Europe, Across Country, Summer Months among the Alps, Scrambles Amongst the Alps,* and so on. A. W. Moore had his *Alps in 1864* printed only for private circulation. The Walkers wrote a few papers in the *Alpine Journal*, Hudson hardly anything at all. As a woman Lucy Walker could not be a member of the Alpine Club, nor could she send papers to the *Alpine Journal*. And yet, in spite of such restraints, mountain books reached a very high literary standard at the very moment when mountaineering, after having been a kind of supernatural revelation, was acquiring the character of a creed, with its dogmas, its rites, its ministers and its heretics.

However sacrilegious it may sound, the worst adversaries of mountaineering were the guides. Much has been written about them and most texts fall little short of hagiography. And yet, as soon as modern mountaineering began, guides did everything within their power for various reasons to oppose it. To climb the Aiguille Verte was obviously much more tiring and dangerous than to go to the Jardin de Talèfre. Devising new climbs required imagination and foresight. Now, it is a fact that not only were hardly any routes discovered by local peasants, unless prompted or led by tourists, but they usually did much to prevent the tourists from having their own way.

Guides were seen at their worst in their dealings with the Matterhorn, during the long battle waged against the mountain between 1862 and 1865. From the very beginning they said, and continued to say, that 'it was impossible to climb it'. It was this unshakable belief that never gave their employers a fair chance. Had an unprejudiced man gone up to the foot of the Hörnli ridge—which Vaughan Hawkins did—he would have realized that the gradient is far less steep than when seen from a long distance. But the guides refused to have anything to do with it. Taugwalder asked for 200 Swiss francs —a very large sum for those days—whether the top was reached or not. Christian Almer curtly asked Whymper: 'Why don't you try to go up a mountain which can be climbed?' On the Italian side of the Matterhorn the natives took a different view of the question; they suddenly realized that to climb so impressive a peak would be a source of gain for the whole valley. The idea of making the first ascent of the mountain from its Italian side appealed also to their patriotic feelings, while it seems that the Zermatt men remained totally indifferent to this aspect of the question. In fact, no Swiss party went up the mountain before Thioly in 1872.

In the Italian valley, the guides were spurred on by the local priest, Aimé Gorret. He was an enterprising young man with a broader mind and a stronger will than most peasants. This is one of the numerous instances when the more cultured man always takes the lead in mountaineering districts: the same had happened with Dr Paccard in Chamonix, the Abbé Murith on the Vélan, the Abbé Clément in Champéry, Father Placidus a Spescha in the Grisons. Then the great Breuil guide, J. A. Carrel, realized the importance of the matter and tried to impose his iron will on all the parties who felt attracted by the Matterhorn. He had made up his mind to climb the mountain and yet acted in a way which is another proof of the lack of real mountaineering spirit among early guides. Carrel had an intelligence and a courage considerably above the average, but he could not bear the idea of sharing the glory of success with anyone—least of all with a foreigner who might know the mountains well. His pride and his well-founded self-confidence were

7. View from the
Col des Montets.
(Photo: Malcolm
Barnes)

8. Weisshorn at sunrise. First ascended by Tyndall in 1861. (Photo: Malcolm Barnes)

strengthened by what may be termed a complete lack of moral rectitude. Accordingly, when engaged by Tyndall in 1861, he deeply resented the presence of Bennen in the party, accepted the money of his employer but acted as a drag during the climb, refused to give advice, did all he could to make the attempt fail and eventually succeeded in his aim. He tried the same trick on Whymper with the same results: Carrel's ill-will, together with bad weather, account for Whymper's failure on several occasions. But in 1865, Carrel was engaged by Felice Giordano, an Italian geologist who wanted to climb the Matterhorn with Quintino Sella, who was the Finance Minister of the Kingdom of Italy and a passionate lover of mountains. Carrel's pride and patriotism were gratified by such notable employers and, as Whymper was just arriving at Breuil to make another attempt, Carrel was unusually polite and friendly while secretly planning the other men's success. He then contrived to spirit away all the Breuil guides and porters, so that Whymper, taken in by Carrel's subtle lies, found himself alone in the Italian village. Carrel failed in being first on the top of the Matterhorn and there is some poetic justice in his failure.

The whole story of the Matterhorn has acquired its sinister aspect from the part played by the guides. After the tragedy on the Hörnli ridge, the two Taugwalders came very much into the public eye. They behaved in a repulsive way in the hours following the accident, though it is probably unfair to pay much attention to the shameless babble of two men who were mad with terror. The son was a nonentity and it seems that the father was hardly, if at all, above the average level of the period, which was low. 'Old' Taugwalder was under fifty and had done a number of climbs with great English mountaineers, but one always gathers that something was wrong with his performance. He was with Leslie Stephen on the Allalin in 1860, but not as first guide. This responsible post had been taken by a man from Saas, Moritz Anthamatten. Taugwalder seems to have made rather heavy weather of the descent to the Allalin Pass. Now, few mountains are tamer than the Allalin, a very easy and almost dull peak. But Taugwalder thought it necessary to adopt double-roping down the last slope above the pass—a superfluous precaution although one of the first uses on record of the double rope. As further evidence of Taugwalder's deficiencies, Sir Arnold Lunn quotes an episode which had been related to him by John Stogdon: when coming down from the Tête Blanche to Prarayé, Taugwalder unroped himself because there were two inexperienced climbers in the party.

A few days before the Matterhorn tragedy, Taugwalder accompanied Lord Francis Douglas up a peak which was later to be known as the Obergabelhorn. The summit is of snow with overhanging cornices, but most of the ascent is done over rocks and the last pitch consists of a large smooth slab on which good holds are afforded by numerous cracks where one can safely insert one's fingers and the tips of one's boots. Now, on the top Taugwalder did not take the precaution of probing the ice of this hitherto untrodden summit, with the result that, while the three men were eating their lunch, Douglas broke through the cornice. As the rope was not belayed—the summit being too large to make this appear necessary—Taugwalder was immediately dragged down by the young climber. The second guide, J. Vienin, succeeded in holding them both and in hauling them back to safety.

Taugwalder did not know how to manage a rope. But it must be admitted that few other guides knew. They had been very slow in consenting to rope up with their patrons. For years they had simply held the rope to which the others were tied, so that it afforded little more than moral support when a slip occurred: the guide let go or had it torn from his hand. This practise accounted for the fatal Col du Géant accident in 1860. It took years to teach guides how to belay a rope, how to keep it taut on a glacier, how to avoid as far as possible the tracks of avalanches and falling stones. For years the rope seemed to many guides to be either a nuisance, or something to be slightly ashamed of; parties roped up as late as possible or not at all.

Now, when we consider the accident on the Matterhorn we find that two things are certain: everyone made mistakes, and during the inquests both Whymper and Taugwalder lost their heads. But the Taugwalders had begun by losing their nerve when coming from the mountain. There is today a general belief that Taugwalder did not cut the rope: he, of course, said he did not and so did Whymper. But the latter's depositions are contradictory in certain places. He could not have seen much of what was happening below him. Once he alludes to the sound made by the rope when it broke, but he surely could not have heard it above the noise made by the four unhappy men falling down the north face amid tons of loose stones. One can hardly move on the Matterhorn without sending stones sliding down in every direction. Later in the summer, the younger Taugwalder was at Chamonix with E. N. Buxton, F. C. Grove and R. J. Macdonald. On account of Croz's death, feeling was running very high against him in the valley. While he was drinking at an inn, several local guides came up to him and in an insulting way asked him who had cut the rope. Taugwalder said nothing but walked out. Now, as the man was not conspicuous for cool-headedness and restraint, as was shown by his behaviour after the accident, one is surprised by this stony calm. One wonders whether a violent outburst of rage would not have appeared a better proof of indignant innocence.

For several years after the accident the Zermatt guides boycotted the

Matterhorn. All the early climbers ascended from Breuil. The first party with Swiss guides was that of the Rev. J. M. Elliott, who had two St Niklaus men with him, in July 1868. Leslie Stephen never climbed the Matterhorn 'not because the mountain is very dangerous, but because guides are likely to be very nervous'. In later years Zermatt made up for lost time and even got into the habit of displaying a morbid interest in accidents.

Extraordinary blunders might be committed by almost anyone. In 1862, Leslie Stephen achieved the first crossing of the Jungfraujoch. An attempt from the Scheidegg had revealed numberless gaping crevasses at the foot of the great ice-wall, a maze of blue chasms fringed with long icicles. Among the crevasses dangerously slender séracs tapered up. The party tried to fight its way through these obstacles, failed on account of the crevasses, retreated to the Scheidegg and came back on the following day, dragging a long ladder to bridge some of the chasms. Now, the man who had advocated the use of this dangerous implement was Christian Almer, 'a bold but safe man' according to Whymper, and one of the very first Oberland guides. The party dragged the ladder amongst the séracs from eleven until three o'clock, and a few days later dragged it again up to the Viescherjoch at the same time of the day and under similar séracs. As the mountains are sometimes indulgent to innocent climbers no missile fell on the party and yet, through this piece of sheer lunacy, they were asking for trouble. Séracs are brittle and particularly dangerous during the warmest hours of the day.

The average guiding standard was low, but a few men were head and shoulders above the rest. They were the great figures whose names recur in every climbing narrative of the period: Melchior Anderegg, Michel Croz, Christian Almer, J. J. Bennen and one or two others. Most of them were Oberlanders or Chamoniards. Michel Croz, owing to his connection with Whymper and his tragic death, is one of the best known among the great guides. He was thirty-five when he died. Whymper wrote him: 'Croz was happiest when he was employing his powers to the utmost.' He had both skill and strength, was at his best on ice and loved a hard fight against a difficult mountain; he could take very great risks, feeling that he was justified in doing so. He was extremely quick-tempered, touchy and passionate, but he displayed an unshakable loyalty to his employers. Readers of the *Scrambles* may have been shocked by what Whymper tells of his haughtiness towards the men of Valtournanche, but one must not forget that Croz was a Savoyard and that the men of Chamonix always despised the Italians. Thus, when climbing the Matterhorn, Croz was glad he could defeat an Italian party. But he was on excellent terms with Christian Almer and other Swiss guides, and the difference of language and even of religion created no difficulties. Croz was a devout Catholic—when his body was recovered at the foot of the Matterhorn, a rosary was found in his pocket—and he spoke only French; Almer was a Protestant and knew very little French; yet the two men were friends and respected each other's skill.

Christian Almer was slightly older than Croz. He had begun his career as a chamois-hunter in the Bernese Oberland. In 1854 he tried to overtake Alfred Wills's party during the latter's first ascent of the Wetterhorn. After this spectacular beginning, Almer developed into a 'bold but safe man', 'impossible to ruffle', according to Whymper. Oberlanders are usually steady, slow, reliable people, but Almer was something better and his love for mountains amounted to passion. In order to commemorate the thirtieth anniversary of his first ascent of the Wetterhorn, which also was his first big climb apart from an attempt on the Jungfrau, he took the youngest of his five sons up the mountain; later, to celebrate his golden wedding, he took his wife too and the sturdy old couple were led by their sons.

The best guide of the period was probably Melchior Anderegg, another Oberlander whose perfect icemanship enabled him to perform extraordinary feats of skill and endurance. He was born near Meiringen in 1827 and died there in 1914. He was also a chamois-hunter, a wrestler and a wood-carver; some of his small carvings, including a self-portrait, were presented to the Alpine Club. He was working as boots at the Grimsel inn and leading parties on easy walks when he was discovered by Hinchliff, who took him out and later introduced him to Leslie Stephen and other members of the club, like Mathews, Morshead, Hort and later the Walkers, whose regular guide he became. Anderegg was not accustomed to wait long before addressing his patrons in the familiar manner which is usual in Switzerland. Frank Walker was somewhat surprised one day to hear himself addressed as 'Papa', while Lucy and Horace were called by their Christian names; in the last century, climbers were still extremely formal. But in truth Melchior Anderegg was a born gentleman, who was always on the friendliest terms with the great climbers who employed him. When Leslie Stephen invited him to London, Anderegg conducted himself with perfect composure and dignity amid his new surroundings, although he had never been in a city larger than Berne. He attended several Alpine Club meetings and was also taken climbing in Wales, though he did not feel at home in so strange a district, where his sense of mountain-proportions played him false, causing him to overestimate the lengths of climbs. These early guides were picturesque figures and they always impressed their employers. Acquaintances thus formed often matured into life-long friendships. When Lucy Walker gave up climbing, she continued to visit the Andereggs every year in their native village. If a fatal accident occurred to one of these great guides, English climbers did all they could to help the family of the dead man. Very often they pensioned off a retired guide, as Alfred Wills had done in the case of Auguste Balmat.

How did the vast non-climbing public react to this new passion for the mountains? For several years the atmosphere was peaceful and pleasant. Widely-read weeklies made polite and slightly inadequate comments on new ascents or older climbs. The *Illustrated London News* gave information about ascents of Mont Blanc by W. Young and Colonel Harding in August 1855 and by the photographer Bisson in 1862. In 1858 it published an article on the Matterhorn by G. Barnard. Barnard knew a good deal about the mountain: 'If ever this vast crag is climbed by Hudson, Kennedy or other brave hand,' he wrote, 'it will be from the Zermatt side; but it will require a perfectly calm day'. The paper also made flattering remarks about Mrs Stephen Winkworth's ascent of the Jungfrau in 1863. It had been a remarkable feat and, when Mrs Winkworth returned to her hotel, everyone rose to do her honour; being a very modest woman, she felt both surprised and shy.

In another periodical, the dignified *Revue des Deux Mondes*, Emile de Laveleye, the Belgian economist who had met the Walkers, fell into raptures over the Matterhorn: 'It seems totally inaccessible. Merely to look at it makes one giddy. Wild and solitary, it seems to be reared up as a challenge to men, for none of them will ever set foot on that virgin brow which only an eagle may touch with the tip of his wing'. Laveleye had collected useful information about the spot. He had heard of Tyndall's attempt on the Matterhorn and conquest of the Weisshorn: 'Guides', he averred, 'never mention him or Mr Kennedy save with the utmost respect.' The ascent of the Weisshorn was 'one of the hardest and most hazardous feats ever performed in the Alps'. Laveleye had heard more vaguely of Whymper's attempt and of his accident on the Col du Lion. He had even heard of the Alpine Club: 'a society composed of men who enjoy high mountain excursions'.

The Matterhorn accident took place just a month after the publication of Laveleye's article, and everything was changed. It was not the worst Alpine tragedy, but it had been the most spectacular, and it was the signal for a storm of protest. *The Times* kept to the most sensible line by asking Whymper to tell his own story, but the *Illustrated London News* wrote in almost hysterical tones:

'When a nation is bitten with a peculiar passion, it seldom passes out without trouble and painful experiences, and though one or two young men are knocked up for life each year by hill climbing, it is by no means certain that a member of the Alpine Club . . . will not endeavour to surmount a "virgin peak" of some wondrous mountain in the year 1875 and render a family heirless and a mother unhappy for life.'

In the French *Journal Illustré*, a certain M. Babinet took up the cudgels: 'Is it possible to believe there actually is in London an Alpine Club, the aim of which is to suggest and glorify dangerous attempts at climbing European mountains?' And Anthony Trollope, in his *Travelling Sketches*, did not hesitate to make fun of the men who belonged to the Alpine Club.

Of all critics, however, the one whose execrations were loudest was Ruskin. In 1865 he published a second edition of *Sesame and Lilies*. His onslaught against mountaineering had already been violent in the first: 'You have made racecourses of the cathedrals of the earth. The Alps which your own poets used to love so reverently, you look upon as soaped poles in bear gardens, which you set yourselves to climb and slide down with shrieks of delight.' Now several motives united in rousing the fury of the great art-critic: a sincere concern over the 'desecration' of the high Alps, an element of jealousy—for he prided himself on having discovered the Matterhorn, the self-righteous attitude of the man who had always said: 'I told you this was bound to happen!' a secret regret at not being a climber himself, and finally a tendency always to tilt against some man or some idea. He felt little real sympathy for the four men who had been killed; they were climbers and they had invited the fate which overtook them.

There is little force in any of the objections which Ruskin raises in his preface of 1865: 'The real ground for reprehension of Alpine climbing,' he argues, 'is that with less cause, it excites more vanity than any other athletic skill.' Climbers have turned Switzerland—a grave, pure, barren country—into a 'ground of delight'. Now Switzerland is not a barren country; its austerity was a hoary legend, and surely 'ground of delight' was not the expression to use at a time when rescue parties were carrying three mangled bodies down to Zermatt, though they had failed to recover a fourth which must have been lacerated by the rocks. The paradox is that, after writing as he had done, Ruskin, who never felt the binding force of an idea, became a member of the Alpine Club and remained one for several years.

The Matterhorn accident suggested a new and exciting notion to non-climbers: Alpine ropes are liable to break or be cut, though it is surprising to think of the violent jerks they can sustain. Thus it came about that the cut rope became one of the typical Alpine features of novels written by non-climbers, and occasionally by a climber. In *Tartarin on the Alps*, Alphonse

Daudet has the rope simultaneously cut by the two men who are tied to it. The cut rope makes a majestic reappearance in one of the short stories of *La Croix du Cervin*, by Charles Gos—a story which greatly agitated the guides of Zermatt. It comes out again in the fantastic setting of Rex Warner's *Aerodrome*, where the villain of the plot, having had his rope duly cut by his rival, falls an unrecorded number of hundreds of feet without being killed.[1]

But a few non-climbers had begun to discover the inner significance of mountaineering. Théophile Gautier, the French writer and artist who had always been attracted by the mountains and had often described them in his magnificent prose, came to Zermatt in 1868. While strolling through the village just before dinner, he met a rather striking group:

'A tall young man, strong and thin, dressed in brown corduroy, with gaiters up to the knees, a soft felt hat pulled down over his eyes, looking a perfect gentleman in spite of the unavoidable carelessness of his clothes. He was a member of the Alpine Club and had just successfully ascended the Matterhorn . . . His guides were walking behind him with their ropes coiled round their shoulders, holding their axes, their iron-spiked poles and all that was required to attack so wild a peak. These three resolute sunburnt faces were resplendent with the joy of their triumph over great difficulties . . . The guides entered the hotel and the Englishman remained for a few moments on its threshold, leaning against the wall with complete unconcern, looking perfectly carefree, just as if he were coming from his club in Pall Mall . . . While watching this handsome youth, probably rich and certainly used to comfort and refinement, who had just been risking his life with complete indifference in a useless dangerous enterprise, we thought of the resistless passion which drives a few men to undertake terrific scrambles. No example can deter them. When going up towards the Matterhorn, this young man had certainly seen the graves of his three countrymen in the Zermatt churchyard. But a peak can exercise the same irresistible power of attraction as an abyss.'

This sketch is the first description in French of a home-coming climbing party. It is as clear-cut as a snapshot. The young man was the Rev. J. M. Elliott; his guides were J. M. Lochmatter, who was killed on the Dent Blanche in 1882 and Peter Knubel. Elliott was twenty-seven and though not actually a member of the Alpine Club, he was admitted in November of the

---

[1] In 1870, the French architect Viollet-le-Duc, crossing the Schwartzberggletscher above Mattmark, fell into a crevasse, had a long talk with his extremely inefficient Macugnaga guide while falling and then cut the rope because he felt stifled and the guide could not belay him. The story, as related by Viollet-le-Duc himself, may be true, though it sounds highly improbable.

same year. The last sentence of Gautier rings tragically true: less than a year later, Elliott was killed on the Schreckhorn. He had thought he could climb unroped, but near the summit he slipped and was dashed headlong to the glacier 1,000 feet below. One feels the suggestion of a haunting anxiety in Gautier's pathetic lines; for Continental writers there would always be something almost ominous in mountaineering.

Yet within twenty years of the foundation of the Alpine Club in London, most Continental countries had founded their own, even if they were sometimes conceived on different lines. First in the field was Switzerland in 1863. One of the founders and the first president of the Swiss Alpine Club was Dr Melchior Ulrich, the pioneer of the Saas-Fee district; other members were G. Studer and Dr Simler. The inaugural meeting was held at Olten. The idea behind the Swiss Alpine Club was to form a broader and more democratic association than the Alpine Club; in fact, Continental organizations are not clubs in the strict sense of the word. An Italian Club was started in Turin in December of the same year; its principal founders were Quintino Sella, Felice Giordano, who played such an important part in the history of the Matterhorn, Gastaldi and the Conte di Saint-Robert, a well-known mathematician. The whole manner in which the club had been founded had been quite in keeping with Italian traditions: it had been secret, one might almost say conspiratorial. After this, in a stirring manifesto, the club announced its desire to promote the knowledge and worship of the Italian Alps by the youth of Italy. Most of the early members were intellectuals, writers or scientists.

France came late to mountaineering. The Club Alpin Français was founded in 1874 by Dr Millot, Armand-Delille, Boileau de Castelnau and others. Here, also, a patriotic motive appeared in the club's slogan: '*Pour la patrie par la montagne.*' One of the new principles established by the French Club was to open its door to women. The Ladies' Alpine Club was founded in England in 1912 and the first president was Mrs Aubrey le Blond.

The Austrian and German Clubs had been founded in 1869 and they were to be united in 1929.

Thus it was that, in spite of criticism and attack, the art and practice of mountaineering had won recognition in nearly all the principal countries of Europe.

CHAPTER EIGHT

NEW WAYS AND MEANS

MOUNTAINEERING was now accepted in most countries as a new, fairly dangerous and aimless species of pastime. No excuse could be advanced on the ground of scientific research, as the two activities had now completely separated, although there was a growing number of scientists among the members of the various Alpine Clubs, whether in England or abroad, but mostly in France. But none of them climbed merely to collect material. Even the Italian naturalist, Felice Giordano, who published a book on the geology of the Matterhorn, had been very keen to get Carrel and his party to the summit of the mountain, not to collect specimens of gneiss but to hoist an Italian flag. Most climbers were intellectuals: lawyers, professors, officers, civil servants, clergymen or diplomats. Such men were numerous in the Alpine Club and that accounts for the high literary standard of the *Alpine Journal*. Yet, however strange it may appear, there were few professional writers among them. The exceptions were John Ruskin and Matthew Arnold, who both joined the club for a few years, but neither was a great climber and their qualifications were just 'literary'. The only well-known Swiss writer who was a member of the Swiss Alpine Club was Emile Rambert, a literary critic from Lausanne. There were none in France, where mountaineering has never been taken seriously by the uninitiated. This early and generally-persisting separation may account for the poor quality of Alpine fiction. There are few mountain novels in any language.

By 1885, let us say, roughly all the great summits had been climbed: it would be useless and dull to give a list of the main peaks with the dates of their conquest. The campaign for the Chamonix Aiguilles had begun by 1865. In 1871, Leslie Stephen, Loppé and Walroth with three guides climbed the Mont Mallet, and James Eccles, Loppé's brother-in-law, with two guides, climbed the Aiguille du Plan. There were several long-protracted sieges. C. T. Dent failed eighteen times on the Dru before reaching the top of the sheer red-granite spire. The last great summit to be climbed was the Meije.

There were many lower peaks which were still untouched. Yet height is not everything, and by a caprice of mountain nature, the lower peaks are often more difficult than the higher ones. The Petit Dru, the Petite Dent de Veisivi, and the Klein Doldenhorn, among others, are more tricky than their greater brothers and sisters. Most of the Chamonix Aiguilles and all the Dolomites are well below 4,000 metres, yet they are the most difficult peaks in the Alps.

New districts were still being opened up. Prior to 1860, very little of Dauphiny had been explored. Durand and, later, Puiseux had climbed the Pelvoux; but after each climb the natives had forgotten all about it and continued to swear that the Pelvoux was still a virgin peak, or, as an early explorer of the district, Count A. F. de Nantes, wrote, 'a peak trodden only by chamois and angels'. T. G. Bonney went to Dauphiny in 1860, met Jean Reynaud, who was to climb with Whymper, and the guide Sémiond and obtained some idea of the aspects of the peaks, but bad weather prevented his doing anything more serious. He came back in 1864, climbed one of the Aiguilles d'Arves and met Whymper, A. W. Moore and Walker, who were completing the long tour during which they had traversed the Barre des Ecrins and various passes.

In 1870 a new mountain siege began, that of the Meije. The mountain had impressed many travellers by its beauty, but all of them immediately became aware of its uncompromising aloofness. The siege went on for seven years, English, French, American, and Italian climbers all attempting it. Now this mountain has many summits. The Pic Central was reached in 1870, at the first attempt, by an American party consisting of Miss Brevoort, her nephew, W. A. B. Coolidge, and their three guides. Other parties then swarmed up ridges, glaciers and faces and all of them were defeated by the sheer difficulty of the pitches or by bad weather. The greatest climbers of the period and the best guides met in La Bérarde or La Grave. Eventually, the Grand Pic de la Meije was ascended in 1877 by a Frenchman, Emmanuel Boileau de Castelnau. He was twenty when he conquered the Meije. He came from an old and very aristocratic family of the south of France, a branch of which had taken refuge in England in the seventeenth century at the time of the Revocation of the Edict of Nantes: the Castelnaus were Protestant. His parents were very rigid and their only son had a rather stern upbringing. Eventually he developed a taste for exploration, and as Asia, Africa or the Poles were too far away, he focused his desires upon the Alps and decided he wanted to climb them. However strange this desire might have seemed to the father, he accepted this unexpected decision—at this time in France there were almost no mountaineers—and he kept his son supplied with money, just asking that he be reasonably well informed of what the boy was planning.

'I was not yet sixteen', the son wrote later, 'and yet I travelled by myself according to my own plans, selecting my guides, paying my hotel bills and ascending the most difficult peaks.' He ascended the Jungfrau, the Finsteraarhorn, the Matterhorn, the Dent Blanche, the Gran Paradiso and the Ecrins and Mont Blanc four times. He was elected to the Alpine Club. His rough, unpublished notes reveal the pluck, coolness and clearheadedness of a boy still under twenty who was already a much better mountaineer than his very indifferent guides. Once he met Garth Marshall in the Grands Mulets hut, three weeks before the latter was killed on the Brouillard Glacier.

In 1875 Boileau de Castelnau attempted the ascent of the Meije with Henri Duhamel, who was hardly older than himself. They failed after a long protracted fight up the north face. Later in the year, Boileau de Castelnau ascended the Ecrins. In 1876 he continued his exploration Dauphiny, traversing the Olan and the Tête de l'Etret. In 1877 he tried the Meije again, this time with the two Gaspards, father and son. Boileau led practically throughout. The elder Gaspard was terrified and almost refused to go on, though he rallied eventually and followed the young man. They failed with the peak within their grasp, for they were too late to continue. Boileau came back a week later and was successful. They had to bivouac on the descent; the weather changed, it snowed and the bivouac was a grim ordeal.

Coolidge soon heard that the mountain on which he had failed several times had been climbed, and he was indignant. He wrote disparagingly of the ascent, describing Boileau de Castelnau as 'a young Frenchman who was a chamois hunter rather than a peak hunter'. It is true that Boileau de Castelnau was a good shot, but obviously Coolidge had not the faintest idea of the social standing of the Boileau de Castelnau family. The young climber paid no attention to the outburst.

Strangely enough, he abandoned mountaineering after his ascent of the Meije and turned his interests elsewhere. He studied medicine in a desultory way, but was fascinated by newly devized machines, such as bicycles, cars and, much later, planes. He took part in many early motor races. He died in 1923.

The year after Boileau de Castelnau's expedition, two very strong parties, led respectively by Coolidge, and by P. Guillemin and Salvador de Quatrefages, ascended the peak, and this success was followed by others in the Dauphiny Alps.

During the last third of the nineteenth century one could glimpse the shape of things to come as a new Alpine playground became popular: the Dolomites. So far, they had been little visited or admired. In the eighteen-fifties, Gilbert and Churchill had described the valleys. These men were not mountaineers, but they had been impressed by the strange aspect of a range which had acquired a name only recently. The name derived from Commander Déodat-Tancrède de Grattet de Dolomieu, a Knight of Malta and a leading geologist (1751–1801) who, at the end of the eighteenth century, had studied the rocks of which the mountains were made. But as for the mountain ranges which bear his name, he never so much as saw them, though he travelled through the Western Alps. Horace-Benedict de Saussure's son, also a keen geologist, gave the name of *Dolomie* to the rock Dolomieu had identified, and the name was extended to the mountains situated in the north-east of Italy when it was realized that they were made of that particular rock.

The Dolomites were strange, smooth, sheer, limestone towers which looked perfectly unassailable. The landscapes were uncanny, with rocks either white or shot with every possible shade of pink, scarlet and purple, with few glaciers. Leslie Stephen, D. W. Freshfield, John Ball, F. F. Tuckett, C. Tucker and others conquered the first summits, among them the Adamello, the Cima di Ball and the Presanella. Local guides were more enterprising than elsewhere in the Alps. They were chamois hunters and shepherds, as everywhere else, but they were definitely attracted by their own mountains, and they thought it worth while to find a technique by which to conquer them. Besides, the difference between guides and climbers was much less marked there than in Switzerland or Savoy. The three brothers Klotz, F. Lacidelli, the two Innerkofflers, Santo Siorpaes, Angelo Dimai and Tita Piaz were among the best known of these men.

Towards 1870, a taste for finding hitherto unknown routes and new means of progression developed. This was the first district where rope-soled shoes were used, to make the most of the tiny holds grudgingly offered by smooth rocks. Later, this was the district where rubber soles (vibrams) first came into use. Many climbers were entranced by the sheer precipices and made the Dolomites their mountain paradise. Reading of climbs in the area, one realizes that the authors felt they had been given access to one of the earth's most secluded gardens. In recent times a leading guide, Gino Solda, told Gaston Rebuffat what the north face of the Cima Grande di Lavaredo was like: 'The first part is an overhang, the second is perpendicular.' This encouraging description was not exaggerated in the least, and that is more or less the kind of problem to be faced everywhere in the Dolomites.

By 1888 one of the most surprising climbers of all times blazed his trail up many strikingly difficult faces in that district and in the Austrian Alps before he disappeared on the Weisshorn when he was barely nineteen: Georg Winkler. He did most of his climbs by himself, overcoming the most incredible pitches. His outstanding achievement was the first ascent of the most difficult of the Vajolet Towers, which took the name of Winklerthurm; the climb was not repeated for many years. He also climbed in Switzerland and in 1956 his body came out of the glacier at the foot of the Weisshorn and was easily identifiable.

Winkler, who was small, made up for his short stature by using a grapnel tied to a rope, which he threw up to get a hold; he then hauled himself up. It was an extremely dangerous and risky device which had been used by Whymper too, whose book possibly supplied Winkler with the idea. It probably accounted for Whymper's spectacular fall from the Col du Lion, and possibly for Winkler's death; no one can tell. Obviously, something less dangerous and more efficient had to be found to enable climbers to overcome the difficult Dolomite pitches. Thus artificial climbing began, when rough and unwieldy pitons were manufactured and gradually altered and made more reliable. The rope technique was also carefully studied and the double rope, used by Mummery in the Western Alps, became the easiest and safest way to come down steep walls and overhangs. Compared with what was to happen forty years later, the use of artificial means was still more than modest.

Men like Norman Neruda, Leone Sinigaglia and the Zsigmondy brothers spoke of the Dolomites as of consecrated ground, which accounts for the violent quarrels which followed. Norman Neruda was killed in 1898, while scaling the Funffingerspitze by a most difficult route. He had been climbing in the Dolomites for five years, either with Christian Klucker or guideless, with his English wife. Otto and Emil Zsigmondy, two young Austrian climbers, made many fine expeditions in the same range and, according to Emil's book, *Die Gefahren des Alpen*, they had some deadly struggles against tremendous odds, until 1885 when he was killed on the Meije. The great Dolomite guide was Sepp Innerkoffler, an excellent though erratic climber who, when his patron could no longer continue a gruelling climb, used to leave him on a ledge where he had room to sit, then complete the ascent by himself. It was Sinigaglia's opinion that new routes up those mountains were so difficult that tourist and guide had to be almost as good as one another if there was to be any chance of success.

A number of first-rate mountaineers specialized in the Dolomites or the German Alps, such as Hans Fiechtl, who gave his name to the first pitons, Hans Pfann and, best of all, Hans Dülfer, who was killed when twenty-two, during the first World War. He had been one of the first to be obsessed by the most direct route to the summit. He also discovered a new and very efficient climbing technique. A severe climb, for him, was something of a work of art and he evolved a climbing style of great perfection.

Mountaineering has often led to heated arguments. A clash occurred in 1911, and the two rivals were Tita Piaz, the Dolomite guide, and Dr Paul Preuss. Preuss had taken an uncompromising attitude about artificial climbing: he did not accept it, and he went very far in his denunciation. Pitons were anathema to him, the double rope was almost a moral sin and he even rejected the idea of a roped party: they were all unfair means to conquer a mountain. They should never be used, not even to contrive the safety of the second man in the party. Preuss argued from an ethical, as well as from an aesthetic, point of view. He had a right to do so, as his most spectacular achievement had been the solitary first ascent of the Campanile Basso. His refusal of any help whatever when climbing a mountain was part of his general conception of the world, a *Weltanschauung* based on his respect and veneration for the mountains: under such conditions the reliance on pitons or the double rope was little short of sacrilege.

The answer to his conception, on which he had written a long essay, came from Tita Piaz. Piaz had tried to become a schoolmaster while attempting his first climbs. He was one of the very first to repeat Winkler's ascent of the Winklerthurm, adding to it the traverse of the three Vajolet Towers. What he achieved in that range was stupendous. On the other hand, he must have been unbearable company. His early intellectual background had turned him into a dangerous school-marm. His book, though very readable, is full of quotations in Latin, which he probably knew, in Greek, which he very likely did not know, and in English, of which he had no idea. He was quite convinced that he was the greatest mountaineer in the world—which was taking a great deal for granted. One of the redeeming sides of his strange and difficult personality was his sense of humour. He loved mountains for what they were, and never tried to develop a mountain philosophy. His attitude was purely experimental: as they were there, they had to be climbed. Having read Preuss' paper, he became really angry and answered with asperity. His position was one of commonsense versus a rather cloudy idealism. Both men knew a great deal about mountains, but Piaz had a more practical conception of the whole problem. He was for roped parties and for descending on the double rope. He was less straightforward about pitons because, when he wrote, in 1911, the piton technique was still vague and pitons themselves not quite reliable. Preuss' attitude might have been accepted by climbers of his class—that is, the very highest, and nothing but the highest. It could not apply to ordinary mountaineers, and much less to men who could live fascinating hours ascending a mountain. The final answer was a tragic one: Preuss was killed in 1913, on the north face of the Manndlkogel in the Salzkammergut. Though quite young (just twenty-seven), he had made more than 1,200 ascents, many of which were first ascents of difficult north faces. A graduate of Munich University, Paul Preuss was an excellent writer, with a great sense of humour, and a gift for well-documented discussion. Tita Piaz died at sixty-nine, killed in a motorcycle accident.

With the opening up of new districts and the growing knowledge of older ones, pioneers discovered new possibilities in the Alps, while an increasing number of climbers followed the well-known routes. The new men were developing personal techniques and tastes which left their mark on mountaineering history. Several of them, when writing of their adventures, also explained how they conceived the ethics of mountaineering: it is by no means too big a word, as a new conception of life—and death—was emerging from their various interpretations. The indignation which had overtaken many readers of mountain tales after the Matterhorn accident and Ruskin's impassioned invocation had slowly subsided. It was now possible and even necessary to explain the new aims and methods of mountaineering. So many great things had been achieved that the previously 'unassailable' peaks were now in process of becoming 'an easy day for a lady'. English climbers strictly avoided transcendental explanations: climbing was regarded as one of the most perfect means of realizing one's possibilities to the full. A strenuous climb was a complete test of a man's physical strength and moral endurance. Obstacles were not to be avoided but faced and overcome, so long as this struggle did not form a disguise for suicide; mountains could teach invaluable lessons, one of the most precious being that they usually exact severe penalities for any mistake or unjustified confidence. Courage and daring were the best ways to ensure victory. Such was the gospel preached by most of the great mountaineers of the period.

The greatest of them was Mummery. He came to the Alps when he was sixteen and made the first ascent of the Zmutt ridge of the Matterhorn when he was twenty-three. He disappeared on Nanga Parbat in the Himalayas after making some of the most daring ascents in the Alps and the Caucasus. He was then still under forty. What most distinguished Mummery from the men who had begun their Alpine careers fifteen years earlier, was his complete and justified reliance on his own skill and knowledge of the mountains. He had succeeded in impressing upon his guides the fact that he did not need a leader but only another man on the rope. He was perfectly able to lead a party, find a way or scale any forbidding pitch. Once Julius Kugy, when coming down the Theodule with Alexander Burgener, met on the path to Zermatt a tall thin man riding on a donkey; his long legs reached to the ground on either side. 'Who is this poor fellow?' Kugy inquired. 'It's Mummery,' replied Burgener. 'He climbs even better than I do.'

Mummery's book gives an impression of happiness born of a realization of his athletic gifts and his understanding of the mountain landscape. He never wrote like a poet; he never attempted to. Yet his narratives of the first crossing of the Col du Lion and the ascent of the ice-slopes of the Aiguille du Plan are graphic enough to enable any reader to feel how desperate such expeditions were. Mummery felt this better than anyone, but his enjoyment was all the greater, since he knew he was equal to his task; he never expressed any love of danger for danger's sake but simply his will to go anywhere and see anything. He had a powerful imagination and a keen sense of humour which never deserted him and made him aware of unsuspected details in the most dangerous climbs. He was full of ingenuity and could find new devices to ensure safety when going over difficult pitches. But, of course, his standard of difficulty was very high. His death on Nanga Parbat deprived mountaineering of one of its most inspiring leaders—if such a term can be used for a pastime which is the embodiment of individualism. Mummery will always be remembered for his first ascents of the Dent du Requin, the Grands Charmoz, the Grépon, the Teufelsgrat, and the Zmutt ridge of the Matterhorn.

C. T. Dent is remembered above all as the man who made the first ascent of the Aiguille du Dru. Although a first-class mountaineer, he was very different from Mummery; he lacked the other's fiery touch, nor did he yield to the call of the mountains with Mummery's zest. Dent's expeditions had an almost austerely classic perfection. He chose to climb outstanding summits of unquestionable difficulty. In private life Dent was a surgeon of great repute and skill, as well known in medical as in mountaineering circles. He took great pains to write and polish *Above the Snow Line*, wishing to make it attractive to the largest possible number of readers, even to non-climbers. While Mummery's alpine career hardly met with any ill-will from the mountains until its very end, Dent had to wage a long and protracted war against his greatest conquest, the Dru. 'The Dru', he wrote, 'is a magnificent mountain with its vast dark precipice on the north face, with its long line of cliffs, broken, jagged and sparsely wrinkled with gullies free from even a patch or trace of snow'.

There is no doubt as to the uncommon severity of the climb. Dent and Hartley with Alexander Burgener and Franz Andermatten attacked the peak in 1873, but they did not reach its summit until 1878, when they had made eighteen attempts. At the very end of the last scramble, when he realized that the top lay within his reach and that in a few minutes it would be beneath his feet, Dent's self-control almost broke:

'On again, while he could hardly stand still on the great steps the leader set his teeth to hack out. There came a short troublesome bit of snow scramble where the heaped up cornice had fallen back from the final rock. There we paused for a moment, for the summit was but a few feet from us, and Hartley, who was ahead, courteously allowed me to unrope and go first. In a few seconds I clutched at the last broken rocks and hauled myself up to the sloping summit. There for a moment I stood alone gazing down on Chamonix. The holiday dream of five years was accomplished; the Aiguille du Dru was climbed. Where in the wide world would you find a sport able to yield pleasure like this? . . . The pleasures of the Alps endure long after the actual experience, and are but invested; whether the interest can be derived by anyone but the actual investor is a matter for others to decide.'

Dent also climbed the Zinal Rothhorn from Zermatt and the Lenzspitze. Mummery and Dent displayed perfect intellectual control of superb physical gifts. Both tried new routes and new summits because they knew they were difficult. Once Dent had a most strenuous day of twenty-one hours, going up a new ridge of the Bietschhorn and coming down in pouring rain. He also made the first ascent of the Portjengrat, a splendid granite ridge above the Saas valley. In all these climbs, as little as possible was left to chance, yet the safety margin varied with the climber and in Mummery's case it could be pretty narrow.

It became narrower still with subsequent climbers who specialized in finding routes up the most forbidding faces. This was the beginning of a still newer conception of climbing. By 1875 mountaineers began to realize what a powerful and intoxicating joy could be derived from a fight against odds almost too great to overcome. This sense of joy may have been partly due to the discovery of the large number of snares which a mountain could set for a climber; it was also the outcome of a passion for the unknown. Such were the inspirations under which Oakley Maund and Thomas Middlemore tackled some of the most forbidding rock-faces of the Mont Blanc range. Middlemore's crossing of the Col des Grandes Jorasses made his Alpine Club colleagues realize that mountaineering had found a new mode of expression. With his guide, Jaun, and their porter he spent his time dodging falling stones. He was stunned by one of them, another scratched his hand, two ice-axes out of three were carried away so that they could hardly belay the rope, and eventually Jaun fell into a crevasse. One wonders here at the extraordinary lack of foresight displayed by both Middlemore and his guide, or at their complete indifference to the most elementary rules of prudence. When they reached the col from the Italian side, the party discovered that they had been going up a gully which concentrated all the stones falling from the ridge of rotten rocks forming the Col des Grandes Jorasses.

A similar expedition was the ascent of the north-east face of the Aiguille Verte by Middlemore, Oakley Maund and Henri Cordier, with Jaun, Maurer and J. Anderegg. The uncompromising steepness of the climb made it doubly dangerous, first because it was steep and then because falling stones gathered a tremendous impetus on such a gradient; an avalanche of stones almost eradicated the party while they were crossing the bergschrund. By the end of the afternoon, a heavy hail shower made the ice even more slippery than before and stones more numerous, and yet, by sheer luck, the six men succeeded in reaching the top unhurt.

This habit of climbing against any odds, taking any risk and forcing a way up at any cost, began to develop and became most frequent among Continental climbers, particularly the Germans and Austrians. The three Zsigmondy brothers were among the most reckless of all. They were athletic young men who, in spite of their university years—Continental university life is very detrimental to sporting activities—had managed to preserve their physical condition unimpaired by days spent in laboratories and libraries. The best climber of the family was Emil, a young surgeon who had studied abroad for several years; his foreign colleagues had been impressed by his appealing personality. He usually climbed with his brothers and L. Purtscheller, an Austrian professor of gymnastics. Their favourite playgrounds were the Austrian Alps and later the Dolomites; their ascent of the Kleine Zinne was a long fight against bad rocks and bad weather, so was that of the Zsigmondyspitze in the Zillertal. Later, they went up many great French and Swiss peaks. When one reads Emil Zsigmondy's book, *Die Gefahren der Alpen*, one is appalled by the number of hair-raising experiences the brothers went through. They seem to have had personal knowledge of every possible mountaineering mishap: they were caught in storms on the Saas Maor, hurt by falling stones, caught by falling séracs, overwhelmed by avalanches, almost frozen to death by a blizzard on the Marmolada; they lost their way in fog on the Dachstein and their compass went out of action; they had to bivouac in a storm on Monte Rosa; they fell into a crevasse on the Passo della Lobbia. Dent said of Emil Zsigmondy that 'he was too venturesome to be imitated'. His book reads like a long list of minor tragedies which continued until at last he fell to his death on the Meije in 1885, while trying to scale a virgin precipice. Purtscheller, who climbed with the Zsigmondys, went on climbing until he had a magnificent list of great peaks to his credit, but he was badly injured when climbing the Dru and died a few months later in 1900.

Another adept of this almost fantastic contempt for danger was Guido Lammer, an Austrian who, however strange it may seem, died of extreme old age during the last war, having been one of the first exponents of the demented Nazi cult of strength and will. He courted death and danger for their own sake. His book, *Jungborn*, leaves the reader under the impression that he has been listening to the strangely methodical ravings of a madman.

Once, when climbing the north-west face of the Matterhorn with his friend Lorria, they were swept away by an avalanche and thrown on to the Stockje glacier. They were both badly bruised, with minor, though very painful, injuries. Lorria was unconscious and Lammer, with a sprained foot, had to go in search of help. He dragged himself on all fours the whole way to the Staffel Alp, and this long and excruciating journey was like a waking nightmare, yet the impression survives that he experienced a morbid pleasure in his own pain. This kind of perversion was more or less the farthest limit of the cult, but it was a cult that spread and was frequently found in action after the first World War.

Such conceptions of mountaineering were still unusual. Climbers were becoming good athletes, they enjoyed difficult expeditions but they often saw in mountaineering a means of enabling them to visit the greatest possible number of ranges and of knowing them intimately. They did not specialize in one particular valley. D. W. Freshfield went *From Thonon to Trent* and Martin Conway (later Lord Conway of Allington) visited *The Alps from End to End*. The Duke of Abruzzi climbed in all parts of the world, besides making daring first ascents of various Alpine peaks. D. W. Freshfield once wrote to me that he was 'a topographer: a geographer mixed with a mountaineer', a fact which accounts for his important expeditions overseas. Yet he made several first ascents, the Presanella, the Monte Sissone, the Tour Ronde and the Cima di Brenta. He never cared for what he called 'stunt climbing', but made minute observations in whole districts of North Italy and the Engadine and then described them in a book which has become a classic. He retained all through his long life a devastating sense of humour which enabled him to poke fun at his adversaries, whoever they were:

> Here is a cheer for the New Mountaineer,
> That very well advertised man,
> His method is risky, I fear,
> But he 'does' all the peaks that he can.
> And anyhow gets his reward,
> A pyramid proud for his bones,
> Or else to be 'busted' by Ford
> Or drawn, as an angel, by Jones.
> 'The New School' (*Quips for Cranks*).

He had begun climbing at a time when it was still unusual to venture above the high passes. When he was sixteen he had been taken by his parents on long walking expeditions through the Alps and he had at once conceived a great passion for the mountains and everything connected with them. His wide knowledge and ready grasp of any new Alpine problem made him one of the leading personalities in Alpine circles.

Lord Conway of Allington must also be reckoned as one of the greatest authorities on the Alps. He climbed in many other parts of the world, and throughout a 'varied life' he returned to the mountains for inspiration. His professional interests were political or artistic. He published many books on the history of art and even more on mountain exploration. His conception of the climber was:

'One who loves first and foremost to wander far and wide among the mountains, does not willingly sleep two consecutive nights in the same inn, hates centres and gets tired of a district, always wants to see what is on the other side of any range of hills, prefers passes to peaks, but hates not getting to the top of anything he starts for, chooses the easiest and most normal route, likes to know the names of all the peaks in view and cannot bear to see a group of peaks, none of which he has climbed.'

Accordingly, he saw all that was worth seeing in any district and tried to link together his knowledge of various valleys so that he could find what was round the corner. He termed himself an 'inquisitive climber'; he wrote guide-books and found names for nameless peaks both in the Alps and abroad. He never climbed without guides, but he usually took them to ranges and districts they did not know, so that they could not climb by mere routine. When he traversed the Alps 'from end to end', starting from Turin and working his way up to the Gross Glockner in three months, he took with him two Gurkhas to turn them into instructors for native mountain regiments in India. The whole expedition was full of surprises. The Gurkhas quickly took to climbing and even more quickly to discussing the various local cheeses with as much competence as the two European guides. They led the party with brilliance over Mont Blanc, and they proved to be good mountaineers and cheerful companions. The experience was, in short, a complete success.

Yet Lord Conway's approach to the hills was more mystical than technical. His first view of the Blümlisalp had opened for him a strange unearthly kingdom, too beautiful and too remote to be trodden by human foot. He came to mountaineering through hero worship, out of his admiration for Tyndall. Another revelation came when he had to take charge of the burial of F. M. Balfour and his guide, who had been killed on the Aiguille Blanche de Peuteret. Balfour had been his friend in Cambridge, and Conway was in Courmayeur when the bodies were recovered. 'The great mountains did not seem inimical, as the Cervin used to be. No! They put on an aspect of higher dignity. They withdrew themselves again into that other world to which years ago they had seemed to belong.' Mountains have a peace of their own. Lord Conway went to see the place where the two men had been found: 'A pall of noontide glory enveloped the mountains. Hours passed in a dream.' There was no bitterness in him. Mountains were too far removed from man to be interpreted by human standards; they were a closed universe in which man might be tolerated, but only after great effort and understanding on his part. In spite of his extremely technical and well-organized expeditions and climbs, Lord Conway remained a mystic in his description and his interpretation of the mountains. His major work, *A Quest for the Divine*, made them a stage in a long mystical initiation.

By this time several women had achieved notoriety as climbers. Lucy Walker was still conquering peaks when the Misses Pigeon, Miss Katherine Richardson, Mrs Main, Miss Meta Brevoort, and Mlle Paillon began their Alpine careers. Miss Richardson was the first woman to climb the Meije. When she ascended the Aiguilles d'Arves with her French friend Mlle Paillon, she stepped aside just before reaching the top, saying to her companion: 'I already have the Meije; you take the Aiguille d'Arves'. In 1888, Miss Richardson made the first ascent of the north ridge of the Aiguille de Bionnassay with two of the best Courmayeur guides, Emile Rey and J. B. Bich: this was the first really great first ascent achieved by a woman in the range of Mont Blanc.

It took some time for women climbers to be accorded proper recognition in the world of mountaineering. The public at large did not contest the importance of their achievements—when they were able to understand them—but they pointed out how 'unwomanly' it was to indulge in such strenuous forms of exercise. Women would ruin their complexions, endanger their reputations, scratch their nails and acquire an ungainly carriage. The idea of dressing in man's apparel was still thought very fast, and Mary Paillon, when recommending it, was quite aware she was probably going too far. Most women went on climbing in long heavy skirts, wide hats, veils and gloves. The hardiest of them wore riding breeches under their skirts and used to remove the skirts when they reached the limit of civilization, the highest chalets and the last cows. They were then hung over their rucksacks or hidden beneath stones. Once an avalanche carried Mrs Main's skirt away while she was coming down with her party: it was a most unpleasant accident. In 1869, Anna and Ellen Pigeon made the first crossing of the Sesia Joch in the Monte Rosa range. The guide lost his way and the porter lost his nerve, so that one of the two sisters thought it safer to come down last on the rope, belaying the second man who was shaking with terror. Later, she wrote to Coolidge: 'Now people are accustomed to lady climbers and even solitary ones. We were the first, I think, to go unattended by a male protector and we got on very well, but then two together must be pleasanter than one alone, when you must have guides.'

Continental climbers were not always as reckless as the Zsigmondys or Lammer. The best French climbers specialized for many years in the Dauphiny ranges, probably because these mountains were still very little known while the Chamonix peaks were already overcrowded. After the conquest of the Meije by Boileau de Castelnau, the two outstanding names were those of Henri Duhamel and Henri Cordier. The latter often climbed with Middlemore and Oakley Maund and was with them when they scaled the Argentière faces of the Aiguille Verte and of Les Droites. He was killed in 1877, falling into the Plaret torrent through a broken snow-bridge. He had been among the best mountaineers of his time, in spite of his short sight, which eventually caused his death, when he was unable to detect from a distance the state of the snow-bridge through which he fell.

Swiss climbers were becoming more and more numerous, though the time when they had been the outstanding pioneers was past. Yet most of the men who had founded the Swiss Alpine Club were still climbing and younger ones were coming to the front. The most important among the members of the new generation was Emile Javelle. He was French by birth and had been naturalized Swiss; he taught literature in Lausanne and began his Alpine career when he was twenty-one. His first big expedition was the Matterhorn, in 1870. He had taken pupils to Zermatt and had fallen under the spell of the mountain: he immediately decided to climb it though it was a difficult and expensive undertaking and Javelle had no money. He borrowed right and left and eventually obtained enough to pay his guide, Nicholas Knubel, who was to be killed on the Lyskamm a few years later. The Matterhorn threw Javelle into an ecstasy of admiration. The weird sensation of being alone on a tremendous peak which had such a striking history, the beauty of the view which is almost unique in the Alps on account of its lack of foreground, the difficult pitches of the climb, all these experiences filled him with rapture.

He wrote an account of this unforgettable day and became more intent than ever on continuing his exploration of the high mountains. Yet his climbing notes are not impressive; he loved the mountains, tried hard to put his love into words and often failed. His choice of words was limited and not very effective. 'Richness and majesty! . . . diaphanous substance': such is the general impression conveyed by Monte Rosa. 'Splendid boundless view': the Adler Pass. He climbed many great summits and made important first ascents, such as the Tour Noir. The latter was one of his finest performances. He went up the Swiss, or eastern face of the mountain, above the Neuvaz glacier, and had to make a long and rather tricky traverse. The huge tower of hard red granite impressed him enormously. He noted the 'numerous arêtes of terrifying thinness; nothing', he added, 'looks accessible except the Aiguille d'Argentière'. Such was the view. A whole world of Aiguilles rose before his eyes. On the summit of the Tour Noir, Javelle thought he heard a sort of heavenly message and drank to the full the intoxicating joy of conquest:

'O you men, my brothers, who are to come here, remember that I, too, was a living, loving soul; I saw for one brief moment what you are seeing; I, too, throbbed with emotion as I gazed at Beauty and the mystery . . . of Beauty . . . Oh, while you are in the light of life, utter my name; bring me back to life for one second in your thoughts! You rocks, which are to stand for so long, allow this remembrance of me to endure for a time!'

Javelle, who was to die young, was always obsessed by a haunting sense of the shortness of life. His ascent of Mont Blanc was the fulfilment of twenty years of passionate longing or, as he put it: 'Mad love for the wild mountains. A perpetual sacred fire: my passion for inaccessible peaks and eternal rhythm, universal consciousness and God's infinity.' He had done the climb by the already much-trodden normal route, yet as happens when one loves mountains for their own sakes and not for climbing them in record time or by some sensational route, he felt the mystic atmosphere of the great peak, in spite of the tracks in the snow and—possibly—the sardine tins. A few years later, when climbing in Corsica, he caught a chill which developed into tuberculosis and he died in 1883 at the age of thirty-six, leaving unpublished narratives of his climbs which were edited by his friend Rambert. Javelle had no opportunity for giving more than a faint idea of the writer he might have become. His style and choice of images was lax, vague and overburdened with an emotional overflow. There was no literary Alpine tradition on the Continent and, owing to the adoration of his Swiss colleagues, Javelle's imperfect style created one. His descriptions were imitated by Swiss and later by French writers. Javelle was responsible for several clichés, among which was the questionable habit of making fun of other parties—usually English— which had been quicker than his on a mountain. This was to last for years.

German tourists began to force their way up many mountains. They trained at home in the Bavarian or Austrian Alps and developed an extremely daring technique. One of the greatest among them was Paul Güssfeldt, an explorer and mathematician. He went up the Grandes Jorasses and the Grand Paradis in winter, usually under appalling conditions. For several years he besieged Mont Blanc and succeeded in climbing it by several new routes, all of them of great severity. In 1892 he traversed the mountain from Courmayeur to St

Gervais, taking five days on the way. The Brenva ice-ridge, discovered by Moore and Walker in 1865, was extremely difficult and the wall of séracs was worse. When he reached it, Güssfeldt felt 'a prison gloom' closing over him and he coolly took the note-book out of his pocket to write: 'Hopeless situation.' Yet his guide, Emile Rey, managed to extricate the party from the maze, as going back was quite out of the question. The following year Güssfeldt made, with Christian Klucker, the first ascent of the Aiguille Blanche de Peuteret, one of the most beautiful and most dangerous spires on the southern face of Mont Blanc. The climb took eighty-eight hours. Among other outstanding German climbers were R. von Lendenfeld, Schultz, Moritz von Kuffner—who was an Austrian—and Karl Blodig. The latter made a point of climbing all the 4,000-metre summits in the Alps. When he had made the complete collection, a few new ones were invented; unnamed rock spires were promoted to the dignity of peaks and given names. Several of these, in the range of Mont Blanc, were of the utmost severity, but, though he was over sixty at the time, Blodig collected these also with true German thoroughness. The ascents of the Grande Rocheuse and the Aiguille du Jardin, which he made without guide or companion, included the crossing of the Col Armand Charlet. The whole expedition is one of the most difficult in the district; according to the terse comment of a great climber, Jacques Lagarde, it was 'proof that one can perform very great feats with very silly motives'.

Towards the end of the nineteenth century two outstanding climbers, Julius Kugy and Guido Rey, began their long and eventful careers. Kugy, who was born an Austrian in Trieste and who died an Italian during the last war, and Guido Rey, the Italian nobleman, had much in common. Both were possessed of a wide culture. Both felt a passionate love for all that was connected with the mountains. Kugy spent months hunting for a mythical scabious in the Julian Alps; Guido Rey lived for part of his life under the shadow of the Matterhorn in Breuil, where he gradually gathered a complete knowledge of the district. Both men took endless pains to discover every detail of mountain lore and all about the people who lived in the high valleys, their history, customs, and legends. Both retained, throughout their lives, a sense of wonder in the presence of the great peaks. Rey found a touchingly childish way of doing the Furggen ridge of the Matterhorn, having himself lowered past the overhang on a rope ladder; while Kugy was more than thirty and already a well-known Alpinist when he climbed the Matterhorn for the first time, finding the Hörnli ridge difficult and impressive, and glad of it. All of which is proof that neither of them was *blasé* from too close a contact with the great peaks. They both felt an inordinate joy when surmounting difficulties, conquering peaks, discovering routes. They both idealized their guides and their mountains. They both kept old traditions alive and became inspiring leaders for younger men. Kugy, in all his mountain descriptions, evinced an endless youthfulness and freshness of impression, mixed with a fine sense of humour, which enabled him to snatch at any fleeting impression. He opened up the Julian and Illyrian Alps, a crowd of unknown peaks of great beauty and difficulty, though not very high. When he came to the Western Alps he discovered several new routes and did most of the big climbs. Guido Rey made a few new ascents, such as the Ciamarella, the north face of the Bessanese—a hideous shaly wall of loose scree—and the Punta Bianca on the Tiefenmatten ridge. Yet he is best remembered as a poet. The impassioned descriptions he wrote of his climbs on the Matterhorn are slightly flamboyant. His Italian style is much more colourful and fervid than Kugy's simple colloquial German. It is always dangerous to push comparisons too far, but it is true to say that both Rey and Kugy were leading personalities, who handed on the love of adventure to younger men. Their books are mountain classics; so are their climbs.

The end of the nineteenth century saw the completion of the main exploration of the Alps. All the great peaks had been climbed, so had most of the secondary ones, and many new routes had been found up all of them. Problems were set in a perfectly straight-forward way; such and such a peak had so many ridges and so many faces and routes had to be forced up every one of them. Usually, ridges were conquered first, as was the case with Mont Blanc and the Matterhorn. Faces were often more difficult on account of their unrelieved steepness and sometimes because of falling stones. The most exciting playground was afforded by the Chamonix Aiguilles, where the greatest degree of difficulty was to some extent relieved by the dependability of the superb red granite. Apart from the Dru, where holds are known to give way, it is as firm as concrete.

While climbers and their methods were rapidly improving, guides, too, were following the general trend and doing something to deserve their title, and in some districts the skill of the guides reached a very high level. This age saw a number of those well-nigh life-long associations between tourist and guide, which make such wonderful reading. There had already been several such associations, like that between Wills and Auguste Balmat, or that between the Walkers and Melchoir Anderegg and—however strange it may sound—between Ruskin and J. M. Couttet. Now the habit became much more frequent and the guides had, as a result, a better opportunity for training and reaching greater efficiency. This second generation of guides learned at last how to use ropes and ice-axes and how to time a climb. Their greater familiarity with ice enabled them to avoid some of their predecessors' errors when crossing glaciers or ascending slopes. Most of the old shackles had been dropped. Parties were no longer weighed down by endless processions of useless guides and porters. One had discovered how to organize an expedition and how to rope up so as to ensure greater safety on ice and rock. There can be no cast-iron rules to prevent any sort of accident. On a mountain one is always at the mercy of storms or falling stones and often of avalanches.

Several great men stood out among an increasing number of good guides and they did much to improve the standard both of amateurs and professionals. The most striking figure was that of Alexander Burgener of Eisten in the valley of Saas. He took to guiding in his native valley when he was twenty-two, in 1868, and one of his first expeditions was the Mittaghorn with a party of schoolboys. The climb is an easy but steep one and Burgender came down by a new route to the great delight of the children, but the new route was an avalanche couloir, for which reason he was soundly rated by the curé Imseng, who supervised the expedition. Among the boys was Heinrich Dübi, who became a leading Swiss climber and mountain historian. From that day on, Burgener's name is to be found in the accounts of many extremely severe ascents. Julius Kugy was impressed by his 'royal aspect'. Moritz von Kuffner, who climbed the Mont Maudit ridge behind him, was so struck by Burgener's tremendous will-power that he hardly realized how tricky the route was.

Burgener's greatest achievement was probably that he climbed year after year with Mummery and C. T. Dent. He was with Mummery on the Zmutt and Furggen ridges of the Matterhorn, on the Col du Lion, on the Teufelsgrat of the Taeschhorn, on the Grands Charmoz, on the Grépon; he was with Dent on the Portjengrat, the Südlenzspitze, on all the attempts upon and the final ascent of the Dru. Burgener's courage, enterprise and endurance were beyond praise and he actually loved the mountains he was climbing All those who climbed with him were impressed by his enormous bulk, his rough, uncouth aspect, his face lost in a tremendous breard, the flow of his invective when thing were looking dubious, and his unshakable confidence in himself when tackling terrible snow slopes or dangerous rocks. When Burgener uttered warnings like: 'We *must* arrive, Mr Mummery, otherwise we are both done for !' there was not the slightest doubt that the situation was very grave indeed. Dent, who was a good judge of men, described his guide as 'a man who united well in himself qualities of strength, carefulness, perseverance and activity and possessed in addition the numerous attributes of observation, experience and desire for improvement in his art, which together make up what is spoken of as the natural instinct of guides'. Some of his colleagues were nimbler or quicker uphill; few were as steady and as reliable. When he was sixty-four, he was killed by an avalanche below the Bergli hut in the Oberland: he was swept away by a tidal wave on an easy mountain when going up an easy slope with indifferent tourists, after having defeated many magnificent summits with the finest climbers of the age.

Though rather hard and extremely proud of his own remarkable achievements, Burgener had always felt for Mummery an admiration which came near to worship and he deeply mourned his death on Nanga Parbat. Burgener's patrons have drawn wonderfully life-like sketches of the big bear in action. One shows us Burgener 'with a yell of anguish, bounding off' to catch a precious knife which had slipped from his grasp. Now this race took place on the summit ridge of the Portjengrat, a rather awkward spot for such a display of speed. Another depicts Burgener pinning his colleague Maurer to the rock with one hand to prevent his slipping into one of the ice-glazed upper gullies of the Dru; and again we hear Burgener yelling to Mrs Mummery, when they were going down the Taeschhorn in a storm, after the first traverse of the Teufelsgrat, 'Go ahead anyway; I could a cow here hold'.

Another Swiss guide, Christian Klucker, left an unforgettable impression on his employers. An Engadine shepherd who studied for a few years in Samaden, he took to guiding at the age of twenty-one. He had done his first climb when he was thirteen, acting as porter to his father who had been engaged by two Englishmen, D. W. Freshfield and F. F. Tuckett, who had brought François Devouassoud from Chamonix, but who needed a second guide. Klucker, who possessed some culture, excellent manners, a good knowledge of the mountains and an appealing personality, soon became an outstanding guide. After doing many climbs in the Engadine he was taken away from his district by a German mountaineer who brought him to Zermatt. Klucker hated the place, though he took his employer up most of the big peaks and was presented with his poems as a reward. He then began a lasting association with Norman Neruda, a young man of Swedish origin, with whom he climbed mainly in the Engadine and the Dolomites. Local guides were usually terrified by the very difficult rock-faces of the Badile or the Cengalo; yet Klucker succeeded in scaling many of them. Later, he was taken to the Canadian Rockies by Whymper, although the latter had reached the stage in his career when he no longer tried to reach the summits himself but just sent his guides ahead. Klucker also climbed with Güssfeldt and led through their long traverse of Mont Blanc; he did this again with Farrar. At the end of his career, Klucker wrote the *Adventures of an Alpine Guide,* an attractive book and one of the few ever written by one of his profession. It is a great pity that guides usually have neither time nor skill nor desire to compile their memoirs, for they often write interesting letters and have a very efficient way of judging their employers' capacities and achievements.

D. W. Freshfield drew a fine portrait of his Chamonix guide, François Devouassoud. Though perhaps not an outstanding climber, Devouassoud was certainly more than a good guide. He loved exploration and always felt at home in the mountains, whether in Sikkim or Algeria or on the Ruwenzori. Though he started guiding very early, in 1849, he knew how to manage a rope and how to proceed on snow slopes. He was thus able to save the lives of several of his employers. He was at his best on ice. But this grave, refined man, who had a keen sense of humour and a taste for culture, was not only an excellent leader on a mountain, he was an ideal companion on long expeditions.

The great guides of the period were a striking and picturesque group of men. The men of the Val d'Aosta, Maquignaz, Emile Rey, J. Croux, and A. Castagneri, were remarkable climbers who scaled the dark precipices of the south face of Mont Blanc. Daniel Maquignaz made the first ascent of the Dent du Géant with the Sella family and accompanied J. P. Farrar in his ascent of the Péteret ridge, an endless fight against ice-glazed rocks and snow arêtes under a raging gale. Emile Rey, 'the man who was always lucky', often climbed with Güssfeldt and died on the Dent du Géant when his luck gave out. Many of those guides were killed when climbing; Castagneri disappeared with the Conte di Villanova and his other guide and nothing was ever found of the party. These men were poorly served by the flowery epitaphs, full of superlatives and far-fetched images, which were carved on their graves or memorial tablets in Courmayeur and Valtournanche.

Among the guides of the Julian Alps one may mention Anton Oitzinger, whose biography has been written by Julius Kugy—not only a guide but a chamois-hunter and a fighter against Bulgarian bandits. But it would be hard to find personalities more picturesque than those of the two French guides of which we must now speak. J. J. Blanc le Greffier, of Bonneval-sur-Arc, was a man of masterful temperament, with an indomitable pride; he was strictly conscientious in every way and always took command of a situation, giving orders not only to the members of his own party, but to every party within earshot. He was also a keen chamois-hunter and a first-class smuggler. C. F. Meade, who often climbed with him before adopting his son Pierre as his guide and friend, wrote of him that: 'He was a passionate lover of the mountains and it was characteristic of him that his last words were: *"Tout ce que je regrette en abandonnant cette terre, ce sont les montagnes et les chamois"* (The only things I regret when leaving this world are the mountains and the chamois).'

Joseph Ravanel of Chamonix, who was called Ravanel-le-Rouge on account of his flaming hair and moustache, was another striking figure. He led most of the great first climbs in the district and was an excellent though rough climber. He went up almost anything with much noise, scraping the rocks with his boots, rattling his ice-axe and rucksack, swearing and grumbling. He had many accidents and always recovered, having as many lives as a cat, and he became one of the outstanding personalities in the valley. The old Couvercle hut, a tiny red box built under a huge overhanging rock, was almost a family possession. When Ravanel was out climbing, his termagant of a wife took his place and went up to the hut, scaling the steep rock staircase of the Egralets in elastic-sided boots and black-feathered hat, carrying a handbag and a large umbrella. The family ran the hut in the most dictatorial way, but no one dared to lodge a complaint with the French Alpine Club which owned it, as the Rouge had an unaccountable charm of his own. He was guide to King Albert of the Belgians; he had climbed with C. F. Meade, Owen Glynn Jones, had done the Grépon fifty-seven times and jumped out of the Montenvers train a fraction of a second before it crashed over a bridge in 1927. Young climbers and young guides loved to hear his tall stories. Above all, he was one of the most reliable guides of his time.

It would be possible to give a long list of guides who led important expeditions during the last years of the nineteenth century. And yet, during the same period, guideless climbing was becoming more and more frequent. There had already been guideless parties. Charles Hudson and E. S. Kennedy had made several great ascents without guides. At a time when good guides were few and consequently heavily booked up throughout the season, and bad guides fairly numerous and liable to commit dangerous blunders, it was normal for well-trained athletes to try their own strength without local help or hindrance. They knew the mountains as well as most of the guides and often much better, a fact which was not realized by a large part of the public. This began a controversy, which is still being waged under various headings. The people who objected to guideless climbing were in the first place guides—for obvious reasons. Then came numerous persons who did not know the difference between a hard climb and a walk, and would call a stroll along a tame mountain path a 'guideless climb'. Untrained tourists fell to their death while picking edelweiss, leaning over a precipice or stepping backwards into the air to come within the range of a companion's camera: I saw this kind of accident happen on the path leading from the Montenvers to the Mer de Glace. Such accidents have nothing to do with mountaineering proper but their frequency and foolishness cause them to be listed side by side with the Breithorn accident of 1927, when a guideless party of four young men fell from the Younggrat, or Emil Zsigmondy's death on the Meije in 1885. This kind of confusion had led to great misunderstanding.

As early as 1870, A. G. Girdlestone published *The High Alps without Guides*. His expeditions had been mostly across high passes. Yet he climbed the Wetterhorn and Mont Blanc, which reminded him of the verse in the Book of Revelation: 'I saw a great white throne.' He travelled up and down the Alps, enjoying the delightful sensation of being his own master, free to exert his physical powers when and where he wished, and feeling equal to his task. However, his book seemed extravagant enough at the time and there were many protests from orthodox quarters. But as years went by, the best mountaineers ceased to limit their activities to guided expeditions. Mummery did major climbs without the company of any professional. He had none when, with G. Hastings and Norman Collie, he made the first traverse of the Col des Courtes and the first guideless ascent of the Brenva route. The latter climb compelled them to bivouac twice, which meant three fights across the sérac wall on the upper part of the glacier. The same party, with the addition of W. C. Slingsby, made the first ascent of the Dent du Requin, the first ascent of the Aiguille du Plan from the south-west, the first traverse of the Grépon. This team was one of the best that ever visited the Alps. Norman Collie was a man with a striking and manifold personality. He was a great scientist, a gifted artist, an art specialist and, according to Colonel Strutt, a leader with 'inspired direction', equally good on rocks and ice.

Frederick Gardiner and the brothers Pilkington were also eminent guideless climbers; they made their most important expeditions in Dauphiny, among which was the forth ascent of the Meije. The Zsigmondy brothers, G. Lammer and Georg Winkler, were among the great Continental guideless pioneers. In France, Pierre Puiseux—Victor Puiseux's son—was the first guideless mountaineer. He ascended many great peaks, though he never attempted new routes. In private life he was an astronomer of repute.

Guideless climbing had many opponents, including W. A. B. Coolidge, one of the greatest and earliest specialists of Alpine history, who at an early age began a tempestuous climbing career under the guidance of his aunt. He soon got together a team of excellent guides with Christian Almer and (later) Almer's son, with François Devouassoud from time to time. He had violent quarrels with other mountaineers and was usually against someone or something. He was at daggers drawn with Whymper. Coolidge could not tolerate the idea of guideless climbing, probably because he had always been able to find excellent guides, and he violently abused men who could do without professionals. Nor could Guido Rey, because of his sentimental admiration for the guides of Valtournanche, accept the idea of climbing without them; he was, in fact, so prejudiced in their favour that he saw nothing extraordinary in their getting drunk, even on a mountain.

German critics—W. Lehner among them—have taken great pains to explain that the great climbs achieved by Englishmen in the eighties and nineties were chiefly due to the fact that, being very rich, they could hire the best guides, while German climbers were 'free, jolly students' who climbed alone. This is completely false. Great German mountaineers like the Schlagint-weits, Häberlin, Güssfeldt, von Kuffner and Moritz de Dechy were quite able to afford good guides in Switzerland and, in fact, they hired the best men. German guideless climbing developed in the Bavarian Alps, where the natives knew no more about their mountains than the townsfolk. Both learned to-gether how to tackle the very difficult peaks of the district. So did the Italians in the Dolomites. The Zsigmondy brothers were Austrians and, although they were students for a time, it is fair to add that this happy state does not usually exceed six or seven years at the most.

According to Lehner, the Matterhorn accident meant the end of all out-standing English expeditions for five or six years: a statement which is con-trary to the facts, as the Brenva was climbed by an English party on the day of the accident, the Aiguille de Bionnassay a week later and Mont Blanc was traversed by way of the Glacier du Dôme three weeks afterwards. An Italian critic, Paolo Lioy, wrote in 1885: 'Our own Alps surpass in beauty and majesty all the other mountains', and he went on to observe that Italian climbers were supreme; after which he quoted seven names, which did not, however, testify to any outstanding supremacy. Thus the end of the century saw the appearance of a new and not quite desirable aspect of mountaineering: nationalistic prejudice.

This period also saw the birth of scientific climbing technique. It had been rather timidly evolved during the last eight or ten years but it was now to develop on a considerable scale. Earlier in the century, climbing a peak had meant finding the easiest way to the summit. Later, new but possibly equally easy routes had been much in demand. When Hudson and Kennedy had tried to reach Mont Blanc, first over the Vallée Blanche and then over the Bosses ridge, they had been actually prospecting for some slope of easier access than the Mur de la Côte. The route up the Glacier du Dôme which had been opened down to Courmayeur by Buxton, Grove and Macdonald with three guides in 1865, was also fairly easy and it has become the normal route from the Valley of Aosta. But a few weeks before, when the two Walkers, with Moore and Mathews and their guides, had forced their way up the Brenva glacier, they had opened a new chapter in Alpine history: before leaving Courmayeur, they knew that this new route, if practicable at all, would prove extremely severe. Mountains were now to be climbed by every route and preferably by the difficult ones. A great challenge had been taken up.

The doctrine of 'climbing style' is a modern one, with serious drawbacks; the doctrine of 'speed' is less modern but has been lately pushed to fantastic consequences. The knowledge of a few sound fundamental principles had been collected all through the infancy of mountaineering, through years of gruelling work. For instance, the conclusion had been reached that it was often safer and quicker to climb rock ridges instead of snow slopes or couloirs: it actually saved time and toil as there were no steps to cut. Early climbers had often accepted the risks of cutting their way up or down for hours, and this was the practice of Leslie Stephen's party when crossing the high Oberland passes. When Tyndall and Hutchinson climbed the Piz Morteratsch with two guides in 1864, they went up a rock buttress, but though Tyndall was for going down the same way, the guides preferred to hack steps in a slippery snow couloir with the result that the party was swept away by an avalanche and it was only by an extraordinary piece of luck that they succeeded in stopping themselves a fraction of a second before they would have been hurled into a crevasse.

In the meantime it was discovered that progress on rocks could be very disconcerting. When Leslie Stephen described his caterpillar-like climb along the ridge of the Zinal Rothhorn, one felt he was explaining a very puzzling experience to an audience that did not know more than he did about such unexpected antics. And yet he was actually addressing the Alpine Club. Years went by and climbers became familiar with the various attitudes forced upon them. When they began scaling the Chamonix or Cortina rock-precipices in earnest, they practised at once and without demur any queer sort of gymnastics. For years the Mummery Crack on the lower part of the Grépon was considered to be one of the worst pitches in the Alps. It is a narrow chimney into which a climber can insert one arm and the tip of one boot; with the other arm and the other leg he has to scrape the rock to find almost non-existent holds on the outside wall—a faith-and-friction slab of the worst type. There are two more or less similar pitches on the same Aiguille, the Rateau de Chèvre and the Fissure du Sommet. Yet a few years later, similar pitches were not only taken for granted but almost welcomed, especially in

9. Ice formations on Mont Blanc. (Photo: Gaston Rebuffat)

10. Ascending the Bosses Ridge on Mont Blanc. (Photo: Gaston Rebuffat)

the Dolomites, where climbers had always been compelled to overcome great difficulties on smooth limestone precipices.

The tools required by climbers were now carefully improved. Throughout the early years of mountaineering, all the members of climbing parties had used alpenstocks; in addition, the guides carried short-handled, and later long-handled axes, the latter affording a better hold. Somewhere between 1860 and 1865, ice-axes, as we understand the term today, came into existence as a cross between the alpenstock and the guide's axe. On the Matterhorn in 1865, Whymper and his English companions had ice-axes, according to his sketches in *Scrambles* and to Lord Francis Douglas's photograph. He had also carried an ice-axe on the Barre des Ecrins, but he had an alpenstock when he fell on the Col du Lion. Leslie Stephen climbed the Zinal Rothhorn with an ice-axe and the Jungfraujoch with an alpenstock. Moore and the Walkers had only alpenstocks on the Brenva glacier.

There were long heated discussions as to the respective merits of either instrument, and Whymper devoted several pages of his book to the question. Leslie Stephen, in an *Alpine Journal* paper entitled 'The Best Form of Alpenstock' (by which word he meant ice-axe!), explained that his own climbing weapon was a pole of four feet six inches, with a strong iron axe at the top. The sketch which was printed with the article showed that the axe was more or less like the spike at the top of modern ice-axes. E. S. Kennedy suggested they they should be made on the lines of an American backswoodsman's axe, which was strong, elegant and easy to wield. There were long discussions as to the advisability of entrusting beginners with ice-axes, for not knowing how to use them, they might prove a danger to themselves and to the other members of the party; but H. B. George wisely pointed out that such people were equally dangerous with alpenstocks. Besides, alpenstocks were cumbersome on rocks, no one knowing what to do with them. They were supposed to be useful as jumping poles when it came to crossing a crevasse, and as support when sliding down slopes of snow or scree; but in fact they were hardly used at all for the first purpose and ice-axes were strong and long enough for the second. Incidentally, English ice-axes were made by Leaver at Maidenhead, and cost from one guinea to twenty-five shillings.

With new and more reliable equipment, Alpine technique became less amateurish. Guides gradually discarded the habit of making sitting glissades over known slopes. But ladders were still in demand; in fact, Dent dragged a ladder up the Dru during one of his attempts, and Dunod took three to an unrecorded height on the Grépon and probably hated the process. There are still several fixed ladders across the bigest crevasses of the Jonction, on the normal route up Mont Blanc.

The art of rope management was progressively discovered after years of trial and error. In his *Scrambles*, Whymper had given a long and minute description of how to manage a rope so as to ensure maximum security. He dwelt at great length on the compelling necessity of keeping it quite taut when crossing a glacier, especially one covered with snow. Leslie Stephen held the same opinion in the last chapter of the *Playground of Europe*: 'The Dangers of Mountaineering'. They both explained how it is possible to belay a rope on a steep ice-slope or on rocks, and how to avoid a jerk if a member of the party suddenly slips. It became more and more clear how important it was to rope up a convenient number of people; how dangerous it might be to have too small a party on a glacier or too large a party on rocks. Rope-management is minute and tricky; it requires extremely quick reactions; it is a matter of tact and intuition; as well as of strength.

All sorts of new possibilities were discovered when once climbers had conceived the idea of roping, or rather double roping, down steep places. There had been an awkward first attempt at double roping by old Peter Taugwalder when he had come down the last ice-slope of the Allalin Pass, but he had just slid down, holding both ends of the rope which he had doubled round some rock-knob. There was no attempt at wrapping the rope round himself in the elaborate way which was found to ensure perfect safety. It seems that Mummery was one of the first who used the complete method and the modern term (double rope—*rappel* in French) when coming down the Grands Charmoz and the Grépon. Though the use of the double rope may have been carried too far, it has enabled climbers to save time, a vital thing in a big climb. Very soon, the use of the double rope compelled climbers to add to their equipment various devices which came later under the heading of 'artificial aids'. Now, as they never knew whether they would find a convenient rock around which to double their spare rope without the risk of its sticking or breaking, they sometimes carried wooden pegs which they hammered into crannies with the head of an ice-axe. Later, the wooden pegs gave way to steel pitons which had to be wedged into the fissures with a steel hammer or a special ice-axe, the head of which was constructed like a hammer.

By 1865 some parties were still climbing very tricky passages unroped. When R. Fowler went up the Aiguille du Chardonnet and the Verte by the Grande Rocheuse route, he and his three guides roped only for a short time when coming down. In many cases parties were roped up in a most objectionable way: the tourists had the rope tied round their waists, but the guides merely held it in one hand, so that the whole process was worse than useless. In 1860 three English tourists and one guide were killed on the Col du

Géant owing to this stupid practice. One of the tourists slipped and dragged the others down at a place which was not very steep; the first and third guides tried to hold them, failed and let go the rope, so as not to be dragged down by the doomed men. The second guide probably got entangled in the rope and fell with the others. Good guides and good climbers refused to accept this senseless practice. Neither Melchior Anderegg nor Croz nor Almer used a rope that way, and it is impossible to imagine Whymper, Leslie Stephen or A. W. Moore allowing their guides to take so light a view of their responsibilities. Besides, guides were also liable to slip. The practice was the outcome of two equal misconceptions: guides had no wish to endanger their own lives when climbing with incompetent people who might slip, while climbers felt vaguely ashamed when tied to a rope and led like a dog on a leash. It took a long time for both parties to realize that mountaineering is team work and that a 'rope' is a living unit, acting as a whole, each member of it co-operating in a single effort.

As to the actual rope, the manilla or hemp cable tied round the climbers' waists, it was the subject of endless technical discussion. Only after long experience was it decided what was the most suitable material and length, and what were the best knots. The whole matter is too complicated and technical to be explained here; moreover it still is and will always be in a process of evolution. New materials have been discovered. By the end of the century the last word in rope texture was silk; now it is nylon.

With the increasing number of climbers, steps had to be taken to make the approach to the hills a little less complicated and exhausting. The various continental alpine clubs undertook to build huts. Until then, there had been no choice other than sleeping in the highest chalets or in a draughty bivouac under an overhanging rock. In both cases, firewood had to be carried up. The Swiss Alpine Club during the first twenty-five years of its existence contrived to build thirty-eight huts, of which the earliest was the Grünhorn hut on the Tödi (1863), followed by the Trift hut, neat the Dammastock (1864). The Matterhorn (Hörnli) hut was built in 1865, the Mountet in 1871, the Weisshorn hut in 1876, the Concordia on the Aletsch glacier and the Boval hut in 1877. By 1890 the French Alpine Club had erected thirty-three huts, mostly in Dauphiny; there were no real mountain huts in the Mont Blanc district, but only small hotels, perched too low to be of much value. The first real 'refuge' was the Couvercle, erected in 1904. The Italian, German and Austrian clubs also had many huts and hotels scattered over the various Alpine ranges, as far as the Karst and the Julian Alps. Most of those buildings were very small and primitive; they consisted of a cave to which a door had been added, or three stone walls under an overhanging rock, or a low corrugated iron shed. There were few blankets, all of them dirty, or a few sheep fleeces dirtier still. A small oven, one or two saucepans, hardly any crockery, a few stools, a small heap of wood, an axe and a spade were the scanty pieces of furniture one could expect to find in such hovels. Few people could shelter in them. Very soon they proved to be much too small and had to be rebuilt on a larger scale.

Some of the huts and some of the hotels in the high valleys have preserved their early archives: such is the case with the hotel at Zinal, the Monte Rosa Hotel at Zermatt, and the Nesthorn Hotel at Ried in the Lötschental. Few records are more touching then these mountain archives in which people complain of bad coffee or bad weather, record new climbs by immensely difficult ridges or merely little walks along the mule-paths. W. A. B. Coolidge, Clinton Dent, Leslie Stephen, the Misses Pigeon, the three Walkers, Lord Conway and his Gurkhas, J. P. Farrar, the Zsigmondys, A. G. Girldestone, W. F. Donkin, William Penhall, Miss Stratton, A. W. Moore, Geoffrey Winthrop Young and H. E. G. Tyndale have all signed in the book at Ried.

Various climbs were made easier by the fixing of ropes or ladders or chains to the rocks, a rather questionable process. It was carried to an insane extent in the Austrian Alps. The Matterhorn received a complete decoration of these devices, both on the Hörnli ridge and on the Italian ridge. The Dent du Géant was also provided with a fair length of cable. It is even true that the large quantity of rope attached to the Matterhorn has made the mountain even more dangerous than it was before, owing to the overcrowding which has resulted from the assumption that it had become an easy climb. I once found eighty people on the summit ridge, and many of them were beginners who did not know how to prevent their ropes from sending down masses of loose stones.

A type of building which now began to appear on the mountains was the observatory. The best known are the observatories on Mont Blanc, the history of which has been a stormy one. In 1886, Joseph Vallot, a topographer and scientist, went up the mountain to make observations. The weather suddenly changed and a blizzard compelled him to come down. He tried again a year later, camped for three days very high and failed again, or at least could not collect all the information he needed. He then made up his mind to have a real observatory built high enough to enable scientists to defy the elements. The town of Chamonix gave him permission to build it, on condition that he also built a hut nearby for the use of non-scientific climbers. His cousin Henri Vallot, an engineer, drew up the plans for both buildings, which were erected on two small rocks below the Bosses du Dromadaire, as these were the last rocks on the mountain and one could not build on ice. Everything was completed by 1890; it had been a great undertaking owing to the exceptional height at which the workmen had to work, and the very low temperatures they often had to face. The first climber who slept in the hut, even before its completion, was an Italian priest who had made several great mountain expeditions, the Abbé Achille Ratti, who was to become Pope Pius XI. On that day he was traversing Mont Blanc.

The members of the Vallot family had fiery tempers. Joseph Vallot invited his cousin to visit the observatory built according to sketches, and they then drew up a legal deed, giving Joseph and his descendants full rights over Mont Blanc, and Henri and his descendants full rights over the rest of the range: no trespassing was to be allowed.

Both buildings were enlarged and moved several times from one rock to the other. The hut, after being for long 'the highest pigsty in Europe', has been replaced by a more adequate building. But as everything is made of aluminium, without wood lining, to save weight and to avoid fire, the temperature inside is appallingly low.

The first scientist to use the Vallot observatory was a French astronomer, Dr Janssen. Very soon, however, he wanted to erect another observatory on the very top of the mountain. In spite of the complete absence of rocks—'nothing even as big as the stone of a prune' said Whymper, who went up to see the new hut built—he came to the conclusion that it was possible to lay a light shed on ice without it sinking. The new observatory was erected according to his desires, but Dr Janssen, who was then very old and a cripple, was able to visit it only three times, and had to be drawn up on a sort of sledge. The new observatory was short-lived and its existence was tragic. The cold froze the instruments; in spite of all calculations, the hut sank into the ice and was slowly crushed; a man was killed there by lightning. An earthquake in 1907 was felt as high as the top of the mountain and it hastened the sinking of the hut. Dr Janssen was then dead and a committee of scientists, with Joseph Vallot as chairman, decided to salvage what could be dug out of the ice and destroy what was left of the smaller observatory. A few instruments were brought down and a few planks were used as fuel: such was the end of Dr Janssen's creation.

Until the last years of the nineteenth century, the only mountain names in use were those which had been handed down through the ages. The habit of giving a name to any rock spire or snow-summit is quite modern. It took centuries to give a name to Mont Blanc itself. Until 1881 the cluster of crags now known as the Grépon, the Grands Charmoz, the Petits Charmoz, the Aiguille de l'M and the Pic Albert, which towers up between the Montenvers and the Glacier des Nantillons, was just known as 'les Charmoz'. Then Mummery climbed the two higher peaks and tried to discover a way of identifying them, with the result that those names came into use. The numberless jagged peaks round Chamonix made this habit very helpful at first; later it was carried too far. The habit was not restricted to this very intricate district. While it is hard to divide into new points the massive summits of the Oberland, the process has been carried very far in Valais and to an almost fantastic extent in the Dolomites.

The custom began when a galaxy of new names was bestowed on Monte Rosa, quite early in the nineteenth century. A little later the Dom received its religious appellation (*Dom* = a cathedral) from the priest of Zermatt, the Abbé Berchtold. Until then none but outstanding peaks had names and they were of the same type all over the Alps: such were Mont Blanc, Monte Rosa (*Roese* or *Ruiz*, a Val d'Aosta name for a glacier), the Dent Blanche, the Weisshorn, or the various Rothhorns or Aiguilles Rouges which dot the map as far as the Škrlatica in the Julian Alps. Most summits are given vague, almost featureless names connected with the nearest village, like the Matterhorn or the Dent d'Hérens. The Aiguille du Dru derived its name from a small meadow at its foot, the Plan du Dru, *dru* meaning thick grass. It is not a primitive instinct to give names to mountains which are so far above human regions. Some of the oldest names in the Alps occur in the Chamonix district and they stress the reason why people cared so little for the great peaks: the Mont Maudit and the Mont Mallet are both 'accursed mountains'.

When the process of climbing not only major peaks, but also secondary summits, became pre-eminent, it was necessary to identify the points which had been reached. There was no romantic appeal in a mere trigonometrical figure like Point 3759, which might be one of the spires which rear up their heads at the back of the Chamonix Aiguilles. When the naturalists of the Hôtel des Neuchâtelois left the Aar glaciers, they had scattered their own and their friends' names all over the place: there was an Agassizhorn, a Hugisattel, and so on. For a long time the highest summit of Monte Rosa was just that, the Höchstespitze; later it was named the Dufourspitze after General Dufour who was the head of the Swiss Federal Suvey. Little by little new names were suggested to the mapping authorities. One of the specialists of the Zermatt and Saas districts was Lord Conway, who coined a number of new names, the aptness and local colour of which were so perfect that they were immediately accepted by the Swiss survey: the Wellenkuppe, an anonymous peak which had been first climbed by Lord Francis Douglas a few days before he was killed on the Matterhorn, the Lenzspitze (Spring Point), first climbed by Dent, the Stecknadelhorn (Pin Point) because it stood next to the Nadelhorn (Needle Point), the Windjoch (Wind-swept Pass) across which a gale is always blowing even while the surrounding sky is perfectly calm.

Later, arêtes and even faces were given names, and some of them have a story. When Stafford Anderson reached the summit of the Dent Blanche by a new route along a steep ridge of crumbling rocks, his guide Ulrich Almer summed up the situation in a solemn statement: *'Wir sind vier Esel!'* (We are four asses!). The name stuck and the ridge is now known as the Viereselgrat. A similar story is related in Chamonix: when Joseph Vallot was mapping the district, he pointed out to his guide a granite spire which looked quite unassailable and asked him: 'If you were asked to go up that which route would you take?' The guide replied 'He who asked me to make such a climb would be a madman' (*un fou*). Hence the name, Aiguille du Fou. The peak has been climbed subsequently. The Teufelsgrat (Devil's Ridge) on the Taeschhorn tells its own story. When Mummery made the first ascent of a forbidding rocky spire above the Glacier du Géant in 1893, he gave it the name of Dent du Requin. The name attracted much attention, and later a French mountaineer, E. Fontaine, bestowed the names of Caïman and Crocodile on other equally forbidding Aiguilles in the neighbourhood. The same man named the Aiguille Mummery after the great climber and the Aiguille Ravanel after his own guide, Ravanel-le-Rouge. Another French climber, E. Beaujard, is responsible for the Aiguille de la République and the Pointe des Deux Aigles; the former name was suggested by his patriotic feelings, the latter by the fact that two eagles had flown round the peak during his climb. Eagles played the same part in the naming of the Adlerpass by the Abbé Imseng. The Col des Hirondelles owes its lovely name to Leslie Stephen, who found a little company of dead swallows on the snow at the foot of the pass when he made the first ascent.

The passion for new names went very far. Almost every small *gendarme* which rears up its head along an arête has been given a name. A fringe of unbelievably sharp rocks soar up on both sides of the Dru. They are not very high but extremely difficult of access and more difficult still to scale; they have been given as a whole the lovely name of Les Flammes de Pierre. Yet a few of them have been ascended and one has received the rather cumbersome appellation of Pointe Michelle-Micheline: these two Christian names happening to belong respectively to the wife and the sister of the men who climbed them. The present habit is simply to give to a peak the name of the first man who climbed it: hence the Pointe Lagarde, Pointe de Lépiney,

Younggrat (several of them), Winkler Turm, Voie Mallory, Voie Ryan, and so on. Most of those modern names came into use after 1920.

For the larger part of the non-climbing public at the end of the nineteenth century, mountains still spelt romance and incalculable danger. They were still wrapped in a kind of pall which too frequent accidents had drawn round them. I have no desire to rewrite a recent work on Alpine tragedies, nor to add further chapters to it. Yet it is a fact that tragedies did happen. Garth Marshall and one of his guides were killed on the Glacier du Brouillard in 1874; Lewis, Paterson and their three guides on the Lyskamm in 1877; Marinelli and his guides were swept down by an avalanche on the south face of Monte Rosa in 1881; during a single summer, that of 1882, William Penhall and his guide fell from the Wetterhorn, W. E. Gabbett and his two guides from the Dent Blanche, and F. M. Balfour from the Aiguille Blanche de Peuteret. There were many other black summers. Six young Swiss climbers died together on the Jungfrau in 1895.

Accidents were usually commented upon with a mixture of horror and contempt. When a party of eleven men died of cold and exposure on Mont Blanc in 1870, the *Illustrated London News* published an article beginning in the following offhand way: 'Another Alpine accident and another railway accident.' After the grim series of deaths in 1882, the *Guardian* spoke of 'the fatal desire of ascending a virgin peak'. In Meredith's novel *The Amazing Marriage*, the hero sprains his ankle in the Tyrol; when he is picked up, he lamely observes: 'I suppose I ought to have taken a guide,' and he receives the haughty answer: 'There's not a doubt of that . . . These freaks get us a bad name on the Continent.' In point of fact, the man had only been walking along a mule-path. Later a French novelist named Paul Hervieu coined the silly phrase *'l'alpe homicide'*, which provided sensational papers with a good headline for mountain accidents.

The disaster on the Matterhorn provoked Queen Victoria to write in her diary: 'Four poor Englishmen, including a brother of Lord Queensbery, have lost their lives in Switzerland, descending over a dangerous place from the Matterhorn and falling over a precipice.' But after the three accidents of 1882 she made her secretary, Sir Henry Ponsonby, write to Gladstone to inquire whether she could not do anything to register her strong disapproval of such dangerous ventures. Gladstone replied that he could see no way by which the Queen might take action. But discussions raged in the Press after each new tragedy. The worst aspect of such controversies was the fact that they robbed mountaineering of some of its dignity and fastened a garish label to it. A somewhat gruesome taste developed in Alpine resorts. Mountaineering accidents became 'news' and people evinced a morbid pleasure in discussing the details of the various tragedies. To say that in doing this they often showed bad taste and heartlessness is probably an understatement.

This attitude went so far that Meredith needed real courage when he advocated the cult of mountaineering in some of his novels. Although not a climber himself, he was a friend of Leslie Stephen and had heard his narratives of mountain expeditions. And so, while Ruskin was renewing his condemnation of mountaineering in *Fors Clavigera* and *Praeterita*, Meredith sounded a completely different note in *Harry Richmond*:

'Carry your fever to the Alps, you of minds deseased; . . . mount, rack the limbs, wrestle it out among the snow peaks; taste dangers, sweat, earn rest; learn to discover ungrudgingly that haggard fatigue is the fair vision you have run to earth and that rest is your utmost reward. . . . Poetic rhapsodists in the vales below may tell of the joy and grandeur of the upper regions, they cannot pluck you the medical herb. He gets that for himself who wanders the marshy ledge at nightfall to behold the distant Sennhüttchen twinkle, who leaps the green-eyed crevasses and in the solitude of an emerald alp stretches a salt hand to the mountain kine.'

Again, in *The Amazing Marriage*, he called mountaineering 'the noblest of pleasures . . . Up in those mountains one walks with the divinities'. In *The Egoist*, Vernon Whitford was a portrait of Leslie Stephen. By the end of the century, even non-climbers were able to realize or at least to imagine the splendours and miseries of mountaineering.

CHAPTER NINE

WINTER MOUNTAINEERING

UNTIL about 1870 scarcely anybody thought that mountains could be ascended after the end of the summer or, at the very latest, the end of September when the summer had been exceptionally dry. As soon as snow fell in the valleys the mountains were out of bounds. Mountaineers were few, and fewer still were those daring enough to accept that the mountains were still there for their pleasure even in the midst of winter. Yet, a handful of men thought that it might be interesting to go and see what they looked like under snow. They took to climbing before they could walk: by which I mean that winter mountaineering was born before skis were imported into western Europe.

The peasants of Valais and Oberland had had to contrive some means enabling themselves to move over the thick layer of snow which covered their fields and the mountain slopes in winter, and they made rough snow-shoes or racquets. Among summer visitors who were deeply in love with mountains, some realized that a totally virgin world would be revealed to them if they had the pluck to come to Switzerland or Savoy in January. Leslie Stephen wrote in October 1875 to his friend Gabriel Loppé, the Chamonix painter:

'I have conceived an idea which I want to mention to you. You often told me how beautiful the Oberland is during the winter. I have a sort of hunger for mountains and for the Oberland above all. I think I could leave London in January. Could you come and join me in Interlaken or Meiringen at that time?'[1]

It proved feasible and the trip was highly successful. For several years Leslie Stephen came back in winter, escorted by friends. In 1888, D. W. Freshfield accompanied him and Loppé photographed them both against a snowy background. When Leslie Stephen wrote to thank him, he commented on the photo in the following way:

'I think I am superb among the frost-covered trees (engivrés): is that the

[1] The originals belong to Mme Savine-Loppé, the painter's grand-daughter, who allowed me to use them. They are in French.

word?[1] And Freshfield is more than superb, he is sublime. He is Milton's Satan defying the Angel Gabriel, except that he stands on snow-covered ground, instead of Hell's fires. . . . I have had delightful associations with the Alps in winter'.

Walking over soft powdery snow, shod with rather primitive racquets, was quite exhausting, and yet the party tried to ascend a few mountains. Everything was different, the ground, the light, the colours and the climate. A 'dreamlike impression is everywhere pervading and predominant', wrote Leslie Stephen. Yet sometimes dreams can become nightmares and Stephen experienced this when his party tried to ascend the Galenstock in winter. Exhausted by an endless trudge up snow-covered slopes. Loppé became mountain sick and practically unable to continue. Things might have taken a very grim turn had he not recovered quickly after a short rest and some food.

Very daring climbs had been undertaken. In 1876, Miss Stratton ascended Mont Blanc with Jean Charlet and two other guides. She eventually married Charlet, who took the name of Charlet-Stratton. Mrs Aubrey le Blond also ascended Mont Blanc, and the Aiguille du Midi from Montenvers; in 1888 Miss Jackson, among other ascents, traversed the Jungfrau.

By that time, winter mountaineering had already been saddened by accidents. In 1864, a party including Philip Gosset, a Swiss friend of his, Boissonnet, the guide Joseph Bennen and three others, tried to ascend the Haut-de-Cry, a very dull mountain above Martigny. It is perfectly tame and uninteresting in summer: in winter it is both uninteresting and dangerous. On the ascent the party crossed a snow-filled couloir, not taking proper precautions, as nobody knew what precautions there were. The two guides, who led, sank into fresh snow and struggled violently to free themselves. This started an avalanche, which promptly overwhelmed the whole party. Eventually, two men were killed, Boissonnet and Bennen. Clearly, much had to be learned before winter mountaineering could be practised in reasonable safety. Local men knew no more than visitors from abroad; they never ventured above snow level after the cattle had been brought down, so there was nothing to induce them to go uphill.

At that juncture skis arrived to solve the problem of winter mountaineering. Skis as a means of progress on snow are quite old. A pre-historic ski has been found in a Swedish bog, and a hunter on ski is to be seen on a runic stone.

---

[1] *Engivré* does not exist in French, which is a pity. The next sentence is in English in the original.

There are drawings representing skiers in the earliest editions of Olaus Magnus' Chronicles (1555) and from then on descriptions and drawings have emerged at intervals. In 1647 a Danish maritime firm sent out a ship to reconnoitre the Norwegian coast. A French doctor, M. de la Martinière, happened to be in Copenhagen when they were recruiting a crew and he was accepted as surgeon. When he was back in France in 1671, he published *Nouveaux Voyages dans le Septentrion,* in which he records that, when he had entered Russian Lapland:

'We saw a Lapp hunting, sliding on snow as quickly as our sledge without foundering, thanks to his skates of bark, some seven feet long and four inches broad, flat underneath and hollowed out on top to place the foot. He held a spear in one hand and a bow in the other; on his back was a quiver full of arrows and he was followed by a huge black cat'.

This is one of the earliest descriptions of a skier in western literature.

At the same time, Henry Oldenburg, Secretary of the Royal Society, described skis while reporting a journey to Lapland, though he did not give these articles their local name, merely calling them snow-shoes. The first and longest description occurs in Johann Scheffer's *Laponia,* published in Latin in Strasbourg in 1674, translated the same year into French and in 1704 into English; it seems to have been a best-seller. Scheffer was quite an authority on ski. He used their local name, *skider* and *skier* for short, as well as *scheitter* in German. His description is accurate. He had brought home a pair and, as he was very thorough, one may assume that he tried them out, so that Alsace was really the first skiing resort in Europe, which is unexpected. Here is his description: 'The longer sole must be about one foot longer than the height of the man who uses it. The longer one is rubbed over with pitch or resin; the other is free from it. They are not quite straight but slightly curved up above, where one's puts one foot.' This is what he said of the bindings:

'The Laps usually tie the soles to their feet with a small hoop of pliant wood which goes from one side of the sole to the other, and is nailed to the thick of the wood. . . . The foot, once thrust into that circle, is fixed to the sole by a strap tied to the heel. Shod with their soles, they hold a stick, the lower end of which is stuck into a round bit of wood, to prevent it from sinking into the snow. They use the stick to steer themselves and to get impetus when starting.'

It has never been clearly understood why the skis were of unequal lengths. Here is the description of the Lapps' progress over the snow:

'They go straight up or down, turning over heaps of snow. Their speed is surprising over long stretches of snow-covered ground. They proceed not only on the flat, but also on high, precipitous and extremely rough ground, and they come down at great speed and without falling, which is past belief.'

Going up should be very difficult, but they have mastered the problem:

'They line their soles with the skins of young reindeers, which are most useful when they go uphill, as the hairs are brushed back, sticking out like hedgehogs' quills, and curving back so as to prevent them from slipping backwards.'

This very accurate description probably impressed readers, as all through the eighteenth century travellers to Lapland—there were not many, of course —always mentioned these curious wooden soles.

Among these travellers were a few interesting people. One of the first to follow Scheffer's route was Jean-Francois Regnard, a well-known French playwright. In 1681 he published his delightful *Voyage en Laponie*. As he went to Laponia in summer, he did not see skiers, but he was shown skis:

'A pair of those long wooden boards on which Lapps run with such extraordinary speed. They are very thick, about two *aunes* long and half a foot broad. They curve up in front and are pierced in the middle to admit a bit of leather which keeps the foot firm and tight. The Lapp who stands on them holds a long stick with a round piece of wood at one end, to prevent sinking in the snow, and an iron spear-head at the other. He uses the stick to give himself impetus at the start, to prop himself up when running and stop himself at will'.

La Mottraye, one of Charles XII's followers. Maupertuis, the President of the Berlin academy and Voltaire's favourite victim, and several others went north, saw skis and described them. In 1773, a Mr Joseph Marshall published his *Travels through Holland, Sweden, Lapland and Poland* in three large volumes. He has a few words on the subject: 'Many (of the peasants) have wooden shoes of their own making.' A very enterprising young man, the Chevalier de Bougrenet de la Tocnaye, of a very illustrious family, went to Sweden at the very end of the eighteenth century, saw skiers and conceived a brilliant idea: 'In the province of Bergen', he wrote in his *Promenade d'un Francais en Suède et en Norvège* (1801), 'in winter, the post is carried by a man who, equipped with these big skates, can cover distances at singular speed. . . . Time will come when other nations in Europe will know how to use these instruments, so useful and inexpensive.' Chamonix, as the biggest French skiing resort, should at least have erected a memorial slab to Bougrenet de la Tocnaye.

Years passed and skiing, before becoming a sport, became a kind of dream. In 1835 Balzac brought out *Seraphita*. The heroine of this short novel is an angel who used skis: at the beginning of the story, Seraphita and her companion Minna are skiing on the hills surrounding a fjord, the rough map of which Balzac drew on his manuscript:

'Were they human creatures or arrows? They whisked over the snow on long planks tied to their feet. . . . The person whom Minna had addressed as Seraphita balanced over her right heel to raise the plank about a *toise* long and as narrow as a child's foot, fixed to her shoe by two sealskin straps. The plank was about two inches thick, lined with reindeer hide, the hair of which, standing on end in the snow, suddenly stopped her.'

They proceed to ski down:

'A wonderful skill controlled their race or, rather, their flight. When they came to a snow-covered crevasse, Seraphita would grab Minna and promptly sail over the thin cover of the chasm, not weighing more than a bird. Sometimes, pushing her companion forward, she would make a turn to avoid a crevasse.'

Balzac's sources have not been discovered yet, though it seems likely that he had read Regnard. He never went to Norway or Sweden, and in the northern countries he visited skis were unknown. He had probably heard the account of someone who had travelled in Scandinavia and seen skiers in action. The novel was widely read and the episode quoted attracted the painter Tony Johannot, who illustrated the novel: he made a lovely drawing of the two girls on skis. Yet, for some fifty years more, skis remained unknown outside Sweden and Norway.

In 1883, Wilhelm Paulcke, a young German who was spending the winter in Davos, was given a pair of Norwegian skis, which he tried out at once, realizing how immensely useful they could be. For several years, and mostly in the Grisons, various pioneers experimented and discovered that skis were much more than amusing gadgets and that they were just round the corner from some fascinating development in mountain discovery.

In 1894, Dr Conan Doyle—not yet Sir Arthur—was in Davos, keeping his sick wife company and writing the *Brigadier Gerard* novels. To while away the time he luged in winter and tried organising a small golf course in summer. He discovered skis and how to use them while reading Dr Nansen's book on Greenland, and he thought it might be interesting to try skiing. He looked for possible skiers in the neighbourhood and the two brothers Branger were pointed out to him: they had made a number of winter ascents on racquets. Eventually the three men left on March 23, 1894, to traverse the Maienfelder Furka on skis. There were very tricky sections on the track which leads from Davos to Arosa.

During the following years a number of keen mountain lovers mastered the new means of conveyance to some extent and evolved a technique, a very primitive one of course. The whole point was how to find how to reach in winter the places which had so far only been reached in summer. Wilhelm Paulcke, together with de Beauclair, Lohmuller, Ehlert and Monnich skied across the main Oberland range. The next year, Paulcke and Helbling went very high on Monte Rosa. In 1897 Dr Paul Payot and his guide Joseph Ravanel-le-Rouge crossed the Col du Géant in winter. People refused to believe them until their tracks were detected on the Mont Fréty above Courmayeur. Then skiing moved ahead quickly: during the 1911–12 winter some forty pairs of skis were fitted and sold in Switzerland.

It seems that the very first skiers, once they had evolved an Alpine technique, which was obviously different from the Scandinavian one, concentrated on long tours which got them over many high passes. Dr Roget, who was half-English and half-Genevese, traversed the whole Bernese Oberland. He was one of the first to follow the High Level Route in winter; he went round the Bernina and traversed from Arosa to Bellinzona across the San Bernardino. Marcel Kurz's winter ascents and trips are too numerous to be listed. Eventually it was assumed that all summits could be ascended in winter: it was merely a matter of carrying one step farther the doctrine which had been unconsciously stated when the Brenva route had been opened by the Walkers and Moore: all the routes up to a summit had to be found, not merely the easiest. The first winter ascents followed the classical summer routes. Things were difficult enough without being made worse by too great a display of imagination.

While summer mountaineering was becoming slightly less strenuous, thanks to good huts which could be reached by good paths, where hot meals were sometimes obtainable, nothing of this kind could be found in winter. Huts could be used, but wood had to be carried up to them; bivouac equipment was primitive, and very little was known about frost-bite and its treatment. Yet a number of fine climbs were accomplished. The Schreckhorn was climbed in January 1879 by Coolidge with the three Almers; the Bernina in 1880 by C. E. B. Watson; while Vittorio Sella traversed the Matterhorn in 1882, ascended Monte Rosa in 1884 and traversed it in 1889. Beaujard, with Ravanel-le-Rouge, followed the High Level Route on ski in 1908. Owen Glynne Jones went up the Moore route on the Dent Blanche in April; Hasler made the first winter ascent of the Aiguille Verte in 1900 and the next year ascended the three main Oberland giants. Ryan ascended the Weisshorn in 1902. The Meije held out long and was not ascended until 1926, when Pierre Dalloz and D. Armand-Delille reached its summit. The latter also made the first winter ascent of the Ecrins. In 1936 Giusto Gervasutti made the first winter solitary ascent of the Italian ridge of the Matterhorn.

The early use of ski in the Alps had very important consequences. Shortly after they had began cutting a still shy figure on various gentle slopes, officers stationed in the French Alps thought that it might be vital to adapt the new device to military use. Lieutenant Wideman, a Swede of the Foreign Legion, stationed at Embrun, in the French Alps, studied the use both of racquets and skis, and decided that the latter were by far the best. With them he made the first winter ascent of the Mont St Guillaume. Another pioneer was Lieutenant Dunod, who traversed the Lautaret in 1897. The first senior officer who fully realized how vitally important ski could be was General Baron Berge, the military Governor of Lyons, who in 1892 studied the subject and organized mountain troops, stationed at various strategical points. Skis were manufactured in Briançon and Grenoble, but civilians on the whole were not much interested at first. Later, a Swedish military mission came to France and one of its members, Captain Lilienhaeck, found followers among the French troops. The first military skiing competition was held in 1902 and the French War Office organised a skiing school in Briançon under Captains Clerc and Bernard, with a Norwegian instructor, Captain Angell. When war broke out in 1914 Angell enlisted in the Foreign Legion and fought for France, and Captain Trygwe Gran, who had been the skiing specialist in Captain Scott's expedition, fought in the British Army.

Much was done to develop a taste for skiing among the younger Alpine population, and little by little children took to it. When they reached the age of military service, an increasing number of recruits applied for service in the Alpine ski troops. In 1907 the Army and the French Alpine Club organized the first international ski competition at Mont Genèvre. There were 3,000 spectators and General Galliéni was President.

After the war of 1914–18, military skiing increased by leaps and bounds. Each *chasseur* battalion had its skiing section. General Dosse created the Sections d'Eclaireurs Skieurs (SES) and eventually, in 1932, succeeded in putting together an Ecole de Haute Montagne (EHM), to give a technical and tactical training to selected recruits, so that they could lead military operations in the mountains all the year round.

Eventually, in 1935, the EHM was stationed at Chamonix and had to try to decide what was the best kind of equipment for mountain operations. In this way the equipment evolved which, a few years later, was found to be perfectly adequate for fighting conditions in Norway. The first instructors were Captain Pourchier, who died in the Struthof concentration camp, Lieutenant Villiers d'Isle-Adam, who was killed at Dunkirk, and Lieutenant (now General) Jacques Faure, an inspired leader during the war in Algeria. He was several times French military champion for long distance skiing, and he captained the French military ski team. Here is the description he gave of the activities of EHM:

'We were not restricted to mere technique. The school was to become the centre where young officers of the Alpine army were to get to know each other, to forge powerful ties of friendship, become integrated into a whole and get to know better the part they were to play. The mountain was to be no mere stadium for difficult performances, but a realm in which technique, physical effort, daring, self-control and poise could be perfectly blended in an atmosphere of mutual trust and truthfulness. . . . Men of my generation are immensely in its debt, for it gave us two priceless things: pride in our calling, and joy in life, through doing our job properly. It enabled us to understand better what an extraordinary school for human training a mountain is. . . . As I was commanding the National Military Ski Team, each winter brought me back to the valley of Chamonix. Mont Blanc kept all its mystery, but it was also a friend, the witness of so many days filled with deep meaning and true happiness.'

The part played by the EHM in clandestine fighting during the war will be told later in this book.

Another skiing and mountaineering school was organized shortly before the Second World War. It was eventually called the Ecole Nationale de Ski et d'Alpinisme (ENSA). At that stage there was already an organisation for training future instructors. It was first sited on the Col de Voza, above the valley of Chamonix, and the principal instructor was the Austrian Rebyska. Quite a number of the best French skiers attended the course. Then, under various names, and under the direction of the Fédération Française de Ski, the school flourished in Val d'Isère, and later in the Alpe d'Huez, even during the war years. Eventually, in 1954, it became formally the ENSA, working first in Chamonix in summer and Alpe d'Huez in winter; then it moved to Les Praz-de-Chamonix and finally to Chamonix itself in 1952. The present Director is Jean Franco, who was the leader of the French expeditions to Makalu and Jannu. It is attended each year by an increasing number of pupils, both French and foreign. They do the most difficult climbs in both summer and winter.

CHAPTER TEN

'OBEY THE LAW'

EVERY sport, including mountaineering, gets the literature and the adepts it deserves. After a time it becames possible to weigh with some accuracy its splendours and its miseries through the narratives or interpretations of its adepts whether these have been put forward boldly or stammered out like painful confessions. A spiritual reality slowly emerges from almost inarticulate utterances. One of the striking aspects of mountaineering is the fact that one can hardly find two climbers who indulge in it for identical reasons.

Many go up the mountains simply because their friends do so, and they feel that it is an obvious thing to do; it is, for example, a normal week-end entertainment. This frequently occurs in countries like Switzerland, Austria, south-eastern France, or southern Germany, where mountains are within easy reach. One might almost say that such people climb from lack of imagination. They often accomplish very great climbs, consider them ordinary achievement, and feel no pride in them afterwards.

But most climbers hold a more personal view of mountaineering and many have taken the trouble to give some shape, literary or otherwise, to their ideas. The latter are varied and it is difficult to arrive at a comprehensive interpretation of them. Yet it may be useful to try to ascertain why people climb. Since the days when great mountains began to inspire a keen interest, one notion has had time to die out completely; strangely enough, it is the very notion which was first taken as justifying the pursuit of mountaineering, the advancement of science. Apart from this, every old incentive to climb has remained active, although under more or less different aspects.

Why does one climb? There have been many replies, several of them inadequate, since climbers are often inarticulate or they articulate badly. The French writer Samivel, who was also a good climber, has attempted to offer what he calls a 'coldly realistic' explanation of the usefulness of mountains. His words are not cold but I have been unable to detect their realism under a downpour of excited adjectives and italics in a language which sometimes borders on gibberish. The author is a poet who thinks he is a philosopher. A more convincing and much shorter text is the cry of ecstasy

uttered by Whymper's porter Luc Meynet, the hunchback of Breuil, when he
exclaimed: 'O you, my beautiful mountains!'

In 1899 A. D. Godley composed the following verse:

'Place me somewhere in the Valais, 'mid the mountains west of Binn,
West of Binn and east of Savoy, in a decent kind of inn,
With a peak or two for climbing, and a glacier to explore—
Any mountains will content me, though they've all been climbed before—
Yes! I care not any more
Though they've all been done before
And the names they keep in bottles may be numbered by the score.'

This is probably one of the purest forms of mountain love: the deep
affection awakened by the beauty of Alpine forms has not been in any way
adulterated. And these lines convey more than the pleasure inspired by a
beautiful landscape. Light and perfunctory as they may appear, they express
one kind of complete communion with nature, deeper than what may be
hinted at in more ambitious verses. Mountain landscapes are disconcerting
and one requires both vision and feeling to grasp their secret. Alpine scenery
above the snow-line is almost impossible to imagine, difficult to describe and
hopeless to paint. It is a world apart, removed from earthly contacts, different
from anything one may have seen elsewhere. When going high, one feels
that one may catch a glimpse of the very features of Nature herself; and she
has discarded the veils which she wears in settings less stark and bare.

Nature reigns supreme. The solitude of a great glacier is one of its potent
charms in an age when life is so overcrowded that one has difficulty even in
preserving the integrity of one's mind. But the climber can wander for hours
and even for days, alone in a world of rocks and snow and sun. The remote
presence of another party makes little difference; the scale is so huge that
three or four tiny figures in the distance are just dwarfed to nothingness.
Sounds, too, are engulfed in the vast silence which they only serve to enhance.
Yet the silence on mountain heights is never complete. The tinkling of a
breaking icicle, the thud of a stone falling on to a patch of snow, the clear
clatter of a pebble hurtling down an ice-slope, the gurgle of a stream under
the ice, render even more overpowering the hush of windless days. The mind
becomes more alert, readier to take in the mystic peace which encom-
passes it.

Solitude gives greater power to the longing for independence that every
climber carries at the bottom of his heart. He is far from human help or
hindrance; he faces the mountains alone, relying on nothing but his own
strength and skill to reach his goal, the summit. Whatever help he can

derive from his climbing implements is small compared with the mighty defences of the mountains. Yet it is a fair contest in which the climber is at least protected from human interference.

Some people climb in order to find isolation from the madding crowd and the world as a whole. Desiring escape from a life monopolized by man, they find themselves in a hard geological world in which everything is instinct with eternity. They seek to lose their identities in the wastes of snow and ice. Others climb mountains to recapture their memories. 'Something of our personality has gone into every mountain on which we have spent out strength and on which our thoughts have rested, and something of its personality has come into ours and had its small effect on everything that has come within our influence,' wrote R. L. G. Irving in *Relativity in Mountaineering*.

Every climb is an adventure. However well known the route, however numerous former parties may have been, one can rely only partly on past experience. Mountains are alive, and they change from day to day, even from hour to hour. Past experience is useful but is never proof against danger. Mountains refuse to be enslaved by any law. One has to put up with their independence, trust to common sense and also to luck.

The will to master a sluggish, shy or rebellious nature is a powerful incentive, and probably one of the strongest incentives to climbing. There is more in it than mere pride: a kind of ascetic longing, not always conscious, urges a man to accept with pleasure, and often with delight, deadly fatigue, cold, heat, breathlessness, lack of sleep, hunger, thirst and the constant threat of danger. There is a moral satisfaction in the knowledge that sheer will-power has compelled the body to undergo such trials without faltering. Many are the climbers who preserve a radiant memory of some hard ascent achieved under adverse conditions, of some victory snatched out of the teeth of a gale, of hours of fighting through a blizzard, of a summit reached in so thick a mist that one knew it was the summit only because the snow or rocks sloped down in every direction. But the climb was done and it had been hard. It was a victory, not so much over the mountains—which are never really defeated—as over oneself. Every climber can remember nights in a hut when he fervently prayed for rain or anything, even an earthquake, that would save him from the ordeal of the next day. Getting up at one or two in the morning and preparing for the climb is a torture one goes through with clenched teeth, and the first hour is even worse, when one doggedly keeps going, staggering over a steep crumbling moraine or up the lower reaches of a glacier. The mind is a blank; through it tinkles only some idiotic slogan which acts as a drug, for too clear a thought might snap the unconscious will to continue. After one hour, and usually at sunrise, the first battle is won and the mind is taking in again all the new and delightful impressions born on a mountain. Over-civilized beings feel happy under the obligation of going back for a short time to primitive life. A friend of mine became almost lyrical when telling how delightful it was to shovel peas into one's mouth with a piton.

The very element of danger is also a strong incentive. A constant threat can materialize at any moment, even on easy expeditions. The fight against great odds is a perpetual gamble; indeed some instinct for gambling is a necessary factor in mountaineering.

An Alpine expedition, even when many parties have already accomplished it, is always something of a exploration. Any peak one has not yet climbed oneself is new, can show itself in the most stupendous aspects and usually does. It is always a quest for the unknown, to quench a thirst for new sensations and new landscapes. The more one climbs, the more one longs for such new aspects of a world one never can see frequently enough. One has but to read a few of the innumerable descriptions of climbs on Mont Blanc to realize how many people have felt in different ways the inspiring beauty of the great mountain. On fine days, parties can be seen literally in queues on the Bosses ridge; yet nothing can really soil or tarnish a mountain such as this.

There is nothing more human, more instinctive or more unpredictable than the love of mountains. Pride and self-sufficiency come into it, as well as 'the joy of comradeship and the thrill of strife', to quote Geoffrey Winthrop Young's poem, *The Treasure of the Heights*. Or, as he wrote elsewhere, 'we may take from the mountains when the time comes for memory and reflection, a perfected home for our thoughts, more generous, more liberal even than their own, great spaces of air and height and freedom'. Mountains enable man's soul and mind to find a perfect fulfilment to their aspirations. Mallory once wrote that 'a day well spent in the Alps is like a great symphony.' I have already quoted his serene interpretation of the message of the mountains: 'To struggle and to understand—never the last without the other; such is the law . . . and we understand . . . a little more. So ancient, wise and terrible— and yet kind we see them, with steps for children's feet.'

The French climber Pierre Dalloz has also tried to formulate the message, but his restless and passionate spirit has found expression in a succession of images and sensations which are in strong contrast to Mallory's:

'Mountains are not the infinite but they suggest it. They have been confused with altitude; as well confuse the soul with the faces that reveal it, or truth with the evidence of itself.

'When the blood throbs in our temples, and the ice-cold air dries up our throat and penetrates our whole being like a fluid, life-giving, infinitely precious;

'When we no more feel hunger, but only thirst, when nothing exists for us but effort, thought and gesture;

'When the cold freezes the ice-axe to the hand and the horizon is blurred by the tears with which it fills the eyes;

'When the face the earth shows us is like the face of a living thing, but the lined face of one who has suffered much;

'When in a single picture are laid bare the old rents and wounds, the intricate joints and foldings that built up the mountain chains, the meetings and the partings of the waters;

'When all life, animal and vegetable, is absorbed into the great crucible below;

'When there comes up from the valleys to die at our feet the voice of geological ages, the groan of the labouring earth, made up of countless murmurs from below, the plaints of erosion, of water and of the wind;

'. . . When the silence itself is so complete and so perfect that it pains our senses;

'When we feel a tremor thrill through space itself;

'When we see the stars shining in the light of day;

'When the light shoots straight down to us out of unfathomable dark, transparent depths, like a light whose reflector has been lost;

'When the light strikes directly in our eyes without hurting us, but is reflected from the newly fallen snow with blinding violence;

'Then we know altitude again.

'. . . In the serenity of altitude, like many of our predecessors, we sought appeasement for the passion of our twentieth year . . .

'It gave us the complete fulfilment of our dream, it proved to us our worth, and in spite of the event which had robbed us of war[1] it allowed us to taste the intoxicating pleasures of the heroic life. . . . This craving for altitude, for danger and for death, for the inexplicable mystery of self, is a new form of the sin of knowledge, the oldest of all sins, which cost us our happiness and our certitude.'

Another French climber, Georges Sonnier, wrote: '[Among mountains] the time of desire and restlessness is dead . . . It is better to deserve a triumph than to seize it by sheer strength. Every real conquest comes from the soul.' A statement which Scott Russell echoed in different words:

---

[1] That of 1914–18: Dalloz was just too young to be called up.

'Our arrival on the summit seemed to be a flat and most inadequate climax. To stand there was nothing; it was the making of the ascent to which I had looked forward and that was over. A long-cherished hope had by its realization been annihilated; something was missing now—an absurd feeling perhaps, but nevertheless sincere.'

Other elements combine in the will to climb. An intensely personal feeling, it can be tinged with the finer shades of any personality, and this accounts for the various conceptions which have developed among modern climbers. Mountain-lovers may have heard a message: 'To the God-starved, [the mountains] often spell God; to the hungry they are love and to the confined they are freedom,' wrote Wilfrid Noyce in *Mountains and Men*. One of the finest mountain books, Scott Russell's *Mountain Prospect*, was written in a Japanese prison camp. The author's best means of preserving his sanity and self-control was to concentrate on a landscape which was the embodiment of liberty and solitude, the two major dreams of a prisoner in an overcrowded camp.

Yet one must avoid placing the mountains in too spiritual a world apart: mountains are not the infinite, as Pierre Dalloz said; neither are they a path towards moral perfection. A long tradition has tended to smother them in a cloud of confused and sentimental notions dating back to the eighteenth century, when it was decreed that mountain-dwellers were pure and saintly. A better knowledge of the high valleys enabled later travellers to discover that they were neither purer nor more saintly than those who lived in the plains. But such traditions never die; henceforth, mountains were reputed to exercise a moral influence on climbers. All sorts of legends blossomed out of this optimistic belief. Mountains were credited with bringing understanding among men. The French novelist François Mauriac—who was by no means a climber—went so far as to write in a preface: 'Above a certain height it is impossible to nourish evil thoughts; there are some thoughts which cannot flourish except in the lowlands . . . on the peaks a coarse creature becomes less coarse and a noble being may sometimes meet God.' A surprising recollection of the antiquated eighteenth-century assumption by the pen of a man who stood as the champion of Roman Catholicism!

On the other hand Jacques Boell, the French mountaineer for whom Mauriac wrote his preface, pointed out in a straightforward way: 'After almost twenty years of climbing and mixing with fellow-enthusiasts, I do not know of a single idealist among us who goes in for difficult climbs with the idea of improving himself.' Obviously mountains teach self-reliance, clearheadedness, foresight, how to pack a rucksack and how to control one's temper when one is tired, exasperated, cold, thirsty or scared. The conscious effect of their lesson does not go much farther. An Italian professor of mathematics who has recently been placed among the Blessed by the church of Rome, Contardo Ferrini, was quite matter-of-fact when he wrote:

'Allow me to take this child to our Alps. By overcoming Nature's obstacles, he will be taught how to overcome the other obstacles life will throw in his way; he will discover how to enjoy the rising sun from the ridge of a peak and the setting sun when it sets fire to the great glaciers . . . He will come down a man and his moral conscience will not be any the worse for it.'

Ferrini had done some climbing and knew what he was writing about. For an Italian and a future saint he was remarkably modest and realistic.

Discussions one overhears in mountain huts might even convince the sunniest optimist of the total intellectual helplessness of many climbers. What can be expected of persons who, when offered an interesting rock-climb as an alternative to a tougher peak, when the weather was rapidly deteriorating, replied: 'Nothing doing! I only do sixth grade climbs'? Or of the man who argued about the number of pitons he had to hammer into the north wall of such and such a peak to save half an hour on his time-table? I have actually heard these remarks in Alpine huts, and yet the persons in question really loved mountains in their own way and enjoyed their climbs. Jacques Lagarde, the French climber and critic, once wrote in a review that 'one finds in a mountain just what one has brought to it'. While making allowances for the hard, clear-cut formula which was characteristic of its author, one must admit that it is the best and probably the only explanation of so many different kinds of mountain love.

During the early years of the twentieth century the number of new and difficult climbs accomplished every year was large and a galaxy of remarkable mountaineers appeared in every country. With the removal of former hindrances, the constant evolution of climbing technique and the help given by higher and more numerous huts, mountaineering had now achieved great efficiency. Even more than before, it was becoming a matter of personalities, a fact which made its development dependent on many unexpected factors.

Guideless climbing had been accepted as a means to further development. Yet there were various ways of climbing without guides and all of them were to be tested. The results were of widely differing value. R. L. G. Irving, who was a master at Winchester, had given up climbing with guides on account of boredom and expense. For a time he climbed without any companion, but the nervous strain was too great; then at last he discovered a new method. He decided to train recruits and, with this in view, travelled in the Alps for five successive summers with two of his Winchester pupils. One of them was George Mallory, who was then seventeen. Irving took them up various peaks, some easy, some very difficult. The first ascent was that of the Velan and it ended in failure, as the two boys collapsed with mountain-sickness. Yet by the end of the summer they had become hardened climbers. Irving's methods were severely criticized by more orthodox members of the Alpine Club, who went as far as to publish a note of protest in the *Alpine Journal*, in which they disclaimed any responsibility for methods of training so drastic. Yet it seems that Irving's ideas have been adopted by various organizations.

It was not surprising that Mallory, after such an introduction to the Alps, should have become the climber and writer he was. As a mountaineer he gave his full measure. After the summers during which he served as a recruit under Irving, he developed into a remarkable leader. He always wondered why mountains meant so much to him and tried to give form to their message. Some of his friends thought that he tried too hard and argued too much: 'He was often in the clouds, but always trying to get above them,' wrote Irving. Yet climbs meant far more to him than reaching summits in good time. Irving says:

'In the wonderful season of 1911 we were on Mont Blanc again; this time three of us. Six years after, when he was at the front in Flanders, Mallory wrote an account of this climb. For him, it was a triumph of mind and will over the body. Something eaten at the hut the night before had poisoned him; he felt rotten all the long morning. In places, his description reads like a confession of deadly sins. He accidentally upset our lovely hot breakfast at 12,000 feet; then he fell asleep when I thought he was holding my rope as I cut steps in steep ice. But his will and nervous energy kept him going to the end. Even when the difficulties and excitement were over, her refused to shirk a last plod to the summit when an easy descent to Chamonix was open to us. This is how he ends his account: ". . . Have we vanquished an enemy? None but ourselves. Have we gained success? That word means nothing here."'

This was exactly the state of mind in which Mallory went out to Everest. There was also a possible wish to escape from the close, suffocating atmosphere of the Bloomsbury group, of which he was one, dancing attendance on Lytton Strachey. He took part in three successive expeditions and then disappeared on the mountain with his companion.

Another way of facing new mountain problems was discovered in France shortly before the First World War. Up to that time the level of French guide-less climbing had been very low. Apart from a few exceptions like Pierre Puiseux, E. Thorant (who was killed on the Grand Pic de la Meije), Maurice Paillon and J. Capdepon, very little had been achieved by French climbers, even on French mountains. Things began to change by 1907. An increasing number of young men, intent on discovering for themselves what mountains meant, began risking the ascent of great peaks without professional leaders. Various names may be quoted, amongst others the brothers Jacquemart, G. Paimparey, Philipe Le Bec. These men undertook long traverses among the Chamonix Aiguilles and later in the Oberland. By 1913 Le Bec and Jacques de Lépiney took the lead and began their great Alpine career with a few friends. There was already a girl in the party, Mme Alice Damesme (she was not then married), who in 1913 made a first ascent in the Aiguilles Rouges of Chamonix with J. de Lépiney and her fiancé. The outbreak of the war put everything back, but a few months earlier these young people had founded the 'Groupe des Rochassiers'. During the First World War, when some of the members were on leave, they achieved a few great climbs, all of them extremely severe and requiring unshakable will-power, endurance and imagination. They ascended the Trident du Tacul, for example, and forced a new route up the Aiguille du Peigne. Danger and death were in the air and these new ascents were made in an atmosphere of constant risk; falling rock or an exploding shell were equal means of destruction. Yet with traditional hatred of extreme solutions, French climbers usually stopped short of suicidal expeditions. When they described their adventures in the club magazines, they had re-course to deliberate and even exaggerated understatement. A 'solution élégante' (the word is not as stale in French as in English) meant a desperate attempt to force one's way up a snow- or rock-face of unusual severity.

Early results were encouraging and a new step was taken at the end of the war, when life was becoming normal again. At that time the leading climbers were Jacques de Lépiney, who was later joined by his younger brother Tom, Paul Chevalier, Henry Bregeault and Phillipe Le Bec. In 1919, during a bivouac on the Peuteret Ridge, they decided to found the Groupe de Haute Montagne—GHM for short—an enlarged and improved successor to the earlier Groupe des Rochassiers. Conceived in such auspicious and impres-sive surroundings, the new group was to be a superlative Club Alpin Français, to which none but first-class climbers would gain admittance. The club was in due course founded, and later developed into an independent and exclusive association. Technically all the members were men—or women—who could lead a rope on severe climbs; most of them climbed always with-out guides. The standard of difficulty, which was very high, was calculated to ensure the greatest Alpine efficiency among the members. The group published a periodical, *Alpinisme,* extremely well edited, illustrated with superb photographs and containing a great wealth of information. Yet one vaguely feels that the contributors are taking mountains too much as a purely practical problem. A scientific diagram which explains the succession of couloirs and traverses up a precipice may be illuminating, but it can hardly be said to convey any mountain message, anything of spiritual or aesthetic significance.

Within a few years, the high ideals and strenuous methods of the GHM began to bear fruit. A number of young French climbers were becoming outstanding figures in the mountaineering world. Most of them were intellectuals and all of them in climbing were using their brains as much as their limbs. Their narratives reveal men of strong personality, of great and often justified self-confidence, a business-like knowledge of mountains, but a kind of shyness in expressing their innermost reaction to the mountains. Pierre Dalloz is one of the few members of the group who have succeeded in breaking the crust of self-consciousness. He has written two short mountain essays, from one of which an extract has already been quoted.

The brothers de Lépiney have related several of their climbs in the range of Mont Blanc. These were well-organized assaults on heavily-defended fortresses, but the authors' clear-headedness, their measured style, reflecting a constant control of the faculties, and their cool appreciation of danger, convey an impression of poise and strength. However sombre a situation might be, it is never reflected in their style. De Lépiney writes:

'My impetus is stopped by an ice slab from which a few snow-covered rocks hardly emerge. I do not like the idea of asking for Picard's ice-axe; he is standing motionless on the spot where he helped me up. With the utmost care I climb on by means of tiny ice-coated holds. Anyone can realize what would be the painful results for the party should the first man fall in such a place. Crouching beneath a projecting rock, my feet in the snow, I wait for my companions; an impressive moment made uncomfortable by the cold.'

Yet sometimes the author succeeds in drawing a very vivid portrait of one of the members of the party struggling up a difficult pitch. Snapshots have too often discouraged such an effort, and references to climbing companions do not go much further than the mention of names. One of the most striking members of the group was Jacques Lagarde.

'With his calm, wilful temper, his bold and perfect technique and that intrepid courage which challenges bad luck, Lagarde is not what we call an athlete. He is rather tall, slim and wiry, and one would expect him to be better at skilful evading action than in a desperate struggle. And yet his resistance to fatigue, cold and snow is almost unique. Instead of trying to find a way of circumventing an obstacle, he loves a route which goes straight up, compelling him to fight his way to the very summit.'

The great climbs made by members of the GHM can be counted by the score; they took place in every possible Alpine district, from Chamonix to the Dolomites and from the Engadine to Dauphiny. The most severe of these expeditions were carefully prepared long before the event and the results were sometimes surprising. When Lagarde and Armand Charlet were planning to lead two ropes up the Nant Blanc face of the Aiguille Verte,—a sheer precipice of ice, swept at times by avalanches—they went up in a plane to reconnoitre the place. Charlet, who was abominably sick the whole time, saw nothing; as for Lagarde, he noticed with dismay that from the air any mountain, even the easiest, looks completely forbidding and unassailable—a fact which did not help them much in planning their route.

Although lists of names do not convey much to the reader, a few of these climbers are to be remembered, those who opened new routes and loved the mountains to the end. Edy Stofer, who was smothered by an avalanche on the Col de la Fourche; Léon Zwingelstein, the solitary climber who was killed on the Pic d'Olan; Bobi Arsandaux, who fell from the Verte because his rope was too old and broke on a belay; E. de Gigord, who fell from the Younggrat on the Breithorn; Choisy, who, after taking a leading part in a rescue party on the Dru, was killed on the Meije; Jean Morin, one of the finest of French climbers between the two wars, whose plane was lost at sea between Algiers and Gibraltar in 1943, when coming back from a mission to the Free French headquarters; finally Georges Vernet, who died in Dachau, and Captain Pourchier, who died at Schirmeck.

One of the most original features of GHM activity is the part played by women climbers. Several women were among the early members. Besides Mme Damesme, there were Mme Loustalot, who was killed on the Aiguille Verte with her husband; Mrs Miriam Underhill (*née* O'Brien); Mme Micheline Morin (Jean Morin's sister); Mme Nea Morin (*née* Barnard and Jean Morin's wife); Signorina Pietrasanta, and others. After being for a few years members of guideless parties, some of these young women started climbing with only women as their comrades. The venture was not quite without precedent, for, according to Colonel Strutt, Mrs Aubrey Le Blond (under her three names of Burnaby, Main and Aubrey le Blond) and Lady MacDonnell climbed the Piz Palü before 1900 without a man in their party. The new manless parties ascended difficult peaks and found new routes. Mrs Underhill climbed the Mönch with Mlle Morin, and climbed the Roche Méane and the Matterhorn with Mme Damesme. Mme Damesme and Mlle Morin climbed the Vajolettürme in the Dolomites, the Aiguille Verte and the Meije, as well as the Aiguille de Blaitière and many other peaks, with Mme Morin. One of the most daring woman climbers is Mlle L. Boulaz of Geneva, who has accomplished the most difficult expeditions in the Alps sometimes with, sometimes without a man in the party. Dorothy Pilley (Mrs I. A. Richards) has also often climbed with two other women. There were few comments on such expeditions; specialists accepted them as satisfactory new solutions to old problems while non-specialists failed to see what was so original about them. These parties never had accidents. Though Mrs Underhill once wrote that 'a few women are a little ahead of a few of the worst men,' she and her companions know how reliable women may be.

The years which elapsed between the two world wars were the great period of guideless climbing in every country and under all conditions. Alpine clubs were founded among the students of German and Swiss universities. All the men who became outstanding mountaineers and led the great overseas expeditions had trained in the Alps without guides.

Throughout this period, one is struck by the number of attempts, at once wilful and systematic, made by the same climber on the same mountain or, at least, the same sort of climb. Whereas, in former years, mountaineers had pitted their strength against any peak, snow or rock, modern climbers are specialists who work out their own technique and keep to it, so that they tackle only those peaks on which they can display their special gifts to the best advantage. Yet one of the most versatile of specialists was Geoffrey Winthrop Young. In his book *On High Hills* one can find a number of main lines along which his extraordinary mountain career developed. The author was a poet as well as a climber, and his logical mind enabled him to get the most out of any mountain expedition. His idea of traversing the Lyskamm and Castor and Pollux in both directions on one expedition, in order to punish a lazy and incompetent guide, or of climbing three groups of Chamonix Aiguilles in succession on the same day, in order to experience the intellectual satisfaction of a performance almost geometrically perfect, were not merely spectacuar. One gathers that, owing to his exceptional physical and intellectual poise, he could drain complete enjoyment out of every instant spent on a great mountain, and that he wished to drink it to the full. This accounts for his discovery of so many ways up the Weisshorn and other great peaks, ridges of great severity which appeal to his exacting mind. It accounts, too, for his conquest of the south face of the Taeschhorn with V. J. Ryan in 1906, at a time when neither rope-soled shoes nor pitons were in use.

This was one of the most daring and desperate climbs in the Alps, and has been repeated very seldom, by crack parties aware of fighting a relentless battle against tremendous odds. René Dittert thought that it was the worst climb he had ever attempted, as unreliable rocks made bad pitches even worse than they looked. The 1906 party, after hours of extremely severe climbing, came to an overhang; climbing out and over it seemed to be beyond human possibility. With almost incredible skill, the first guide, Franz Lochmatter, managed to pass the ice-glazed rocks; it was a demented struggle and yet to retreat was altogether out of the question. When it was G. W. Young's turn, he had to repeat the same struggle, for the rope gave him little more than moral support.

'I reached up and back with both arms, got hold of a finger-grip, and gained another inch. Infinitesimal inches they seemed, each a supreme effort, until my nose and chin scratched up against a fillet of the cornice. Then the arms gave out completely, so much at the end of their strength that they dropped lifeless. But the teeth of the upper jaw held on a broken spillikin and, with the stronger succour of the rope, supported me for the seconds while the blood was running back into my arms.

'Wrestle by wrestle it went on. Every reserve of force seemed exhausted, but the impulse was now supplied by a flicker of hope. Until at last, I felt my knee catch over a moulding on the edge, and I could sink forward for an instant's rest, with racked clothes clinging over the rough, steep, upward but *backward* curving of the dome. It is impossible to suggest the relief of that feeling, the proof that the only solid surface which still kept me in touch with existence had ceased to thrust itself out for ever as a barrier overhead, and was actually giving back below me in semi-support.'

The passage is typical of its author, who could both sustain such an effort and keep his mind clear and detached enough to analyse and memorize each detail. When the First World War had temporarily broken his career, owing to the severe wounds he had received, he was justified in writing:

> 'I dream my feet upon the starry ways;
>   My heart rests in the hill.
> I may not grudge the little left undone;
>   I hold the heights, I keep the dreams I won.'

Yet his indomitable spirit was not broken and he succeeded in climbing again for several summers.

Few mountaineers had the gifts necessary for such concentration. Yet there have been a number of specialists in certain ranges or in certain techniques who have devoted most of their Alpine careers to solving a particular problem. The brothers Gugliermina, climbing sometimes with, sometimes without guides, waged a long campaign against the southern face of the Monte Rosa group, and then against the southern arêtes of Mont Blanc. They succeeded in reconnoitring and traversing new cols and reaching the various Monte Rosa summits along still virgin ridges, but they achieved even more striking results when ascending Mont Blanc, first by the Brouillard and then by the Innominata ridges, traversing and naming on their way the Col Emile Rey and the Pic Luigi Amedeo. These last were climbs of unquestionable difficulty, along endless wind-swept arêtes. Yet in their ardent stories of these ascents, they showed themselves keenly aware of the wild beauty of the scenery, its huge and yet well-proportioned details and the radiant light in which they basked, even at grips with the worst pitches. Their excitement sometimes carried them far. When attempting a new ascent of the Aiguille Verte, they described themselves as 'knights-errant out to assault the strength of La Belle Dame sans Merci'. They were excellent photographers, and referring to their bedroom, the walls of which were covered with photos of the Matterhorn, they said that the room was 'invaded by Cervins'. The prints had been named in the heroic style: *Semiramis, Helen, Ophelia, Brunhild, Lalage, Penthesilea, Cordelia, Elsa* . . . etc.

Most climbers are more sedate and do not indulge in such wildly romantic fantasy. G. I. Finch's accounts of his expeditions impress the reader by their cool effectiveness. A remarkable climber, he delighted in the difficult routes which he found up many great peaks, in many districts, even as far as Corsica.

So did Frank Symthe. Besides his several expeditions to the Himalayas and the Canadian Rockies, he did much strenuous climbing in the Alps, such as the traverse of the Aiguille Blanche de Peuteret, the Innominata ridge, and a new route up and down the Bietschhorn. He was extremely quick uphill, his endurance was great, he was inured to cold, fatigue and mountain-sickness to a high degree, and he had a strong sense of humour, no mean asset on any long climb. Another great asset was his deep enjoyment of Alpine scenery, even under the worst conditions: he could feel the beauty of a dreadful storm on the Schreckhorn, during which he was struck by a flash of lightning, or of a ski-run at Verbier under heavy snow.

In 1927 and 1928, with Professor Graham Brown, Smythe found two new routes in the Mont Blanc range, leading straight up the ice-precipices of Mont Blanc and Mont Blanc de Courmayeur from the Brenva glacier. The routes branched off at a small pinnacle of red granite which they named the

Sentinelle Rouge. Both expeditions were among the most notable of the century. During most of the time Frank Smythe led up ice couloirs where stones were likely to come down at any moment, up hard blue-ice ridges, or across walls of séracs of questionable reliability. It meant hours of step-cutting; speed was vital, since parts of both routes became death traps when the sun fell upon shaky séracs higher up on the face. The route up the Mont Blanc de Courmayeur was the worst, an experience so nerve-racking that both climbers were haunted by a ghostly presence and vaguely felt that there was a third man on their rope.

Professor Graham Brown, in spite of his numerous great climbs in various districts, was devoted to Mont Blanc, on which he had done eighteen different routes. Climbing usually with the guide Alexander Graven, he ascended all the difficult routes on the south face, including a second climb of the Mont Blanc de Courmayeur without a bivouac under the Sentinelle Rouge. Ten days after this, he opened up another new route on the same forbidding face, the Via della Pera. The 'Pear' is a vaguely triangular mass of rocks directly under the summit of the Mont Blanc de Courmayeur. Its three sides are overhung by walls of séracs and one has to climb under their constant threat, and the second party to make this ascent, consisting of the Swiss André Roch and R. Gréloz, had a narrow escape from an avalanche of ice-blocks. Professor Graham Brown also climbed the final ice-cone of Mont Blanc on the Chamonix side, half-way between the Bosses ridge and the Corridor. He wrote to me: 'I had always thought it strange that a face so often seen had never been climbed straight up.'

Another major climb was accomplished by a British party: this was the north face of the Dent Blanche ascended by Mr and Mrs I. A. Richards, with a guide from Evolène, Joseph Georges le Skieur.

Several first-class mountaineers stand out among the large company of Swiss climbers; among them are André Roch, G. de Rham, E. R. Blanchet, R. Gréloz, R. Dittert and others. They have attempted with success what were apparently the most unassailable faces, and yet they have sufficient self-respect or common sense not to go beyond the limit of justifiable risk, though they have borrowed the technique of the most reckless German climbers. André Roch coolly analysed the process which brought so many mountaineers to their deaths: 'Out of thirty climbers who succeeded in ascending the south arête of the Aiguille Noire de Péteret,' he said, 'more than half were killed on other mountains.' It is certainly too many. Apart from the usual arguments against suicidal climbs, such a high percentage of accidents is due to grave technical faults. Brilliant young climbers plan their expeditions long before the event, then when the day comes they find themselves short of time and

11. The Bosses Ridge and the Aiguille du Bionnassay. (Photo: Gaston Rebuffat)

12. *Right*: Aiguille du Géant, (*below*) Tour Ronde and Mont Blanc (south face). (Photos: Malcolm Barnes)

try to carry out their plans regardless of the condition the mountains are in. They fight on to the limit of their strength and have no energy left to resist a sudden change of the weather; or they slip just because they are exhausted. It might almost be said, in the manner of Talleyrand's celebrated formula: such accidents are worse than tragedies, they are blunders. André Roch sums up the position as follows: 'The art of mountaineering consists in doing well even the most difficult climbs.' A French mountaineer named Alain de Chatelus, after describing many dangerous climbs which he carried out with two brilliant Chamonix guides, Georges and Jean-Paul Charlet (father and son), congratulates them and himself on having pursued 'nineteen summers in the Alps without an incident', which is doubtless the sanest way of talking about great feats of mountaineering.

The new technique and the new notions which have made mountaineering what it is today have had a strong influence on the guides. The average level of guiding is far higher now than it was forty years ago. When Guido Rey reached the top of the Dru in 1905, his guide, Ange Maquignaz, sadly confessed: 'You know, such mountains are *much* too difficult!' No guide would have thought this—or at least have said it—ten or fifteen years later. Guides may prefer rocks to ice, or vice versa, but the Dru is among the normal climbs of the district. Of course it will always be recognized as a difficult one, and in 1924 Alfred Couttet, one of the good local guides, was killed there because one of his holds broke. On the whole, guides have kept pace with the times, for better or for worse.

A few have attained the level of historical figures. Among these we may count Andreas Fischer, a striking personality in a tragic family. His father, Johann Fischer, was killed with Garth Marshall on the Brouillard glacier; his brother disappeared with Donkin in the Caucasus. Yet in spite of this Andreas, who deeply loved the mountains, persisted in becoming a guide. At the same time he studied with a view to becoming a schoolmaster and the fairly easy examinations he had to pass gave him the taste for further study. He went to the University of Berne, specialized in comparative literature, wrote a thesis on *Napoleon and Goethe* and became a schoolmaster. Meanwhile he remained a guide and led important expeditions in several districts. A delightful companion in the Alps, he published several scholarly works and good narratives of mountain adventures. In 1912 his party was overwhelmed by a storm on the Aletschhorn; they wandered long in a blizzard, then Fischer slipped and the whole party was carried down a slope. Fischer himself broke his neck. He died at once.

Guido Rey has drawn a memorable portrait of another picturesque guide with whom he often climbed: Tita Piaz, one of the first Dolomite specialists, 'the exponent of a new form of mountaineering, a master in those short but terrific climbs which are anything between difficult and impossible'. He was a restless and passionate creature, immensely proud of his achievements, well read and cultured. He lectured in Germany, wrote articles in Alpine papers, talked politics, rode on a motor-bicycle (the height of luxury before the First World War) and charged exorbitant prices. An extraordinary climber, he made a fetish of speed, ordered his companions about like children and was apt on occasions to fly into furious passions. Once, when taking an American couple up a very stiff climb, he shouted to the lady, who was finding the pitch too difficult: 'Stop wailing! Do you think you are on the stage?' He was a tower of strength and did not in the least mind keeping his employers waiting for a solid hour while he ate his lunch before starting: a new and slightly disconcerting figure for men who were used to the guides of the old school.

It seems that one of the greatest guides of all time was Franz Lochmatter of St Nicholas, the man whom G. W. Young termed 'the greatest of mountaineers, the best of friends'. The whole Lochmatter family lived—and died—for the mountains. Franz's father and eldest brother had been killed in 1882 on the Dent Blanche. Three other brothers were guides and Franz took to guiding when he was very young. He developed a technique of his own, a perfection of poise and harmony which enabled him to overcome almost any obstacle with apparent ease. G. W. Young wrote that 'he never struggled'. He always gave the impression of being on his own ground, however difficult the climb was, and he always succeeded in displaying even greater efficiency when the going grew abnormally severe or when the weather broke. He then managed to extricate his party from any forbidding pitch—as he did on the south face of the Taeschhorn—or to bring them back safely through a blizzard, until the day when his luck gave out and he fell from the Weisshorn, on an easy place, through a trifling technical oversight. And yet he had led parties up all the difficult routes and many new ones, on Chamonix aiguilles, Dauphiny peaks, the Mischabels or Monte Rosa. He was tall, thin and of refined appearance. Most of the men who had climbed with him became his friends and most of his colleagues worshipped him.

Another outstanding St Nicholas man is Joseph Knubel. He was more or less discovered and trained as a guide by G. W. Young and as a skier by Arnold Lunn. He was of medium size, thin, lithe, diffident, extremely courteous, well-groomed even on a mountain, and as nimble as a cat, even when he was no longer young. He was liable to grow outwardly excited and to indulge in a flow of fervid exclamations and gloomy prophecies. Then he calmed down and set to work with perfect coolness and thoroughness. He was less self-assertive than was Franz Lochmatter, less impressive of aspect, less striking to watch; yet he was one of the finest rock-climbers of his generation.

Among the younger men Armand Charlet, of Argentière, at the head of the valley of Chamonix, is head and shoulders above anyone else. His name has been associated for almost fifty years with the toughest climbs in the range of Mont Blanc. All those who have been with him on a mountain have been struck by his impressive, almost tragic face, his intelligence and culture, and above all by his speed and poise when climbing. In 1938 my party happened to cross the wall of séracs on the Glacier du Géant behind Charlet and Wilfrid Noyce. They were almost running. Charlet was holding his ice-axe horizontally, just to balance himself; he did not cut steps—he and his companion were secure enough with crampons— and his swift, graceful, perfectly poised movements suggested dancing steps rather than the uphill toil which one expects on a glacier. On difficult rocks he can do almost anything with his ice-axe, which he uses as a climbing pole, a belay or an additional foothold. His fantastic will-power has enabled him to conquer forbidding routes or to extricate his parties from desperate predicaments. He has had several bad accidents, twice when going out with rescue parties, but has always recovered and continued climbing. Mountains are not only a profession with him, but a passion: he is one of the very few professionals who have descovered new routes for the sheer joy of climbing. Wilfrid Noyce wrote of him: 'It was amusing to note how Armand's pre-eminence was recognized by the other guides and the hut-keeper. His word was law'. And again: 'It would be hard to dissociate Armand from Mont Blanc.'

Chamonix is the one French climbing centre with numerous and, on the whole, good guides. The only outstanding figure outside the Mont Blanc valley is Pierre Blanc of Bonneval-sur-Arc. The son of Blanc Greffier, he has been for years at the top of his profession. He had been farther afield than any French guide; C. F. Meade had him as companion and friend, and took him to the Valais, the Dolomites and three times to the Himalayas. In 1907 they attempted to climb the Guglia di Brenta: 'Its appearance', wrote Meade, 'is sensational, for it towers into the sky, some say like the finger of a god; others less romantically compare it to a factory chimney.' Owing to an unexpected iron ring which had been hammered into the rock and which, as they subsequently discovered, had been left by a man who had fallen from that spot to his death, they were able to force their way up a most appalling limestone precipice of unrelieved steepness: 'How long this nightmare lasted, it is difficult to say.' Meade's narrative leaves an impression of incredible obstacles. Blanc worked magnificently in extricating himself and his companion from this death-trap. He is a very capable and upright man, who can rise to any situation and face any climb; he impresses complete strangers by the force of his personality. During the occupation of his native valley, after 1942, and during the subsequent fighting, he hid weapons for men of the Resistance army, risking discovery by the German parties which constantly searched the villages. These are only a few of the great names.

Lately, the whole question of the relative positions of the amateur and the guide has taken a completely new turn. It has never been easy to draw a line between them, especially in Switzerland, where many men, not professional guides, have held guide diplomas. Among these is André Roch, an engineer who specializes in the study of avalanches in the research centre of the Weissfluhjoch, above Davos, while in the Valais many doctors, priests or schoolmasters hold the diploma. Since the time when ENSA, in its various successive forms, was started in France, the same thing has happened. Each year a number of young men, whose main profession is not guiding, nevertheless pass their guiding exams after having attended courses at ENSA. Since May 1968 the present French inspector of guiding has been M. Paul Keller, who led the Jannu Expedition; he is also a Protestant pastor. On the other hand, a number of amateurs have taken to professional guiding. Edouard Frendo, who was an NCO of the Chasseurs Alpins and a military mountain instructor, was a guide for several years before retiring to Aix-les-Bains; he was killed recently in a car crash. Most of the leading French guides—Rebuffat, Terray, Lachenal, Leroux and others—were amateurs first. Rebuffat and Terray, among others, went through a semi-military organisation, Jeunesse et Montagne, which, during the German occupation of France, tried officially to give some sort of physical and moral training to youths and to save them from forced labour in Germany; unofficially, they were trained to become leaders when the time came to re-enter the war and fight along the Alps.

Under such conditions the old guide-and-client team has been greatly modified. A number of leading guides are not mountain born. Rebuffat originates in Marseilles—and he may not know that one of his eighteenth century ancestors was a conventual chaplain of the Order of Malta. Terray was born in Grenoble, where his father was a doctor; Lachenal came from Annecy, and Livacic from Yugoslavia. The novelist Frison-Roche, who was always a guide, came from Paris, though his family was from Savoy. On the other hand, a good many amateurs who never thought it necessary to train for the guide's diploma, have become as good as or much better than any professional.

Such is the case of Pierre Mazeaud, for instance, a magistrate and a politician who, during the summer of 1969—an exceptionally fine one—ascended Mont Blanc seven times by all the difficult routes, and has led new and extremely strenuous climbs in the Dolomites and elsewhere. He was one of the three survivors of the Pilier du Fresnay tragedy in 1961. With modern means of conveyance it is possible to train during week-ends on the low but tricky rocks of Fontainebleau or the Saussois in Burgundy. Many similar training grounds have been found all over Europe, including Great Britain, from Tunbridge Wells to Skye and all the difficult routes up Scottish and Welsh mountains; this is the reason why so many British mountaineers are outstanding as rock climbers before they have the opportunity of tackling ice.

At the same time, the guides' attitude towards mountains has changed a great deal. Some outstanding figures are well above the accepted notion of what a first-class guide should be. Apart from being one of the most accomplished climbers, Gaston Rebuffat is an exceptional and a highly gifted author. Listening to his lectures is a treat; without a gesture, using an extremely wide and well-chosen vocabulary, avoiding any sensational effect, he succeeds in making his audience see and feel what he wishes to convey. Together with Armand Charlet, Guido Magnone and Jean Franco, he has been elected to the Alpine Club.

Walter Bonatti's extraordinary feats in most Alpine and oversea ranges are accompanied by a keen feeling for mountain beauty. His book, *Le mie montagne* is in the very highest rank of mountain literature, without the exasperating and swashbuckling style which Tita Piaz, among others, indulged in. The present guide is different beyond recognition even from guides of the last generation.

Though the average level of guiding in the Alps is now fairly high, when selecting a guide for a climb one ought to ascertain whether the prospective man is a record-breaker of some sort and, if he is, to avoid climbing with him at any cost. A few years ago, a Zermatt guide prided himself on having done the Matterhorn twice in one day. One can easily imagine what an ordeal it was for the first party, compelled to leave the hut at midnight or 1 a.m.—which is quite unnecessary—mercilessly spurred on, denied rest, roundly abused if they were slow or dizzy, and hurried down so that their guide could collect his second set of victims. It might be interesting to know whether any member of either party enjoyed the climb very much. As for the guide, he pocketed 300 Swiss francs and was interviewed by several newspapers. Such freaks have frequently been in action in the Dolomites, where short but difficult climbs can be tackled in very spectacular ways. Of course, climbers are often responsible for their fate. An American tourist took a guide to go up and down the Matterhorn in five hours; he succeeded and then went to bed for several days: the kind of crime 'for which the death penalty is inadequate', according to E. L. Strutt.

Climbing equipment has now reached a high level of efficiency. One of the characteristics of the present time is the number of books devoted to mountain technique. As early as 1892, Dent published *Mountaineering,* an excellent summary, pages of which are still worthy of serious consideration. Mummery devoted a chapter of his *Climbs* to the same subject. G. Wherry, under the strange title of *Alpine Notes and the Climbing Foot,* published a book to explain among other things, how useful feet are when climbing and how one must take care of them and how one must use them. He had given first-aid to Farrar's porter, Maquignaz, whom he had met on the top of Mont Blanc, after the party had traversed the mountain under very bad conditions. G. W. Young's book, *Mountain Craft* was a standard book for a time; the French Alpine Club brought out two volumes on mountain technique and equipment; the Swiss Alpine Club has issued several. There have been many more in German, and the Italian climbers Chabod and Gervasutti have published *Alpinismo.* The best and most recent book on the subject is *Mountaineering* by Alan Blackshaw.

With the increasing popularity of mountaineering, the various Alpine Clubs have continued to build refuges, and it is necessary to make them really serviceable. The new ones have been built as high as possible, such as the Tour Rouge hut at the foot of the Grépon on the Mer de Glace side, Envers-des-Aiguilles in the same vicinity, or the one on the Col de Bertol. Dauphiny is very much behind Savoy and Switzerland in this matter.

A new aspect of the problem has developed since the Second World War. Ruskin, for some obscure reason, wrote that the Alps best display their beauty in places where it can be admired by children, cripples or old men—or words to that effect. Whether it is a blessing or not, children cripples and old men are now able to grasp the full beauty of the Alps: telepheriques enable them to reach the top of the Aiguille du Midi and cross the Vallée Blanche, or reach the foot of the Grands Montets ridge above Chamonix and Argentière. When the weather is fine, you queue up for hours to get into the cars. If the weather remains fine, people just get excited and queue up again to get down, and there is a large crowd at the summit. If the weather changes for the worse, which is not infrequent, anything may happen, as people unused to mountains do not realize that the temperature may quickly fall below freezing point. Under the best conditions, as the top of the Aiguille du Midi is at 3,700 metres, the temperature is always low, while it is grilling hot in the valley. Such sudden falls of temperature have caused accidents, and so has the speed at which the cabins are pulled up. Moreover, people without mountain training and equipment have drifted along the snow ridge immediately below the summit in high heels or sandals, with rather unpleasant results. Even when one is properly equipped, the Vallée Blanche is not to be trifled with: it is a dangerous glacier, with huge hidden crevasses.

Together with the large increase in the number of mountaineers and mountain tourists, huts have been rebuilt and some of them have been turned into large and comfortable hotels: the Torino Hotel, for instance, on the Col du Géant, which can now be reached by telepherique from either side. The crowd there is unbelievable, and a ski school operates throughout the summer. The view is, of course, magnificent. Numerous real mountaineers also use the facilities, as the telepheriques have greatly shortened the approach to all the climbs in the district. But even without achieving the palatial state of the new Torino Hotel, many huts have been enlarged and altered beyond recognition, which is a blessing even for the most hardened mountaineers. Mattresses are reasonably soft and clean, and there are huts where it is actually possible to wash a little—the Requin and the Couvercle huts among others. Quite a number of Italian huts in the Dolomites are charmingly situated, with easy access from the valleys, even reachable by motor; they had been built during the first World War and kept in good repair. Most huts are now provided with telephone and radio communication.

All such changes have been made possible by the use of helicopters, which parachute their loads near the huts, which are kept constantly in touch with the valley, and are able to summon help at great speed when there is an accident. Casualties can be picked up by helicopter and brought to hospital within a very short time. The Swiss pilot Hermann Geiger specialised in mountain rescue by air, using first a Fiesler-Storch plane on skis, and then a helicopter. The number of people he rescued runs into hundreds, but he was killed eventually when landing at Sion, after more than 20,000 flying hours.

Anything is dragged up to a hut. Once, at the Requin hut, I saw a huge St Bernard dog which had been brought by guides from Courmayeur. It was supposed to help them in the search for a party which had disappeared somewhere in the neighbourhood. They hauled the dog up to the dormitory and it distributed its fleas everywhere. In the morning, the roping up of the dog was little short of a tragedy; it hated the process and its barks should have brought down the whole wall of séracs. Needless to say, the lost party was never found. Frank Smythe had been in the hut a few days before and had also met the reluctant St Bernard.

Of course, many huts are well out of reach of the crowds. To pass a peaceful evening or an idle day on the narrow terraces of Bertol or the Mischabel huts, gazing at the surrounding peaks, at the valleys far below, green expanses dotted with white or brown specks, while the shadows of the mountains slowly lengthen over the glaciers and the ice becomes blue, then crimson and gold, then mauve and at last ashen grey, vaguely thinking of the climb one has just done or of the climb one is about to do, is something very near to heaven. You are cut off from the world; you allow your thoughts to drift in an aimless way through a brain which is just sufficiently dazed by fatigue and sunshine to be able to take in the surrounding landscape without concerning itself about anything very much. Hours fly by, the sun sets, someone goes in to cook the dinner and you suddenly realize that the afternoon is over, that night is falling and that within a few hours you have to be up and ready to put on the rope once more and start for a new climb.

Non-climbers have come to the point where they take a lively interest in mountaineering affairs. A proof of this was afforded by the way in which the Press reacted all over the world when, in November 1946, an American passenger plane crashed on a glacier in the Bernese Oberland. The most detailed reports of the search were eagerly perused. By a fantastic piece of good fortune, no one had been badly injured in the plane when it landed and no one was badly frostbitten, in spite of low temperatures during the days and nights spent on the glacier. The Swiss rescue parties had great difficulty in making their way up a glacier deeply covered with snow. The passengers were ultimately taken down in small planes which could land on a limited surface. I had been sent to the scene of the mishap as a journalist and my party was the only one which climbed high enough up the mountain to witness something of the rescue operations. Most journalists who reached the valley where the rescue operations were being directed realized for the first time that in November mountains must be scaled with care; their readers also realized it with a shock when they were presented with an account of this sensational episode.

Films have done much to create and develop an interest in the high Alps. But this kind of initiation has serious drawbacks, as mountain films are for various reasons very unsatisfactory. The filming of mountains began at an early date—in 1913 a film of the ascent of the Matterhorn was shown in the West End Cinema in London. It had been made by F. Burlingham for the

British and Colonial Kinematograph Co. Burlingham had taken five guides up the mountain laden with a 15-kilogram camera, a 10-kilogram tripod and 1,500 feet of film. They were on the move for nineteen hours and filming on the summit and the shoulder had been very arduous on account of a violent gale. Then Burlingham had gone to Chamonix and filmed Mont Blanc with seven guides and 2,000 feet of film. The results were good, as everything had been filmed on the spot by a man who had a good knowledge of the mountains and respected them. According to a letter in the Coolidge archives, Burlingham also filmed an ascent of the Jungfrau. Later, a French photographer, named Munoz, filmed the very spectacular climb of the Kingspitze in the Engelhörner. Finally the Vallot family had a film made of one of their expeditions to Mont Blanc; this is still extant in Chamonix, although there is hardly anything left on the diapositive but ghost-like shapes floating through mist.

Shortly after the First World War, photographers who were good mountaineers began filming in earnest, and fine films were made on the Dent du Requin, the Grépon, the Mummery and Ravanel Aiguilles, the last-named starring Armand Charlet. These were fine pictures. Specialists could recognize or discover every detail of the routes and study the climbing technique of the actors, a fascinating process when one could watch Armand Charlet hauling himself up over a narrow ledge. A production which centred round the Aiguilles du Diable was little short of a masterpiece, and Charlet was again the star. But, on the whole, such films hold little appeal for the general public and are consequently little known.

German film producers invented what they called mountaineering: 'invented' because their conception of mountaineering had nothing in common with what even German climbers had previously meant by that word. *The Holy Mountain*, *Piz Palü*, *Mont Blanc* and other films were among the worst absurdities conceived by demented minds. The photography was usually superb, but that was all. The star was the notorious Leni Riefenstal, who always gave a morbid aspect to her parts. The part of the hero was often taken by Luiz Trenker, a Tyrolese guide who had become an actor and a writer, and the stories were in exceptionally bad taste, with ludicrous episodes. In *Piz Palü*, for example, one of the characters had his leg broken by an avalanche: he had been indulging in the dangerous habit of climbing up avalanche couloirs, ignoring the fact that if once does it often enough one is bound to meet the avalanche at least once and this is usually enough. So, with one broken leg, he promptly broke his ice-axe across his sound knee to make splints. I saw the film in Chamonix, and when this brilliant piece of first-aid work was thrown on the screen, a young guide at the back of the hall called ironically for the name of the maker of such an axe. In *Mont Blanc* we are shown that the only way to cross a deep crevasse is to climb down one side and up the other, and that, if you have been careless enough to leave the door of the Vallot hut open in a blizzard, you will meet your fate when you are stunned by the same door on crossing the Jonction, the door having been wrenched away by the wind. It is only to be expected that the large public which saw and liked such films on account of their magnificent photography was assured that mountaineering was only another name for suicide. Possibly for murder, too. Trenker played the leading part in a film called *The Challenge*, which was a misrepresentation of the first ascent of the Matterhorn. Trenker acted Carrel; the whole story was a libel on Whymper, and it was even hinted that *he* had cut the rope when his companions fell.

A French film, *Premier de Cordée*, based on Frison-Roche's novel, was made during the war. The photography is excellent, all of it being taken in the range of Mont Blanc, where the story is set. But we are disconcerted after one of the characters has exclaimed: 'This pitch is beyond human capacity!' to be shown easy slabs of rough granite with plenty of holds, crannies and belays. The atmosphere is conventional and stilted.

Raymond Lambert directed the filming of *The White Tower*, made after J. R. Ullman's novel. It was filmed in Chamonix, the Aiguille Verte acting as the Tower. The least said the better: a bad novel and a worse film, as seen by anyone with any experience of mountaineering.

During the last few years, filming and mountain technique have become much better and more subtle, and these rather babbling early films have been left well behind. Documentary films have lost the shy style of the early productions, which seemed to be pleading for forgiveness: 'I am so short that I won't bore you long!' There are now several mountain films of normal length and more than normal interest.

Gaston Rebuffat, with Georges and Pierre Tairraz, Lionel Terray and Marcel Ichac, have produced beautiful films—*Etoiles et tempêtes, Entre terre et ciel, Les Etoiles de Midi*—which enable film-goers to grasp the technique of big climbs and also the dreamlike or nightmare atmosphere of high mountains. The ascent of the great north faces of the Matterhorn, the Jorasses or the Eiger, the west spur of the Dru, the traverse of Mont Blanc or the Matterhorn, and the ascent of the Grand Capucin, have been filmed by specialists. They become alive on the screen, full of sincerity and poetry. Some sequences have an unforgettable beauty, as for instance Gaston Rebuffat's long walk with a youth he is training, first across woodland and waterfalls, then across the fantastic realms of ice which surround the Aiguille Verte. His bivouac in an igloo on the very top of Mont Blanc with Haroun Tazieff, the volcano specialist, is shot with the most extraordinary colours of sunset and dawn. A number of minute details can be underlined in any climbing sequence, which stress the complexity of such climbs.

When mountain films deal with fiction, they still hesitate between accuracy and uncontrolled imagination. In 1958 Rebuffat directed and acted in *Third Man on the Mountain*, the film version of J. R. Ullman's novel, *Banner in the Sky*, a re-hash of the story of the first ascent of the Matterhorn meant for children too backward to read Whymper's *Scrambles*. Yet the novel is better than *The White Tower*. The film was shot in Chamonix and Zermatt, Rebuffat taking the part of the character based on Michel Croz. Of course, he displayed an acrobatic skill far beyond anything Croz could have dreamed of in 1865. There is some discrepancy between the fact that the story is meant for children and yet is scened where they have no place, because it is much too dangerous, but the landscapes are superb. Another mountain film, *The Mountain*, made after Troyat's *La neige en deuil*, though filmed in Chamonix, is full of inaccuracies and Spencer Tracy cannot give the impression of really being an old guide.

Apart from films, mountains become familiar to the general public through accounts of accidents; these are either very brief or very inaccurate, and sometimes both. They combine with the films to create a melodramatic atmosphere, leading too many people to believe that mountains are no more than death traps, and that guides are chiefly required to recover dead bodies. Visitors arriving at Zermatt are at once directed to the museum, which is almost a mortuary, and to the churchyard . . . which is just a churchyard. All this amounts to a libel on the Alps, a libel so unfair that we feel something should be done to correct an impression which is at once morbid and inaccurate.

PART III

'THE LAST ALPINE PROBLEM'

CHAPTER ELEVEN

NEW TECHNIQUES

SHORTLY before the First World War, Alpine magazines began discussing what they called 'the exhaustion of the Alps', meaning that all climbing possibilities had been fully explored and that nothing remained to be done by enterprising spirits who did not care to follow the beaten tracks. By this time mountaineering in other continents had acquired great importance, but this pursuit was out of the question for the great majority of European climbers, on account of distance and expense. Further, at a time when anyone could cross the whole of Europe (Russia excepted) and America without a passport, there were many diplomatic regulations to comply with before setting out for the mountains of the Caucasus, Tibet or China. Tibet itself had been completely closed to Europeans until 1905. New alternatives in climbing had to be found.

Mountains do not change, but the spirit in which they are faced often does. A new technique came into being, a technique largely determined by the cult of danger: it was the unavoidable consequence of the First World War and the discovery of new and difficult routes up every important peak. The more dangerous routes were sought after with industry and ingenuity and, under certain conditions, danger for danger's sake became one of the strongest incentives to climb. This conception developed first in the Dolomites, where the small scale of most climbs and the almost complete absence of glaciers allowed very severe expeditions to be made without the added risk of ice-glazed rocks and very low temperatures at night, when parties had to bivouac on precarious ledges.

New methods of climbing were invented and taught in various mountaineering centres. One of them, which called for great athletic prowess, had been evolved by certain Germans, the most remarkable among them being Hans Dülfer, who invented an efficient though athletic way of ascending steep rock-chimneys. Later came Paul Bauer, another outstanding climber best known through the Himalayan expeditions he directed.

The present age being a mechanical one, several new devices for rendering difficult climbs less precarious have been discovered. Such was the piton, a long steel nail, carefully designed, which is driven into a cranny to provide an extra hold or belay. A hole was made in its head so that the rope could be threaded through it and made secure. But such a device involved the temporary unroping of the first man, so that the end of the rope should be free. Obviously it was a tricky task to unrope, thread the rope through the hole and rope up again on a very nasty pitch. C. F. Meade and Pierre Blanc went through the process on the Guglia di Brenta and thought it extremely unpleasant. But a new device was then found. A steel ring, fitted with a spring which allows it to open and shut automatically, is fastened into the hole of the piton and the rope is forced into the ring. It is called a *mousqueton* in French, a *karabiner* in German. The last man on the rope recovers the ironmongery. These contrivances are generally useful and safe when well hammered in, but they are never quite reliable on ice. A great German climber, Tony Schmid, was killed because a piton he had driven into an ice-wall worked loose in spite of all efforts to keep it in. Pitons can be used to swarm up an overhang or to gain height when there are no holds within reach; on such occasions the second man hauls up the first, the piton acting as a pulley.

A much more complicated contrivance has been devised to enable a climber to overcome extremely difficult pitches provided there are enough cracks or crannies. The man is tied to two ropes, one on his right, the other on his left, preferably of different colours and sizes. Pitons are hammered in alternately right and left. Then he hooks each rope into the corresponding *karabiner* and is hoisted up by the second man who, pulling from below, hauls on each rope in turn. It is, of course, easier said than done, since all the hammering is carried out while standing on almost non-existent holds. The process is very slow but fairly reliable. It provides the only way of crossing the worst slabs. One may object that it is not real mountaineering, and this may be true; but everyone knows that children love to hammer nails into a wall, purely for the pleasure of the thing. Besides, double-rope climbing is done in places where the climber cannot fail to grasp the fact that the mountains have every advantage.

Various devices have been contrived to supplement holds on completely smooth pitches. Stirrups, like rope-ladder rungs, can be fixed to pitons, affording a reliable foothold on sheer precipices. There are means of progression up a fixed rope, called prussiking, after Dr Karl Prussik, a German climber who at the end of the nineteenth century invented a very simple and reliable knot which can be pushed up and cannot slide down. It is used to fasten stirrups to a rope. Sometimes steel *jumars*, a sort of clasp, are used to get a good grip on the rope.

Few faces or ridges are now out of human reach, thanks to the new climbing methods. The latest mountaineering books give long lists of new routes up the most forbidding pitches; fantastic feats have been accomplished in the

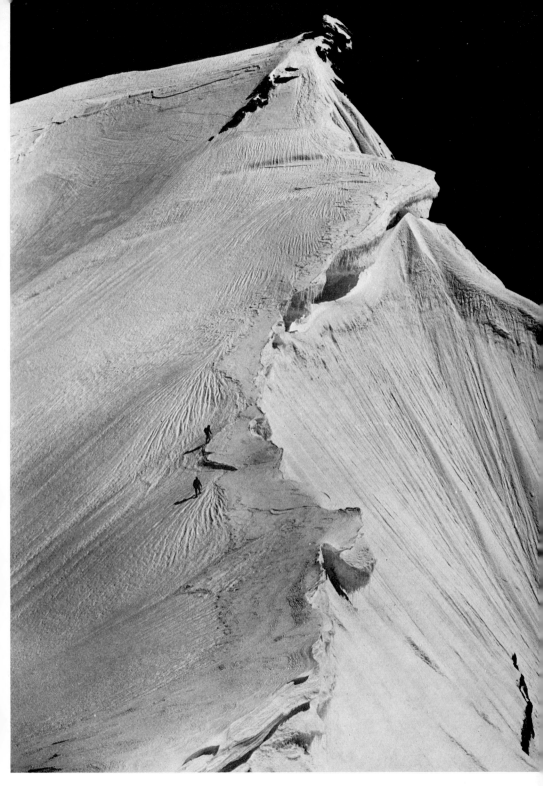

13. Snow effects on Mont Blanc. (Photo: Gaston Rebuffat)

14-15. The Eiger from the air, with (centre) the North Face. (Photo: Eidg. Landestopographie, Bern)

16. Séracs. (Photo: Gaston Rebuffat)

Dolomites, in the Bavarian Alps and in the Illyrian Alps. Climbs like the Guglia di Amicis, the difficult routes up the Wilde Kaiser in Bavaria, the Cresta dei Draghi in the Julian Alps, or the crags of Marche-les-Dames in the Belgian Ardennes, are among these new and nerve-racking climbs. King Albert of the Belgians was killed at Marche-les-Dames, climbing alone and grasping a rock which gave way and fell on him. Most of the limestone ranges are swept by falling stones; but no guide-book has ever thought of mentioning another kind of danger which seems to be far from negligible—that of adders and wasps' nests. These pests do not live at great heights, but low, stony hills in warm countries are likely to offer them pleasant homes, and meeting an adder face to face on an exposed precipice is likely to be bewildering, to say the least.

The present age is not only a mechanical one. A passion for science, however unrelated and often uncertain it is, forms another of its aspects, if only as a legacy of the almost ecstatic belief in science which was cherished by the materialism of the eighties and nineties. Now it takes a long time for scientific theory to percolate to the ordinary individual, and in an age when the newest discoveries have shown how many things still remain unexplained, a man who has a smattering of science comes to the happy conclusion that science accounts for everything and that figures make a new Gospel. They are, at all events, safe labels to be pinned up everywhere. They were consequently pinned to mountains, with characteristic German thoroughness and lack of discrimination, by a brilliant young Munich climber Willy Welzenbach. In 1925 he evolved a system of 'grading' mountains. He was tactful enough to limit it to pure rock-climbs, assuming that the conditions on such routes never alter—a questionable hypothesis—and he accordingly graded them from I (the easiest routes, on which one hardly uses one's hands) to VI ('the limit of human capability', which sounds rather ambitious, though his own capabilities were very great). All this was easy to remember and made technical descriptions of the climbs both short and precise. Each grade has a lower and a higher level. The marks I to VI were chosen because German and Swiss examination papers are marked on this basis: had a Frenchman conceived the idea, he would have used the 1 to 20 scale.

Even if we accept the premise, which is not self-evident, that the grading is done in good faith, we nevertheless cannot lose sight of the fact that there is much childishness in the procedure, and even more vanity. No one has been told who were the omniscient climbers who decreed what were the limits of human capability, and the notion is so vague that a climber always tries to degrade a pitch he has conquered, just to show how much better he is than the last man, so that few climbers pin a No. VI label to one particular place. Of course, their judgment may have been pronounced in good faith. But even if Welzenbach had really climbed all the Bavarian peaks, could he—or any one—compare the various routes down to the minutest details?

Another aspect of the question—an important and probably a major aspect —is that such 'grading' promoted violent national rivalries. One of the notions implicit in the idea was that rock-climbs are more difficult than climbs on ice, and that Bavarian and Dolomite climbers are therefore the hardiest in the world. Enthusiasts immediately imported the new scale of values into Italy and began grading the Dolomites. Things became lively when someone attempted to grade the French mountains. This gave birth to impassioned discussions, in which fantastic arguments were advanced. One of the French disciples of Welzenbach suggested, for instance, that this desire was only an aspect of that constant longing of the human mind to arrive at the easiest and most precise way of reckoning in figures. To which an opponent replied that no lover had ever thought of grading the beauty of his mistress or of saying: 'Her divine face is of a VI+quality!' Georges Sonnier writes: 'Hard-working mountain clerks have conceived as their supreme object the desire to stick a figure as a label to the name of each mountain.'

Welzenbach's calculations were meant to apply only to dry rocks, completely free of ice; hence, when an enthusiast tried to express in grades the traverse of the Meije, he had to leave out the Pic Zsigmondy, as it is always ice-glazed. The same enthusiast stated that the quality of the rocks did not come into his calculations: a very dangerous statement for the man who should climb with him! Chabod, when publishing *Alpinismo*, made careful reservations on these matters. He suggested, for example, that, when attempting the grading of the Western Alps, one should take into considera-tion the total length of the climb, the altitude, the distance to the hut, the length of the approach, etc. In one of the worst climbs in the Alps—the north face of the Grandes Jorasses—Gervasutti, who was a member of the third party to reach the top, said that 'there were no Grade VI pitches'. And yet, in his account of his ascent, we read that the party took two hours to climb a hundred feet! Ideas certainly differ as to 'the limit of human capability'.

The system of grading appears to afford some help to climbers, but it also provides them with worry and further opportunities for getting into trouble, not to speak of the rivalry which it engenders. Even in a district where it may mean something, it has created or developed an unpleasant desire to do more than is enjoyable, simply in order to rise to a higher grade.

To find an adequate means of expressing the nature of a climb might be a useful achievement, because pure description cannot tell everything, since mountains (in their technical aspect and in climbing condition) change very quickly. But these very changes make any permanent formulae futile or at least extremely hard to arrive at, so that we find ourselves, after a short time, in a vicious circle. Meanwhile, the abuses of the system were obvious. Some countries began to bestow a kind of ecstatic worship on 'grade six' heroes. In Germany, Welzenbach was hailed as a new Siegfried, and his tragic death on Nanga Parbat was followed in Alpine periodicals by eulogies that were not merely morbid, but hardly sane.

The strong appeal of danger is now heard by an increasing number of climbers. Thus the Guglia di Amicis, in the Dolomites, which for long was thought to be 'beyond human capability' has now been climbed by all its faces. In 1931, the scaling of this pinnacle became the special object of a small association of specialists; twenty-one in number, among them being five women. Mme Jean Morin led a party up the Guglia. Naturally, this quest for danger has not been limited to the lower ranges. Its adepts have been led to wage incredible campaigns in every climbing centre, under every climbing condition, in order to assure themselves of their perfect mastery of the mountains and of their own nerves. Several of them, when relating their expeditions, quoted Mummery and insisted that they were among his followers. Thus did Chabod and Gervasutti in *Alpinismo*, in which they translated long passages from his book; so also Pfann. Mummery's influence is still powerful, owing to the superb new routes he opened and the technique which he worked out.

The trouble with grading is that a climb inevitably loses part of its severity after it has been done several times. Chimneys and *dièdres* get known and guide books even warn climbers that such and such a pitch has to be done left foot first, so that the right hand can grab a tiny hold. Also, positive help comes from the pitons which have been left in the rocks by earlier parties. As a rule, the second man of the party pulls them out but, either because they are too difficult to recover or the party is in a hurry because of approaching bad weather, or for some other reason, it is not always possible to do so.

Recently, Reinhold Messner, a top climber from South Tyrol, wrote a paper about *The Devaluation of Grade VI*. According to him, the climbs which had been given the fascinating VI a few years ago, after their first ascent, have now lost it—not all of them perhaps, but most of them. 'Extremely difficult' ascents have now been permanently tamed as large numbers of pitons have been hammered into the rocks by numerous parties. The number of pitons required for a climb depends on the courage—or lack of courage—of the party that attempts the pitches. According to Messner, 'real courage and climbing ability can only be displayed by the climber who is alone on a high face, scaling an extremely difficult pitch thirty metres above the last piton'.

Some routes are more fashionable than others; thus more pitons are used to scale them, and so they lose grade.

Mountains are devalued because mountaineers are no longer what they were. According to Pierre Mazeaud, there is no sense in comparing the men who climbed the great north faces some twenty years ago with those who now scale the direct routes with a much more adequate equipment. One cannot compare a climber of 1970 with Cassin or even with Mummery. Everything is different and each man has been necessary to all those who have come after him. It is not possible to speak of an evolution in mountaineering, and even less of progress. Mountains are always different and unexpected. The new technique enables climbers to tackle more selective routes, but unexpected difficulties, which did not occur during the first ascent, may intervene. Basically, it is a conflict between two generations and two attitudes of mind. This is a further example of the fact that grading does not solve all problems, and would not be more accurate by adding a seventh or higher grade in the Alpine scale of values. It would just push the problem one step further.

The grading system has had another effect. While new routes are opened by the dozen, a number of former classical climbs are deserted. No one would dare to confess to an ambition to go up the Tour Noir or the ordinary route of the Weissmies, primarily because they are easy climbs, with magnificent views (but that does not count) and their approaches are extremely long. Until the Grand Montet telepherique was built, the whole Argentière district was practically deserted, on account of the long and tedious pull up to the hut. Today, parties queue up at the foot of the Aiguille Lachenal or the Rebuffat route on the Aiguille du Midi (south face), while quite a number of formerly popular routes are out of fashion.

Lately, several technical problems have come to the fore. Here are two. In Italy, the admission of women to the Academic Club is under discussion. Women are already admitted to the Italian Alpine Club, and there are several women whose Alpine and scholarly achievements should amply qualify them for admission to the Holy of Holies. The problem has been discussed in the *Rivista Mensile* and the women's part has been taken up by Massimo Mila who, apart from being a first-rate mountaineer, is a professor of music at the Turin Conservatory. The solution should come soon. Even in Switzerland, one of the least feminist countries in the world, the Swiss Alpine Club sometimes invites members of the Swiss Ladies Alpine Club to its lectures. It is fair to add that members of the Swiss women's club have been given equal rights in huts, telepheriques, mountain railways and so on. In other countries, the United States, Canada and France, women have always been admitted.

The membership problem has developed in Great Britain too, where the Alpine Club has been faced with a number of unexpected situations. I have already mentioned that professionals have been elected as members, and even as honorary members. When British mountaineers came back to the Alps after the Second World War, it soon became obvious that they were among the very best climbers, and they have kept to that very high level: Bonnington, Brown, Haston, Whillans, Kor, Evans, Bourdillon and Band are among the greatest of modern mountaineers. Bourdillon was killed on the Jäggihorn in 1956, when he was thirty-two, and John Clough on the south face of Annapurna when he was thirty. Evans married Denise Morin, the daughter of Jean Morin and Nea Barnard, who were both among the pre-war stars. Mme Morin, who was one of the first to lead all-women parties, does so still, climbing mostly with her daughter Denise Evans and scaling the stiffest Dolomite precipices.

The new climbers founded the Alpine Climbing Group (ACG) in 1953 from a nucleus of university men and the Rock and Ice Club. The first President was Tom Bourdillon. Since then, most of the big personalities in British climbing have served as Presidents. The Secretary Mr. Estcourt wrote to me:

'The constitution is based on the GHM's and membership is on climbing qualifications alone; the member's record is reviewed every five years and if he appears to have given up hard climbing he is retired. As a result of this and the fact that there are few professional climbers in Britain, very few people stay full members for more than ten years. Hence the group and committee are all very young, not often outside their twenties.

'In 1966 we merged with the Alpine Club. All this has meant in effect that ACG members get all the advantages of AC membership (meetings, insurance, etc.), but no right to vote at the Annual General Meeting. In addition, on retirement (or earlier), ACG members can become full AC members merely by paying more money (no chance of being blackballed). The advantage to the ACG is mainly financial and on insurance. The advantage to the AC is that we provide a net that catches most of the best climbers and channel them into the AC eventually, by the time they have given up climbing. Two ACG representatives also sit in the AC committee and it provides a very useful quick way for able young climbers to get to the mountaineering establishments. The ACG at the moment has about seventy members.'

This means that youth and vitality have been brought into the oldest mountaineering organisation in the world.

Shortly after the end of the Second World War, a number of American mountaineers took to the Alps. There had always been some American climbers at Zermatt and Chamonix and two Americans, William Howard and Jeremiah van Rensselaer, ascended Mont Blanc as early as 1819. John Auldjo, who published such an amusing account of his own ascent in 1827, was born in Canada, and another American, William Oxnard Moseley, was killed on the Matterhorn in 1879; his name was given to the spot from which he fell—the Moseley slab. There were many good American climbers between the two wars, but none of outstanding fame. The new generation is quite different. There are several important climbing centres in the United States, the most famous of which is in the Yosemite National Park. The rocks are of limestone and climbers can find any degree of difficulty. With such a training behind them, it is not surprising that American climbers can tackle the severest climbs in the Alps.

Two Americans were quite outstanding, and during their brief lives they have made some of the most difficult ascents in the Alps: John Harlin and Gary Hemming. Harlin was thirty-one when he fell to his death while opening a new direct route up the north face of the Eiger. Harlin's death is vividly recorded by his comrade, Douglas Haston, in *The Mountain World* for 1966–7. He had lived a very picturesque life, studying at Stanford University and starting a career in several directions at once, one of them as a Paris fashion designer. Then he enlisted in the American Air Force for five years, and while stationed in Germany he succeeded in carrying out many severe climbs in the Dolomites, at Chamonix and in the Swiss Alps. All those who met him and climbed with him remember him vividly as proud, intelligent, energetic and charming.

Gary Hemming was born in California and studied at the University of California. Eventually he became a student at Grenoble university, possibly because it was a good university, but most likely because it was so close to the Alps. He was supposed to study philosophy and philology, but he specialized rather in the mountains of the Chamonix range. He attended ENSA, but did not acquire his guide's diploma because he refused to shave off a rather striking beard. This did not prevent him from tackling some of the most difficult peaks, among other things a solitary ascent of the Walker spur on the Jorasses in winter. He failed at this, but eventually accomplished the first American ascent of that route in the summer of 1961. He made a number of extremely difficult first ascents and solitary ascents of some of the most difficult ice routes. He was very much noticed for the leading part he played when rescuing two German climbers marooned on the Dru. His curious dress, his beard and his general deportment earned him the nickname of Alpine Beatnik, and he was a well-known figure in Chamonix. He was a charming companion, both on the mountains and in the valley, though he could be moody, sullen and temperamental. He was not at peace with himself and was quarrelsome in the extreme. He quarrelled with John Harlin, probably because both were too highly strung to stand one another.

Hemming had several colourful episodes in his brief life, one of them leading him to climb to the window of a French girl who had probably encouraged him, since he was good-looking, clever and amusing, and also into prison, for the indignant family telephoned the police. He was released shortly afterwards. In 1969 he was found dead in the Grand Teton National Park, having clearly committed suicide. He was then thirty-four.

CHAPTER TWELVE

THE MATTERHORN

THE Matterhorn, which made such a spectacular entry in Alpine history, has remained one of the main attractions of the Alps. Within a few years of Whymper's success, three ridges had been ascended and the west face had been climbed by Penhall as early as 1879. Then, while the pioneers waited and looked hard at the mountain, an ever increasing number of parties climbed the Hörnli and Italian ridges and also the much more difficult Zmutt ridge. Eventually logical-minded people came to the conclusion that the fourth (Furggen) ridge had not been properly climbed and that there were three virgin faces left.

The Furggen ridge had been attempted several times. Mummery with Burgener had gone high, but they had then found themselves under the projecting rocks which are the key to the climb. These they could not over-come. They gave up the fight and traversed across the east face, a most dangerous route on account of the constant rain of falling stones; yet they eventually reached the Swiss ridge and the summit. Guido Rey made a similar attempt, failed almost at the same place, but did not accept defeat. He went up the mountain by the Italian ridge and had himself lowered past the overhang on a rope ladder; then having actually reached the place where he had had to stop on his first attempt, he climbed back to the top. With perfect honesty he never laid claim to a genuine ascent of the ridge. There were several less spectacular attempts, but all failed more or less at the same spot and for the same reason.

An Italian climber, Mario Piacenza, also fell under the spell of the Furggen ridge. Most of the guides of Valtournanche, to whom he explained his wish to try and scale it, told him it was out of the question to force a way up such overhangs and they refused to have anything to do with the project. Yet three of them were more optimistic and for several summers explorations were carried out secretly in the best Italian conspiratorial tradition. In 1911, an extremely dry summer, the climb actually took place, the whole ascent being carried out under a constant bombardment of stones. One gathers that Piacenza and his guides, Carrel and Gaspard, performed a wild race from cover to cover while the going was easy enough to allow quick progress. Then came an overhanging rock. The three men climbed on to one another's shoulders to reach a small hold very high up, round which they could belay the rope. The whole process was extremely risky. There were several other bad pitches, on which no belay was safe and the rock was crumbling to pieces. Eventually they reached a place where they found Rey's old ladder: a proof that the worst part of the climb was over. The summit was now within easy reach. It was a fine achievement, yet Piacenza's comments were bitter: 'The Swiss parties on the Hörnli ridge', he said, 'greeted us without the cordiality of the Italian guides of the southwest ridge. The glory about to accrue to the men of Valtournanche is lost for ever to the men of Zermatt.' How could he know that the parties on the Hörnli ridge were Swiss? This attitude of mind was still rare, but it became more common.

Then began the attempts to solve what was for a time 'the last Alpine problem'. Periodically, this title has been bestowed on the latest difficult climb. There were several 'last problems' on the Matterhorn; above all, the problem of the three faces. The most spectacular of them was the north face, that dark ice mirror which towers above the Zermatt valley. It is of unrelieved steepness. The ice has levelled its surface, making it almost smooth; the narrow ledges slant outwardly, affording very little help to climbers. The whole face is swept by falling stones, a tediously repetitive statement when discussing any part of the Matterhorn. There had been several attempts to scale it, led by great climbers like E. R. Blanchet, but all had been defeated.

In 1931, two young Germans, the brothers Schmid, attempted the climb. They had bicycled from Munich to Zermatt, where they camped at the foot of the Hörnli ridge to save expense. They had brought a large number of pitons and *karabiners*. Such climbs require a great supply of artificial belays, as the mountain offers none of its own. Speed was a vital factor, so vital, that during part of the climb, the young men relied on their crampons in spite of the steepness of the face, and dispensed with cutting steps in order to save time: the first man went up to the end of the rope's length, drove in a piton to get some security and then took in his brother's rope as he came up. The key to the first part of the climb was a long narrow gully; in order to reach it, they had to traverse on ice-glazed rocks on which hand-holds had to be chipped. The gully proved to be a channel for streaming water and falling stones. The Schmids' luck held and they succeeded in dodging the stones. By that time the afternoon was almost spent and a site for a bivouac had to be found before nightfall. With great difficulty they succeeded in finding a slightly protruding rock on which they could anchor themselves with pitons and double rope, and they managed to get into their sleeping bags. Hours dragged by; they were chilled to the bone and could hardly stretch their cramped limbs.

They resumed the climb at seven in the morning, on rocks which became more and more difficult while the steepness of the slope increased constantly. Holds were tiny and insecure and they had now reached bands of rotten snow which looked as if they might slip away at any moment. Meanwhile, the weather was deteriorating and mist was creeping down the face of the mountain. A storm would have meant death. Their one chance of safety was to reach the summit and they tried to increase the pace, in spite of their immense weariness. They were now following narrow, snow-filled cracks leading straight upwards. Suddenly, they noticed that the slope was easing; they were within a few feet of the summit ridge, which they reached just as the storm broke overhead. They hid under a rock near the cross, discarding their axes and crampons, and waited until the worst was over. As soon as there was a lull, they traversed the ridge and hurried down the fixed ropes. A second storm broke while they were climbing down the Shoulder. They entered the Solvay hut tired out and wet to the skin. In spite of the raging storm, they slept in the hut for two nights and a day, and then waded through drifts of fresh snow down to Zermatt, where they met with a triumphal reception.

This climb created a stir throughout the mountain world. The two brothers had taken enormous risks; the ascent had been a game of hide-and-seek with death. But they had had extraordinary luck and the fact that the weather had kept fine until they were safe on the easy summit ridge. The German papers went into hysterics over the Schmids' achievement and showered on the young heroes eulogies in which Teutonic mythology played a conspciuous part. Franz Schmid told his story in *Nordwand*: Hübel retold it in *Der Riese von Zermatt* (*The Giant of Zermatt*), while several other volumes were devoted to the subject. Franz Schmid's text is simple to the point of dreariness; his worshippers were less restrained. But the tragedy which had been avoided on the Matterhorn happened elsewhere: Toni Schmid was killed while leading a difficult winter ascent on the Wiessbachhorn.

In 1933 an Austrian was killed while attempting to make the second ascent of the north face of the Matterhorn, and his body was very difficult to recover. Two years later, a Munich party consisting of J. Schmiedbauer and T. Liess made the second ascent, with two bivouacs. The next party to attempt the climb after the war reached the summit without a bivouac: it consisted of Gaston Rebuffat and R. Simond, climbing just ahead of two other parties, one Austrian and the other German. There was no nationalistic rivalry between them. The French team was quicker than the two others: they started first and kept first, but it was a mere matter of hours in spite of the storm which lashed them during the first part of the climb, and again during part of the way down the Hörnli ridge.

The first solitary ascent was made by a young Austrian who specialised in such climbs: Diether Marchardt. He took less than six hours to scale the face. He was a quiet, cultured, unassuming young man and an outstanding climber. He was killed in 1962 on the north face of the Eiger.

In 1965 Zermatt was in dire need of every kind of advertisement. The year before the village had fallen prey to a serious epidemic of typhoid, due to the pollution of the water supply by workmen's huts built high above the springs supplying Zermatt with its water. Many visitors had been ill and one had died. In order to make the world forget this unpleasant episode, the local authorities gave the greatest possible publicity to the centenary of the first ascent of the Matterhorn, organising all sorts of celebrations, ceremonies, speeches, a televised ascent of the Hörnli ridge and various other features. The main event was getting Bonatti to make the first winter solitary ascent of the north face of the Matterhorn. He made it between February 18th and 22nd. He would have done it even if there had been no centenary to commemorate. However, it was a terrible ordeal, as he had to go three times over each difficult pitch in order to fetch his rucksack, which he had to haul up whenever he could not carry it with him. His route was different from the one the Schmids had followed. Bonatti, who is highly strung, temperamental, and a prey to nerves, needed all his self-control and courage to resist the depressing atmosphere of winter solitude. When he eventually reached the summit, he fell into a sort of trance: 'Now,' he wrote, 'as in a dream, I held out my arms to the cross, until I felt its metallic body close to my breast: and I fell on my knees, shedding silent tears.'

During the summer centenary celebrations, Yvette Vaucher, climbing with Michel Vaucher, her husband, was the first woman to ascend the north face. The mountain was in very bad condition and their bivouac very unpleasant.

Would it sound disrespectful here to mention the mountaineering feats of Mitza, a small cat who for some time lived in the Solvay hut and used to escort parties to the summit? Sometimes, she was given a lift in a rucksack, to get up the fixed ropes. Eventually, a guide brought her down to the Luigi-Amadeo hut on the Italian ridge.

The ascent of the north face by the German party immediately awakened the Italians to action, for there were still two virgin faces. A few weeks after the Schmids' expedition, E. Benedetti, with L. Carrel and M. Bich, started to climb the south face from Rionde. The main difference between the south and north faces lies in the fact that on the former there is less ice and more stones. Otherwise, it was just another, equally threatening death-trap. The party climbed almost without a break for thirteen hours and did not bivouac.

The story of the east face is worse. It was climbed in 1931, too, by G. Mazzotti, L. Carrel and H. Gaspard. They intended to climb straight up the forbidding wall. Stones were as numerous as elsewhere, possibly more so. Yet the lower part of the scramble, up to the level of the Swiss shoulder, was fairly easy. But then the party came to a steep overhang and the usual nightmare began. For hours they hammered pitons into crumbling rocks, climbing by inches, encountering unscalable pitches, being forced into even more perilous traverses under a constant shower of stones. Night came before they had found a way out, and they had to bivouac on precarious ledges, hooked up to pitons. They were not secure, as the rocks were rotten, and it was a miserable night. After daybreak, they found a means of pushing their way up to the summit. The fight across the last pitch, a few hundred feet, had lasted more than ten hours.

The last route on the Matterhorn was found in 1941 by an Italian party of three men, A. Deffeyes, A. Cretier and L. Carrel, who had been in most of these spectacular climbs. Starting from the shoulder on the Swiss ridge, they reached the top after having crept round the four faces in succession, beginning with the east face. Of course, the party had to dodge a maximum of falling stones from the beginning of the climb to the end.

Some of these ascents, brilliant feats of mountaineering frequently done against great odds, often reflected Nazi ideals, with German climbers indulging in a sort of rapture of despair and a mystic contemplation of death. A young Bavarian, who was killed later on the north face of the Morgenhorn, said to a Swiss acquaintance a few days before his death: 'For us Germans there is nothing more to lose.' They usually worked themselves up into a kind of nervous frenzy when attempting a big climb, bringing all their national ideals and national heroes into play, beginning with Hitler. Terror can be a drug and they drained it to the dregs. They drew a further emotional thrill from their sentimental conception of comradeship, as exemplified by a climbing party. German books made an almost sickening use of all the implications of *Bergkameradschaft*. Italy adopted the German technique and conceptions, which fitted well into the Fascist doctrines, but they gave them up eventually. Some never accepted them. Gervasutti persistently refused to stop climbing with his French friend, Lucien Devies.

This craving for excitement and peril had harrowing results. Indulged in to the point of mania, it destroyed the nerve of many of its adepts. According to R. L. G. Irving:

'A Munich expert estimated that after seven years of very difficult climbing, a man was fit for nothing more, if he was still alive. My own experience has been that the thrill of climbing a step near the limit of my powers has settled down in what I can describe as discomfort. If a man depends on difficulty and the thrill of danger or of high achievement, he must keep pushing his standard of difficulty up till he can go no higher. If he has got so far without falling off himself, then his enthusiasm must begin to fall from him unless he has advanced in appreciation of what I may call more absolute values of mountaineering.' (*Relativity in Mountaineering*)

After the Second World War, the hyper-nationalistic attitude mostly disappeared, making the general atmosphere purer and more pleasant. Of course, personal rivalry is very strong, but it is quite unavoidable, and it has been one of the time-honoured curses of mountain history and of all other aspects of history. The first ascent of Mont Blanc underlined a deep jealousy between the two men who were the first on top, and how many mountaineers were at daggers drawn with Coolidge and Whymper, not to mention the fact that Whymper was at daggers drawn with Coolidge?

CHAPTER THIRTEEN

THE DRU

THE Dru is not only one of the most beautiful mountains in the Alps, it is one of the most obvious. It is seen from anywhere in the Chamonix valley and its aspect changes dramatically with the viewpoint. The sheer pyramid of reddish granite, with a huge hollow near the top, its sloping floor harbouring a small, steep glacier, has always filled with awe both the tourist and the climber. In the eighteenth century, a young Duke of Hamilton was raced up its lower rocks by a friend; it was a rather childish attempt, of course, but it evinces a genuine admiration for the mountain and perhaps some measure of wonder or terror. The two young men did not reach very high and they cannot really be credited with a first attempt of the north face. It never yielded easily to a siege that dragged on for years. I have mentioned the eighteen attempts by C. T. Dent over a period of five years before he reached the top of the Grand Dru in 1878. All the other routes involved a similarly protracted effort.

The north face, with the large white hollow in its dark red wall, was the first to be attempted, starting either from the foot of the mountain or from the summit. All the attempts failed. In 1932, a party of Germans fell at the very beginning of the climb and two men were killed. Two years later, André Roch and Robert Gréloz succeeded in descending the face. It was an extremely daring enterprise, for they simply did not know what insuperable obstacle they might meet on the way, with their retreat towards the summit cut off by the sheer rock precipices down which they had double-roped. They took 780 ft. of rope with them. All the ledges were ice-glazed. One of their ropes was severed by a falling stone and another got stuck, so that they had to cut it and abandon it. Eventually they came level with the cave.

'How very different from what we expected!' wrote André Roch. 'It is just an extremely steep slope of blue ice, stuck into semi-cylindrical, over-hanging, black walls. At the back of the higher part of the cave, a spire of rock, resembling a huge matchstick, has broken from the wall to plant itself vertically into the slope. Judging from the present standard of mountaineering, our children may be ready to scale the match.'

A storm broke as the daylight failed and they were benighted on a tiny sloping ledge, trying to find a perch in total darkness. They hooked themselves to pitons, using the double rope to make themselves a little more secure. All through the night melt water poured over them and small pebbles rattled down. When dawn broke at last, they were almost at the end of their endurance, but the last precipices were mercifully easy; they were able to slide down on the double rope and reach the lower glacier, where friends were waiting for them with hot coffee.

Three years later, two Frenchmen, Pierre Allain and Raymond Leininger, succeeded in ascending the forbidding wall, and a second party made the same ascent in 1936: its members were Raymond Lambert and Mlle Loulou Boulaz, who had made most of the outstanding climbs in the Mont Blanc range. They had to bivouac twice. Lambert's description of the climb suggests an endless succession of long, smooth, steep cracks, of tiny ledges and awkward traverses. Every step was difficult and the whole climb was fraught with danger. One bad pitch succeeded another for hours on end. No relief could be derived from an easy occasional scramble: there was none. Yet they reached the summit and descended by the usual route, very tired, but filled with intense joy. When they reached the Montenvers, after crossing the Charpoua Glacier and the Mer de Glace in worn-out rope-soled shoes (nothing worse can be imagined), they had been on the move for fifty hours. The weather had remained fine during the whole period.

A climb like this might leave the impression of a struggle against odds too severe for human strength. The courting of danger seems to hold even greater attraction than the single desire to climb. Yet the Dru is a straightforward mountain: the rocks are good, though steep, there are few falling stones and no avalanches, for the mountain is without snow, except after violent storms, when the mountains of Chamonix must be left strictly alone for at least three days.

The Dru has retained its prestige intact. After the double conquest of the north face, it became one of the classic, though difficult, climbs of the Mont Blanc range. Gaston Rebuffat climbed it once with the President of the Belgian Alpine Club. They had started late in the day, as the weather had been more than doubtful the day before, and it was early afternoon when they reached the foot of the rocks. By that time the weather was beautiful, and though it was a north face the temperature was quite high. They went up very quickly, feeling very fit and in perfect spirits. Their only bivouac was on the normal route on the descent.

Yves Seigneur opened a new route up the north face, the most direct route. He attempted it once, failed, returned and succeeded in February in a temperature of $-20°$ centigrade. He bivouacked eight times, once in the big hollow, three-quarters of the way up.

The next route to be attempted was the west face, the one which is seen at its best from the Montenvers, a sheer wall which can only be scaled by artificial means so that there were heated discussions about the moral implications involved in using pitons. Now, whether climbers like it or not, pitons have to be accepted in the same way as one makes use of crampons or of the double rope for descending: both the latter aroused much heated criticism years ago and both are now taken for granted.

Two very strong French parties, Schatz and Couzy forming one, and Georges Livanos and Robert Gabriel the other, all of whom were specialists in artificial climbing, tried to scale the west face and were defeated, as it proved to be even worse than what they had expected. Another team attacked: Guido Magnone, Marcel Linné, Lucien Debernardi and Adrien Dagory. In spite of the Italian-sounding names of two members of the party, all were French. For three years they tried to force their way up and failed. These successive summers were very wet, with plenty of snow, and mountains are very resourceful when they want to defeat human beings. At the end of the summer of 1950, as a result of a rather bad earthquake, a heavy landslide swept over part of the mountain and when the party returned in 1951, they had to force their way through a nightmarish landscape of broken rocks precariously heaped and always ready to move and to start stone avalanches. One attempt after another failed, and the party was frequently compelled to race down under violent storms. Bivouacs became increasingly unpleasant.

The west face combines to an extraordinary degree some of the worst difficulties of the Mont Blanc range with a steepness only to be found in the Dolomites. Eventually, the party discovered the key to the ascent and on July 17, 1953, they launched the final attack. It lasted for three days and at the end of the third afternoon the four men reached the summit, exhausted, but victorious and happy, having accomplished what they had been looking for. A year later, Joe Brown and Don Whillans repeated the ascent with one bivouac, helped to some extent by a number of pitons left in the rocks by Magnone's party. And in 1965, after various failures due to bad weather, John Harlin and Royal Robin opened a direct route up the face. It was very hard and tricky, 'tense, dangerous climbing', wrote Harlin. He was hit by a stone and it was touch and go whether he could continue; but there was no alternative in that death trap, and he pushed up, the pain vanishing gradually. He summed up his climb as: 'Small man, damn big mountain.'

There are other routes up the Dru. The west face is separated from the south face (the normal route) by a huge ridge, which is the south-west pillar of the mountain. Just like the west face, it is as steep as a Dolomite wall, with enormous overhangs above precipices over 3,000 feet high. The rock is excellent, but with very few holds. A new siege began. This time, it was led by Walter Bonatti. For years, he had felt a passionate love for the mountain and the fact that the west face had been climbed did not annoy him in the least, for there were other possible routes, equally difficult or more difficult. He had tried the pillars several times and failed. In 1953, after an exhausting expedition to the Karakoram and the ascent of K2, he came home almost on the verge of a nervous breakdown, feeling as if he were about to abandon mountaineering. Suddenly, after a bivouac on the Pic Eccles, he felt better and decided he would attempt the ascent alone: it was a moral as well as a physical challenge.

Now the month of August 1955 was horrible, one of the worst in a number of wet summers. Several successive storms compelled Bonatti to postpone his ascent and retreat to the Charpoua hut. Finally, he got started, after a long fight with himself. Things looked dark and got darker still. On the first day, he injured his left hand and his methylated spirit flask got unscrewed and wrought appalling damage to the food in his rucksack. Solitude weighed on him heavily. The climb was becoming more and more difficult, but strangely enough he felt a sort of encouragement in the struggle and lashed up his will to win, in spite of his maimed hand. He lived through five bivouacs. Finally, on the sixth day he reached the summit, meeting friends there who had gone up the normal route to welcome him. There was a sixth bivouac on the way down. By that time, together with the joy of victory, Bonatti had recovered the physical and moral fitness he dreaded losing.

This extremely difficult climb has been repeated several times: Gaston Rebuffat, climbing with Christain Molier and Pierre Creton, had it filmed in his *Entre Terre et Ciel*. As usual, the speed has increased and the number of bivouacs has diminished. The climb has also been repeated by Joe Brown, and again by Chris Bonington and Paul Ross, who were pelted by snow avalanches. Japanese teams ascended both the north face and the Bonatti pillar in 1965. Rather pointlessly, the author of the Alpine chronicle of *La Montagne* wrote that they had taken rather more time than European climbers. One wonders whether finicky people will think of fining climbers who take too much time over their climbs.

On the whole, there is not much to find in accounts of accidents: usually, the press pounces on the subject, often giving a totally unreal account of what has happened. Accidents have been too frequent on the Dru, even on the normal route, which is not easy. There is no point in going over a number of maccabre episodes. Yet, in 1966 a rescue which had to be organized in the west face would have been almost humorous, had not one of the rescuers been killed in an unaccountable way, and everybody very much the worse for wear. Two young Germans, well equipped, left Montenvers on August 13, 1966, to ascend the west face. After three bivouacs, they apparently decided that they had had enough and settled on their bivouac ledge, waiting to be rescued. During the previous day, there had been the usual number of storms to be expected during a rainy summer, and there was plenty of snow on the rocks. German friends of the two climbers who were in the valley reported what had happened to the rescue organisations, and several helicopters hovered about the face and located the two men. They got the impression that one man was injured. The ledge they were on was difficult to reach—everything is difficult on the Dru.

From three directions teams of rescuers hurried towards the apparently helpless Germans: members of the EHM, directed by Colonel Gonnet, guides led by René Desmaison, who had made the first solitary ascent of the face, a team from ENSA, and various amateur parties, British, French, American and German, who were all men of outstanding mountaineering skill. Among them was a strange, irrepressible character, Gary Hemming. One of the German volunteers, Wolfgang Egle, an excellent mountaineer, just before the two men were reached, got entangled in his rope and was strangled. Meanwhile, Hemming's party and, from a different side, Desmaison's, succeeded in reaching the two Germans, discovering with mixed feelings that they were neither sick nor injured, and that they had ample provisions of food and woollies. They had simply been overcome by fear and had thought it easier to wait until they were rescued. Eventually, two parties brought them down.

The whole episode had taken a week. It did not end there, as there were violent subsequent quarrels. Of course, the whole thing had happened because the two young Germans had attempted to climb something for which they were neither physically nor morally able. As often happens, the rescue entailed fierce, endless arguments between all those who had taken part in it, and the two most active members were those who met with most abuse. Mountains seldom bring peace. Another unexpected aspect of the climb was the fact that an American led a French rescue party on a very tricky bit of the Dru, that Holy of Holies of the French Alps.

CHAPTER FOURTEEN

THE GRANDES JORASSES

THE Grandes Jorasses are almost invisible from the bottom of the Chamonix valley: only a tiny bit of the highest peak can be seen from Les Tines. But when you reach Montenvers their huge wall makes the most stupendous background to the landscape of the Mer de Glace. They are both beautiful and awe-inspiring. In uncomprising steepness, they soar up, shining in their coating of ice or ice-glaze. They form a straight-forward mountain: they look dangerous and they are dangerous.

In the eighteenth century, a guide whose real name was Jean-Baptiste Lombard was nicknamed Jorasses or le Grand Jorasse. He was one of Saussure's guides and became the hero of an extremely melodramatic poem by Samuel Rogers, in his *Italy*. I have never succeeded in discovering whether he was nicknamed after the mountain because he was very tall, or whether this very high peak got its name from the man. Saussure and his contemporaries were the first to refer to the mountain by that name.

However, throughout the eighteenth century mountaineers strictly refrained from having anything to do with the big rock face. Leslie Stephen saw it from very near when climbing the Col des Hirondelles and Mont Mallet and kept away. While most Chamonix mountains are free from falling stones, because the rocks are good and have had most of their loose stones swept off by innumerable parties, the Jorasses are alive with stone avalanches. They rumble like thunder day and night. The whole situation was tersely summed up by Armand Charlet, who said: *'Ce n'est pas de l'alpinisme, c'est la guerre'* (This is not mountaineering, it's war).

The summit ridge has several peaks, Pointe Walker, Pointe Croz, Pointe Whymper, and steep buttresses lead up to them. On the extreme left a large hanging glacier, the Linceul, also leads up to the final ridge. Logically, each buttress and the glacier provide routes.

The first attempt was made as early as 1928 by Armand Charlet. With a party made up, besides himself, of an American and three Italians, including a guide, he tried to go up the buttress across the face, leading to the Pointe Croz, but could not go very high. He was using no pitons, no artificial devices of any kind and such a climb could not be tackled without them. Nothing more was done for three years. Then, in 1931, the German offensive was launched and was conducted throughout the Alps. Two parties went to Chamonix and by the beginning of August two men had been swept down by an avalanche and killed. The other party, which consisted of Kröner and Heckmair, who was later to make history in the Alps, reached a point a little higher than Charlet, but failed to go further, though they managed to come down alive. They were out of work, practically without money and had scarcely anything to eat during their attempt. Many more tried to force a way up, including one of the brothers Schmid, of Matterhorn fame, Welzenbach, Armand Charlet again, and others.

The Italian parties, which had now arrived on the spot, included Chabod and Boccalette, Benedetti and Cretier, and two Valtournanche guides: the team which had attacked the south face of the Matterhorn. They all failed when they reached the extraordinarily steep slabs above the bergschrund of the Pointe Croz.

So many motives are at work in the minds of those who attempt such climbs that I asked René (now Senator) Chabod whether he could formulate the reasons which had led him to face the Grandes Jorasses several times and persevere until he succeeded in scaling the huge wall. Here is his letter, which he has permitted me to publish. (the original is in French).

'I began the struggle for the north face of the Jorasses in 1932 with my friend Gabriel Boccalette (who was killed in 1932 on the Aiguille du Triolet). One day, while we were studying the face, I asked him: If we were certain that nobody would ever hear of our having conquered it, should we yet try to scale it? Neither of us dared to reply. On the one hand, there was our passion for mountaineering for the sake of the mountains, but on the other we were urged towards the terrible face by pride, by team spirit, by our wish to succeed before others, as we were representatives of Western and Italian mountaineering. As for myself, I was also spurred on by the Aostan aspect of the question: being a native of the Val d'Aosta, I wanted to be among the first on the top of a mountain which is half-French, half-Aostan.

'In 1935, I wrote: "I should say I don't feel very enthusiastic because I do not like to endanger my old skin merely for a mountain—even *that* mountain, but my friend Gervasutti had made up his mind, so I had to go with him. Am I a victim of friendship? Exactly so, a victim of friendship and also of the foolish ambition to make a first climb. Now that the first climb has been accomplished by others and we have been forestalled, I am committed to do the second, so as not to lose face." In a word, I was in for it: I had wanted to tackle the face of a Val d'Aosta climb, I was bound by promise to Gervasutti, so that now there could be no backing out.

'Of course, I did not exactly start in a suicidal frame of mind. On our 1934 climb, when we gave up the attempt from lack of daring, we had discovered that it was quite possible to come down. So that on our second attempt we were for doing everything within our power, but we knew that we could come down if we failed. We found the conditions so bad—mainly on account of the awful weather—that we had to go on at all costs, to the very limit of our capacities. But had the weather been good the face would not have been as difficult as we thought. Of course, I speak of the 1935 route, leading to the Pointe Croz, not of the Eperon Walker, which I have not done.

'Our mistake was that we had been too timorous in 1934: had we then gone on, we should have conquered, with less danger than during our second attempt in 1935. Owing to our rate of progress in 1934, we should have reached the top before the blizzard in which Peters and Haringer were caught. In 1935 we ran great risks on account of the weather, but I must repeat that we did not attack in a suicidal frame of mind. Personally, I did not then think that one is justified in taking enormous ricks for a second climb and I just went because I was committed.

'Now that the climb is done, I think I ought to have answered "yes" to the question I put to Boccalette, for I experienced some of my finest mountain impressions when I was climbing the Jorasses: it is a wonderful climb. And I thank my sense of duty, of friendship, of personal dignity which conquered the sinking feeling I had in the Leschaux hut when I heard that we had been defeated by the Germans.'

This is an essential document for the study of contemporary mountaineering. Senator Chabod, who is a lawyer, has included all the arguments with the greatest clarity and precision.

At the opening of the 1934 season a number of parties gathered at the Leschaux hut, at the foot of the wall. Armand Charlet and Robert Gréloz made another attempt: they went higher than anyone previously but could not succeed in forcing a very difficult pitch and had to come down. A few days later, the whole spur leading to the Pointe Croz was literally swarming with parties. The quickest party was that of Armand Charlet, who was trying this time with a second Chamonix guide: they again ran into an obstacle impossible to overcome, observed a change in the weather and descended at top speed. René Chabod and Gervasutti were also attempting the climb and they, too, noted the changing weather; they came down and bitterly regretted it. According to the letter I have just quoted, René Chabod thought they might have reached the top before the weather became too bad.

On the same day, an Austrian and a German party were attempting the climb. The Germans were Peters and Haringer. When the weather took the change for the worse that Charlet and Chabod had observed, the Germans went on. Through the thickening fog they were dimly descried still going up very slowly. Night fell; in the morning a fierce gale was blowing, and it continued for days. Then Peters staggered back to Leschaux, alone and half dead. He had spent four nights and five days on the face. His companion had slipped on an ice slab just when he had taken off the rope, and he had fallen to his death on the rocks below; the body was recovered later at the foot of the great wall. This was the second casualty in the contest, not to mention the two Germans who had gone to train on the north face of the Dru and had been killed in a fall. Wild tales began to circulate in the valley of Chamonix.

Meanwhile, a new party had appeared on the mountain, consisting of two French climbers, Edouard Frendo, an instructor in the military mountain school at Chamonix, and Maurice Fourastier, a schoolmaster from Algeria. Both were noted climbers. They went out to reconnoitre the face with the idea of attempting to descend it, but various factors, including the usual change of weather, defeated them.

In 1935, the final contest took place. Peters, the survivor of the accident which had cost Haringer his life, had found a second man and both went again to the Leschaux hut. Whether or not they had tried to keep their coming a secret is not known; however, the news spread quickly in Chamonix and within a few hours had reached Geneva and Courmayeur. Frendo was waiting for Fourastier, but the latter's holidays had not yet begun. As he was coming from the neighbourhood of Algiers, the journey would take at least three days, and in the existing circumstances Frendo felt he had to act at once. He found another companion, Chaix, who was also a military instructor and they both hurried to Leschaux, where a Swiss party, consisting of André Roch and Robert Gréloz, had just arrived. They decided to join forces and attempt the climb as quickly as possible, so as to forestall the Germans.

Frendo's description of the ascent gives the impression of a breathless rush. Things were going well when the French party suddenly heard a cry ahead of them. Roch, who was leading at the moment, yelled: 'Come quickly! Gréloz has dislocated his shoulder'. It was awkward, for the injured man was apparently in great pain. The two Frenchmen came level with him and hooked themselves up to pitons driven into the rock. Frendo, who had some knowledge of first-aid, pulled the shoulder back into place and then, probably without much discussion, the French party gave up the climb, in spite of a very legitimate hope of success, to help the injured man and his companion down.

Meanwhile, the Germans were progressing. They had already bivouacked twice and had succeeded in reaching the top of the face on the day before the two defeated parties had left. The weather had remained good all through the climb. The problem of the Grandes Jorasses was solved. Three other parties reached the top within a few days: René Chabod and Gervasutti, who were already in the hut when they heard of the Germans' success and decided to go up all the same, then Mlle Loulou Boulaz from Geneva, with her guide Raymond Lambert, and lastly a Munich party a few days later.

The Jorasses were now on the way to becoming a feasible, though extremely difficult climb. Of course, none but the toughest and the very best parties would stand the slightest chance of success. Soon a second way up was found. After his failure in 1935, Frendo tried the new route up the Eperon Walker. The risks are similar and as great as on the first route. On August 4, 1938, an Italian party led by Cassin, one of the very best Alpine climbers and a specialist of the sheer Dolomite rock faces, arrived at the Requin hut with two companions, Esposito and Tizzoni. They knew nothing of the Chamonix district, had never been there before, and in a vague fashion asked the hut keeper where the Grandes Jorasses were. Even more vaguely, the man made a sweeping gesture and said: 'somewhere there'. He had not recognised the Italians and he thought that their question was a joke. He was greatly surprised when, the next evening, he saw a bivouac light fairly high up on the Walker spur; by the next night the light had crept up the face. On August 6th the party reached the summit ridge, where it was caught by a violent storm which compelled the men to bivouac on the way down. Finally, they reached Courmayeur on August 7th. They had raced up the spur using their Dolomite technique, hammering pitons where they could not find holds. The two main routes up the face were now open, and more could be found.

The second attempt to ascend the Walker Spur was made by Edouard Frendo in 1943. This time he was accompanied by Gaston Rebuffat, a very young and very skilful climber. There had been an interval of several years: in 1940, as an officer of Chasseurs Alpins, Frendo had a very different sort of work to do. Fourastier was in the army which landed in Italy and was very badly wounded at Monte Cassino. Frendo and Rebuffat's attempt was a failure and more than two years were spent in doing what was very different from climbing mountains for one's pleasure.

In July 1945, Frendo and Rebuffat tried again. The weather kept fine all the time, which meant intense cold. It was a difficult and tricky climb, over ice-glazed rocks, and the two men were compelled to go all out. Frendo slipped and his fall was checked by Rebuffat in the nick of time. They eventually reached the summit ridge in a light mist, when the weather was about to change. For Rebuffat it meant the fulfilment of an old cherished dream. Two years later he ascended the first route, leading a party of pupils from the

School of Alpinism. It was a beautiful climb, and the weather and the rocks were in good condition. Yet, Fate struck. They had reached the summit in one day and they were about to bivouac on the way down, when a large block fell on the party, killing one man and injuring two others, including Rebuffat, who sustained a broken knee, a broken foot and broken ribs.

In 1947, Gurekian, Malet and Revel succeeded in scaling the face without a bivouac, reaching the top before night fell. Barral and Gevril traversed the summit ridge two years later, also avoiding a bivouac.

Most great climbers have now gone up either route, if not both. It would be useless to make a complete list of those who have forced their way up to one summit or the other. Pierre Allain, René Ferlet, Guy Poulet and Poincenot made the ascent in 1946. Allain, in his account of the climb, is perfectly candid: according to him a climb is a race. You have to try and do better than those who have climbed before, be quicker and, if you can, avoid a bivouac, not only for safety's sake, but merely to save time. Terray and Lachenal found a new route to overcome the difficulties of the top of the Walker Spur. Among other parties, one can mention those of Jean Couzy and René Desmaison, Hermann Buhl and Kuno Rainer. Rebuffat returned to the mountain with Paul Habran. The first woman up the Walker Spur was again Mlle Boulaz, who had already been the first woman up the first route. This time she was climbing with Pierre Bonant, Claude Asper and Raymond Dreier from Geneva. They were caught by a severe storm.

Joe Brown went up the Walker route with Don Whillans, Chris Bonington with John Clough, and Gary Hemming with Harry Kendal. Walter Bonatti proved to be quite a specialist of the peak, ascending it at least three times. In August 1949 he went up the Walker Spur with Oggioni, Villa and Bianchi. The weather was fine and remained so, but they had to fight back against a deadly cold wind. In 1964, Bonatti came back, this time with Michel Vaucher, the Genevese mountaineer, and they went up the buttress leading to Pointe Whymper. They had to face an unexpected kind of danger: an earthquake. The whole mountain trembled and groaned, and a rock, the size of a church, slowly started moving and eventually toppled down. They had a hair-breadth escape. Snow avalanches kept sweeping the face, though an ice-cold wind should have frozen the snow. They took four days on the face and had to bivouac on the way down. Finally, Bonatti, together with Cosimo Zapelli, made the first winter ascent of the face. The first solitary ascent was accomplished on July 8, 1968, by Alessandro Gogna from Genoa, a twenty-year-old student who is the infant prodigy of Italian mountaineering. He was reading for an engineering degree but has lately abandoned the University to devote all his life to mountaineering.

Climbs, even very severe ones, can provide humorous episodes. One of them took place on the Jorasses. Jacques Batkin, nicknamed La Farine because his Polish name sounded unfamiliar and because he had once trundled flour sacks for the Grands Moulins de Corbeil, a big mill near Paris, attempted the north face with a friend, during an extremely rainy summer. An American party was also on the mountain on the same day. During the night they heard shouts or moans which they interpreted as SOS and, as soon as they could see their way, they decided to abandon their climb and summon a rescue party, as the weather was quickly deteriorating. The Chamonix rescue organisation was contacted and a helicopter was sent up. The two men were promptly discovered; and they were apparently motionless. When the rescue caught a glimpse of them it appeared that the men who were to be rescued were calmly proceeding up the mountain, apparently none the worse for their bivouac. Violent shouts were exchanged while the rescuers were pursuing the rescued-who-did-not-want-to-be-rescued. Finally, the latter convinced the rescuers that they were all right, and the race stopped. La Farine and his partner eventually reached the Jorasses hut, on the Italian south face, where they were met and feasted by Italian guides who has also heard of that strange episode. The next day, they went down to Courmayeur. There was one more problem to solve: who was to pay for the rescue party? Unhappily, I left Chamonix the next day and did not hear the end of the story. I think La Farine refused to pay. He was Desmaison's companion when they attempted the second winter ascent of the Spur, starting with fine weather and intense cold, and were compelled to race down when they were already very high, as a blizzard was threatening.

In January 1968, René Desmaison and Robert Flamaty forced their way up a new route, the Linceul, the long ice slope to the extreme left of the Jorasses. In spite of the cold and the short days, they had selected winter to do it, to be more or less immune from falling stones. It took them eight days. When they were about to reach the ridge connecting the Col des Hirondelles to the summit of the Jorasses, over the top of the Linceul route, they heard over the radio that the weather, which had already broken, would worsen during the next forty-eight hours. The only solution was to reach the top and then come down the Chamonix side as quickly as possible, sliding down the Linceul on the double rope. Before they could reach the summit ridge, above the Linceul, a snow avalanche fell on them, not hurting them but carrying away the rucksack containing their small bivouac tent. Under such conditions, the only possiblity of survival was to reach the foot of the mountain the same day, which they did, racing down against time.

René Desmaison's name is going to be mentioned often in the following pages; in his early thirties, he is one of the outstanding French professionals, with a faultless technique and a deep and subtle understanding of the mountain world. Quite lately he has scaled for the first time a very difficult pinnacle of disintegrating rock, the Corne du Chamois above Sixt.

In 1965, Pierre Mazeaud and Roberto Sorgato ascended the face. Some time before, I called on Pierre Mazeaud at his office. A large air photo of the Jorasses was pinned on the wall. I asked him a few questions about the route he was planning. Staring at the photo with an entranced look on his face, he said: *Il n'y a que ça de vrai!* (There is no truth but that!)

Two more women are numbered among those those have scaled the Jorasses face, Mme Yvette Vaucher and Mlle Ring. During the surprising beautiful 1969 summer 140 parties ascended or attempted the north face!

CHAPTER FIFTEEN

THE NORTH FACE OF THE EIGER

THE ascent of the north face of the Matterhorn set mountaineers thinking. There are plenty of north faces in the Alps, and many of them had been left untouched, not because they had been overlooked, but because they looked and were, quite murderous. One of the most obvious and among the worst is the north face of the Eiger. It is seen from very far off, from Berne, for instance, as a dark stain on the huge, silvery ice wall of the Oberland. It looks uncompromisingly steep. Seen from Grindelwald, which clusters at its foot, the height of the wall seems overwhelming. The rocks which compose it are rotten and often overhang. Gaston Rebuffat wrote: 'On the Eiger, bad weather is part of the condition of the mountain'. And again: 'A heap of black stones and glassy ice, it stands contemptuously alone. No one loves it. And yet men have died to conquer it'.

Roughly speaking, there are two main routes up the face: one along the east ridge and the other straight up the wall. The ridge was ascended in 1932 by a first-rate Swiss party, the climbers Lauper and Zürcher, with the guides Graven and Knubel. They found it very difficult but interesting. So far, the wall had been left untouched.

In 1935 two young Bavarians, Karl Mehringer and Max Sedelmayer, arrived at Grindelwald to attempt the climb. Thinking of the glory which had accrued to Franz Schmid after his Matterhorn expedition, they longed to be victorious on this other north face, to be presented to Hitler and obtain parts in films. They waited long for good weather; at last, the usual Oberland clouds cleared and they started. Throughout the Eiger tragedy, the parties in action could be watched through the loopholes of the Jungfrau railways and the contrast between the comparative comfort and civilization of a railway station and the appalling agonies of these young men, slowly dying in the snow a short distance away, gives a deeper horror to the whole story.

The two climbers drew level with the Eigerwand station and bivouacked. On the following day, they met with greater difficulties and gained but little height. On the third day, they hardly progressed at all. That night a storm broke. The mountain was hidden in fog and showers of hail fell; then it began to snow. Avalanches of waterlogged snow swept the face and the clouds closed over it. Two days later, there was a short lull and the mountain showed clear for a few moments. People obtained a glimpse of the two men, who were now a little higher and about to bivouac for the fifth time. Then the fog came down again and swamped everything. Further days elapsed and the weather cleared for good, revealing a mountain wrapped in bright fresh snow. A Swiss military pilot flew up as close to the rocks as possible. The pilot saw one of the men frozen to death, standing in the snow; the other was probably buried in it at his feet. There was nothing to be done. Owners of telescopes in Grindelwald charged extra prices for a view of the bodies.

The next summer, ten young Germans and Austrians came to Grindelwald and camped at the foot of the wall. From this point a party of two made a training climb, but they fell off and one of them was killed. The weather was atrocious throughout the summer, so bad that after waiting for a change and seeing none on the way, several members of the party left. Of the four who remained, two were Bavarians, Hinterstoisser and Kurz, the youngest of the party, and two were Austrians. They were feeling happy and confident in the result of the climb. At last the weather became fine and they left to reconnoitre the route; at the end of the day, when they were coming down, Hinterstoisser, who was the last man down on the rope, suffered a fall of 120 feet. His luck still held: he sustained nothing worse than a bruised knee. The whole party set out in earnest a few days later. They went up quickly and climbed well. The first bivouac was cold, but apparently there was nothing wrong. Then in the morning the weather changed, clouds came down and hid the group.

The clouds did not lift until the next day when, during a break, the whole group was seen coming down, and they could be watched intermittently. The weather grew worse for two days. From the Eigergletscher station three guides started on an extremely perilous attempt to reach the party. They failed actually to reach them, but they came within shouting distance, and found that only one man was still alive, Kurz. He explained that his three companions had died the day before. One had fallen down the face, another was frozen above him, the third had fractured his skull in falling and was hanging dead on the rope.

In the morning the three guides came back, traversing across the face from the station and risking their lives under incessant avalanches. Kurz was still alive but quite helpless, caught as he was between the two corpses, with one arm completely frostbitten. The guides shouted directions to him and for hours, with infinite courage, in spite of his deadly weariness and the great pain he was enduring, Kurz endeavoured to reach his rescuers, who could not pass an unclimbable overhang. He had to cut the rope which tied him to the dead man below and come down on it. The guides were able to pass him a few pitons; and then, when he had done almost enough to win his way to safety, he began to lose consciousness. One of the guides, climbing on his comrade's shoulders, was able to touch the tip of Kurz's crampons with his ice-axe, but could not get higher. Suddenly, the rope stuck, and Kurz was unable to descend further. He was completely exhausted and he let go. He died, caught in the rope after hours of tremendous effort.

Later another German party, about to attempt the climb, suddenly came across Hinterstoisser's body somewhere near the bergschrund at the foot of the mountain, and 'the finest day of the season was wasted, bringing him down to the valley', wrote one of them with disgust.

The Bernese authorities put the north face of the Eiger out of bounds, threatening to fine any party that should attempt it again. But the grim enthusiasm which animated prospective climbers could hardly be damped by the threat of a twenty-five francs fine or whatever the sum might be. In 1938 Austrians and Germans tried the ascent and eventually reached the summit. It was typical. The two Germans, Heckmair and Vörg, suddenly came across their 'rivals', according to the term they used in describing their ascent. They had done everything to keep their coming to Grindelwald a secret. The two Austrians, Harrer and Kasparek, were probably not more pleased than the Germans, but they had no choice in the matter. Heckmair wrote: 'We, the sons of the older Reich, united with our countrymen of the Eastern Border to march together to victory'. After the second bivouac, the march to victory continued under the constant threat of storms and avalanches. They scarcely had the time to eat. They watched the avalanches of fresh snow and timed them, so as to rush as quickly as possible in the estimated interval between the falls. On the third day, a terrific storm broke. The cold was so intense that the men's wet clothes froze almost at once, wrapping them in icy sheets. Yet, as they were very high by then, falling stones were less frequent. When they at last reached the summit at four in the afternoon, they were so exhausted that they could hardly feel the elation of victory, and could only gather strength enough to rush down the normal route through a raging blizzard. Joy and pride came later. They were duly praised, and the eager desire of all those who had come before them and had died on the face was at last gratified: the four men were presented to Hitler, who congratulated them on their achievement. This was their most splendid reward. They were not given parts in films.

War broke out and put a temporary stop to further attempts: the Swiss authorities maintained their opposition to such climbs, on account of the risks incurred by the rescue parties. The next ascent was not made until 1947 and was accomplished by two French guides, Lionel Terray and Louis Lachenal.

Terray had suffered a bad accident, which had almost paralysed one of his fingers. However, he recovered in time to be able to tackle the worst climb in the Alps. By that time, very little was known about the route followed by the victorious pre-war party, and the French team had to improvise, with the result that they followed a route that was partly new and thus made a new first ascent. The rocks, as usual, were made extremely dangerous by a succession of storms which pelted the face with hail and snow. It was a merciless fight against a tough enemy. A blissful lack of imagination enabled the two men to carry on without being too obsessed by an atmosphere redolent with tragedy. The rocks were either too loose to take a piton securely, or too tough to have anything hammered in.

During the first part of the ascent, the two men hurried upwards in a constant hail shower. However, they succeeded in reaching the last pitches of the Mitteleggi ridge and pushed along to the summit, almost unable to realize that success was theirs. And yet, all was not over. They got lost on the way down from the summit and wandered for hours down chimneys and along ledges, always in dread that they might come upon a cliff too high to be double-roped down. They felt that they were too exhausted to be able to reclimb any pitch they had descended, if the way proved hopeless. However, they eventually reached the Scheidegg Hotel, where they were met by an army of journalists, intent on having the whole story: so many years had elapsed since the first ascent of the terrible north face.

By slow stages the face became popular among the best climbers. At the end of July 1952, nine men attacked on the same day, in four parties. Five were French, climbing on two ropes: and their members were among the best of contemporary climbers, Gaston Rebuffat, Paul Habran, Pierre Leroux, Guido Magnone and Jean Bruneau. Habran was the only amateur of the group. The Austrian party was also quite outstanding, with Hermann Buhl and Sepp Jochler. The German party consisted of the two brothers Maag, who were not on the same level as the others. Rebuffat had come to Grindelwald with Leroux a few days before to have a look at the face. They had not been able to go very high on account of innumerable falling stones, but they had not been awed by the mountain, in spite of its legend and its repelling aspect. They came back in great form, Rebuffat and Habran having just climbed the Jorasses.

The weather was beautiful for once and a cold wind promised marvels, but did not keep its promise. The beginning of the climb was easy. These very strong parties went up very quickly and had a fair chance of reaching the summit ridge, with just one bivouac, when voices were heard above them. Rebuffat discovered one, and then another party ahead of them. The Germans and the Austrians had started separately, but had joined forces later. They were much slower than the French teams and rather badly equipped. Nevertheless, they refused to let the others pass them. Buhl, though an excellent mountaineer, who had done the Walker Spur on the Jorasses in very bad conditions, was surprisingly slow and his companion, Jochler, led most of the time. The two Germans, good climbers though very young, were pleasant lads and, when coming to a bad pitch, suggested by gestures, as they knew no French and the others knew no German, that they should all rope up together, an offer which Rebuffat accepted. It was later in the afternoon when they reached a bivouac site. Rebuffat gave a pull-over to one of the Germans, whose only over-garment was a light anorak.

During the night the weather deteriorated and, when a dirty dawn swept away the night, snow began to fall. They fought their way up under worsening conditions. Rebuffat was hit by a falling stone and needed all his strength and self-control not to let go under the impact. Avalanches were thundering down the whole face. Fixed ropes left by former parties were stiff in their coating of ice. The second bivouac was organised under pouring snow. The two French parties had to take charge of the Germans, who had no food left and were quite exhausted and slightly frost-bitten. During the night, the temperature fell further but the weather cleared. The next day, with Buhl leading the whole team, they crept up ice-glazed or snow-covered rocks and it was six in the evening when the French parties reached the summit. Contrary to what had happened to Terray, they had no difficulty in finding the fairly easy route down and reached the Eigergletscher station safely.

A few days later, Erich Vanis, one of the best Austrian climbers, made the ascent in more or less similar conditions.

In 1957 occurred another tragedy of the kind in which the Eiger specialises. An Italian party and a German party attempted separately to climb the face and eventually joined forces higher up. The two parties were very slow; the weather became bad, as usual, but even then they made no attempt to come down. They were seen from the Scheidegg and a rescue party was organised. Meanwhile, they were still climbing very slowly. One of the Italians, Longhi, was quite exhausted apart from being shaken and injured by a fall; his hands were frostbitten. His companion, Corti, decided to push on and find help. The Germans, Nothdurft and Franz Meyer were also very tired, but they went on with Corti. Higher up the latter was hit by a falling stone and the Germans decided to leave him where he was and go up for help. What happened to the Germans remained a mystery for several years.

A rescue party, unaware of what had happened on the mountain, was organised at the Scheidegg, and it took a very long time to get ready.

Meanwhile, Lionel Terray, who was in Grindelwald with two Dutch climbers, was asked to help. The rescue party was well equipped. They organised a clever device to send down a long cable with a sort of basket; with this they would try and reach the climbers, who were known to be very high in the face, from above. A small crowd of specialists was gathering on the summit of the Eiger. Among its members was Ricardo Cassin, who had arrived at top speed from Lecco to help his countrymen. One of Terray's Dutch companions acted as interpreter. The next day, after a biouvac in ice-cold wind, someone went down on the cable and succeeded in getting within shouting distance of the men marooned in the face. A young German guide volunteered to be let down and eventually, with great difficulty, he reached Corti and succeeded in hauling him back to the top. Though injured and frostbitten, he was in a less terrible state than one might have expected after such an ordeal.

Terray volunteered to go down and try to reach Longhi, who was still alive and whose voice was heard from time to time. The weather was getting worse, night was falling and the rescuers abandoned their attempt: even the task of getting Corti down the mountain required a tremendous effort. Longhi died alone of cold, exposure and despair. Could he have been saved? His body was recovered later.

For months one wondered what had happened to the two Germans, who were both excellent mountaineers. Wild tales circulated. In September 1961, when collecting part of the equipment left on the top of the Eiger, a guide who had gone down some distance in the west face suddenly discovered the two dead bodies, side by side, on a rock ledge. They had reached the summit and died of cold and exhaustion, probably in their sleep, during a last bivouac. They were within one hour at most of the Eigergletscher station and safety.

The first winter ascent was made between March 6 and 12, 1961, by Toni Hiebeler, Toni Kinshofer, Walter Almberger and Anderl Manhardt: a long, terrible ordeal, extremely well led by an outstanding team. Climbers then tried solitary ascents of the face. In 1962 the Austrian climber Diether Marchart was killed on such an attempt: he was twenty-three.

Eventually, the first successful solitary ascent was accomplished in August 1963 by Michel Darbellay, a young guide from Orsières (Valais). He had already tried to ascend the face with Michel Vaucher and two young women, Mme Attinger, who shortly afterwards married Vaucher, and Mlle Boullaz, all of them outstanding mountaineers. On the wall, when he was alone, Darbellay displayed a magnificent technique and extraordinary speed, which is a safety factor on that storm-haunted peak. Very early in the climb, Darbellay overtook a German party which had started a day ahead of him. He passed them and pushed on, following Terray's route, which is more difficult

17. On the Midi-Plan arête. (Photo: Ed. Novos)

18. Mont Blanc, south face, and the Vallée Blanche. (Photo: Gaston Rebuffat)

19. Rebuffat on the south face of the Aiguille du Midi. (Photo: P. Tairraz)

20. Col du Diable, with the Vallée Blanche below. (Photo: Gaston Rebuffat)

than the ordinary one, but free from ice-glaze. The weather was fine and remained so throughout that day and the next, which is a rare occurrence. The drawback was the intense cold, which cramped the young man during a long night on a narrow ledge. The solitude and the necessity to concentrate on countless details make a solitary climb doubly exhausting. Darbellay had a whole night to consider them. Yet, the hours of darkness eventually ended. Leaving his ledge by six o'clock, he reached the summit by eight. When coming down the ordinary route, at a leisurely pace, he met a Wengen guide who was coming up to bring him some food, which was very welcome, since Darbellay had climbed very light and the last of his food had been eaten long before.

By the end of 1964, 144 climbers had succeeded in reaching the top of the north face of the Eiger, and twenty-five had died in the attempt, sometimes after a successful climb. A new attitude was developing. Since the first ascent, the routes up the face had been experimental: the first party had passed where it was possible to pass, and that was hard enough. Lionel Terray had found another itinerary because he did not know where the usual route was or because he had lost it. Now the mountaineers decided that climbing the face was not enough: the new idea was to find a *direttissima* route up the face. This geometrical obsession is a craze in the Dolomites. On granite mountains climbers had mostly thought of following the various ridges or spurs. There are no spurs on the huge sunless face of the Eiger, so that a sort of ideal line had to be drawn up the face and followed as closely as possible. Various parties, German, Swiss, and Italian, tried this ideal line of ascent and either gave up or finished by using the normal route. Things changed when British and American mountaineers took up the challenge.

Chris Bonington, Joe Brown, L. S. Clough, Peter Gillman, Douglas Haston, J. D. Layton and others opened or repeated the most difficult routes in the Western Alps and Dolomites. They brought a classical and very conservative Alpine Club to accept modern notions of mountaineering, and they brought British mountaineering back very much to the fore. The other important event in contemporary Alpine history was the arrival of the Americans. In the fight for the north faces there were two outstanding American mountaineers, Gary Hemming and John Harlin. John Harlin was attracted by the Eiger. In 1962 he ascended the North Wall with Konrad Kirch, following the usual route up the face, and it was, as usual, a most gruelling experience. They had to force their way up through snowstorms, but Harlin was able to study the surrounding parts of the wall, and from that day he was intent on coming back to find a more direct route.

Other parties were also training for the big attempt. Among them were

Chris Bonington and Ian Clough, who had already ascended the usual route up the face, Layton Kor, Peter Gillman, Dougal Haston, all of them great ice specialists who had been fascinated by the mountain. Harlin was the most intent of them all, and he wrote once: 'In placing those pitons and in stretching for the infrequent holds on the great smooth wall, life effervesced in me.' The new route was to be attempted with a new technique, fitting the gigantic size of the mountain, and the climb was to be achieved in winter, to avoid loose stone. The whole equipment was carefully thought out. The new route had been reconnoitred by helicopter, flying as near as possible to the rocks. This very long ascent was likely to require ten days and probably more.

The Anglo-American team consisted of Harlin, Kor and Haston. Bonington went out as a photographer. The four men had been meticulously and progressively trained. They were about to start when they suddenly heard that a German party, eight men strong, was actually on the new route. There was no time to waste, and the party, scattered all over Switzerland and England, promptly re-assembled at the Scheidegg, where they met the Germans. The latter had been some way up, organising their itinerary with fixed ropes and extra pitons, and they had come down during a spell of bad weather. When it cleared, shortly afterwards, both parties left, Kor and Haston following the line of fixed ropes but not using them.

It was the beginning of a strange climb, run on completely new, almost Himalayan lines. The Anglo-American team soon came level with the Germans. They climbed either together or separately. Sometimes they shared bivouacs. Conditions were so severe that they could climb very little each day and often spent whole days hooking fixed ropes to the rocks in order to be able to push on the next day. Once or twice a week, two or three men would go down to the Scheidegg for a rest, a wash and a decent hot meal; then they would come back to their wretched bivouac and start climbing again the next day. Sometimes they were storm-bound for several days in their snow caves. One day, John Harlin heard over the radio that a friend of his, the Swiss guide Hilti von Almen, had been killed in a skiing accident, and he went down to attend the burial service, changing back into climbing kit on reaching the Scheidegg.

Unlike the British team, the members of which were well-known, hardened climbers, the Germans were practically unknown in the climbing world. They had never climbed the Eiger or any of the big western peaks. They had specialised in extremely severe, though rather low north faces, usually climbed in winter. They were Peter Haag, Lorg Lehne, Karl Golikow, Siegfried Hupfauer, Gunter Schnaidt, Gunter Strobek, Rolf Rozenkopf and Roland Vottler, all between twenty and thirty. Days passed.

On March 22nd, Peter Gillman, who was the British radio reporter, was following the progress of the team through the Scheidegg telescope. Suddenly, 'in a chill moment that turned the world upside down, he saw a figure dressed in red falling through the air, clear of the face: It was stretched out and was turning over slowly, gently, and with awful finality'. Kor was at the Scheidegg. He and Bonington, dreading the worst, skied down, reaching the foot of the mountain to find John Harlin's body. Two days later he was buried in Leysin, where he had been teaching in an international climbing school. The ascent went on, which was much criticised. Yet as it was obvious that the German team would not have stopped for anything, Harlin's companions also resumed the climb, as a kind of homage to the man who had given his life to ascend the face. Eventually the summit was reached on March 25th. Haston was the one Englishman among the five who made it.

What had happened to John Harlin will never be known for certain. He was prussiking up, using his jumars: they may have frayed the rope, which may also have been worn out by friction on the rocks.

The newly-opened route has been followed several times, and in the summer of 1969 a Japanese party, including a girl, Dr Michiko Imai, went up the new route, taking one month to complete the ascent. The girl was twenty-seven and all her companions were also quite young. They had something like one ton of equipment to drag along. An Austrian and a Swiss team, going up the ordinary route, were much helped by the ropes the Japanese had left on the lower part of the wall. Purists objected strongly to such mechanical help and the long ropes left fastened to the rocks. The discussion is purely academic: it is very difficult to know what is permissible on a mountain and what is not. As soon as pitons are morally tolerated—as they cannot be physically banned—everything follows as a matter of course.

The last feat accomplished on the Eiger—not on the north face but the north-west—was one accomplished by a young Valais guide, Sylvain Saudan. On March 9, 1970, he descended the face on skis. Having been dropped by a helicopter near the Eigerjoch, not without great difficulty and danger, he climbed to the top and then skied down to Eigergletscher. When Cassin had come to help the rescue party haul up Corti, he had been greatly impressed by the large slabs of the north-west face, and their coating of green ice. Saudan skied over a repellent mixture of ice, emerging rocks, windslabs and fresh snow, always ready to avalanche. Yet he managed to negotiate the long steep slope without injury or frostbite.

CHAPTER SIXTEEN

PIZ BADILE

Piz Badile was ignored for a long time, standing as it does at the far end of a remote district, and few mountaineers went to inspect its threatening north-east face. It lived a quiet, secluded life until daring climbers went very much off the beaten tracks to have a look at it and realised that here was one more 'last problem', and a problem not easy to solve. The mountain towers above the Val Bregaglia (Bergell in German) which leads down from Maloja to Lake Como over the Swiss-Italian frontier. There is a hut above the village of Promontogno, and from the hut there is a very stiff pull to the foot of the mountain. The south face is easy, with a tame glacier creeping down to Val Masino. The north-east face—the Swiss side of the Badile—is one of the biggest Alpine precipices. Not that its height is tremendous—3,308 metres—but the rock is hard, smooth compact limestone with few holds, and it is extremely difficult to drive a piton into it.

The mountain has a respectable early history. The south face was scaled by Coolidge with the Devouassoud brothers. A second ridge was climbed by another well-known team, von Rydzewsky with Christian Klucker and Emil Rey, and a third by von Rydzewsky alone with Emil Rey. There were one or two more attempts. The north-east face was left untouched until 1937, when Ricardo Cassin, with Esposito and Ratti, after strenuous Dolomite climbs, came to Promontogno and tackled the great, partly overhanging wall. Two young Como mountaineers, Molteni and Valsecchi, were already fighting their way up the mountain. Cassin and his team overtook them and they joined forces, but the younger men were already very tired, after a bad night in the hut and a first bivouac. The weather changed, and during the second bivouac they had to face a terrific gale blowing over the district. Cassin managed to pull the whole party through and they reached the summit the next day, but that was too late for the Como youths. Molteni died of exhaustion on reaching the summit and his friend just before they reached the hut. And the rest was silence for several years.

The war put this frontier ridge out of bounds on either side. Then, in 1948, Gaston Rebuffat and Bernard Pierre decided to re-open Cassin's route. Though Bernard Pierre at that time had had only a few seasons in the Alps, he had already ascended the north face of the Dru and the north face of the

Aiguille de la Brenva, the latter with Rebuffat. They were both keen to take up the challenge of Piz Badile, and in spite of an extremely rainy summer they left Chamonix for that remote district, right at the back of the Grisons. The long drive to Promontogno made them even keener to pit their strength against the big mountain. The hut had been burnt down during the war (a fire not due to enemy action, as it was on Swiss territory). They had to start from the village of Sciora, much lower than the hut.

After an easy beginning, the whole face proved to be a matter of pitons and of balancing on extremely precarious perches. They were able to pitch their first bivouac slightly higher than Cassin's, more or less half-way up, and just below the place where the wall becomes steeper still. 'Shrivelled with cold, hanging on to Piz Badile by a piton, like a picture on a wall, we were living only through our longing for sunrise', wrote Gaston Rebuffat. The night was endless. The next day, they were soon confronted with the main problem of the climb, a perpendicular *dièdre* which took hours to overcome. When they were wondering whether it might just be possible to reach the summit before nightfall, they noticed that the sky was clouding, and almost at once a storm broke over them. They were soon wet to the skin, stuck on a precarious ledge with lightning striking right and left. Rain turned to snow. The storm, its fury spent, abated, driven away towards the Bernina. But almost at once another one began to bellow and streaks of fire pierced the night. But even storms on a mountain come to an end. In the morning, the weather cleared; by midday they reached the summit, then descended to the hut by the normal, easy route.

In spite of the storm which had delayed them, they had taken less time than Cassin's party. In July 1949, Bonatti and Barzaghi also ascended the face, bivouacking only once, probably because there was no storm to delay them. Their main trouble proved to be an endless succession of stone avalanches which made the big *dièdres* extremely unsafe. During the second day they fought their way up through occasional showers of hail and snow, but the weather cleared when they reached the summit.

Badile by way of this face became slowly, if not popular, at least one of the peaks a great mountaineer should have ascended. Growing intimacy with the mountain reduced the time required to reach the summit. The first party who succeeded in avoiding a bivouac altogether was that of Lionel Terray and Louis Lachenal in 1950. They went up at top speed, lashed on to an even fiercer pace when nearing the top by an approaching storm. They had taken a little under seven hours and a half. Hermann Buhl made the first solitary ascent in 1951. He found a number of Terray's pitons, which helped him to solve one or two problems, though Terray wrote that he had hardly used pitons at all. Buhl reached the summit in the almost unbelievable time of four hours and a half. The rest of the day he spent in long periods of rest in brilliant sunshine, gazing at the view and leisurely descending the Badile ridge to Promontogno, where he had left his bicycle. Later, Nothdurft, who was to die on the Eiger, climbed the face in three hours and a half. Terray came back, climbing with Suzanne Valentini, an excellent mountaineer, and they went up the face in seven hours.

In accordance with the modern attitude towards mountaineering, something more difficult and more exciting had to be attempted on the Badile, and the answer was a winter ascent. Winter conditions make Piz Badile a much more difficult proposition than in summer. The granite faces are smooth and compact, so that pitons are not to be relied upon, and as the faces are steep but not perpendicular, the heavy winter snow does not slide off, but remains there and turns to ice-glaze or pure ice. Parts of the faces are covered with, or overhung by, huge ice bulges.

In 1961, Pierre Mazeaud attempted the climb with two friends and they failed on account of heavy snow over very steep rocks. Then it was known—such things cannot be kept secret in the Alps—that Badile was the goal of Michel Darbellay. Eventually, by the end of 1967, two extremely strong parties met at the foot of the mountains: Darbellay with two Swiss colleagues, Daniel Trolliet and Camille Bournisien, and three Italians, Gogna, Armando and Calcagno. The two parties worked together, joining forces. The mountains proved to be as bad as, or even worse than they expected. Snow fell most of the time and the temperature fell to —30°. Eventually, on Christmas Day, they had to come down to wait for better weather.

The weather changed a little a few days later. During the whole climb, the parties had followed a Himalayan technique, fixing ropes, organising caves for bivouac sites. In spite of all that, the climb was extremely hard and strenuous. They resumed the climb, having been dropped on the glacier at the foot by helicopter. They greeted the New Year half-way up the face, but the greeting was rather subdued. They had no food left and hardly any rope, which they would have to use if compelled to descend at the last pitch. Yet they eventually managed to reach the summit at midday on January 2nd. It had been a terrible ordeal and they had to bivouac once more on the way down. Darbellay and Calcagno sustained frostbite.

CHAPTER SEVENTEEN

MORE 'LAST PROBLEMS'

THE solution of what had been accepted for several years as 'the last Alpine problems' never meant that the Alps were exhausted, as the development of Alpine technique put within reach a number of faces and ridges which could not have been considered seriously in the thirties. Of course, they are extremely severe, all of them, and most Alpine districts can feature one or more. The two most popular ranges for acrobatic feats are the Dolomites and the Mont Blanc range.

All the great Italian climbers have trained in the Dolomites: men like Gervasutti, Bonatti, Oggioni, Cassin and others. They have induced increasing numbers of enthusiasts to follow in their footsteps. The Dolomites can be climbed when practically everything else in the Alps is snow-bound; they are a good deal lower than the Chamonix or Valais ranges and are therefore less likely to be covered with snow or ice-glaze. On their sheer limestone faces, the new Alpine technique has been tried and brought to a high pitch of efficiency. Competitive mountaineering has always been practised there, with questionable results. In 1959, for example, the north face of the Tre Cime di Lavaredo became a sort of racecourse, with parties hurrying up to the summit, climbing precipices over 1,500 feet high. Cassin and Ratti had found a new route up the face of the Cima Ovest in 1935, but in order to avoid the first overhangs they had followed a side ridge, so that it was not quite a direct approach to the summit. Between July 6 and 11, 1959, Mazeaud and Desmaison found and followed a new route straight to the top. It was a hard, tricky fight, which was repeated during the following days by their friends Kohlman and Lagesse.

Then a Swiss party, Schelbert and Weber, tried another direct route, reached a great height, hammering in pitons and fixing stirrups. They left a document in three languages on the last pitch they reached, claiming the discovery of the route. Then, they double-roped down. Completely ignoring the document, its claims and implications, two Cortina d'Ampezzo 'Squirrels' members of a very exclusive local climbing club, the members of which wear a red pullover embroidered with a white squirrel—Franceschini and Micchielli, —went up the newly-discovered route. While they were forcing their way up, their climb was mentioned over the radio. The two Swiss heard the broadcast and hurried back to Cortina, attacking the Cima Ovest again three days later. The two Squirrels were still hammering their way up, and the two parties indulged in a regular race up the face. Eventually, the climb proved so difficult that the Swiss were compelled to traverse to Cassin's route. They reached the top, climbed down to the place where they had been compelled to abandon the *direttissima* and fought their way up again, along a slightly different itinerary. There is a sort of grim humour in such a race over such unfriendly ground.

Episodes of this kind give a sort of glamour to the story of the progressive discovery of the Dolomites, yet sometimes the various routes scarcely differ from one another, and are sometimes not very far apart. Most of them are extremely strenuous. The great specialist of the Marmolada is Gino Soldà who, with Conforto, discovered the route up the west face in 1936. It is a straight line up the face, geometrically perfect. It was left untouched until 1949, when two parties, Franceschini with a companion, and afterwards Schatz and Couzy, reopened it. Couzy was killed in the Dauphiné in 1958, hit by a falling stone. In 1936 Vintzer had found another and equally difficult route, which was followed again by Georges and Sonia and Livanos. The team specialized in the most uncompromising sixth-grade climbs and they found many in the district.

One of the classical playgrounds of the Dolomites is the Tre Cime di Lavaredo group which happen to consist of four summits and not three. While the Chamonix Aiguilles have always been likened to Gothic steeples, the Lavaredo peaks look like fortified Romanesque castles, with straight, massive, square buttresses. The north face of the Cima Grande had been scaled for the first time in 1931 by Emilio Comici and the Dimai brothers. It is 1,800 feet high; the first part is a stiff overhang and the second is perpendicular. Toni Egger, from the Tyrol, made the first ascent without a bivouac. Soldà is also a specialist of the group, and the Grande is one of his favourite mountains, which he climbs with the dash and elegance of the man who feels perfectly at home on its stupendous wall. He introduced Gaston Rebuffat to that sort of climb, so that the younger man got used, as he put it in *Starlight and Storm*, to dancing 'a fantastic ballet on a perpendicular stone stage . . . The frightful void was no longer a weight tied to my feet, but a pleasant companion'.

Walter Bonatti began his winter mountaineering career in the Dolomites, either alone or with Carlo Mauri. When he came to Cortina d'Ampezzo, the north face of the Cima Grande had already been climbed in winter by Kasparek, but that of the Cima Ovest had never been touched in that season. He attacked it with Mauri, and it became a long protracted struggle in thick powdered snow, with nothing stable round them except the pitons they hammered into the rocks. They bivouacked twice. Then they went up the Grande, which they found in excellent condition, and they scaled it without a bivouac in spite of the cold and the thick snow which made the ascent even more difficult than in summer.

In 1963, Toni Hiebeler spent eight days on the winter ascent of the north-west face of the Civetta, another face of which was scaled in winter, too, by a party under Roberto Sorgato. All over the Dolomites the best climbers are discovering more and more *direttissime*, each more difficult than the last. Aurelio Garobbio wrote that 'there is always something more difficult'. Obviously, for most climbers, one of the characteristics of the present mountaineering era is the will to conquer what had been previously thought invincible: difficulty for difficulty's sake, as a thing in itself, and hardly ever as a means towards an end.

One of the very latest winter achievements (January 1970) is the first winter ascent of the Grivola by the outstanding young Italian mountaineer, Alessandro Gogna, with four companions: Gianni Calcagno, Leo Cerutti, Carmelo di Pietro and Guido Machetto. The Dolomite technique has been imported into other ranges, too, and it was only by 'artificial' climbing that the scaling of many faces and ridges became possible—the south face of the Aiguille du Midi by Rebuffat and Maurice Baquet, for instance. This climb is extremely spectacular owing to the fact that the crowd hauled up the Aiguille du Midi by telepherique can watch the climbers during the whole of their progress up the face. The first ascent took twelve hours. It has now been repeated many times and has become very popular. One day, when I was climbing in the neighbourhood, I watched five parties queuing up for the south face. On one occasion Rebuffat did it twice in one day, first with an American companion, then again with Cassin, who had had no time to let him know in advance that he was coming. The climb has even been filmed for television.

Shortly after the end of the war French parties came back in strength and skill. Herzog, Madeuf and Oudot repeated one of the Sentinelle Rouge routes. When Georges and Claude Kogan climbed the south ridge of the Noire de Peuteret, it was Claude who led all through, displaying her astonishing pluck and talent in one of the stiffest climbs of the whole range.

In 1949, Bonatti tried for the first time the Grand Capucin du Tacul, a tall red granite steeple which towers above one of the faces of the Mont Blanc du Tacul, overlooking the Vallée Blanche. It is quite sheer, just like a Dolomite peak, with the added difficulty of much greater altitude. Bonatti tried several times and eventually reached the top in July 1951, together with Luciano

Ghigo, after three bivouacs. They had to use 'artificial' means all the way. Most great specialists have been attracted by this very severe and beautiful climb. Marcel Ichac, in the film he made with Lionel Terray, *Stars Shine at Midday* (*Les Etoiles de Midi*), filmed the longer part of the ascent, enabling a wide audience to realize what a very difficult climb looks like.

The Mont Blanc range is perhaps not quite inexhaustible, but a large number of new routes have been opened up the various Aiguilles. One of them was the south face of the Fou, between the Blaitière and Plan massifs. John Harlin and Gary Hemming had studied it from afar and they decided that the formidable face was climbable. Eventually, after a first unsuccessful attempt, two parties tried in earnest: John Harlin with Gary Hemming, and Tom Frost with Stew Fulton. After a bivouac during which they were lashed by a tremendous storm, they eventually reached the summit, but all was not over. For some trifling reason—probably because they both were tired and on edge—Harlin and Hemming quarrelled and almost fought. That was the end of their climbing partnership. When Harlin climbed the west face of the Aiguille de Blaitière, he did it with Pierre Mazeaud, whose guest he was in his Chamonix chalet. Mazeaud kept a delightful remembrance of him as a very pleasant young man and a magnificent climber, with a most original technique. They had an almost comfortable bivouac during a stormless night, very high up in the face, and came down the next day after a very enjoyable climb. John Marts went up the south face of the Fou in 1968.

These were major climbs. It is still possible to find minor—and fairly difficult—ones in the Chamonix district. In 1968, during an extremely wet summer, in which most of the long climbs were out of reach in their heavy shrouds of fresh snow, Rebuffat made the last of several 'recreational ascents' above the Argentière glacier. They were up low, steep peaks which had been given very picturesque names, like Minaret, Yatagan and Casque, but were quite neglected. For three years they had provided his parties with interesting climbs in the beautiful landscape of the Argentière Glacier. The larger part of the climbing crowds ignores the latter as it requires a very long approach, even now that the new Grands Montets telepherique has been built.

The very spectacular climbs of the Chamonix district often compel mountaineers to take heavy risks. Wet summers are dangerous on account of heavy snow falls which are likely to dissolve into avalanches, and rocks plastered with ice-glaze. Climbers whose Alpine holidays are strictly limited in time are likely to rush up as soon as the weather shows a more lenient tendency, not waiting for the fresh snow to melt. This is particularly dangerous in Chamonix and the Valais. Dry summers are dangerous for other reasons: the increase in stone falls.

Glaciers have been retreating a great deal for more than two centuries but they are now extending again. This increase has had disastrous consequences: huge slices of ice fell from the Tour Glacier, crushing a group of campers, and later from the Allalin Glacier, destroying the huts of Italian workmen employed on the new Mattmark dam. There were many deaths. Mountainsides seem to be alive with landslides, one of the worst being that which crushed the Roc des Fiz sanatorium above Servoz, at the foot of the steep and dangerous Fiz range. In 1964, an avalanche falling from the Grands Montets face of the Aiguille Verte carried away fourteen men in seven parties, all of them first rate climbers attending an Alpine course of ENSA. No convincing explanation was offered. They may have been swept down by a tremendous wind-slab. Those very difficult climbs have led to a complete reorganization of the rescue parties in the Alps. The best equipment and personel seems to be displayed in Chamonix, where the rescue organization is attended to by a specialized set of *gendarmes* with helicopters and the most modern devices possible. Lately they have succeeded in rescuing parties stranded in the middle of almost vertical walls, lowering a guide parallel with the wall and near enough to hack in it a step to stand in, until the second man was lowered the same way and they could rope up and proceed towards the stranded party, to get them hauled up into the helicopter.

One of the major tragedies of recent times happened in 1961 on the Pilier du Fresnay, a high promontory in the face of Mont Blanc de Courmayeur. On July 7th two extremely strong parties started up the Pilier: Pierre Mazeaud, Antoine Vieille, Robert Guillaume and Pierre Kohlman on two ropes, and Walter Bonatti, Robert Gallieni and Andrea Oggioni making the second party. Oggioni, from Monza, was a guide of first rank who had done outstanding climbs in the Dolomites, Mont Blanc and the Andes. Galliani usually climbed with him and with Bonatti; he was an outstanding and efficient mountaineer. The French party was more than competent and Pierre Mazeaud is one of the very best of present-day mountaineers. The Pilier towers up at high altitude and is only reached after a long and severe approach. Had the weather kept reasonably fine there would have been no problem whatever, but when the parties were within about 100 metres of the summit the weather changed and a furious thunderstorm pinned them where they were, under pouring snow. Kohlman was struck by lightning; he was slightly paralysed, recovered quickly, but had probably undergone some sort of brain shock.

That was the beginning of a long agony. Snow was falling in sheets, piling up on the walls of the small tent in which the climbers huddled together. The cold was intense and, contrary to what could be expected in July, it did not bring along a change of weather. Day changed into night and into day again, and the storm still raged. Exhaustion comes quickly under such conditions. After several days, they decided to try and force their way down to the Gamba hut, in spite of the constant risk of being swept away by an avalanche. Shortly after they started, Vieille, the youngest of the party, died of exhaustion. Kohlman became more and more distracted and was delirious. Mazeaud and Bonatti, the two leaders, grimly set to their task of bringing down their companions. Then Guillaume died. Bonatti and Kohlman went on, but Bonatti alone reached the hut, where he found a rescue party of Italian guides. They had been met by Harlin and Hemming, who had heard of the trouble and had come up to help, but they had been turned down. Mazeaud, Galliani and Oggioni were grimly staggering on. Night had fallen—their eighth night in the mountains—and it was very dark. Suddenly, Oggioni started talking about Monza and his family and slowly died in Mazeaud's arms. Eventually, Mazeaud and Gallieni staggered into the hut, where Mazeaud learned that Kohlman had died just before reaching it.

Six weeks later, when the weather had cleared and most of the snow melted, eight men in four parties reached the summit of the pillar, after a bivouac at the spot where Bonatti and the others had been snowbound. The members of the successful team were Whillans, Bonington, Julien, Desmaison, Poulet, Villard, Piussi and Clough. On February 8, 1967, Desmaison came back and made the first winter ascent, which he completed by reaching the summit of Mont Blanc on the 13th.

CHAPTER EIGHTEEN

MOUNTAINS IN WAR-TIME

MOUNTAIN warfare is probably as old as war itself, which is as old as the hills, and much has been written about military operations in mountain districts, such as the crossing of the Alps by Hannibal, assisted (or more probably, hampered) by his elephants, or of the St Bernard by Bonaparte in 1800.

During the First World War there was hard fighting in the Dolomites, with battles raging high upon the jagged crests. The Austro-Italian front line became fixed in these high places and the armies were locked into each other's positions on fantastic ground. The fighting line was reached with the help of téléphériques or exposed mule-paths, and the danger of avalanches was often added to the expected dangers of war. The fighting units needed an extremely accurate knowledge of mountains and of mountaineering to be able to keep their precarious positions or to attack the enemy. Luis Trenker, before he became a film star, had fought in the Dolomites in the Austrian mountain troops and in *Bergkameraden* he gave some vivid descriptions of these actions.

Mountain warfare was different in 1940 and during the subsequent years. While it had been waged along more or less classic lines in 1916–18, with regular, if complicated transport lines, the battles which were fought in the Alps in 1940, at a time when France was already dissolving into nightmare, were almost improvised rearguard actions. Everything was disorganized, no one could form a precise idea of the situation, and something like terror was engulfing the whole country. It was at that very moment that Italy declared war on the Allies and the Alps became a battle line. There were very few troops, since most of the Chasseurs Alpins had been sent first to Norway, and then, after evacuation, brought back to the Somme. The Alpine frontier was well fortified: the height and the steepness of the slopes, which were more difficult to scale from the Italian than from the French side, could be relied on to aid defence. The assumption that those small, though well situated, fortresses could hold out, proved to be correct.

It is not my intention here to relate the various actions, but only to show what was done with mountain technique in some of them. There are few, if any, official documents on the subject, for the German occupation had one catastrophic result among many others: the accidental or wilful destruction of many military archives. Few documents have been published about mountain warfare. The best of them is *S. E. S. (Section d'Eclaireurs Skieurs)* by Jacques Boell.

I have already mentioned the author's name. He has specialized in the mountains of Oisans and has written several books about them. In 1940 he was called up as an officer of the Chasseurs Alpins, and stationed in the mountain huts above Chamonix. The whole of this district, each stone of which is familiar to mountaineers, was more or less a vast fortress. With the various huts and smaller posts dotted all over the glaciers, no enemy could be expected to come down to the Arve valley. It was in such a setting that Boell heard of the Italian declaration of war. On that very same night the weather broke and all operations along the frontier were carried out under the worst possible conditions. It was winter still, and on the whole the deep snow on the ground and the constant snowfalls assisted the French troops, who, though heavily outnumbered and badly equipped, held out all along the frontier. In fact, a few hours before the armistice was enforced Italian soldiers were actually surrendering in the valley of Larche. Max Aldebert, who was also fighting in the Mont Blanc region, gave the following description of a night on guard:

'I remember one night in June 1940, standing on watch at an altitude of 7,500 feet with the thermometer at 16 degrees Fahrenheit; the wind was blowing wildly through the pass and there was an infinite void on both sides of the ridge. Below me, four square yards of snow and rocks; in front of me, beyond my Tommy gun, a desert of ice, where, in the deceptive light of the moon, each crevasse looked like a man advancing towards me. With ice-cold hands, a flask of brandy inside my anorak and my feet tight with cold inside boots that were too wide for me, I was longing for dawn while peering into the night. The slightest touch of my finger on the trigger would have started a roar of gun-fire in every direction. I was wishing for, and at the same time dreading it with all my strength. In the middle of this transparent, wintry world, where silence has all the combined weight of the slow development of geological forces, of the swish of the wind-blown snow and of the wail of the blizzard tearing itself against the precipices, a heavy loneliness seemed to weigh me down, pinning me to that merciless earth like the dreary stones which surrounded me, with no hope of relief. There are nights which are longer than centuries; nights which leave no feeling of humanity, when the mind becomes almost mineral or part of the calm fury of the elements.

A few operations were carried out to make the enemy aware that, whatever was happening in the north and the east of France, the troops on the

Alpine frontier intended to fight. These were strange battles, led by small groups of men with a perfect knowledge of the mountains they were defending. They took place at the heads of valleys, on passes which were under Italian fire. On the Col de la Galise, at the top of the Val d'Isère, a very small garrison was sent out on June 13, 1940, to clear the neighbourhood of the pass where Italian Alpini were still leading a peaceful life. Seven men volunteered and left on ski, early in the morning, on fine powdery snow. Their arrival was not detected by the Italians, who never reacted until hand-grenades were showered upon them. When the operation was completed and the Italian post was showing signs of panic, the seven men made a hasty retreat on ski. But there are necessities to be complied with, even under fire, like brushing the iced snow from the steel edges of the ski, or fastening the bindings, a slow process because of the complicated strap used by the French army. The two NCOs who were leading the party were excellent skiers, but the men were far less expert, and coming down the pass under fire was dangerous. One of the NCOs decided he would come down as slowly as possible, making many turns in the snow couloirs to draw enemy fire towards him. But he was so good a skier and the snow was in such fine condition that no military resolution could prevent him from sliding down at top speed, leaning forward, in a perfectly straight line, skiing as he would have done in an international competition. For the first time in their lives, the other men succeeded in coming down on their skis without falling and in good time. Their style was probably faulty, but none was wounded. The Italians had been much puzzled by the attack and they made no attempt to invade Val d'Isère.

Another small episode, which brought forward the necessity of Alpine technique under disconcerting conditions, took place between June 21st and 23rd in the Combe d'Enclave, a small glen at the south end of the Mont Blanc range. A group of seven men under a young lieutenant of the Chasseurs Alpins, Jean Bulle, had been sent out to reconnoitre Italian positions, the enemy having forced their way into the higher part of the Val des Glaciers. It was vitally important to keep them away from the passes leading into the Vallée de Montjoie. The whole district was very lightly held on the French side, as most of the troops had been taken away to the north in an attempt to stop the Germans before Lyons.

A small French detachment was holding out in the Val des Glaciers in an extremely precarious position and was threatened with encirclement by much more powerful Italian forces. To make things more awkward, a violent storm broke, covering the summits with fresh snow and coating rock precipices with ice. Yet, in a way, it helped: the Italians thought more about taking shelter than of keeping watch. Bulle left his seven men on a ridge and contrived a means of distracting the Italians' attention from the other party. He came down on the side of the ridge, climbing from one hold to another, then, when he had reached an overhang, sliding down on the double rope in full view of the enemy, looking like a spider dangling at the end of its thread, his tommy-gun slung across his back. Having reached a convenient though precarious position in the middle of the precipice, his feet resting on a tiny ledge, and supported by the double rope, he opened fire on the Italian position. He was a perfect shot and the Italians could not imagine where the bullets were coming from. He then had to reclimb his double rope, at the limit of his strength, after days of exhausting mountain warfare. Yet that could not be the end.

After another night on the ridge, under heavy snow, he realized that a new effort had to be made. The Italians that remained could not be very dangerous, but cold and exposure were worse. The one hope of survival for his men was to descend to the French party lower down, but it meant taking exhausted heavily-laden men along a difficult ridge and then down a long ice-glazed precipice. Bulle had been too tired to recover the double rope he had used the day before, so he decided to descend alone to find the route, collect a rope from the other party and come back to fetch his men. The rocks on the ridge were good, but coming down the face was a long nightmare. It took him a whole hour, forcing his way through heaps of waterlogged snow which he had to brush off to find holds. He succeeded at last in reaching the other party. He left his rucksack and gun with them, was given a rope and climbed back. His men were eagerly awaiting him: he was the only man who could lash them into action and help them down to some sort of safety. They had to double-rope twice. At the last moment, when Bulle was coming down last, and was mercifully near the bottom of the pitch, the rope snapped, but he did not fall more than a few feet. He had saved his men.

In August 1944 Jean Bulle, who was then a Major in the new army which had been formed after the first stages of the Liberation, went out to the German garrison of Albertville to demand their surrender. He never came back. A few days later, when part of the German troops had succeeded in forcing their way out towards Montmelian, Bulle's body was found on the road. He had been shot down in cold blood.

There were other similar instances of the part played by mountain technique during the short tragic fights of 1940. Then a hush fell, officially at least, on actions taken against the enemy until the day when, in August 1944, after the Allied landings in Saint-Raphaël and along the French south coast, the whole south-east of the country was once again in the war, the German and Italian troops fighting a fierce retreating action against the maquis

21. A modern climber's equipment. (Photo: Herbert Maeder)

22. On the face of Piz Badile. (Photo: Herbert Maeder)

organizations sent out to recover French Alpine territory. As early as August 19th, the whole Haute Savoie had been liberated by French maquis units, helped by British and American officers who had been parachuted among them. The Germans in Chamonix urgently called for help, but the twenty lorries of reinforcements were overtaken near Cluses and completely destroyed. The Chamonix garrison surrendered and Georges Charlet, Armand's brother, turned his barn into a prison camp until they were handed over to the French troops. Jean Bulle had started regrouping his men as early as 1942. His murder was a great blow to the young army.

Until the very end of the war there were fights all along the ridges, some of which have been related to Jacques Boell in the book I have already quoted, and some by C. Micholet in *Combats sur les Alpes*. Lieutenant Boell had gone back to his Chasseurs Alpins in September 1944, in Maurienne. His Colonel was Alain Le Ray, one of the climbing companions with whom he had made many great ascents in the Oisans mountains. Le Ray had escaped from a German prison camp and had been one of the first Resistance leaders in Dauphiny. Several well-known names appear in Boell's story: one meets for the first time Lionel Terray. In December 1944 he was in action, climbing with one of his cousins near the Col de Fréjus to try and destroy a post of German snipers who were a constant threat to the local French positions. The operation involved the ascent of an ice-couloir, the top of which was covered with a dangerous cornice likely to collapse on the first man to touch it. They had to extricate themselves from the couloir and tackle an ice-precipice, belaying their rope with their ice-axes; they had no pitons in their military equipment. At the last moment Terray's Bren gun failed to fire, put out of action by the intense cold.

Terray took part in another military operation when he was taken as far as the Italian town of Suza by Captain Poitaut, a regular army officer who had been one of the first maquis leaders in the district. They wanted to see to what extent the Germans had reoccupied the Alpine valleys. Terray was worried because a German attack seemed about to be launched on the Col d'Arnès, above the Avérole hut, and he hated the idea of being too late for the battle. As it turned out, Poitaut and he managed to come back just in time, when the enemy was attacking towards Arnès and was beaten back with heavy casualties. On another occasion, Poitaut went down from the Col de la Bessanèse under a blizzard in order to blow up the Italian téléphérique to the Gastaldi hut, at the foot of the col.

Jacques Boell himself, as ADC to Colonel Le Ray, directed an attack against the Point de Bellecombe in Maurienne, where the attacking troops were led by Lieutenant Frendo, the Jorasses specialist. There were very few men and it was essential to approach the German post in complete silence—a rather difficult undertaking since it involved ascending a long ice-slope with crampons and then a chimney where the ice-glaze had to be scraped off with the tips of their ice-axes. During the ascent of the slope, one of the men slipped and fell headlong, trying wildly to grab at something to stop his fall; rolling down and bumping with constantly increasing violence against the ice, he retained enough self-control not to yell. He escaped with a broken shoulder. Frendo led the first group of men who came into the open in broad daylight to shower grenades on the enemy.

Another episode was quite extraordinary. On March 10, 1945, a small party commanded by Colonel Le Ray with Jacques Boell and Captain Stephane went up the Ronce, above Lanslebourg, to have a look at the neighbouring heights and see, if possible, what the German troops were doing on the Italian side. The weather was beautiful and the snow hard and crisp under their crampons. They descried in the distance a solitary figure climbing towards them. He was a German officer or NCO, and he carried neither a gun nor binoculars. He had no ice-axe either, but a big, old-fashioned alpenstock. The three French officers, wondering what this unexpected mountaineer was up to, waited until they could cover him with their guns; then Captain Stephane pounced on him, shouting: *'Hände hoch!'* (Hands up!). The man was completely taken aback. He had never expected to come upon an enemy party and was horrified by the realisation that a prison camp now awaited him, though he would be there just for a short while, since it was obvious that the war was almost over. He explained that he was a corporal in a medical unit, serving in a front line hospital.

With his three captors, he completed the climb of the Pointe de Ronce and proved to be a good mountaineer in spite of his alpenstock, and a pleasant companion, though he was a prisoner of war. When they had descended to the point where he had been captured, he suddenly jumped over the cornice at the top of a steep couloir and slid down an ice-slope, balancing himself with his alpenstock; he succeeded in remaining upright and disappeared out of reach into a narrow rock gully. It was an extraordinary mountaineering feat. The three officers did not shoot at him, admiring the courage and coolness of a man who preferred possible death to a prison camp. Eventually, through other prisoners and a Germany army magazine, it was known that the man had not been killed but only slightly injured after his spectacular flight. His name was Anton Hörnle.

Years later, the second part of the story came out. When Marcel Ichac filmed *Les Etoiles de Midi*, one of the sequences was Hörnle's escape. The film was shown in Germany and a doctor from Nurtingen in Bavaria wrote to the West Germany TV, which had shown extracts from the film, telling them that Hörnle had been serving under him when he had escaped, that he was still alive and had settled in Constance. By that time Colonel Le Ray was a General and French Military Attaché in Bonn. The Bavarian TV organized an interview with the two men, who met again after their brief acquaintance on a summit in wartime. The sequence was both picturesque and moving.

The most extraordinary episode of this strange Alpine war took place on February 15, 1945, between the Col du Midi and the Col du Géant in the Mont Blanc range. The German-Austrian *Gebirgsjäger* were holding the Torino hut near the top of the Col du Géant; their goal was the Col du Midi, held by French Chasseurs Alpins supplied by téléphérique from Chamonix. The German idea was to destroy the téléphérique, hoist mortars to the pass and bomb Chamonix. The Austrian officer in command, Captain Singel, had about seventy men with him. On the Col du Midi there was a tiny detachment of seven Chasseurs, boys between seventeen and twenty-four. Lower down, the Requin hut and the Montenvers were equally lightly held. A patrol from the Col du Midi noticed German reinforcements coming up from Courmayeur and they telephoned Chamonix to report and ask for reinforcements. By nightfall, Lieutenant Rachel with twelve officers and men came up the téléphérique. The small hut on the col was a most primitive shanty, wind-swept and ice-cold, overlooking on one side the dizzy precipices of the north face of the Aiguille du Midi and on the other the long easy snow-slopes of the Vallée Blanche. When the post had too many visitors, late-comers were sent to slightly less primitive lodgings a few minutes away, built for the Duc de Broglie to study cosmic rays. The Chasseurs named this hut 'The Cosmics', though they probably had not the faintest idea what the term meant! There were also a few igloos serving as air-raid shelters—for there really were such raids. By 1.30 a.m., on February 17th, the Germans were signalled, skiing up on both sides of the slope leading from the Col du Géant. There were no stars and a gale was blowing.

Six members of the S.E.S. left the col at once, led by Lieutenant Rachel, who thought it better to attack the enemy than wait for him. They were on foot, carrying both their skis and their Bren guns. They went in the direction of the German ascent. Suddenly Rachel vaguely descried motionless white shapes crouching in the snow, and from that moment began a long nightmare, a struggle in pitch darkness between opponents who could hardly see each other. They were all dressed in the white skiing overalls worn by mountain troops in winter; shots were fired at random. At one moment, Rachel's detachment, thinking they were being met by the second small troop from the Col du Midi, suddenly came under tracer fire, but since the Alpins had no such ammunition, it was clear that the new detachment was German and about to surround them. They took evading action and began retreating towards the Col du Midi, diving into the night, dodging bewildered Germans who could do little in spite of their larger numbers.

As day was about to break, it became vital to get back to the Col du Midi, as open fighting would have been suicidal in broad daylight. The whole group succeeded in doing so and reached its goal completely exhausted by a mad fight at a very high altitude.

The last group to leave the col had succeeded in establishing itself in some rocks. At dawn, the Germans tried to storm them; they were excellent climbers and started up the precipice. Singel was shot dead in this action. At the same moment, a small French reconnaissance plane flew up the Vallée Blanche and dropped grenades on the already wavering Germans. It was the end. They retreated towards the Col du Géant, leaving nine dead in the snow. One of the Alpins had been wounded and captured; he was still alive when recovered by his companions, but he died shortly after. This was the only French casualty in 'the highest fight in the world'.

There were many similar operations. When the war ended the French troops had entered the Val d'Aosta and later Turin.

Another feature of the war which must be mentioned in any history of mountaineering is the escape of prisoners of war from Italy across the main range of the Alps in 1943 and 1944. Here, too, documents are not easy to procure.

The luckier men succeeded in entering Switzerland by Chiasso and the places near the Lake of Lugano or Lake Maggiore, but no figures have been given so far, so that it is not possible to find exactly how many had to work their way across more complicated and dangerous ground. It is known, at any rate, that 1,600 men found their way into Switzerland through the various passes at the top of the Viège valleys. In addition, between April 1943 and April 1945, 1,500 refugees entered Switzerland in the region of the Simplon, many of them being British escapers, according to official reports. There were many other districts through which it was possible to escape from enemy territory.

The Alps were in very bad condition in 1943. Huge crevasses were gaping beneath a thin layer of snow. Trained mountaineers could have avoided the worst dangers, but the men who went that way had no mountain experience whatever. They were exhausted by months in prison camps and weeks in hiding, ill-fed, badly clothed (some of them were wearing shorts in January) with dilapidated shoes. Many of them were Australians and South Africans who had never seen snow, and it goes without saying that they had never crossed a glacier. They had no ice-axes; sometimes they were given ropes, but they did not know how to use them. Italian 'guides' were not guides at all, but usually smugglers, who charged exorbitant prices and never went farther than the frontier. And since, in many cases, the way down was much worse than the way up, while the guides retreated safely towards Italy, the fugitives had to force a way down some of the worst glaciers in the Alps.

It seems that few accounts of the crossings have been written and few records have been kept, according to the replies received from official quarters. Yet no history of mountaineering can be complete without devoting some space to these adventures. After many enquiries, I have been lucky enough to make contact with the Swiss Major Kenzelmann, who commanded the Viège districts during the war, and I am very grateful for the information he passed on to me.

It seems that very few of the men who found their way into Switzerland had any previous knowledge of mountains. The one exception seems to be Kenneth Grinling, a New Zealander who, after having been hidden for two years in France near Bourg d'Oisans, made up his mind to reach the Swiss frontier in October 1943, to avoid being deported to Germany. His tale was published in the *New Zealand Alpine Journal*. He had to cross five or six passes in late autumn conditions, but he was a good climber, owned an ice-axe, a pair of crampons and good boots; and from a mountaineer's point of view the whole journey meant just a long bout of solitary climbing through valleys and low passes, culminating in the traverse of the Col du Chardonnet at the north end of the Mont Blanc range. The fact that the whole country was occupied by the Germans added much danger to the expedition. Throughout his journey, Grinling was sheltered and fed by the peasants, who never failed to hide these fugitives from the invader.

On reaching the valley of Chamonix over the Col de Voza, Grinling kept to high forest paths on the side of Mont Blanc. There was one agonizing moment of suspense when he had to cross the Arveyron, by the railway bridge, in broad daylight. The Glacier d'Argentière was not closely patrolled by the Germans, since one of their men had lately fallen into a crevasse and it had been hard work to extricate him. Benoît Simon, an ex-guide, took Grinling to his Lavancher hotel and put him on his way to the Col du Chardonnet. Grinling knew the place, had already traversed the col and felt almost at home in the familiar but impressive surroundings. This is how he describes his climb:

'How thankful I was for my crampons as I cut steps up ice-walls and tackled passages which I should never have looked at in normal times!

'The exhilaration of that experience was something I shall never forget. What a relief it was to have finished with the caution of the hunted which I had had to observe for the last two days! Even had there been anyone to see me, there was little danger of being overtaken in that rough going. Here I was at grips with the honest and familiar difficulties of ice and rock, and not with the nerve-wearing uncertainties and risks of gendarmes and patrols.

'The full moon lit up the scene in brilliant relief, and the silence and solitude can be imagined only by those who have an intimate acquaintance with the high hills. Great peaks rose all around—the Aiguille du Chardonnet, the Aiguille d'Argentière, Mont Dolent in the distance, Les Droites, Les Courtes and the Aiguille Verte with its great couloir—in their lofty remoteness both awesome and reassuring. One's very insignificance seemed a guarantee of safe-conduct and the sheer beauty of the night lifted one above earthly cares.'

Yet the whole experience was far from being pleasant. The small hours of the morning at such a height, in the middle of October, were deadly cold. The glacier was seamed with huge crevasses and Grinling had a very hard time practising a kind of tight-rope dance on thin, hard, slippery ledges, though he felt cold and exhausted from having already climbed alone for more than nine hours. The lower part of the glacier was a maze of crevasses and séracs, through which he wormed his way with great difficulty: 'I went down where the ice joins the rock. It was like cutting steps in concrete. I also had to chip hand-grips for my left hand to cling to while I used my right cutting below me.' Yet he succeeded in reaching the Saleinaz hut, and later, Orsières.

By that time most of the other Swiss frontier districts were dealing every day with large groups of fugitives. In the Saas and Zermatt districts, the first refugees had been a party of fifty-seven Italian Alpini arriving from Breuil on September 17th, complete with weapons, ammunition and food. They had come up the Testa Grigia. Then, on the 20th, twenty-two British soldiers reached the Monte Moro (9,390 feet); the pass was in very bad condition and the men who had crossed it came down in the last stages of exhaustion. Thenceforward, big detachments arrived incessantly. On the 22nd eight groups reached Switzerland through all the local passes, the Breuiljoch (10,722 feet), the Lysjoch (13,800 feet), the Felikjoch (13,345 feet), and others. The group which ascended the latter pass was headed by a Colonel. Altitude and snow-glare had made the climb a grim ordeal. On the 23rd, thirty-two men crossed the Felikjoch. One of them had made the crossing with his feet wrapped only in rags and was terribly frostbitten. The long procession continued, eighty-six men coming down to Saas-Grund on the 25th, seventy on the following day.

And then things became more complicated still. On September 27th, German troops reached Breuil, making the traverse of the Theodul Pass almost impossible. They were also very close to St Jacques d'Ayas and Macugnaga and paths up the other cols were becoming more and more risky. But the refugees still arrived. Seventy-nine of them reached Saas on October 4th, together with twelve Yugoslavs who made a very bad impression on the Swiss soldiers. On the other hand, these soldiers were impressed by the quiet, dignified bearing of the British, who were in rags and deadly tired, but never complained about anything, who shared between the whole group the clothes, cigarettes, chocolate which were given them and always made the same request: to be given means to wash and shave. One of them, being given an old black suit by a Saas-Fee guide, said that he felt he was going to a smart dinner-party. The guide, who told me the story, had been much impressed by his quiet humour.

With the heavy autumn snow-falls, conditions became worse still. On November 2nd a group of forty-three men reached the Monte Moro, but twelve others had to be left behind, worn out by cold, fatigue and mountain-sickness. On the pass they had found the dead body of one of their companions who had attempted the crossing before them and had died of exposure and exhaustion.

The number of fatal accidents will never be known. Observation was maintained from the Gornergrat, Schönbühl, Fluh Alp, the Britannia hut, the Furggalp and the Almageller Alp, and Swiss soldiers were sent out to bring down the parties as soon as they were sighted. There were a few extraordinary escapes. My Zermatt guide, Karl Franzen, told me a story of which he happened to have first-hand knowledge, having actually met the party concerned. A dozen New Zealanders had reached the Lysjoch (13,645 feet) under the guidance of an Italian who, as usual, refused to set foot upon Swiss territory. To descend from the Lysjoch they had to follow the whole length of the Grenzgletscher, which is probably one of the worst in the Alps; great crevasses turn it into a dangerous sieve. The descent was slow, with the chance of catastrophe at every step. Yet nothing serious happened until the moment when the party was confronted with a crevasse larger and deeper than all the others. For some reason—there might be many, and all of them good—they could neither jump it nor go round it. The officer in the group suggested that the only thing to do was to go down one wall and try to climb up again on the other, and he asked for a volunteer. The youngest member of the party went down on the rope and after a short time called out from below that everything was all right and that they had just to come down. The crevasse, instead of going straight down to unfathomable depths, as crevasses usually do, curved round in a kind of tunnel and had another way out below the end of the barrier of séracs. Such freaks of nature may be frequent, of course, but climbers usually avoid crevasses as much as possible. This piece of good fortune enabled the party to slide down the ice wall, to pass through the tunnel and arrive at the Bétemps hut where Swiss mountain troops, my guide among them, interviewed them and heard this extraordinary story. The men themselves did not suspect how unusual their story was.

Crevasses were not always so merciful. At about the same date, two young English soldiers attempted to cross the Monte Moro. The autumn snow had covered the track across the ice. They strayed and one of them fell into a crevasse, going down until he was stopped by the narrowing of the space between the walls. He managed to climb back by a violent effort, cutting notches in the ice with his pocket-knife—an exhausting task—up the damp, cold, slippery sides of the crevasse. When at last he emerged from his dreadful predicament, he found no trace of his companion. He walked down, expecting to find him in the first inhabited place, where he might have gone to fetch help. He accordingly reached the Swiss military post in the valley, but no one had been seen. A search party was sent out at once, but nothing whatever was found and there was no reply to their shouts. The other man had probably fallen into another crevasse, and that one had no way out.

Such fatal accidents were probably numerous. Months later, when winter snow began to melt, bodies were recovered on various mountain paths leading up to the cols; more were found on Monte Moro and such places. They were always difficult to identify as most of the fugitives had destroyed their papers and sometimes thrown away their identity discs. Near Sondrio, in the Bernina district, eight dead bodies were found; they were six British soldiers and two Americans. Out of one group of twenty who escaped from a North Italian camp, only two succeeded in reaching Switzerland.

When winter closed in it became almost impossible to cross those very high cols. Yet, as late as November 3rd, eleven men reached Saas, having wandered for two days in heavy snow without food or shelter. A few more arrived the following day, completely worn out.

The exodus continued throughout the winter, the fugitives crossing the lower Tessin passes, though they, too, were under snow. A Swiss friend of mine, who was stationed between the Valetta and the Passo di San Jurio, saw groups arriving all through the winter of 1943–44. They were very mixed parties, consisting of British, French, Yugoslavs, Greeks, even Ukrainians, all of them very young; they had all spent several months in hiding in Italy, coming from prison camps near Merano or Bolzano, and the language they used amongst themselves was mainly Italian. On most occasions the parties which reached the passes were led by cockneys, who had taken the lead as a matter of course and succeeded in shepherding their groups to safety after days of wanderings among the mountains and hours of climbing in deep snow to avoid the German patrols. They were usually very badly frost-bitten.

All those frontier crossings, even when not actually tragic, were gruelling experiences for men who suddenly discovered all that is exhausting in mountaineering. Weariness is seldom mentioned in accounts of climbing adventure; a polite fiction ignores it. Under such new and unexpected conditions, this time-honoured tradition disappeared or was unsuspected. One of the few tales ever published on the subject, the one by Julian Hall from which I have already quoted, is striking evidence of all the new impressions suggested by the mountains to one who had no previous knowledge of them and could describe his impression in a most effective way. Julian Hall crossed the Felikjoch early in October 1943. This is how he arrived at the Gnifetti hut:

'There were no longer rocks in our path, or stones. There were peaks in the distance and stars overhead, but in our way was snow, soft, interminable, barren and white. One had to climb, but I couldn't keep my foothold. I slithered. I struggled. I felt a fool. Time passed: how many hours I couldn't say. I was deeply distressed. Ice, precipices, crevasses—to those things I had looked forward with dread: I knew that they would test my endurance. But I hadn't reckoned with the enmity of snow; sheer, passive, gentle snow in which I was unable to walk. Perhaps it was the lack of nails in my boots (in one of them I had but three), perhaps it was the faulty placing of my feet. The snow was beating me. I was not angry. I was scarcely even ashamed. I was merely sick of it, heartily sick of it. My body loathed what it was trying to do and was doing so badly, so wearily. I had lost my stick, I didn't know where we were, or how far we had come, or what the time was. I dragged myself forward, slipped backwards, waited; I no longer cared what became of me, I was struggling without hope or plan. Three of the others were pulling me on a rope. Goliath (the guide) shouted encouragements. *"La cabana"* was near. *"La cabana!"* What did I care for *"la cabana"*? For me there existed nothing but snow—this cursed snow in which I couldn't walk, could scarcely be dragged without falling. I didn't want to get to the *cabana* or to Switzerland. I wanted only one thing—to walk no further, to get my feet out of the snow.'

Such thoughts do probably occur to most climbers but are always suppressed in their accounts of climbs made under normal circumstances, and yet they are the frequent underlying ground to any other impression. Any climber, however experienced he is, will remember days when he could think of no greater blessing than to be allowed to stop. Endless dull slopes in the middle of a dull landscape—or, at any rate, a landscape deprived of any appeal on account of more urgent thoughts—the exhausting trudge uphill, hardly relieved by the added danger of ice, can make any climb a kind of endless nightmare. Julian Hall continues:

'It was a world of white and grey, a drab and uninhabited world: a rack of clouds below us with mountains peering through it, mountains which were names but no more. It was a clumsy, graceless and tedious spectacle. It brought no exhilaration to the mind. It looked dead, inanimate. The clouds looked inert. We turned and set out on our journey.

'A long, broad and gentle slope. Nothing to do but mount it steadily, step by step, hour by hour, placing our feet in the snow. I didn't slither, for now we had ropes, and I followed in the footsteps of the leaders; but I suffered as much as I had suffered in the night; for now I was so weary and stiff that to walk at all was painful. My feet were like lead. It was as though they were chained. I staggered rather than walked. Five minutes' stagger, and then I must rest. Again five minutes, perhaps less. A longer rest, a shorter five minutes, the sky was turning golden where it met the earth, a single peak glowed pink like a rose. If I ever reached the crest of this slope, I should be at the foot of a steep rocky barrier. Was that our goal? Was Switzerland at the top of it? My neighbours thought that it was.

'They were right. That barrier was the end of our climb. It was the Felik-joch. Goliath and his friend cut steps for us to climb. "Don't look round," they said, "watch where you are going." It was dangerous. There was ice. This was the ascent of which they had warned us at Champoluc. Dangerous it may have been, but it wasn't hard work. It didn't take the heart out of me as mere snow had done. I climbed very slowly, I was practically crawling but I didn't feel tired or distressed. I was exhilarated. I reached the crest. This was Switzerland. Everyone was laughing, talking. The morning was up. The day was awake. The barren world had come to life.

'France, Italy, Switzerland—three countries partook of this lonely spectacle, three countries and not a man or a habitation within sight. A wilderness of peaks, like the score of a symphony whose notes are waiting to be played. A mighty skeleton. A world without a name. A collective monosyllable, the Alps.'

Of course the way down proved to be even worse than the way up. The guide, however helpful he might have been on the Italian side, calmly told his party: '[They] had nothing to do but descend at [their] leisure. [They] were free, [they] needed no guide.' One wonders for what reason a man who obviously knew the mountains well told this palpable lie: the glacier which descends from the Felikjoch on the Swiss side is hardly better than the Grenzgletscher. But the party was sighted by Swiss soldiers, who went up to fetch them.

The text I have just quoted deserves a very high rank in mountaineering literature. For one thing it registers a completely original impression of the Matterhorn, a mountain which has been heavily overloaded with legend and history. Julian Hall brings it back into its true perspective:

'As Shakespeare's kings are to kings who have nʊ Shakespeare, so is the Matterhorn to its Alpine fellows. Your historian and your mountaineer know the one. The whole world knows the other. A name, a legend, a picture, a memory. The Matterhorn is all those things. I had seen it (not with pleasure or with awe, but listlessly, with chains on my feet) before I knew what it was. Now, in my freedom, I knew its name and the name was familiar to me and moving like that of a Greek tragedy or the number of a Beethoven Symphony.'

While following more or less the same route a few days earlier, another party had a harrowing experience. Colonel de Burgh and Captain Phillips arrived at Champoluc in the Val d'Ayas by the middle of September, 1943, and they were put in touch with two local smugglers who agreed to lead them into Switzerland across the Lysjoch or the Felikjoch. Neither of them had ever done any climbing before and they were as badly equipped as possible. They were first taken to a farm high up the mountain-side, where under ice-cold wind:

'On the top of a high peak we halted again, and in spite of utter weariness we were astonished at the sight around us. Below, a few hundred feet, was a sea of billowing, pure-white cloud. Out of it great jagged black islands of rock, like giants' teeth, stood up towards the sky. On the east the whole was tinged with a lovely pink darkening to red near the rising sun.'

The route was leading up to dangerously steep ice-slopes on which a slip would have meant death. The party eventually reached the derelict hut and rested for a short while, feeling horribly cold and weary. Then they set off again towards the pass. But the sky darkened, they were caught in the mist and the smugglers lost their way in the blizzard. After much shouting, and feeling completely unable to find the pass, they decided to return to the hut. They were lucky enough to find it. Colonel de Burgh and his companion reached it utterly exhausted and badly frostbitten. The blizzard raged for several days; food became scarce, then disappeared; the whole undertaking seemed hopeless and the party was actually on its way down to Italy when the sky suddenly cleared. They returned to the hut and very early next morning were again on their way towards Switzerland.

The second ascent was worse than the first because of a heavy layer of fresh, waterlogged snow on every possible ledge and always likely to avalanche. Colonel de Burgh writes:

'We came to a knife-edge stretching away and up in front of us, rising five hundred feet or more. On the right nothing, black rocks a thousand feet below; on the left a slope of shining white snow almost perpendicular. I stared fascinated at the edge so narrow that it looked impossible. But on we went, and I know my tired brain could not register enough fear or I should never have been able to go another step'.

It was a long endless nightmare. Yet, after hours of excruciating work, they made the pass. The place they had reached was somewhere near the top of the Grenzgletscher. Colonel de Burgh and his companion knew nothing of the lurking danger of the place and they thought that they would soon reach the grey moraine of the Gornergletscher which they could descry in the distance. The smugglers left them to fight their way down alone.

'Suddenly, in a clear patch of smooth unwrinkled snow I went down again. This time I had a dream as the snow dropped from under me. As I fell, I threw myself back clutching, but the snow came with me and down I went. My thoughts were numbed and detached, but I remember wondering whether icicles grew upside down and if I should be impaled. Then I crashed; I knew no more for seconds, it must have been. The snow had broken my fall, but I had not got away scot-free. My left arm was injured. I was more anxious than frightened now. It was gloomy but not dark and a trickle of water ran below me and under the ice. Far above was daylight and the sun and silence. The walls about me graded from black to dark green as the ice rose towards the light. . . . I got up and moved along the narrow passage of the crevasse; as I moved, I stumbled over a long block of ice. I looked down. In a thin casing of frozen glass lay a man. I could see his shadowy form and his face; his eyes were shut; he was grinning. It did not impress me much; I wondered who he was and passed on. There were two more. One I saw very clearly, young and fair-haired, in what appeared to be an Italian uniform. He was looking at me; his eyes were open and he smiled. I liked him. I felt he was glad to see me. I sat down on his—his what?—his robe of ice and, nursing my broken arm, began to talk to him. But suddenly I found that I, too was gradually becoming robed in ice.'

In a vague, dazed way, he tried to get back to a more logical train of thought, to yell to his companion above and to concentrate on his will to live. But his shouts did not seem to reach above the ice-wall and he began to loose control over his mind and to feel past caring for anything, even his own hope of escape. Then he lost consciousness altogether.

The deadly spell was lifted when he recovered consciousness, on the glacier above, being nursed back to life by his companion and the two Italians, who had come back, summoned by the shouts of the other officer. The latter had been unable to rescue de Burgh unaided, for hauling a man from a crevasse is a hard and difficult piece of work which requires not only strength but skill and the thorough knowledge of how to handle a rope. Eventually, after a slow, painful descent, the party reached the Gornergletscher, where they were picked up by Swiss soldiers who led them to solid earth, fed them and had tea brought down to them from the Gornergrat. Then they were accompanied to Zermatt, where they arrived completely dazed and exhausted.

At the same time, the Resistance was mustering its forces everywhere. Few accounts of that secret warfare have survived. However, one of them enables the reader to grasp the fury of the winter mountains. In 1942, Alfred Southon, a young private serving in the tanks, was captured in Libya. A year later, when Italy collapsed, he succeeded in escaping from his prison camp and joining a group of the Italian Resistance in the north-west of the country. For several months, together with other British escaped prisoners, he fought alongside the Italian partisans, living in villages where the population was very friendly, helping them as much as they could. When the SS arrived in the district, however, they were immediately outnumbered and their guerilla operations became impossible. About forty young men, British and Italian, decided to cross the Col de la Galise into Val d'Isère in France: it was December 1944 and Dauphiné had been liberated. French and American organisations had their headquarters in Val d'Isère and were in close touch with the Italians on the other side. But the snow was already thick on the mountains and none of the British knew anything about mountaineering.

Fairly easy at the start, the path up to the col became more and more difficult. The weather changed, snow began to fall and the cold was intense. Soon the group was in the midst of a raging blizzard. They broke up into small parties, some of which just disappeared into a howling inferno of fog and snow. Eventually Alfred Southon and Walter Rattue, who had been his constant companion since the prison camp, were cut off from the main party, together with two Italians, one of whom was Carlo de Forville, the principal guide. In spite of their courage and endurance, the two Englishmen came to the point where they could not make another step. Their companion decided to leave them under a rock and push on to Val d'Isère and organize a rescue party.

The two men began to wait, and the wait was endless. Huddled in their rock shelter, they listened intently to the faintest sound that might mean that help was on its way. Hours turned into days, and they did not know how many. They had no food left and they sucked snow, and the cold numbed them. The blizzard did not abate. Slowly they sank into a sort of stupor, almost without consciousness. When they could put a few thoughts together, they wondered why no one came. And they still waited. Further days elapsed; with the greatest difficulty, Rattue managed to write a short farewell letter to his father and became unconscious. Southon saw that the blisters of his frost-bites were bursting and that the snow about him was stained with blood, but he hardly paid any attention to the fact. Rattue muttered a few words and died, slipping painlessly into the final numbness of death. Southon was now alone in his ice grave, and he tried to hold on to life. He shouted, tried to move, but the wind carried his shouts away and he fell back.

Suddenly he thought he heard voices: was it the wind or a new nightmare? No, it was human help at last! Someone had shouted, quite close to him. He mustered his failing strength and managed to make himself heard. It was the rescue party from Val d'Isère at last. Two men were standing at the entrance to the icy grave, contemplating with horror the living man and the dead. They picked Southon up and carried him down to a chalet, which they took only a few minutes to reach. Had Southon known it was there, he could have crawled there, possibly taking an hour, but it would have meant safety and life. But he did not know and Rattue had died. Southon had waited for ten days. Of the men who had gone down for help only Forville had arrived. The rest of the group had been lost somewhere in the wintry wilderness.

Diebold, the chief ski instructor of the Val d'Isère, who was also the director of the rescue organization, took Southon down the next day on his back; Southon lost both feet and several fingers.

Very few narratives of Alpine escapes seem to have been written. Yet they might be landmarks in one of the strangest aspects of the war. It might also be interesting to know whether any of the men who came into such unexpected contact with high mountains felt any desire to renew this first acquaintance.

CHAPTER NINETEEN

MOUNTAINS AND LITERATURE

I N concluding this long inquiry into the history of mountaineering we may ask ourselves one further question: has mountaineering found adequate expression in literature? I take mountaineering in a different sense from the mere love of mountains, as it has to be judged by very different standards. Lovers of mountains have often tried to give literary form to their feelings, but the literary expression of an impulse to climb derives from an altogether different emotion. Lord Conway's first impression on seeing a great snow peak, the Blümlisalp, gave proof of this:

'I felt it as no part of this earth', he said, 'or in any way belonging to the world of experience. Here at last was the other world visible, inaccessible, no doubt, but authentically there; actual yet incredible, veritably solid with an aspect of eternal endurance, yet also ethereal; overwhelmingly magnificent but attractive too. No dimmest idea of climbing them entered my mind.'

Again, one of the finest mountain poems is Shelley's *Mont Blanc*. Now, in the preface of *Laon and Cythna*, Shelley wrote: 'I have trodden the glaciers of the Alps and lived under the eye of Mont Blanc': it was literally true, but the glaciers were the Mer de Glace and the lower part of the Glacier des Bossons, and he did not live under the eye of Mont Blanc for more than three days. That was not mountaineering.

One may also wonder whether there is such a thing as Alpine literature. Mountaineers have to fight against the great temptation of silence. General Faure once wrote to me:

'It is a pity that men we met and climbed with never cared to write down what they had told us in a few brief sentences. It is a pity . . . But is it? It was their own private kingdom: one illuminating sentence and then silence . . . How precious was silence during many long hours; how useful it was to enable us to know one another! It was neither hostile nor lifeless; it accompanied our gestures. It was a private world, alive with thoughts, efficient, simple and not lonesome. It was a blessing.

'Yet, we must be thankful that some of us have broken the silence and have written down our thoughts, for they have to be uttered and brought into full light. Of course, some have turned their struggles and contests into mere bathos but, with very few exceptions, most have been sincere. One of the gifts bestowed by the hills is their suppression of tiresome bores. Some mountaineers do show off, but their number is very small'.

The best mountain literature has always required a dual struggle: against oneself and against the obstacles put up by the mountains. Against oneself since, having vanquished one's own physical deficiencies during a climb, one has to vanquish a sluggish, shy or restless mind, to find the right tone to convey to the reader some idea of the rushing stream of thoughts, sensations and impressions in which surprise, wonder and fear are intermingled.

There have been constant endeavours to create a literary form suitable for the narration of mountain adventure. Why write badly about anything if there is hope of being more effective by writing well? It is only recently that the craze for sham science, which has led to the grading of mountains, has also led enthusiasts to describe their climbs in a purely technical language which requires the use of a glossary. Provided that the author has a good memory or that he has taken down notes in the course of his expedition, he can always sum it up in a few dry sentences. It is so easy and so short that it turns such records into a constant threat to more elaborate forms of composition.

And yet for a little over a century there has been a continuous succession of mountain books, at once well conceived and well written. A few of them have almost made history; they have at least exercised a considerable influence on some of their readers, and have given them a lead throughout their lives. Lord Conway relates in his *Mountain Memories* that he took to climbing through hero-worship: his hero was Tyndall, whom he discovered when reading *The Glaciers of the Alps*. The most important book from this point of view was Whymper's *Scrambles Amongst the Alps*. It attracted a wide public, ranging from young children to elderly people. It is probably still the best-known mountain book. It has been translated into several languages and its French translation—a very bad one, which came out as early as 1875—was the first mountain book ever read in France. The translator had had to coin several new words to express things which had no French equivalents. When Whymper went on lecture-tours in various parts of England, he always left a strong impression upon his audience. A schoolboy, who once heard him at Harrow, wrote as follows: 'There was a lecture on climbing the Alps by the great Mr Whymper, with wonderful pictures of guides and tourists hanging on by the eyelids or standing with their backs to precipices which even in photo made one squirm.' That boy was Winston Churchill.

The *Cambridge History of English Literature* has devoted part of a chapter to mountain books, quoting *Peaks, Passes and Glaciers,* Forbes, Tyndall, Leslie Stephen and several others. It is not going too far to say that such works have become classics, ranking with the greatest travel literature. So did Mummery's *Climbs in the Alps and Caucasus.* This work was also translated into several languages and, as I have already pointed out, it has remained a living inspiration for many great climbers of today; Mummery's very daring technique had endowed his book with some of the qualities of permanency.

This long tradition has remained unbroken. Many books which have been published of late have maintained the level of the older ones; they are written with great literary care, they are not monotonous and the offer many pictures of mountains as seen through young and modern eyes. Each writer has his own way of relating his climbs, his own devices for making the landscapes real or depicting the climbing-party as it progresses along a ridge or cuts its way across an ice-slope. Most of the climbers mentioned in previous chapters have written books and articles to express their own conception of mountaineering, and all of them are to be taken into account, both for their technical value and their literary value. Such are the works of G. W. Young, R. L. G. Irving, Sir Arnold Lunn, Frank Smythe, Dorothy Pilley, Gaston Rebuffat, Sir Douglas Busk, Spencer Chapman, Eric Shipton, Chris Bonington, Joe Brown, and others. A complete list is hardly needed. One thing is certain: technical mountain books certainly come within the scope of literature.

For several years, after the great Himalayan climbs of the fifties, most mountain books dealt only with Everest, Kangchenjunga, Makalu or K2. When most of the biggest mountains had been scaled, readers reverted to the Alps, hoping to find the same thrill they had experienced when reading about far-away ranges. They were right, because this was the time when all the big north faces were being scaled by new routes. This accounts for the wide success of books written by Bonington, Brown, Haston and Gillman, who relate very hard climbs in a straightforward way that makes them even more impressive.

England is practically the one country where this blending of literary skill with the description of climbs had led to constantly felicitous results. Few mountain classics have been written by Continental authors, one of them being Guido Rey's *Matterhorn.* As a reference book it is excellent; so are Rey's other works. But it is hard to accept it as a masterpiece, owing to its uncontrolled sentimentality. The author allows his enthusiasm to run away with him. It is not a question of the love of mountains but of incomplete mastery of style. Rey's passion for the Alps, and above all for the Matterhorn, is exacting. He has woven a golden net of metaphors round the great peak and his odes and invocations are so numerous, his admiration for everything connected with it so complete and indiscriminate, that one wonders why he wrote in prose. *The Matterhorn* should have been an epic in twelve or twenty-four cantos; then everything would have been in keeping with the literary traditions of such works. Rey's conception of god-like men—the guides of Valtournanche, Whymper and himself—paying willing or reluctant homage to a heavenly mountain in their attempt to scale it, would have found a more adequate expression.

French mountain books are exactly the reverse. Guido Rey is hyper-sensitive to mountain beauty: for various reasons, French mountaineers seem to react but very little to it, or to do so with reluctance. They seem to dread putting their feelings into words. By 'French', of course, I mean works written in French, even by French Swiss. Some of these books are marred by an immoderate use of mountain slang. The desire to produce a humorous effect from the narration of climbing adventure has spoiled many an article or longer work. Far too much importance is given to the loss of a tin-opener or the description of the various bores the authors never fail to meet in the mountain huts or on the summit which they have just scaled. Somehow or other, the minute reproduction of jokes usually falls flat. Everything goes into a climb to make it a perfect whole; yet there is probably some lack of proportion in concentrating on its ludicrous aspects. For some unknown reason, some totally insignificant episode may seem important or humorous; yet it is impossible to recapture the feeling when describing the climb in a subsequent narrative: there was really nothing in it but the irresponsibility and light-heartedness born of a perfect day and of a happy frame of mind. Most of the jokes about lanterns, tinned food or tangled ropes cannot live below the snow-line. They melt away. Using such recollections to prop up a story is a thankless task, as nothing of them survives.

A possible exception is however provided by the French painter and writer Samivel, who succeeded in creating one comic Alpine character: Job the Chough. That blue-black creature, which looks as if it had been cut out of a sheet of steel, is the only bird which flies high enough to reach the high summits. Eagles, strangely enough, are never seen at such altitudes under normal conditions and probably not under abnormal conditions either. Choughs are reserved creatures, but they know the time-tables of the Montenvers and Gornergrat trains and the places where climbing parties have their second or third breakfasts. So they fly up to where the flesh-pots may be expected and wait for the moment when tin-openers come into action and cheese-rinds are thrown away. On the Zinal Rothhorn, Samivel met the ancestor of the tribe. Years later, the episode crept into one of his books, *L'Amateur d'abîmes*.

Samivel has written much about mountain ethics, mountain art, mountain metaphysics; but there are too many words which keep jingling and careering through his text. Mountains seem to lose something of their dignity in the over-elaborate setting in which he places them. Yet his books are the only ones which sometimes succeed in recapturing the humorous aspects of a climb.

Narratives which avoid the pitfall of trying to be funny meet with other dangers. The early mountain books are pompous and the modern ones are often dry. They labour under one curse or the other. Javelle's book fell under the first and did much harm, as it was much admired. The older Swiss writers still labour under this handicap. It would appear that the best French mountain books are straightforward narratives from which emerges the sincere impression made by the mountain on the author's mind. They are not always well-written, they are too closely linked with technical descriptions, yet they hint at the author's intellectual or spiritual reactions to the climb. Among the best are Jacques Boell's *High Heaven* (the title of the English translation), Alain de Chatellus' *Alpiniste, est-ce toi?*, E. R. Blanchet's *Hors des chemins battus*, Frendo's *La Face nord des Grandes Jorasses*.

It is possible to go a step higher. There are a few outstanding French works, all of them short. It would seem that their authors could not remain long on the high literary level they had reached. Yet it was unnecessary to write longer, as they achieved much in a few pages. Among such works I would include Pierre Dalloz's short essays *La Pointe Lagarde* and *Zenith* (from which I have already quoted at some length), and also Georges Sonnier's and Tézenas du Montcel's essays.

Pierre Dalloz's works are examples of that blending of a perfect style and a wide knowledge of the mountains which represents the best type of modern mountain literature. It is a pity that he has not written more, for his refinement of thought and style, his power and inward penetration go very far. His essays are as free from dryness as they are from sentimentality, or indeed from any esoteric implications. His writings convey the higher message of the mountain landscape. There is in them a hidden restlessness, a quest towards some indefinite goal, which endows them with subdued poignancy. Here is a characteristic description of the Pointe Lagarde itself, a thin steep pinnacle above the Glacier d'Argentière which Dalloz ascended with Jacques Lagarde, Tom de Lépiney and Henry de Ségogne:

'I soon descried the top pinnacle, shaggy like a mane in the wind, the perfect living crown of a huge ice slab which looked like a powerful forehead. Those soaring rocks were reared between us and the sun like a screen against which pale rays shot down; diverging sheaves of light caught a spot of snow or a crystal-like arête on their way and cast a bejewelled dust which looked like a hazy glittering halo round the summit.'

Georges Sonnier's essay is longer; its constant underlying emotion makes *Où règne la lumière* possibly softer and more sentimental than Dalloz's terse pages. Yet Sonnier's knowledge of the various aspects of mountains is wide enough to prevent his using empty words instead of living images, or allowing his thoughts to drift into unconvincing rhapsodies.

With a totally different conception of climbing, Max Aldebert, another French writer, has lately published a haunting description of a difficult mountain expedition, *Un Fait divers*. In a few pages he has succeeded in analysing the strong devotion he feels for the mountains—a devotion verging on physical love for their beauty and their violence, for the intoxicating influence of air, space and granite, and the passionate will to live which takes possession of the mind when the situation seems hopeless. The simplicity, effectiveness and strength of his tale are quite exceptional.

During the last ten years, Gaston Rebuffat's books and a few others have altered the balance of Alpine literature. *Etoiles et tempêtes, Entre terre et ciel, Mont Blanc jardin féérique, Cervin cime exemplaire,* have become mountain classics. The author has done most of the severest climbs in the Alps, including a number of difficult first ascents. Besides providing an accurate description of his climbs, he has succeeded also in conveying to his readers the impression they made on him. His full knowledge of everything connected with mountains enables him to grasp the tiny details as well as the entirety of a wide landscape. He can also appreciate poetically, as well as psychologically, the human reaction to a big climb, his own attitude as well as that of his companions. Each of his chapters conveys the mood in which the ascent was made, which is sometimes quite surprising. Once he climbed the north face of the Dru with a good friend, who was a keen mountaineer and very quick uphill. The mountain was in good condition and the weather was fine and remained so. In his description, Rebuffat conveys an impression of peace, quiet joy and complete friendliness with Nature. When reading his relaxed and harmonious pages, one cannot suspect the very strenuous climb the two men managed to accomplish in a minimum of time, probably because the writer's mind was so completely peaceful.

When relating his ascent of the Eiger Nordwand, during which he had to lead his own party and protect two friendly but rather green young Germans, while watching all the time for some new danger which could strike at any moment, he managed to retain a perfect balance which was not indifference. He felt that the mountains were dangerous, but not unduly so if you kept your head, and that there was no sense in making it worse than it actually was. He is also aware of the beauty of colour, the shape of a rock, the curve of a snow cornice. He feels a deep joy when taking a receptive friend up some striking pitch and seeing him react the right way to the beauty of their surroundings. For him, a victory over a mountain is an act of love.

Robert Tézenas du Montcel, who was among the leaders of the GHM several years before the Second World War, when he was very young, brought out a book of recollections, the title of which describes the respectful and logical attitude of a sensitive mountaineer, *Ce monde qui n'est pas le nôtre* ('This world which is not our own'). His conception of the mountains is of a realm from which man can always be ejected at any moment. Man is there only on sufferance, but that does not prevent him from admiring a form of beauty which passes all understanding. The tone of the book is quite unique. Factors which to modern climbers seem of great moment were a matter of indifference for Montcel; he is not interested in making a climb in record time, and he is quite prepared to share the delight of a first ascent with a party of friends intent on reaching the same peak by the same route. He has the vision of a poet, and shows complete contempt for all kinds of ostentation. He expresses his passionate love of mountains with a quiet, unassuming elegance. He feels deeply the remoteness of the mountain world, and his attitude towards man's means of making contact with it may be summed up with the words: 'Adventure is not in things, but in ourselves'. Montcel does not reject 'artificial' climbing; he can follow it like any other mountaineer, but he sees in it no more than a means to the same end.

Lionel Terray's book *Les Conquerants de l'inutile* ('Conquistadors of the Useless') was written in a totally different mood. Terray had very little sense of humour, and always seemed to have a grudge against someone and eventually against the mountains, too. A magnificent mountaineer, he climbed the most difficult mountains, not only "because they were there", but also to put to shame an earlier party which might have taken two hours too many over a given pitch. Some of his chapters sound as if written by an angry boy, and others by a boy who is playing a practical joke on some adult. Sometimes, the boy is quite amusing and interesting; at other times, he simply gets on his reader's nerves. Terray had a little fox-terrier named Narcisse; his book reveals that in fact there was a certain amount of narcissism, not about the dog, but about its owner.

There is one branch of mountain literature which is still an almost complete failure, and that is fiction. In whatever language they have tried to recapture the spirit of mountain expeditions, writers have never succeeded in bringing their characters to life. The taste for a mountain setting as the background to a story is not new; mountain scenery can be found in late eighteenth-century novels, in Anne Radcliffe's *Romance of the Forest*, for instance, and in less well-known Gothic romances. A French novelist whose hair-raising stories were widely read by 1790, Ducray-Duminil, brought the hero and heroine of *Celina* to the Glacier de Talèfre on their honeymoon, with Jacques Balmat as their guide. Sotheby wrote a tragedy on *The Monks of the St Bernard* (1801) and Napoleon's brother, Joseph Bonaparte, gave an Alpine setting to his novel *Moïna*. Mary Shelley's *Frankenstein* and Byron's *Manfred* also have glaciers and wild mountains in their backgrounds, Mary described the valley of Chamonix both in *Frankenstein* and *The Last Man*. Nevertheless, mountains in those works always remind the reader of the wild pointed rocks depicted in the Renaissance paintings: they are very steep, fantastic and ugly, and they serve no purpose except that of closing a vista or of being the haunt of hermits —Alpine hermits were much in demand at one time.

The first and one of the cleverest novels by which the mountains were liberated from this conventional interpretation was *Tartarin sur les Alpes* by Alphonse Daudet. Daudet knew the Alps; at least, he had visited the lower slopes. He had never climbed, but he had heard many stories of great ascents, he had talked with guides and, according to family traditions, he had met Whymper. His climbing episodes are convincing enough on the whole, with one exception. When Tartarin and Bompard attempt to climb Mont Blanc, they grow increasingly frightened until, fairly high up, they can stand the strain no longer, and so part from the rest of the caravan and return downwards; they are promptly lost in the fog, wander about aimlessly and at last fall, somewhere near the Col de la Brenva. Immediately they both cut the rope, in spite of the grandiose speeches they had delivered about being tied together for life or death. Bompard slides down the French side and is picked up by a caravan which is descending from the summit. Tartarin falls down the Brenva glacier and eventually turns up in Tarascon a few weeks later, perfectly safe and sound. Now, this is definitely too much! To slide down the Corridor, on the north face of Mont Blanc, is bad enough, though possible. To perform a similar feat on the southern face of the mountain is not. Tartarin had not the slightest chance of being picked up by a caravan: there were none on that route, which parties ventured to ascend only at intervals of several years. Had Tartarin descended alone, he would have been an Alpine marvel: the first party to do so was that of R. W. Lloyd in 1911. On the whole, however, *Tartarin* keeps within credible limits and the satire is both amusing and fair. It came as a revelation to the greater part of the French public.

But in this same year, 1885, another work of fiction took Alpine literature to the lowest depths: this was *L'Alpe homicide*, by Paul Hervieu. First of all, the title in French is both silly and stilted, and so are the stories. Hervieu had never climbed; his knowledge of the mountains was limited and inaccurate; he had done a certain amount of reading and accumulated some old legends and mistaken notions. He went back to the heroic chamois-hunters, and also offered a feeble interpretation of one of the worst Alpine tragedies, the death of three climbers and their eight guides and porters on Mont Blanc in 1870. He added a few extravagant tales of life in the high valleys. Nothing could be more unconvincing than these stories, in which the author takes great care to suggest to his readers that he is deeply moved by the sad fate of his heroes, while in fact he feels nothing at all, not having the slightest real notion of their plight.

There have been several other attempts at describing the Alps in fiction. One of the worst failures was *The Little Dream* by John Galsworthy. Galsworthy had some knowledge of the Alps. He had been to Tyrol, which is the setting of part of *The Dark Flower*. But his short play is the kind of thing which can be written only by one who does not really know what he is writing about. Setting and characters are feeble; as to the symbols, it is almost impossible to grasp their meaning: what one understands appears both childish and far-fetched. The three protagonists, the mountain girl Seelchen (Little Soul), the young climber Lamond and the guide Felsman, indulge in an obscure symbolical discussion. One gathers that Galsworthy understood mountains as the realm of flowers—gentian, rhododendron, edelweiss and dandelion—of pastures and herds of cows. The cow is for him the most Alpine of animals, and the incarnation of the high mountains. The Cow Horn is the highest local peak and is made to utter a complicated rigmarole:

'I am the mountains. Amongst kine and black-brown sheep I live: I am silence and monotony; I am the solemn hills. I am fierceness and the mountain wind; clean pasture and wild rest. Look in my eyes! . . . I stalk the eternal hills. I drink the mountain snows. My eyes are the colour of burned wine; in them lives melancholy . . . The lowing of the kine, the wind, the sound of falling rocks, the running of the torrents; no other talk now. Thought simple and blood hot, strength huge—and the cloak of gravity!'

Seelchen is torn between her love for Felsman and the mountain on one hand, for Lamond and the town on the other, and she yields to both in turn: a new version of 'Come down, O Maid, from younder mountain height!' This is the Dream of the title. It is mixed with many fervent appeals to 'the little grey flower'—the edelweiss—the silent solitude of mountains and so forth.

The local colour is of an almost touching naïvety. Lamond is described as 'young, tanned and good-looking, dressed like a climber and carries a plaid, a rucksack and an ice-axe.' The plaid is probably intended for a bivouac, for Lamond arrives at Seelchen's chalet to climb the Great Horn, a mountain of apparently sixth-grade severity which is pronounced 'not possible by the famous Felsman', who yet agrees to 'start at dawn', which is late. They accordingly leave when the sun is rising, with a lighted lantern, the use of which is not clear. There is a bivouac ahead, owing to the late start.

One last quotation. Lamond is told that the hut is full:

'*Seelchen*. There are seven German gentlemen asleep in there.
'*Lamond*. Oh God!
'*Seelchen*. Please! They are here to see the sunrise.'

Another writer, D. Fawcett, used the mountains as a setting for the philosophical talks which are entitled *The Zermatt Dialogues*. The landscapes —the shoulder of the Matterhorn, the Hörnli hut, the Bétemps hut, the Untergabelhorn, 'a long scramble in the sunlight'—are but frames in which long philosophical discussions are set.

In *Les Faux Monnayeurs*, André Gide alludes to a climb of the Allalin above Saas-Fee where he went in 1917. It has little to do with the plot. A boy of sixteen describes the expedition to a school-friend as follows:

'We are just back from a huge grind: the climb of the Allalin—guides getting roped up, crossing glaciers, crevasses, avalanches, well, all sorts of fun. Spent the night in a hut, heaped on top of other people; needless to say, we could not sleep a wink. The next day, we left at dawn . . . Well, old man! I shall never abuse Switzerland again. When one is up there, losing sight of every bit of vegetation, of everything connected with human avarice and stupidity, one would like to sing, to laugh, to weep, to fly, to dive head foremost into heaven or to kneel down.'

Novelists seem to be stricken with palsy in mountain air. This is not an explanation, of course, but it is difficult to account for their almost continuous bad luck. But there are two or three novels which have avoided this sad fate. One is A. E. W. Mason's *Running Water*, which appeared in 1907, and nothing half as good has ever been published. The mountain episodes—the search-party on the slopes of the Aiguille du Plan, the ascent of the Aiguille d'Argentière and, above all, the blizzard on the Brenva ice-ridge are fine pages, both powerful and convincing. The author had first-hand knowledge of the mountains he was describing. Incidentally, *Running Water* started a violent discussion between the author and W. A. B. Coolidge. In the story, the second ascent of the Brenva glacier is ascribed to a man who, in spite of his being a remarkable climber, proved to be an extremely shady character and who was struck from the list of members of the Alpine Club after being convicted of a criminal offence for which he served a term in prison. Now it happened that the second ascent had actually been made by Coolidge himself, who was deeply offended by A. E. W. Mason's chapters and said so with great asperity.

In spite of numerous attempts, most French novels or short stories dealing with the mountains have failed to show them in their true light. Yet, there is one exception and that is *Le Cas de Jean Bunant* by Edouard Estaunié, a story of little more than fifty pages in which the author has succeeded in summing up the passionate longing a man can feel for the mountains—a longing so ardent that he will take the greatest risks in order to reach his fascinating goal, and willingly die in the attempt. Jean Bunant, an archive keeper, is sent to La Grave to recover from a heart-attack. He has never climbed, but the constant view of the Meije makes him realize the unexpected beauty of the mountain. He falls under its spell, and though he is aware all the time that it may and probably will mean death, he decides to ascend it, out of the sheer ecstasy of his love:

'Before starting Bunant stood on the roadside to look for the last time at the loved one towards which he was going. He was filled with a supernatural ecstasy. He felt so intensely alive that a longer lease of life was immaterial to him.

'"Let us go," he said gently.

'The real climb begins at the foot of the glacier. Two almost vertical rocks, the Enfletchores, help to surmount the first pitch. Before tackling them, Pic called a halt to rope up. Bunant was getting more and more nervous and wanted to resume the climb at once. It was the beginning of a giddy scramble in total darkness. Now, every move made the abyss seem deeper.

'Acting almost automatically, Bunant obeyed Pic's orders. He was ascending. His ears had began to hum. He was breathing more quickly, in a greedy way. The air had never tasted better. At the same time, his body thrilled as it came into contact with stones which were already a part of her, the Meije. He was no longer afraid and he realized that a hero was born in him. Suddenly he saw a vision: the summit, looking higher than ever. It seemed to defy his efforts and to say: "You will never reach me." A dim elation coursed through his veins. All his blood ran back to his heart. He uttered a faint cry and collapsed.

'"Hell!" shouted Pic, propping himself up against a cleft rock.

'With immense care, he and the porter hoisted the body which was swinging at the end of the rope, like a man hanging from a halter. Bunant's eyes were open. His enraptured face almost suggested he could still see his vision.'

The subdued emotion of the tale and the delicacy of the analysis combine to create a masterpiece. The suggestion of the manifold changing beauty of the mountain is unforgettable. 'Bunant discovered how much it changed. It changed more quickly than the sea. Of course, its features were always the same, but the light and the colour were as transient as the expressions of a human face.' This short tale conveys a deeper understanding of the mountains than any long novel.

Another fine achievement is a short story by C. E. Montague published in *Action*. It is the story of a man who wants to commit suicide and decides to stage a fall while climbing above Zinal. But when he is on his way towards death, he discovers a guideless couple vainly trying to find a way out of some impossible pitch and his mountaineering instinct gets the better of his wish to die; he saves the party and abandons his attempted suicide. The author was a good climber himself.

Such stories are quite exceptional. One of the elements which tend to paralyse the novelist who treats of mountain adventures is the fact that real stories—the stories of great climbs or mountain tragedies—are so perfect in all their details that it is difficult to imagine more effective or better-planned episodes. No novelist could invent anything as dramatic as the story of the Dru, the long siege of the west face by Dent and Burgener, the terrible sequence of accidents, especially that of 1928, an eight days' tragedy in the course of which two men died and one was badly injured, and the repeated breathless attempts on the north face. The Eigerwand tells another story in which courage, devotion, irresponsibility, foolhardiness, and nationalistic hysteria combine to create first the grimmest of Alpine tragedies and later 'one of the most disgusting climbs in the Alps', according to Terray.

The result of this state of things was that, at a time when semi-fictitious biographies were so much in fashion, several writers attempted to relate in their own way the lives of some of the great Alpine pioneers. Karl Hänsel wrote *Der Kampf am Matterhorn* (The Struggle for the Matterhorn), and Joseph Peyré *Mallory et son Dieu* (Mallory and his God). Both are unsatisfactory. The first of these leaves the reader under the impression that Whymper was a sentimental, almost neurotic person, united by a quasi-mystical friendship with Lord Francis Douglas; after the young man's death, he is supposed to have led a long heart-broken existence. Whymper is depicted as ascending the Matterhorn several times to commune with the spirit which lingered where the body vanished. The whole story is so strange that one wonders whether the author was not influenced by the fact that Francis Douglas was Lord Alfred Douglas's uncle—though he died before his nephew's birth. Of course, it does not help us to understand the Matterhorn story any better. And that story, anyway, is so simple that no such interpretation is needed: the Matterhorn tragedy was a tale of wasted talent and unsuspected incompetence.

Joseph Peyré's equally irresponsible biography of George Mallory cannot be discussed here at great length, as it deals mostly with Mallory's Everest campaigns. There was a very intellectual and sophisticated trend in Mallory which Peyré never suspected. One of its shortcomings is the fact that the author does not lay sufficient stress on his hero's Alpine climbing seasons. He deals with his subject from an almost purely mystical point of view, which is another error. Mallory wrote very little, but his few articles in the *Alpine Journal* are records which no biographer has a right to leave aside. They are the best key to Mallory's philosophy and love of the mountains. His description of the ascent of the Mont Maudit ridge is one of the greatest Alpine texts ever written. But Peyré's enthusiasm for his hero has carried him too far; he has brought him into a realm of abstract ideas instead of leaving him in his own world, among his own companions and friends. There is always a penalty to pay when one attempts to destroy life, even in complete good faith. Too idealistic an interpretation falls short of the effectiveness and poignancy of a true portrait.

Most mountain fiction has been a failure. It is possible to detect some of the reasons for this. The most obvious is sheer bad luck. A good climber is not often a good writer, endowed with a gift for fiction. Mountaineering is an exacting pursuit and novelists do not often possess the physical gifts required to scale mountains. Few young novelists are climbers. One from an earlier generation, who was once a brilliant climber, Charles Gos, tried to recapture the excitement of past years in his novel. His landscapes are alive while the characters are not.

The same can be said of Frison-Roche's *Premier de Cordée*; a very near miss was J. Peyré's *Matterhorn*. The author felt the curiously morbid atmosphere of Zermatt, tried to render it and almost succeeded. He attempted to show the great mountain in a lurid kind of light, haunted by the spirits of the dead, Whymper's companions and the countless victims who have fallen from its flanks since 1865. The hero, the guide Jos-Mari, is not over-idealized, but all the other characters, including the heroine, are both lifeless and uninteresting. This failure to give life to a story may be explained by the fact that mountains and human beings are not on the same scale. The gap between them is so great that nothing short of genius can bridge it. Sénancour felt this when he wrote in *Obermann*: 'Here (among the mountains) man recovers his transient but indestructible shape; he lives a true life in sublime communion with nature.' But Sénancour never attempted to place a novel in this 'sublime communion'. Obermann merely recorded his thoughts and his ineffectual attempts at 'living for a few hours before dissolving into nothingness'. In the pages devoted to Obermann's stay in the Alps, the mountains stand supreme, and no plot interferes with their overwhelming presence. On the other hand, in the few convincing mountain stories which have been written, the author has succeeded in suggesting their presence rather than describing them in connection with human beings: the latter were shown as actors on a stage, the size of which they realized and dreaded. So far, few novelists who have used the Alps as a setting have evinced any great gift of character drawing.

Some novelists who had no knowledge, or only a slight knowledge of the mountains, have tried to write about them, and it is not very surprising to notice that the result is far from satisfactory, at any rate when judged by readers who happen to know what the author did not. One of the puzzling aspects of mountain lore is that uninitiated writers are apt to go back to hoary tradition to gather what they believe to be local colour. In a short story by Henry Bordeaux, the hero rode up to the tame Mont Fréty on his way to the Col du Géant. Feeling in a happy mood after a good lunch, he burst into song: 'The guide, feeling his responsibility, grew serious. When the concert was over, he said: "Don't do it again, Sir: it might start an avalanche."—"I know, I know," the young man agreed.' But where, on Mont Fréty, could anyone ever start an avalanche?

The old legend of being able to start an avalanche by a mere song has been told and re-told for years. Yet in all the accounts of climbs I have ever read, in all I have heard from friends and guides, of all the glaciers I have actually crossed, I recall only one instance when an avalanche was actually started by human cries: it took place at the Jonction, on Mont Blanc, in 1839 and the shouts were those of Dr Grant.

The latest book in this manner is *The White Tower* by J. R. Ullman, which combines the worst legendary traditions with a few new ones, derived from a confusion between climbing conditions in the Alps and the Himalayas, and also with a very superficial understanding of the national characteristics of climbers. It is another case of the attempt to blend mountaineering and philosophy, a process which has not yet given birth to a masterpiece. The existence (as in *The White Tower*) of any peak in the Alps requiring several bivouacs on the normal route, is too laughable almost to mention.

A completely different attempt was made by Samivel in *L'Amateur d'abîmes,* which I have already mentioned. His starting point was different, too, owing to his wide knowledge of the mountains. He tried to account for the haunting terror that lurks in the High Alps, the terror of the blinding midday sun, which disintegrates a flimsy snow arête on which his heroes are standing. Nothing is to be trusted; danger lies in ambush under every boulder and under every cornice, and one feels vaguely that death's wings are about to close over the ice-slope. But the incipient threat is then expressed by a chorus of Invisible Devils who haunt the mountains. These counterparts—if one may so call them—of the Abominable Snowmen of Himalayan fame are too Machiavellian and too easily vanquished to be very convincing. Yet the author had actually lived through the nightmare he describes during an ascent of Les Droites. When he keeps to the imaginative description of how he broke down a cornice which 'crashed heavily, by tons, rolling in slow torrents into the abyss . . ., like flour, at once heavy and fluid, which he pushed aside with his chest, catching his breath with a gasp', one sees the remembered vision, and feels that the author has, in fact, realized the malignant spell which the mountains can cast. But as soon as the Invisible Devils begin chanting their version of 'double, double, toil and trouble', the whole prospect fades away and one is left with nothing but well-written, empty lines.

The intricacy of climbing experiences makes their literary interpretation all the more difficult. Mountaineering, when it is not a mere quest after danger and difficulties to be overcome, when it is the 'great symphony' Mallory once alluded to, requires a man to exert himself to the utmost both physically and mentally, if he wishes to retain and perhaps record some of the impressions he has gained. Conditions make it all the harder to concentrate on one's mental state. The whole personality comes into action with its moral and intellectual aspirations, its sense of humour—or lack of it—its habits, its reactions to sun, rain and weariness, its common sense and even its obsessions. The violence of a long and protracted effort may wear out the protective crust of coolness and detachment. A wealth of unsuspected impressions may creep into the mind. Or, on the contrary, they may blend into broad inarticulate waves which fill the mind to the exclusion of any thought too precise. When the climb is over and one's mood has become normal, it may be difficult to recapture this state of grace which had nothing to do with the mere recollection of the successive pitches and how they were overcome. On the whole few climbers, thinking of a future story, do as Güssfeldt did under the Brenva séracs, whipping out a note-book and writing 'Hopeless situation.' They trust to memory which often plays them false.

Mountain landscape makes its appeal only to the 'happy few'. One does not accept it in progressive stages, but as a whole. Or one rejects it as a whole. None of the beautiful photographs one has become familiar with can give anything but a faint rendering of its wildest aspects. One needs real understanding to go beyond the striking landscape one has seen in print and reach the vision which belongs to the real one.

While mountaineering was moving towards an entirely new technique and understanding, mountaineering novels suddenly broke out of the conventionality in which they had been smothered too long. After the unconvincing books already mentioned, the novel has reached a more mature stage during the last ten years. Novelists who are also mountaineers have come into their own.

They are not very numerous and their books have not been best sellers. Etienne Bruhl's *Accident à la Meije* is an excellent detective story, with a clever plot completely centred on a traverse of the mountain. The characters are not very subtle, but they were not meant to be, and the account of a climb that began in glorious weather and eventually landed the two heroes in a raging inferno of snow, hail and fog, is a brilliant piece of description.

Hugh Merrick's novels, *The Breaking Strain* and *Out of the Night* have succeeded in bridging the gap between mountaineering and fiction. The story of an easy climb done by an incompetent party, so that everything goes wrong from the beginning, is very convincing. An over-confident young man commits a number of mistakes for which he finally pays with his own life. *Out of the Night* begins and ends with an ascent of the Tour Ronde, a modest but beautifully situated peak above the Col du Geant: the subject is the redemption bestowed by the mountains upon an elderly broken man, who has to revive his youthful energy in order to help a party that has met with an accident; he dies of the effort, but in death achieves freedom and peace.

In Wilfrid Noyce's novel, *The Gods are Angry*, only the first part takes place in the Alps, but it enables the reader to feel the author's talent and power. It was a tragedy that Noyce, a poet, a novelist and an essayist, as well as a great mountaineer, died so young, while climbing in the Pamirs, leaving his message just half expressed. He was an Alpine writer of great promise.

Two French writers have achieved a great deal with mountaineering novels. Jean Morin (a pen name and not the Jean Morin who was a founder of the GHM) brought out *Les royaumes du monde* in 1954. The allusion is to the kingdoms which Satan displayed to Christ during the Temptation in the Wilderness. For a man who longs for solitude, the mountain is the great temptation, a form of pride. The hero, Jean Fouquet, in his solitary quest tries to bring some meaning into his own empty, aimless life. The girl he was in love with had been killed during the war and his closest friend had died in a mountain accident. Yet, while climbing, he becomes aware of a strange message, imparted to him by the mountain: 'Eternity is out of time. You grasp as much in one brief moment as during the endless succession of days and nights. Any man sums up eternity in himself, from the moment he realizes his own predestination in full.' Mountains lead to a sort of spiritual initiation. The novel has depth.

I have already mentioned Georges Sonnier. His novels conjure up the same entrancing atmosphere as his essays. *Meije* is hardly longer than a short story; yet it is packed with delicate, subtle details. *Terre du ciel* is the story of a high altitude bivouac on a Dauphiny peak; it is a succession of disconnected thoughts or recollections in the minds of two young men benighted on a high ledge. One of them tells the story of a friend who had died in a mountain accident and whose deep and mysterious personality permeates the whole book: 'Alban had chosen mountains,' writes Georges Sonnier. 'It would be more to the point to say that he had been chosen by them, if I did not fear accepting the decrees of a strange predestination'. Alban's life was over-shadowed by the Grande Muraille of the Meije; in the end he was killed at its foot. The book is a slow meditation on mountains, on life and death, to the rhythm of the endless hours of a night in the open. Noticeable throughout is the recurrence of the idea of predestination.

Georges Sonnier's latest novel, *Un Médecin de montagne*, is something new in the way of mountain literature. It is a short, tightly-knit book, discreet and subdued in tone. Two men meet in a Oisans hut. The elder is a doctor, who lives in a tiny village, high up in the mountains. He has settled there because he loves mountains and also out of charity for the local population, who feel no gratitude to him whatever. He does not mind, as mountains are really his reward. In the course of a dull, hard, painful life, they are his one reason for remaining alive. Eventually he finds faith, an austere, sober kind of faith, like his own life, and he feels his strength renewed by this communion with the Alpine atmosphere. The book is full of brief, sensitive descriptions, and 'it rings true and clear', as General Faure wrote to me.

Lately, a new book which may have borrowed some ideas from Sonnier's novels, has come out: *La Paroi*, by Pierre Moustiers. The story resembles that of *Un Médecin de montagne*, but the two men, instead of being strangers, are enemies, and the reason why they started climbing together is quite un-convincing. The climb of an unnamed face in the Maritime Alps is not at all credible. It begins like a stiff, short expedition, the kind of thing one does between 6 a.m. and lunch time. Then it expands over three or four bivouacs and the tame mountain enlarges to the size and dangerousness of the Eiger-wand, and the elder man dies of exhaustion and exposure. While climbing desperately steep pitches, the two men talk a great deal about complicated philosophical and political notions, which sound strangely out of place in such circumstances.

And so one returns, in a roundabout way, to a notion I have already put into words: mountains and men have not the same scale of values. There may even be a latent antagonism between them, and the titles of books in which they are associated—*When Men and Mountains Meet* by H. W. Tilman, *Men and Mountains* by Wilfred Noyce, *Memorials of Mountains and Men* by A. P. Harper, *Men, Women and Mountains* by Lord Schuster, ending with Tézenas du Montcel's inspired title, *Ce monde qui n'est pas le nôtre*—seem to point to an unconscious realization of this. Their ways are different. Mountains were not made for men and, if men wish to reach the new realm, they must go through years of mental and physical exertion. One of the first consequences of their joy in having entered the Promised Land was their assumption that they had conquered it—as it was only too obvious that they could not speak of having mastered it. The prevalent interpretation of the mountains has brought them down to man's level: hence all the sentimental nonsense about their moral influence, their 'being built for the human race', or their being 'the cathedrals of the earth', as Ruskin called them. But too many mountaineers have turned the high peaks into 'soaped-poles in bear gardens' to allow the mystical interpretation to go unchallenged. Yet we think that both Ruskin and the soaped-pole addicts are mistaken.

Ethics are made for man and the mountains are not. It is probably wrong to force a moral code upon them. They are neither good nor evil. They simply *are*. Man cannot come to love them through mere reasoning, or through weighing their good against their evil influence, whatever either term may mean.

Mountain landscapes are too widely different from any other not to have laws of their own. Their geological character, which seems inured to time, raises our mind above the ideas, hopes and fears of daily existence. Mountains have their own space and their own time. They are slowly perishing, as anything that lives, lives but to die. But the process is so slow that it is hardly felt at all. A completely new notion of time must be applied to them, since ordinary values are non-existent on their slopes. More than anywhere else— even more than at sea—one grasps to the full the length of one hour and the insignificance of the wavelet of time against the wall of eternity.

23. Two stages of an ascent of Piz Badile by Rebuffat amusingly called 'le grand dièdre des sufferings'. (Photos: Bernard Pierre)

24. In the séracs of Mont Blanc de Tacul. (Photo: P. Tairraz)

CHAPTER TWENTY

CONCLUSION

WHEN one has surveyed the long history of mountaineering, its slow uncertain beginnings and then its quickening pace, which has made modern climbing progress by leaps and bounds, one is faced with a representative example of the development of many technical activities of the human mind. Yet one of the striking aspects of this century and a half of activity is the important part played by the personalities of a few inspired leaders. Round several of them there has developed a kind of hero-worship to which even non-climbers have subscribed, whether consciously or otherwise.

The greatest of all these is Whymper. So much has been written about the Matterhorn accident that people who knew hardly anything of mountains, and have never even climbed a high hill, nevertheless have heard of him. Their knowledge is likely to be vague; some of them actually believe he was killed in the accident. Whymper's rival in glory is de Saussure; many Swiss people still believe he made the first ascent of Mont Blanc. A large monument in Chamonix has been dedicated to him and two streets have been named after him, one in his native town of Geneva and the other in Paris. Incidentally, there are a few Alpine memorials scattered here and there: Jacques Balmat has been given two in Chamonix, and Dr Paccard one, which was unveiled as late as 1932. C. T. Dent has a memorial tablet on the Britannia hut above Saas-Fee, Hinchliff has one at Riffelalp, C. E. Matthews in the garden of what was the Hôtel Couttet at Chamonix, and a huge obelisk has been dedicated to Tyndall at Belalp. Whymper has a tablet outside the Monte Rosa hotel in Zermatt; and Ruskin has one on a huge block at the foot of the Brévent above Chamonix. A bench has been dedicated to H. F. Montagnier at Champéry. Javelle is commemorated by an inscription on a boulder in the moraine of the Glacier de la Neuvaz, at the foot of the Tour Noir, and Rambert is remembered by another at Salvan. This last rock has been so awkwardly chosen that it is seen from nowhere except from the railway line, which is not an ideal vantage-point.

The fame of great mountaineers has led many young people to hero worship and more often to mountain worship. Georges Livanos tells in the first chapter of *Au-delà de la verticale* that he was about fourteen when he discovered the hair-raising tales of *direttissime* in the Dolomites, read them with delight, usually when he was supposed to listen to a lecture on maths or history, and decided that he would be a climber. And yet, apart from mountaineers, few people remember Mummery or Frank Smythe, or what they achieved. It is possible that the conquerors of Mount Everest are more widely known. In France, a rather heavy and mostly political publicity gave a kind of glamour to the conquerors of Annapurna, but it faded as the years elapsed. Some fifteen years after the climb, I heard the following dialogue in a train:

'By the way, X is contesting a constituency at the next election.'

'I say! What has he done?'

'This and that . . . And he is a first-class mountaineer. You know, he was one of the Annapurna people.'

In fact, he was not; for the gentleman was confusing him with Maurice Herzog, even though X was nevertheless a great mountaineer.

'Really? How very interesting! . . .' A long silence followed. Then he added, 'By the way, what is Annapurna?'

Usually, mountaineers do not care. Their names will be handed down to later generations, in that they have been suitably pinned to some summits, routes or crannies. Such is the case with Mummery, Ryan, Young, Gervasutti, Lagarde, Lépiney, Winkler, Comici, Bonatti, Lachenal, Rebuffat, and many others whose names can be found in the mountain maps.

Yet, however fragmentary and inaccurate it may be, a faint knowledge of mountain history has crept down to the non-climbing public. As for the great company of climbers, they are certainly becoming more important and more active. It is not only a question of north-face addicts becoming more numerous: they will never be a majority among lovers of the mountains, even in a distant future. It is very doubtful whether people who climb the north face of the Dru as their second ascent in the Alps will go on for many years. They are likely to become blasé pretty soon, and the real mountaineer is not the man or woman who does fantastic climbs for five years, but the one who goes on for twenty-five years, making great or small climbs every year and being able to enjoy them all. Such was the older state of mind. Such is still the state of mind of the greatest climbers, who see mountains as mountains and not as pincushions for pitons. Most climbers do not merely look for danger when starting up a mountain.

Mountains appeal to many who can hear their strong and manifold message. Never has this appeal been more widely felt than today. Mountaineering seems to be one of the kinds of relaxation which are attracting larger numbers of adepts. And yet it can hardly be explained to incompetent or uninterested persons, as it is almost impossible to make them grasp the delight hidden in the various forms of exertion practised during a climb.

However, when one realizes how many people have discovered mountaineering by themselves, whether in books or by falling under the spell of the landscape, one must admit that there is a mysterious attraction which is stronger than weariness.

In the preface of his Alpine anthology, *The Mountain Way*, R. L. G. Irving wrote as follows:

'The element of discovery is still, and will always be, the most important of all that mountaineering offers . . . On the material side, unclimbed routes and unexplored ranges afford the most obvious way of supplying it. On the non-material side there are treasures of beauty, of knowledge, of vision that have no limit.'

There is one discovery to be made in each new ascent: that of one's own soul. A great ascent enables a man to find his own personality, as do few other experiences in life. An exhausting expedition compels him to throw his whole body and mind into action. He is weighed and may sometimes be found wanting. Climbs are a question not only of skill and strength, but also of moral and intellectual balance. Melodramatic gestures are even less frequent —and useful—on a mountain than anywhere else in normal life. But perfect technique implies more than the knowledge of how to manage a rope or to cut steps. It includes discipline, self-control, alertness of mind and—if possible—the perfection of manners which is a great moral asset. From this point of view one can speak of the high educational value of mountaineering, a doctrine which, in other respects, is perhaps only an outcome of wishful thinking. One may say that mountains hold up a mirror to the man who wishes to climb them. If he perceives his own face in it, so much the better: he has been found worthy of his surroundings, and he can face further climbs with confidence. But he may see distorted features which reveal to him his carefully hidden self, the other man whom he has always avoided meeting, though he has been always dimly aware of his haunting presence. You cannot deceive yourself when climbing; you can even less deceive your climbing companion who is faced with the same trials, and the face in the mirror, whatever it is, cannot be kept secret. Mountains leave no room for play-acting or make-believe.

And so, by a roundabout way, we are led back to the old interpretation of mountains as the 'cathedrals of the earth'. Most emphatically, it may be affirmed that they are not 'built for the human race'. Hence their unsullied beauty, their purity and their eternity. Men have built only to destroy, they have trampled their ideals underfoot and extended the sway of death. Yet, in spite of so many attempts upon their strength, the mountains have remained outside the dominion of man. They have not been tamed and never will be, and when men gain access to them, it is by paying homage to them consciously or unconsciously. Mountains are indeed 'the cathedrals of the earth' but not the cathedrals of men, and though allowing men to climb them, they are always capable of withdrawing their permission. To place the message of the mountains in the category of ethical teaching would be akin to desecration. It would be to offer an interpretation of the Alpine giants, insignificant when set beside the reality which it proposes to explain. It is better to insist on their mystery and dignity, and the fact that they are consecrated ground. They enable and even compel man to realize some aspects and implications of eternity and infinity, the fact that he is not absolute master of the world. And they also point to a hope that there is so much beyond him. The old prayer may still be answered: 'I will lift up mine eyes unto the hills, from whence cometh my help.'

BIBLIOGRAPHY

In spite of its length, this bibliography is not to be regarded as exhaustive. Alpine magazines are numerous; I went through most of those published in England, America, France, Switzerland, Italy and Germany. I have not mentioned all the articles I made use of. Even as regards the *Alpine Journal*, I have not had the space to list the 'Alpine Notes' from which I borrowed. I can merely refer the reader to the indexes of the *Journal*, and express my gratitude to the late Colonel Strutt and to Mr H. E. G. Tyndale for having allowed me to use their publications to such an extent.

I. MANUSCRIPTS

(1) *Alpine Club Library:*
    H. F. Montagnier's MSS and letters.
    Führbücher of various Swiss guides.
(2) *Bibliothèque Publique et Universitaire, Geneva:*
    Deluc Archives.
    Gautier Archives.
    Saussure Archives.
(3) *Stadtbibliothek, Berne:*
    Haller, *Correspondence.*
(4) *Zentralbibliothek, Zurich:*
    W. A. B. Coolidge, Archives.
(5) *Neuchâtel Archives:*
    M. de Meuron, Archives.
(6) *Royal Library of Malta, Valetta:*
    Meyer de Knonau's proofs of Nobility.
(7) *Private Archives:*
    Dr P. Ulrich, Zumikon: M. Ulrich's *Reisebücher.*
    M. & Mme Schroter-Mooser, Hotel Nesthorne-Ried: Guest book.
    Sir John Herschel: Herschel's Diary.
    Baron Boileau de Castelnau: Emmanuel de Castelnau's *Diary.*
(8) *Val d'Illiez Archives:*
    Abbé Clément's letters.

II. PRINTED SOURCES

1674 J. Scheffer, *Laponia*, Strasbourg.
1676 N. Lee, *Sophonisba*, London.

1700 J. J. Scheuchzer, *Itera Alpina Tria*, Zurich.

1748 A. von Haller, *De Stirpium Helvetiae*, Göttingen.

1760 — Needham, *Observations*, Berne.

1773 M. Th. Bourrit, *Description des Glacières de Savoye*, Geneva.

1776 D(eluc) & D(entan), *Relations de divers voyages dans les Alpes du Faucigny*, Geneva.

1779 H. B. de Saussure, *Voyages dans les Alpes*, Vol. I, Neuchâtel.

1781 M. Th. Bourrit, *Description des Alpes Pennines et Rhétiennes*, Geneva.

      L. Ramond de Carbonnières, *Lettres sur l'état politique, civil et naturel de la Suisse*, translated from Wm. Coxe, Vol. I, Paris.

1786 M. Th. Bourrit, *Nouvelle description des Glacières de Savoye*, Geneva.

      M. Th. Bourrit, *Lettre sur le premier voyage au sommet du Mont Blanc*, Geneva.

      H. B. de Saussure, *Voyages dans les Alpes*, Vol. II, Neuchâtel.

1787 H. B. de Saussure, *Relation abrégée d'un voyage au sommet du Mont-Blanc*, Geneva.

1789 L. Ramond de Carbonnières, *Observations sur les Pyrénées*, Paris.

1791 Anon: 'Voyage à Ivolèna', *Journal de Lausanne*.

1796 H. B. de Saussure, *Voyages dans les Alpes*, Vol. IV, Neuchâtel

1797 J. Michaud, *Voyage littéraire au Mont Blanc*, Paris.

1801 L. Ramond de Carbonnières, *Voyage au Mont Perdu*, Paris.

      B. de la Tocnaye, *Voyage d'un Francais en Suède et en Norvège*, Paris.

1802 L. Ramond de Carbonnière, *Voyage au sommet du Mont Perdu*, Paris.

1804 L. Sénancour, *Obermann*, Paris.

1806 Echasseriaux, *Lettres sur le Valais*, Paris.

1808 M. Th. Bourrit, *Itineraire de Genève et de Chamonix*, Geneva.

1810 Murith, *Guide du botaniste qui voyage dans le Valais*, Lausanne.

1813 — Zschokke, *Reise auf die Eisgebirge des Kantons Bern*, Berne.

      M. Beaufoy, 'Narrative of a journey . . . to Mont Blanc', *Annals of Philosophy*.

1818 A. Malczeski, *Lettre au professeur Pictet . . . sur un voyage au Mont Blanc*, Geneva.

1819 Ph. Bridel, *Essai de statistique du canton du Valais*, Lausanne.

1819 L. Zumstein, *Voyage sur le Mont Rose*, Turin.

1821 H. Durnford, 'Mont Blanc', *New Monthly Magazine*.

      Capt. Undrell, 'An Ascent of Mont Blanc', *Annals of Philosophy*.

1822 H. Hamel, *Reise auf den Mont Blanc*, Basle.

1823 F. Clissold, *Narrative of an ascent of Mont Blanc*, London.

1824 A. Malczeski, *Maria*, Warsaw.

      L. von Welden, *Der Monte Rosa*, Vienna.

      Anon, *The Peasants of Chamonix*, London.

1826 Dr E. Clark, 'Narrative of an excursion to the summit of Mont Blanc', *New Monthly Magazine*.

1827 Sir Charles Fellows, *A Narrative of an ascent of Mont Blanc*, London.

      J. Auldjo, *An Ascent of Mont Blanc*, London.

      M. Sherwill, 'An Ascent of Mont Blanc', *New Monthly Magazine*.

1828 Wm. Brockedon, *The Passes of the Alps*, London.
　　　Wm. Hawes, *Narrative of an Ascent of Mont Blanc*, London.
1830 F. Hugi, *Naturhistorische Alpenreise*, Soleure.
　　　Victor Hugo, 'Fragment d'un voyage aux Alpes', *Revue des Deux Mondes*.
1832 A. Dumas, *Impressions de voyage en Suisse*, Paris.
　　　E. B. Wilbraham, 'Narrative of an ascent of Mont Blanc', *The Keepsake*.
1833 Wm. Brockedon, *Journals of Excursions in the Alps*, London.
　　　L. Elie de Beaumont, *Faits pour servir a l'Histoire Naturelle des Glaciers de l'Oisans*, Paris.
1835 H. de Balzac, *Seraphita*, Paris.
　　　R. Shuttleworth, 'Account of a Botanical Excursion in Valais', *Magazine of Zoology and Botany*.
　　　Comte de Tilly, *Ascensions aux Cimes de l'Etna et du Mont Blanc*, Geneva.
　　　R. Viridet, *La Traversée du Rothhorn*, Geneva.
1836 M. Barry, *An Ascent of Mont Blanc*, London.
1840 E. Desor, *Journal d'une course aux glaciers du Mont Rose et du Cervin*, Geneva.
1841 E. Desor, *Ascension de la Jungfrau*, Geneva.
1843 E. Desor, *Ascension du Schreckhorn*, Geneva.
　　　J. D. Forbes, *Travels through the Alps of Savoy*, Edinburgh.
　　　J. Ruskin, *Modern Painters*, Vol. I, London.
1844 R. Töpffer, *Voyages en zigzag*, Paris.
1845 E. Desor, *Nouvelles excursions dans les Alpes*, Geneva.
1846 Comte de Bouillé, *Une Ascension au Mont Blanc*, Nantes.
　　　J. Ruskin, *Modern Painters*, Vol. II, London.
1849 M. Ulrich, *Die Viespertaler*, Zurich.
1850 Dr J. Forbes, *A Physician's Holiday*, London.
　　　M. Ulrich, *Die Seitentäler des Wallis*, Zurich.
1851 J. Ruskin, *The Stones of Venice*, London.
　　　M. Ulrich, *Das Lotschental*, Zurich.
1852 M. Engelhardt, *Monte Rosa*, Paris.
　　　A. Bainbridge, *Alpine Lyrics*, London.
　　　R. Töpffer, *Nouveaux voyages en zigzag*, Paris.
1853 J. D. Forbes, *Norway and its Glaciers*, London.
　　　A. Smith, *The Story of Mont Blanc*, London.
1855 E. Desor, *Le Val d'Anniviers*, Geneva.
　　　J. D. Forbes, *The Tour of Mont Blanc and Monte Rosa*, London.
1856 C. Hudson and E. S. Kennedy, *Where there's a Will, there's a Way*, London.
　　　J. Ruskin, *Modern Painters*, Vols. III & IV, London.
　　　A. Wills, *Wanderings in the High Alps*, London.
1857 T. Hinchliff, *Summer Months among the Alps*, London.
　　　J. D. Forbes, 'Pedestrianism in Switzerland', *The Quarterly Review*.
1858 S. W. King, *The Italian Valleys of the Pennine Alps*, London.
　　　L. Stephen, *The Allalinhorn*, Galton's Vacation Tourists, London.

J. Tyndall, *From Lauterbrunnen to the Eggishorn*, id, London.

1859 E. L. Ames, 'The Fletschhorn and Allalinhorn', *PPG*(I).

L. Davies, 'Ascent of the Dom', *PPG*(I).

Mrs Cole, *A Lady's Tour of Monte Rosa*, London.

J. Tyndall, 'A Day among the Séracs of the Géant', *PPG*(I).

A. Wills, 'The Crossing of the Fenêtre de Saleinaz', id.

1860 J. Ruskin, *Modern Painters*, Vol. V, London.

J. Tyndall, *The Glaciers of the Alps*, London.

A. Wills, *The Eagle's Nest*, London.

1861 Mrs Freshfield, *Alpine By-ways*, London.

V. Hawkins, *A Partial Ascent of the Matterhorn*, Galton's Vacation Tourists (II).

1862 J. F. Hardy, 'First Ascent of the Lyskamm', *PPG*.

J. Tyndall, *Mountaineering in 1861*, London.

1863 J. Ball, *Guide to the Western Alps*, London.

— Coutts-Trotter, 'The Mischabeljoch', *A.J.*, London.

H. B. George, 'Crossing of the Sesiajoch', *A.J.*, London.

R. Spence Watson, 'The Balfrinhorn', *A.J.*, London.

L. Stephen, 'The Weisshorn', *A.J.*, London.

1864 Gilbert and Churchill, *The Dolomites*, London.

1865 J. Adams Reilly, 'Some new Ascents in the Chain of Mont Blanc', *A.J.*, London.

T. G. Bonney, *The High Alps of Dauphiny*, London.

A. J. Butler, 'The Zermatt Churchyard', *The Times*, London.

E. N. Buxton, 'Mont Blanc and the Glacier du Dome', *A.J.*, London.

D. W. Freshfield, *Across Country from Thonon to Trent*, London.

E. de Laveleye, 'Le Mont Rose,' *Revue des deux Mondes*, Paris.

J. Ruskin, *Sesame and Lilies*, London.

1866 D. Dollfus-Ausset, *Observations sur le Col du Théodule*, Strasbourg.

1867 J. Michelet, *La Montagne*, Paris.

A. W. Moore, *The Alps in 1864*, London.

A. W. Moore, 'The First Ascent of the Glacier de la Brenva', *A.J.*, London.

1868 E. Rambert, *Les Alpes Suisses*, Geneva.

1869 Th. Gautier, *Les Vacances du Lundi*, Paris.

F. A. Yeats-Brown, 'Mont Blanc and the Glacier du Miage', *A.J.*, London.

1870 A. G. Girdlestone, *The High Alps without Guides*, London.

1871 G. Meredith, *Henry Richmond*, London.

L. Stephen, *The Playground of Europe*, London.

J. Tyndall, *Hours of Exercise*, London.

E. Whymper, *Scrambles amongst the Alps*, London.

1876 Stephen d'Atve, *Les Fastes du Mont Blanc*, Paris.

1877 E. Boileau de Castelnau, 'La Meije', *Annuaire du CAF*.

F. Gardiner, 'Expeditions in the Saastal', *A.J.*, London.

1878 J. Eccles, 'The Brouillard and Fresnay Glaciers', *A.J.*, London.

H. G. Gotch, 'The Meije', *A.J.*, London.

G. Meredith, *The Egoist*, London.

Schutz and Wilson, *Alpine Ascents and Adventures*, London.

Viollet-le-Duc, 'Un accident de montagne', *Le bien public*.

1881 W. M. Conway, *The Zermatt Pocket-Book*, London.

1884 W.M. Conway, 'Monte Rosa from the South', *A.J.*, London.

Anon, 'The Accident on the Meije', *A.J.*, London.

1885 A. Daudet, *Tartarin sur les Alpes*, Paris.

C. T. Dent, *Above the Snow line*, London.

P. Hervieu, *L'Alpe homicide*, Paris.

P. Lioy, 'L'Alpinista in Italia', *Nuova Antologia*.

1885 H. Seymour King, 'First Ascent of the Aiguille Blanche de Peuterey', *A.J.*, London.

E. Zsigmondy, *Les dangers de l'Alpinisme*, Neuchâtel.

1887 C. D. Cunningham & — Abney, *The Pioneers of the Alps*, London.

1888 C. Slingsby, 'A Day in the Aiguilles Rouges d'Arolla', *A.J.*, London.

1889 W. A. B. Coolidge, *Swiss travels and Swiss Guide-books*, London.

E. Zsigmondy, *Im Hochgebirge*, Leipzig.

1890 W. M. Conway, 'Centrists and Excentrists', *A.J.*, London.

W. A. B. Coolidge, 'Early Ascents of the Dent Blanche', *A.J.*, London.

A. T. Malkin, 'Leaves from his Diary', *A.J.*, London.

1891 W. A. B. Coolidge, *Alpine Studies*, London.

V. Puiseux, 'Histoire du Mont Rose', *Annuaire du CAF*.

1892 E. Javelle, *Souvenirs d'un Alpiniste*, Lausanne.

C. T. Dent, *Mountaineering*, London.

Earl of Minto, 'Zermatt in 1830', *A.J.*, London.

T. Wethered, 'Early Attempts on the Monte Rosa', *A.J.*, London.

1893 E. Carr, 'Two Days on an Ice Slope', *A.J.*, London.

1894 N. Collie, 'The Ascent of the Dent du Requin', *A.J.*, London.

A. Lorria & — Martel, *The Massif de la Bernina*, Zurich.

1895 W. M. Conway, *The Alps from End to End*, London.

G. Hastings, 'Over Mont Blanc by the Brenva Route without a Guide,' *A.J.*, London.

A. F. Mummery, *My Climbs in the Alps and Caucasus*, London.

1896 L. Sinigaglia, *My Climbs, Reminiscences of the Dolomites*, London.

G. Wherry, *Alpine Notes*, London.

1898 D. W. Freshfield, 'Paccard v. Balmat', *A.J.*, London.

F. Gribble, *Early Mountaineers*, London.

P. Güssfeldt, *Mont Blanc*, Geneva.

O. G. Jones, 'The Domgrat', *A.J.*, London.

Mrs N. Neruda, *The Climbs of Norman Neruda*, London.

C. E. Mathews, *The Annals of Mont Blanc*, London.

1899 A. D. Godley, 'Switzerland', *Climbers' Club Journal*, London.

1900 G. Rey, *Il Monte Cervino*.

1901 W. M. Conway & D. W. Freshfield, 'The Future of the Alpine Club', *A.J.*, London.

L. Purtscheller, *Über Fels und Firn*, Munich.

1902 A. Kraebühl, *Hugi*, Munich.

1903 Duke of Abruzzi, 'The First Ascent of the Punta Jolanda', *A.J.*, London.

1904 W. A. B. Coolidge, *Josias Simler*, London.

D. W. Freshfield, 'Mountains and Mankind', *A.J.*, London.

'F. Devouassoud', *A.J.*, London.

1907 A. D. Godley, 'The Alps', *A.J.*, London.

W. A. B. Coolidge, *The Alps in Nature and History*, London.

A. E. W. Mason, *Running Water*, London.

1909 R. L. G. Irving, 'Five Years with Recruit', *A.J.*, London.

1910 C. D. Robertson, 'Alpine Humour', *A.J.*, London.

G. W. Young, *Mountain Craft*, London.

1911 J. P. Farrar, 'The Brenva Face of Mont Blanc', *A.J.*, London.

J. P. Farrar and C. Wilson, 'The Ascent of the Brenva Ridge by Coolidge in 1870', *A.J.*, London.

J. Galsworthy, *The Little Dream*, London.

H. F. Montagnier, 'A Bibliography of the Ascents of Mont Blanc', *A.J.*, London.

'Dr Paccard's Lost Narrative', *A.J.*, London.

1912 W. A. B. Coolidge, *Alpine Studies*, London.

1913 H. Dübi, *Paccard wieder Balmat*, Zurich.

A. Fischer, *Hochgebirgswanderungen*, Frauenfeld.

F. Pieth, K. Huger & Carnot, *P. Placidus a Spescha*, Berne.

F. F. Roget, *Ski Runs in the High Alps*, London.

E. L. Strutt, 'The West Wing of the Bernina', *A.J.*, London.

1914 A. Burlingham, *How to become an Alpinist*, London.

W. A. B. Coolidge, 'Le Origine Storiche de Arolla', *Rivista Mensile*.

G. L. Mallory, 'The Mountaineer as an Artist', *Climbers' Club Journal*.

1915 W. A. B. Coolidge, 'Il Col de Colon', *Rivista Mensile*.

'Il Col de Seillon', *Rivista Mensile*.

1916 W. A. B. Coolidge, 'Il Col d'Hérens', *Rivista Mensile*.

'Le Weisshorn', *Annales Valaisannes*.

H. F. Montagnier, 'A Further Contribution to the Bibliography of Mont Blanc', *A.J.*, London.

1917 W. M. Conway, 'Some Reminiscences of an Old Stager', *A.J.*, London.

W. A. B. Coolidge, *J. Madutz*.

H. F. Montagnier, 'Records of Attempts and Ascents of Monte Rosa', *A.J.*, London.

1918 J. Coaz, 'Aus dem Leben eines Schweizerischen Topographer', *Jahrbuch* CAS.

J. P. Farrar, 'Days of Long Ago: Chas. Hudson', *A.J.*, London.

G. L. Mallory, 'Mont Blanc by the East Buttress of the Mont Maudit', *A.J.*, London.

A. L. Mumm, 'Ruskin and the Alps, *A.J.*, London.

1919 G. L. Mallory, 'A New Route up the Charmoz, *A.J.*, London.

1920 W. A. B. Coolidge, 'The Climbing Years of Francis Gardiner', *A.J.*, London.

H. Dübi, 'Early Swiss Pioneers', *A.J.*, London.

J. P. Farrar, 'The Aiguille Blanche de Peuterey', *A.J.*, London.

D. W. Freshfield, *The Life of H. B. de Saussure*, London.

H. F. Montagnier, 'Ascents of Mont Blanc in 1819', *A.J.*, London.

G. Rey, 'Recits et impressions d'alpinisme-Chambéry Alpinisme Accrobatique', *A.J.*, London.

F. F. Tuckett (publ. by W. A. B. Coolidge), *A Pioneer of the High Alps*, London.

1921 W. A. B. Coolidge, *My Scrap-Book*, Montreux.

G. L. Mallory, 'Our 1919 Journey', *A.J.*, London.

H. F. Montagnier, 'Early History of the Col du Géant', *A.J.*, London.

A. L. Mumm, 'A History of the Alpine Club', *A.J.*, London.

1922 A. Ratti (Pope Pius XI), *Ascensions*, Chambéry.

1923 K. Blodig, *Die Viertausender der Alpen*, Munich.

Ch. Durier, *Le Mont Blanc*, Paris.

D. W. Freshfield, *Quips for Cranks*, London.

W. Lehner, *Die Eroberung der Alpen*, Munich.

D. Pilley and H. Richards, 'The N.E. Arête of the Jungfrau', *A.J.*, London.

1924 P. Dalloz, *La pointe Lagarde*, Strasbourg.

J. and T. de Lépiney, *Sur les Crêtes du Mont Blanc*, Chambéry.

A. L. Mumm, *Alpine Club Registers*, London.

1925 E. von Fellenberg, *Der Ruf der Bergen*, Zurich.

G. I. Finch, *The Making of a Mountaineer*, London.

A. Lunn, *The Mountains of Youth*, London.

1926 J. Estaunié, *Le Silence dans la Campagne (Le Cas de Jean Bunant)*, Paris.

G. Pye, *G. Mallory*, London.

1927 Gugliermina, *Vette*, Varallo.

A. Lunn, *A History of Skiing*, London.

G. W. Young, *On High Hills*, London.

1928 A. Hess, *Trent' anni d'Alpinismo*, Novarre.

Mrs A. Le Blond, *Day In, Day Out*, London.

1929 Mary Paillon, 'Miss K. Richardson', *La Montagne*.

F. S. Smythe, *Climbs and Ski Runs*, London.

E. H. Stevens, 'Dr Paccard's lost Narrative', *A.J.*, London.

1930 T. Blaikie, *The Diary of a Scotch Gardener*, London.

W. S. Churchill, *My Early Life*, London.

1931 C. E. Engel, *La littérature Alpestre en France et en Angleterre aux XVIIIe et XIXe siècles*, Paris.

D. Fawcett, *The Zermatt Dialogues*, London.

Lord Schuster, *Men, Women and Mountains*, London.

1932 E. R. Blanchet, *Hors des Chemins battus*, Paris.
W. M. Conway (Lord Conway), *Episodes of a varied Life*, London.
P. Dalloz, *Haute Montagne*, Paris.
Ch. Klucker, *An Alpine Guide*, London.
C. Simon, *Erlebnisse und Geanken eines alten Bergsteiger,* Zurich.
L. Trenker, *Kameraden der Berge*, Berlin.

1933 T. G. Brown, 'The Alpine Club, 1920–2', *A.J.*, London.
H. F. Montagnier, 'T. Blaikie and Dr Paccard', *A.J.*, London.
Monroe Thorington, *Mont Blanc Sideshow*, Philadelphia.

1934 R. L. G. Irving, *The Romance of Mountaineering*, London.
J. Kugy, *Alpine Pilgrimage*, London.
— Mazzotti, *Dernières Victoires au Cervin*, Paris.
Lord Schuster, 'An Abstract Alpine Subject', *A.J.*, London.

1935 R. Chabod and G. Gervasutti, *Alpinismo*, Rome.
C. E. Engel, *Alpinistes d'Autrefois*, Paris.
Leslie Stephen's Letters to French Friends', *A.J.*, London.
— Franz and — Mair, *Der Mensch am Berg*, Munich.
D. Piley, *Climbing Days*, London.

1936 E. Bruhl, 'A propos de degrés', *La Montagne*.
Monod-Herzen, 'Disquieting Aspects of Modern Mountaineering', *A.J.*, London.
F. Schmidt and S. Schmidbauer, *Nordwand*, Graz.
F. S. Smythe, *The Spirit of the Hills*, London.

1937 Dr Azema, 'La voie Allegra', *Alpinisme*.
E. R. Blanchet, *Au Bout d'un Fil*, Paris.
M. Morin, *Encordées*, Paris.

1938 C. Bailey, 'The Treasure of the Humble', *A.J.*, London.
— Eberhard, *Hochwelt*, Berne.
C. E. Engel, 'Markham Sherwill's Collection of Autographs', *A.J.*, London.
R. L. G. Irving, *The Mountain Way*, London.
J. Kugy, *Son of the Mountains*, London.
Anon, *Über der Eigernordwand*, Munich.

1939 L. S. Amery, *Days of Fresh Air*, London.
C. E. Engel, *Le Mont Blanc, route ancienne et voies nouvelles*, Paris.
F. Frendo, 'Procédés artificiels d'Escalade', *Alpinisme*.
A. Heckmair, 'La Conquête de la Face Nord de l'Eiger', *Alpinisme*.
J. Peyré, *Matterhorn*, Paris.
G. W. Young, *Collected Poems*, London.

1940 C. Gos, *Tragédies Alpestres*, Lausanne.
P. Hübel, *Der Riese von Zermatt*, Innsbruck.
R. L. G. Irving, *The Alps*, London.
J. Kugy, *Im Göttlichen Lächeln des Monte Rosa*, Graz.
C. F. Meade, *Approach to the Hills*, London.

M. Roberts, 'Poetry and Humour of Mountaineering', *A.J.*, London.

F. S. Smythe, *Whymper*, London.

W. Welzenbach, *Ascensions*, Paris.

1941 L. Devies, 'Origine de l'alpinisme sans guide français', *Alpinisme*.

R. Frison-Roche, *Premier du Cordée*, Lyon.

R. L. G. Irving, *Ten Great Mountains*, London.

C. W. Murray, 'In and out of Saas', *A.J.*, London.

L. Pilkington, 'Early Memories', *A.J.*, London.

Samivel, *L'Amateur d'Abîmes*, Lyon.

F. S. Smythe, *Mountaineering Holiday*, London.

F. Spencer Chapman, *From Helvellyn to Himalaya*, London.

E. L. Strutt, 'Memorable Days', *A.J.*, London.

1942 T. G. Brown, 'The Nordend of Monte Rosa', *A.J.*, London.

Pfann, *Führerlose Gipfelfahrten*, Munich.

E. L. Strutt, 'The Eastern Alps', *A.J.*, London.

R. Warner, *The Aerodrome*, London.

J. Weiss, *Murailles et Abîmes*, Neuchâtel.

1943 C. E. Engel, 'Early Lady Climbers', *A.J.*, London.

A. Lunn, *Mountain Jubilee*, London.

A. Roch, *Conquêtes de ma jeunesse*, Neuchâtel.

G. W. Young, 'Mountain Prophets', *A.J.*, London.

1944 T. G. Brown, *Brenva*, London.

C. E. Engel, *La Suisse et ses amis*, Neuchâtel.

R. L. G. Irving, 'When We were very Young', *A.J.*, London.

A. Lunn, *Switzerland and the English*, London.

G. de Rham, 'An Ascent of the South Face of the Täschhorn', *A.J.*, London.

E. H. Stevens, 'J. D. Forbes', *A.J.*, London.

1945 G. R. de Beer, *Escape to Switzerland*, London.

G. de Burgh, 'Smuggler's Way', *Blackwood's Magazine*.

R. Dittert, *Passion des Hautes Cimes*, Lausanne.

C. E. Engel, 'Un Curé Alsacien à Zermatt', *Les Alpes*.

1946 L. S. Amery, *In the Rain and the Sun*, London.

J. Boell, *S.E.S.*, Grenoble.

D. Dangar, 'Christian Almer and Melchior Anderegg', *A.J.*, London.

C. E. Engel, 'The Alpine Archives in Ried', *A.J.*, London.

C. Gos, *Notre Dame des Neiges*, Neuchâtel.

K. Grinling, 'Escape to Switzerland', *New Zealand A.J.*, Wellington.

A. Guex, *Le Rêve de Pierre*, Lausanne.

J. Guex, *La Montagne et ses noms*, Lausanne.

J. Hall, 'La Traversée des Alpes', *Les Alpes*.

R. Lambert, *A l'assaut des 4000*, Geneva.

G. Sonnier, *Où règne la lumière*, Paris.

1947 M. Aldebert, *Conquête de la Haute Montagne*, Paris.

J. Boell, *High Heaven*, London.

A. de Chattelus, *De l'Eiger à l'Iharen*, Paris.

D. Busk, *The Delectable Mountains*, London.

A. Deffeyes, 'Comment nous avons réussi le tour de la Tête du Cervin', *Les Alpes*.

E. Frendo, *La Face Nord des Grandes Jorasses*, Lausanne.

J. Guex, *Dans les Traces de Javelle*, Lausanne.

A. Lunn, *Switzerland in English Prose and Poetry*, London.

C. Micholet, *Combats sur les Alpes*, Thonon.

W. Noyce, *Men and Mountains*, London.

T. H. Peacock, 'Six Months in the Abruzzi Apennines', *A.J.*, London.

J. Peyre, *Mallory et son dieu*, Geneva.

S. Russell, *Mountain Prospect*, London.

Samivel, 'Montagne d'utilité publique', *La Montagne*.

H. W. Tilman, *When Men and Mountains Meet*, London.

G. Rebuffat, *L'Apprenti Montagnard*, Paris.

M. Roberts, 'Early English Travellers in the Graians', *A.J.*, London.

1948　J. Boell, *Paysages d'Oisans*, Marseille.

A. Cicogna, 'A propos des Dolomites', *Alpinisme*.

J. Couzy, 'Dans le domaine de la Verticale', *Alpinisme*.

C. Gos, *Le Cervin*, Neuchâtel.

L. Lachenal, 'Eigerwand', *Alpinisme*.

A. Lunn, *Mountains of Memory*, London.

A. Roch, *Mon carnet de courses*, Lausanne.

P. E. G. Tyndale, *Mountain Paths*, London.

1949　G. R. de Beer, *Travellers in Switzerland*, Oxford.

T. G. Brown, 'The History of the Innominata Face of Mont Blanc', *A.J.*, London.

D. Busk, 'Bad Weather in Chamonix', *A.J.*, London.

S. L. Courtauld, 'The Innominata Face of Mont Blanc', *A.J.*, London.

J. Couzy, 'De la graduation des difficultés rocheuses', *Alpinisme*.

C. E. Engel, *La Vallee de Saas*, Neuchâtel.

N. Hanson, 'Courmayeur, 1948', *A.J.*, London.

B. Pierre, 'The N.E. face of Peak Badile', *Climbers' Club Journal*.

G. Rebuffat, 'La Face NE du Piz Badile', *Alpinisme*.

1950　P. Allain, *Alpinisme de Competition*, Paris.

A. Chamson and M. Aldebert, *Le Royaume des Hautes Terres*, Paris.

A. Charlet, *Ma Vocation Alpine*, Neuchâtel.

R. Clark, *Early Mountain Guides*, London.

C. E. Engel, *A History of Mountaineering in the Alps*, London.

'Sir John Herschel's ascent of the Breithorn', *A.J.*, London.

'Evasions à travers les Alpes', *La Revue de Paris*.

H. Merrick, *The Breaking Strain*, London.

B. Pierre, 'The West Face of the Aiguille Noire de Peuterey', *Climber's Club Journal.*

G. Rebuffat, 'La Face Nord du Cervin', *Alpinisme.*

Lord Schuster, *Postscript to Adventure*, London.

1951 V. Annan, *Leslie Stephen*, London.

S. Brunhuber, *Wände im Winter*, Munich.

1952 A. Borgognone and F. Rossi, *Scalatori*, Milan.

C. E. Engel, *They Came to the Hills*, London.

G. Sonnier, *Meije*, Paris.

1953 H. Buhl, *Achttausender drüber und drunter*, Munich.

R. Clark, *Victorian Mountaineers*, London.

G. Magnone, *La Face Ouest des Drus*, Paris.

Capt. Lestien, 'Les debuts du ski en France', *Papier d'Information des Troupes de Montagne.*

1954 J. Morin, *Les Royaumes de ce monde*, Paris.

1955 G. Rebuffat, *Du Mont Blanc à l'Himalaya*, Paris.

1956 P. Allain, *L'art de l'Alpinisme*, Paris.

E. Fal, *Sesto Grado e sestogradisti*, Milan.

R. Mailleux, *Le Roi Albert Alpiniste*, Bruxelles.

1957 G. R. de Beer and T. G. Brown, *The First Ascent of Mont Blanc*, London.

A. Lunn, *A Century of Mountaineering*, London.

H. Merrick, *Out of the Night*, London.

C. Evans, *On Climbing*, London.

L. Lachenal, *Les Carnets du Vertige*, Paris.

V. Milroy, *Alpine Partisan*, London.

W. Noyce, *The Gods are Angry*, London.

1958 R. Cassin, *Dove la parete strapiomba*, Milan.

G. Livanos, *Au-delà de la Verticale*, Paris.

W. Noyce, *The Springs of Adventure*, London.

1959 J. Boell, *L'Or de la Muzelle*, Paris.

R. Clark, *An Eccentric in the Alps*, London.

G. Rebuffat, *Neige et Roc*, Paris.

G. Sonnier, *Terre du Ciel*, Paris.

P. Vincent, *Echappés à la Montagne*, Bruxelles.

1961 W. Bonatti, *Les mie Montagne*, Bologna.

G. Rebuffat, *Entre Terre et Ciel*, Paris.

G. Rebuffat, *La piste des cimes*, Paris.

C. E. Engel, *Le Mont Blanc*, Paris and London.

1962 I. Clough, 'A Season of Plenty', *A.J.*, London.

P. Mazeaud, *Le Pilier du Fresnay*, Paris.

G. Rebuffat, *Mont Blanc jardin feérique*, Paris.

L. Terray, *Les Conquérants de l'inutile*, Paris.

1963 A. Garobbio, *Uomini del sesto grado*, Milan.
   J. Harlin, 'The Eigerwand', *A.A.J.*
   G. Sonnier, *Un Médecin de montagne*, Paris.
   I Cento del CAI, Milan.
1964 A. Bernardi, *Il Gran Cervino*, Bologna.
   M. Fantin, *I quatordici ottomila*, Bologna.
   A. Roch, *La Haute Route*, Paris.
   A. Oggioni, *La Mani sulla rocca*, Bologna.
   J. Harlin, 'First Ascents in the Mont Blanc Alps', *A.A.J.*
1965 A. Bernardi, *Il Monte Bianco*, Bologna.
   R. Clark, *The Day the Rope Broke*, London.
   K. Gretlaur, 'L'Alpinisme et notre vision du Monde', *Les Alpes*.
   Sir A. Lunn, *Matterhorn Centenary*, London.
   G. Rebuffat, *Cervin Cime exemplaire*, Paris.
   J. Harlin, 'West Face of the Mönch and West face of the Blaitière',
       A.A.J.
   R. Tezenas du Montcel, *Ce monde qui n'est pas le notre*, Paris.
   Y. Vaucher, 'Première Féminine de la face nord du Cervin',
       Les Alpes.
1966 Ch. Bonington, *I chose to climb*, London.
   R. Desmaison, 'Einsamkeit am Dru', *Alpinismus*.
   H. Gilman and D. Haston, *Eiger direct*, London.
   J. Harlin, 'Petit Dru direttissima', *A.A.J.*
       'The North Face of the Petit Dru direct', *A.J.*, London.
   M. Mila, 'La questione delle donne nel CAI', *Rivista Mensile*.
   N. Morin, *A Woman's Reach*, London.
1967 J. Brown, *The Hard Years*, London.
   J. Harlin, 'La Face ouest du Petit Dru', *Les Alpes*.
   M. Holroyd, *Lytton Strachey*, London.
   A. K. Rawlinson, 'The Alpine Club and the ACG', *A.J.*, London.
   G. Rebuffat, 'Quelques premières de récréation', *La Montagne*.
1968 M. Darbellay, 'Première hivernale de la face N.W. du Badile',
       Les Alpes.
   P. Mazeaud, *Schritte Himmelwärts*.
   F. Rho, *Capodamo sulla NE del Badile*, Bologna.
   J. Ulman, *Straight Up*, New York.
1969 A. Gogna, *Grandes Jorasses*, Bologna.
   D. Isherwood, 'Direttissima on the Piz Badile', *A.J.*, London.
   R. Messner, 'Kampf am Grand Capucin', *Alpinismus*.
   P. Moustiers, *La Paroi*, Paris.
   D. Robertson, *Mallory*, London.
   Samivel, *Le fou d'Edenberg*, Paris.
   'Sechs Japaner in der Eigerwand', *Alpinismus*.

1970 R. Dittert, 'Piz Badile', *Mountain World*.
G. Rebuffat, *Neige, noẓ et glace*, Paris.
H. de Ségogne, 'J. Lagarde', *La Montagne*.
G. Sonnier, *L'Homme et la Montagne*, Paris.

P.P.G. = *Peaks, Passes and Glaciers.*
A.J.   = *Alpine Journal.*
A.A.J. = *American Alpine Journal.*

INDEX